ELEMENTARY BUSINESS STATISTICS: THE MODERN APPROACH

PUBLISHED BY PRENTICE-HALL, INC. ENGLEWOOD CLIFFS, NEW JERSEY

ELEMENTARY BUSINESS STATISTICS: THE MODERN APPROACH

JOHN E. FREUND PROFESSOR OF MATHEMATICS, ARIZONA STATE UNIVERSITY

FRANK J. WILLIAMS PROFESSOR OF STATISTICS, SAN FRANCISCO STATE COLLEGE

PRENTICE-HALL INTERNATIONAL, INC., LONDON
PRENTICE-HALL OF AUSTRALIA, PTY., LTD., SYDNEY
PRENTICE-HALL OF CANADA, LTD., TORONTO
PRENTICE-HALL OF INDIA (PRIVATE) LTD., NEW DELHI
PRENTICE-HALL OF JAPAN, INC., TOKYO

Current printing (last digit):
14 13 12 11 10 9 8

Library of Congress Catalog Card Number 64-10228.
Printed in the United States of America. C25300.

TO MICKEY AND JEAN

PREFACE

In the past few decades, the development and the application of new mathematical, statistical, and computer techniques have brought about radical changes in virtually all areas of business. There is much evidence that the schools have been keeping pace remarkably well with these developments; indeed, the rapid modernization of collegiate business training has been among the most spectacular changes in higher education. The extent to which the older, as well as the new, quantitative techniques have entered the traditional business areas is evident from even the most cursory examination of currently popular texts, and nowhere is the new look more evident than in such quantitatively oriented subjects as demand analysis and sales forecasting; production, cost, and pricing analysis; and capital budgeting.

So far as statistics is concerned, recent years have seen its shift from a backward-looking process to one concerning current affairs as well as future operations and their consequences. In today's statistics, experiments are designed, samples selected, data collected and analyzed with reference to decisions that must be made, controls that must be exercised, judgments entailing action that must be taken, and so on. *This forward- and outward-looking attitude, which we have tried to capture in this book, is what we refer to as "the modern approach."*

The level of mathematical difficulty justifies calling this book "elementary"; indeed, in its notation, details of mathematical derivations, and in the selection of topics, it is quite a bit more elementary than the authors' earlier book, *Modern Business Statistics*, published by Prentice-Hall, Inc., in 1958. In some respects, this present book provides less coverage "in depth," but on the other hand, it provides a wider perspective of subjects that have become increasingly important in recent years. Although most of the examples and exercises in this text are drawn from actual problems, many of them have been modified and scaled down somewhat to simplify the computational burden.

The book contains more than enough material for a one-semester or two-quarter course, and it thus permits a good deal of latitude in the selection of topics. We shall resist the temptation to tell anyone specifically what chapters, sections, or subjects to study or teach, but we do want to make the following brief comments: Many topics (no matter how practically important or intellectually stimulating they might be) can be omitted without loss of continuity. This applies particularly to the Technical Notes (which contain most of the mathematical detail) and to the exercises based on them, as well as to some of the special and slightly more advanced topics. For example, the counting problems in the first set of exercises of Chapter 5 may appear more difficult conceptually than the probability problems usually found in elementary texts, but they may be omitted. Of course, there is some loss involved in not doing this combinatorial work, but the loss is more in the understanding of probability itself (which many feel should be part of everyone's general education) than in the understanding of statistical inference or methodology. It is possible also to omit entirely the section in Chapter 5 entitled "Some Further Rules of Probability" which includes the Rule of Bayes and gives the necessary foundation for Bayesian inference. If this is done, the last few pages of the section "Probability Distributions" should be omitted, together with the exercises relating to these topics.

All of the material of Chapter 6 beginning with "A Decision Problem" and, of course, the entire operations research chapter (which is written at the same level of difficulty as the rest of the book) may be omitted.

In connection with this we should add, however, that we have found both student interest and achievement agreeably high in all of this material. Finally, let us point out that those who wish to stress the probability and decision material can omit some of the more traditional topics of business statistics (for example, index numbers and time series) without difficulty.

The authors are greatly indebted to the editorial staff of Prentice-Hall, Inc., for their courteous cooperation in the production of this book; to their many colleagues and students whose helpful suggestions contributed greatly to the final version; and especially to Dean Frank J. Gilliam of Washington and Lee University.

Finally, the authors would like to express their appreciation and indebtedness to Sir Ronald A. Fisher, F.R.S., Cambridge, and to Dr. Frank Yates, F.R.S., Rothamsted, also to Messrs. Oliver & Boyd, Ltd., Edinburgh, for permission to reprint parts of Tables III, IV, and VI from their books, *Statistical Methods for Research Workers* and *Statistical Tables for Biological, Agricultural, and Medical Research;* to Professor E. S. Pearson and the Biometrika trustees for permission to reproduce the material in Tables IVa, IVb, Va, and Vb from their *Biometrika Tables for Statisticians;* to Donald B. Owen and Addison-Wesley, Inc. for permission to reproduce parts of the Table of Random Numbers from their *Handbook of Statistical Tables*.

JOHN E. FREUND
FRANK J. WILLIAMS

CONTENTS

ONE
INTRODUCTION

Modern Statistics

One of the great phenomena of the past few decades has been the growth of statistical methods and statistical ideas. For many years, statistics used to be concerned largely with the collection and presentation of data in tables and charts; today it has evolved to the extent that its impact is felt in almost every area of human activity. This is because modern statistics is looked upon as encompassing a process as old as history itself, *that of decision making in the face of uncertainty.* Needless to say, there are uncertainties wherever we turn—when we predict the outcome of a football game or a national election, when we toss a coin or roll a die, dig for water or oil, experiment with a new product, market a new soap, even when we cross a street, choose a career, or buy a box of cigars.

There is hardly any area in which the impact of statistics has been felt more strongly than in business. Indeed, it would be hard to overestimate the contributions statistical methods have made to the effective planning and control of business activities of all sorts. In the past twenty years the application of statistics has brought about radical changes in production, in the effective use of materials, manpower, and money, in marketing, in business research, and in business management and organization in general. As in science, some understanding of statistics has become an absolute necessity in business; without it, it is virtually impossible to appreciate and to apply most of the important work currently done in business and economic research.

In this introductory text, our attention will be directed largely toward business statistics, and our specific goal is to acquaint the reader with those statistical concepts and methods with which any student of business management should be familiar. Actually, the formal notions of statistics as a way of making rational decisions should be a part of any thoughtful person's equipment. After all, business managers are not the only persons who must make decisions in the face of uncertainty; *everyone* has to make decisions of this sort professionally or as part of his everyday life. It is true that many of the choices we have to make entail only matters of taste and personal preference, in which case there is, of course, no question of a decision's being right or wrong. On the other hand, many choices we have to make between alternatives can be definitely wrong in the sense that there is an actual loss or penalty of some sort—possibly only a minor annoyance, perhaps something as serious as loss of life, or anything between these two extremes. The methods of modern statistics deal with problems of this kind and they do so not only in business, industry, and in the world of everyday life, but also in such fields as medicine, physics, chemistry, agriculture, economics, psychology, government, education, and so on. Although the examples and exercises used in this book will be mostly from the area of business, we shall not hesitate to refer to these other areas from time to time. In this way, the reader will be reminded of the fact that although specialized techniques exist for handling particular kinds of problems, the underlying principles and ideas are identical regardless of the field of application. It is also hoped that exposure to examples from other areas will enable the reader to gain a better understanding of the scope and limitations of empirical (scientific) knowledge in general.

The most important feature of the recent growth of statistics has been the shift in emphasis from methods which merely *describe* to methods which serve to make *generalizations*. In other words, the shift in emphasis has been from *descriptive statistics* to the methods of *statistical infer-*

ence, or *inductive statistics*. Under the heading of "descriptive statistics" we shall include any treatment of data which is designed to summarize or describe some of their important features *without going any further;* that is, in descriptive statistics we shall not attempt to infer anything that goes beyond the actual data. Thus, if someone compiles the necessary data and reports that California fish and game wardens arrested nearly 12,000 persons in 1960, most of them for fishing without a license, and that they paid almost $375,000 in fines and served 5,000 days in jail, his work belongs to the domain of descriptive statistics. This is true also if he calculates that the average cash fine per arrest was about $31.25, but *not* if the data are used to predict the future, estimate fines paid in other states, estimate the number of persons fishing illegally who were not caught, or make other kinds of predictions.

Descriptive statistics is an important branch of statistics and it continues to be widely used in business and other areas of activity. In most cases, however, statistical information arises from samples (from observations made only on some of a large set of items), or from observations made on past happenings. Time, cost, or the *impossibility* of doing otherwise usually requires such a procedure, even though our real interest lies in the whole large set of items from which the sample was obtained, and not in the past but the future. Since generalizations of any kind lie outside the scope of descriptive statistics, we are thus led to the use of statistical inferences in making both short- and long-range plans and in solving many problems of day-to-day operations. To mention but a few examples, the methods of statistical inference are required to estimate the 1969–1970 assessed value of all property in Alameda County, California, to predict the operating lifespan of a washing machine, to forecast the 1980 military requirements for raw materials, or to decide upon an effective dose of an antibiotic.

It must be understood, of course, that when we make a statistical inference, that is, a generalization which goes beyond the limits of our data, we must proceed with considerable caution. We must decide carefully how far we can go in generalizing from a given set of data, whether such generalizations are at all reasonable or justifiable, whether it might be wise to wait until we have more data, and so forth. Indeed, the most important problem of statistical inference is to appraise the risks to which we are exposed by making generalizations from sample data, the probabilities of making wrong decisions or incorrect predictions, and the chances of obtaining estimates which do not lie within permissible limits of error. These various possibilities may seem somewhat frightening, but they cannot be eliminated; *so long as we have to live with uncertainties, we simply must learn how to live with them intelligently.*

Statistics in Business Management

There are literally thousands of practical problems in the major areas of business management (general management, research, finance, production, sales, advertising, etc.) which are of a statistical nature. Of course, not all problems in these areas are statistical, but the list of those which can be solved either partly or entirely by statistical methods is very long. To illustrate, let us consider some of those which might face a fairly large manufacturing company.

In the *general management* area, for example, where long-range planning is of great concern, population trends must be forecast and their effects on consumer markets must be analyzed; in *research and engineering*, costs must be estimated for various projects and manpower, skill, equipment, and time requirements must be anticipated; in the area of *finance*, the profit potential of capital investments must be determined, over-all financial requirements must be projected, and capital markets must be studied so that sound long-range financing and investment plans can be developed. Although we cannot illustrate at this time how statistics is actually used in these areas of application, let us point out that they will be touched upon in the examples in the text and the exercises following the various sections.

In *production*, problems of a statistical nature arise in connection with plant layout and structure, size and location, inventory, production scheduling and control, maintenance, traffic and materials handling, quality assurance, and so forth. Enormous strides have been made in recent years in the application of statistics to the last area, that is, to sampling inspection and quality control. In the area of *sales*, many problems are encountered which require statistical solutions. For instance, sales must be forecast for both present and new products for existing as well as new markets, channels of distribution must be determined, requirements for sales forces must be estimated, and so on. Building a successful *advertising* campaign is also a troublesome task; budgets must be determined, allocations must be made to various media, and the effectiveness of the campaign must be measured (or predicted) by means of survey samples of public response and other statistical techniques.

So far we have been speaking of problems of a statistical nature that are encountered by a manufacturing company of some size. However, similar problems are faced, say, by a large railroad trying to make the best use of its 90,000 freight cars, by a poultry grower trying to decide how to feed his 40,000 hens so that their nutritional needs will be met at the lowest possible cost, or by a mutual investment company trying to decide whether to include in its $400 million portfolio a particular stock.

It is not at all necessary to refer to large organizations to find business applications of statistics. For the smaller businesses, problems usually differ more in degree than in kind from those of their large competitors. Neither the largest supermarket nor the smallest neighborhood grocery store, for example, has unlimited capital or shelf space, and neither can afford to tie these two assets up in the wrong goods. The problem of utilizing capital and shelf space most effectively is as real for the small store as for the large, and it is extremely shortsighted to think that modern management tools (including modern statistical techniques) are of value only to big business. In fact, they could hardly be needed more anywhere else than in small business, where some 350,000 units failed in 1961 and many of the 400,000 new units entering the field in that year were preordained to failure because of inadequate capital, over-extended credit, overloading with the wrong stock, and, generally speaking, no knowledge of the market or the competition.

We shall not elaborate any further, but we hope that we have made it clear that there are many statistical problems in virtually all kinds of business—small or large, and in whatever type of activity. As a matter of fact, it is hard to think of an area of business where statistics cannot make some contribution. As we have pointed out earlier, we shall touch upon many of these applications in the examples in the text and in the exercises the reader will be asked to solve.

Operations Research

In recent years we have seen the birth of a new technology which is partly mathematics, partly statistics, partly engineering, partly industrial know-how, partly philosophy (a new outlook and a new approach), which is called *operations research*. So far as the work in this book is concerned, its most important feature lies in the application of scientific methods to the solution of problems in practically all areas of business management. This is not meant to imply that scientific analysis and intuition are inimical or that intuition, judgment, and experience are no longer desirable or necessary in business management. Many problems met in actual practice do not have one "best" solution, but several good ones, and experience and judgment can be the main factor in choosing one of these alternatives. Intuition, or the "feel" for a situation, is still extremely important and it can spell the difference between the merely good and the excellent in management. On the other hand, the application of these qualities *alone* will no longer suffice to make many of the decisions required for successful management; despite technical difficulties which are often staggering, it has been demonstrated that carefully designed scientific analyses lead to decisions that are generally superior to those intuited by humans working under the burdens of too little time and (or) too little experience.

Of the various forces which are leading to the widespread development of automatic systems in filing and retrieving information, in sorting, comparing, and computing, in making decisions, in operating machinery, ..., two of the most important are an advancing technology and the military situation. War and business may seem like totally unrelated activities, but there are many close analogies; to emphasize the closeness of the relationship we have only to refer to a "military-business" dictionary, which tells us that for "weapons" we read "materials," for "command" we read "management" or "executive," for "enemy" we read "competitor" or (curiously) "customer," for "destroy" we read "outcompete" or "acquire," and so forth. Actually, the idea of organization itself appeared first in politics and warfare, and countless businesses have been organized on traditional military "line and staff" principles.

The idea of applying scientific techniques to the management of a business or the conduct of a war is quite old. In the third century B.C., the King of Syracuse called on Archimedes to help in defending the city against the Romans, and historians generally attribute the ability of the city to resist for three years to Archimedes' great inventive genius. By the late eighteenth century, the mathematical approach to warfare was so well established that it has been written that "a true strategist of that epoch did not know how to lead a corporal's guard across a ditch without a table of logarithms." In business, the need for effectiveness in matching individuals and jobs has long been evident, and years ago scientific methods (based essentially on psychological and statistical techniques) were used in trying to maximize the chances of choosing the best individuals for various kinds of work. The pioneering application of scientific personnel selection dates back to 1897; also in the 1890's, Frederick W. Taylor applied scientific techniques to various problems in industrial operations, achieving the best results of his "scientific management" in the area of production, where the largely physical processes were readily susceptible to definition and measurement, and more easily controllable by direct methods.

During and after World War I a great deal of statistical work was done in both business and government, and by the time of World War II such tools as time and motion study, market research and analysis, and statistical business forecasting were in wide use. The many critical problems of strategy, tactics, organization, logistics, and weapons systems during World War II demanded the application of new techniques, new methods, and new ideas. The solution of these problems depended on so many technological, economic, and political factors, that they could be handled only by *teams* of military strategists, mathematicians, statisticians, economists, physical scientists, psychologists, and others. It is with these teams of experts that we usually associate the beginning of operations research—*the application of modern scientific techniques to problems involving the operations of a "system" looked upon as a whole, namely, the conduct of a war, the management of a firm, the manufacture of a product, and so forth.*

In an elementary textbook like this one, we can at best present some of the more important techniques that are generally included under the heading of operations research. Among them we find such things as "scientific" decision making based on probability, statistics, and the Theory of Games, Linear Programming, the theory of random processes, methods for handling problems concerning inventory, replacement, allocation, transportation, and many other areas of business management. Unfortunately, even the simplest of these new techniques is fairly difficult mathematically, and we shall, therefore, be satisfied to introduce the reader to some of the basic language, concepts, and tools of operations research. After all, a person working in management does not have to be a scientist (and vice versa), but he should be familiar enough with the new concepts and methodology to know where, when, and how they can be applied.

A Word of Caution

The amount of statistical information that is disseminated to the public for one reason or another is almost beyond comprehension, and what part of it is "good" statistics and what part is "bad" statistics is anybody's guess. Certainly, all of it cannot be accepted uncritically. Another important consideration is that sometimes entirely erroneous conclusions are based on sound data. For instance, a certain city once claimed to be the "nation's healthiest city," since its death rate was the lowest in the country. Even if we go along with their definition that healthy means "not dead," there is another factor that was not taken into account: since the city had no hospital its citizens had to be hospitalized elsewhere, and their deaths were recorded in the cities in which death actually occurred. The following are some other examples of *non sequiturs* based on otherwise sound statistical data: *"Statistics show that there were fewer airplane accidents in 1920 than in 1960; hence, flying was safer in 1920 than in 1960." "Since there are more automobile accidents in the daytime than there are at night, it is safer to drive at night." "Recent statistics show that the average income per person in the United States is $1,200; thus, the average income for a family of four persons is $4,800."*

Sometimes the identical statistical data are made the basis for directly opposite conclusions. This is illustrated by the example on page 63, and it is often found in collective bargaining, where the identical figures are used by one side to show that employees are getting rich and by the other side to show that they are on the verge of starvation. In view of examples like these, it is understandable that some persons are inclined to feel that figures can be made to show pretty much what one wants them to show. Sadly enough, this is uncomfortably close to the truth, unless we carefully distinguish between "good" statistics and "bad" statistics, between statistics properly applied and statistics shamefully abused, and between statistics correctly analyzed and statistics unintentionally or intentionally perverted. We shall repeatedly remind the reader of this problem in special sections titled "A Word of Caution," which are given at the end of each chapter.

It is also important to realize that the sound statistical treatment of a problem consists of a good deal more than merely making a few observations on some conveniently available data, performing a few calculations, and reaching a conclusion. Questions as to how the data were collected and how the whole experiment or survey was planned are of prime importance. As elsewhere, we get "nothing for nothing" in statistics, and unless proper care is taken in all phases of an investigation—from the conception and statement of the problem to the planning and design, through the stages of data collection, analysis, and interpretation—no useful or valid conclusion whatever may be reached. *Generally speaking, no amount of fancy mathematical or statistical manipulation can salvage poorly designed surveys or experiments.* Indeed, professional statisticians insist that even the simplest of sampling studies be rigidly conducted according to certain well-defined rules. There is no more justification for calling a study which does not conform to these rules "statistical" than there is for calling a barnacle a ship.

TWO
SUMMARIZING DATA: FREQUENCY DISTRIBUTIONS

Business Decisions and Mass Data

In recent years, business decisions have come to depend more and more on the analysis of very large sets of data. This includes the small business-man who may need information about income patterns in the area which he serves, the market research analyst who may have to deal with the views expressed by thousands of shoppers, the government statistician who must handle, treat, and analyze census data which can only be described as voluminous, and the head of a large corporation who must consider information which would overwhelm him if it were not presented in a compact and usable form. This trend in the use of mass data is due partly to the increasing availability of high-speed computers; indeed, many current applications of statistical methods would have been prac-tically impossible before the advent of modern data processing techniques. The trend is also due partly to an increasing awareness of the need for scientific methods in business management. Of course, we do not always deal with very large sets of data; there are instances where they are costly and hard to obtain; but the problem of putting mass data into a usable form is so important that it deserves special attention.

When dealing with large sets of data, we can often gain much information and obtain a good over-all picture by *grouping* the data into a number of classes, as is illustrated in the following two examples:

1955 Money Income Before Taxes (in dollars)	Number of Spending Units
Under 1,000	261
1,000 – 1,999	331
2,000 – 2,999	359
3,000 – 3,999	384
4,000 – 4,999	407
5,000 – 7,499	703
7,500 – 9,999	277
10,000 and over	292
	3,014

The data which have been grouped here are the 1955 money incomes (before taxes) of 3,014 spending units; the table, itself, was taken from the July, 1956, issue of the *Federal Reserve Bulletin*. This kind of table is called a *frequency distribution* (or simply a *distribution*): it shows the frequencies with which the various incomes are distributed among the chosen classes. Tables of this sort, in which the data are grouped according to numerical size, are called *numerical* or *quantitative* distributions. In contrast, tables like the one given below (taken from the same source), in which the data are sorted according to a number of categories, are called *categorical* or *qualitative* distributions.

Occupation of Head of Spending Unit	Number of Cases
Professional and semiprofessional	313
Managerial	183
Self-employed	262
Clerical and sales	365
Skilled and semiskilled	810
Unskilled and service	299
Farm operator	154
Retired	269
Other	329
	2,984

Although frequency distributions present data in a relatively compact form, give a good over-all picture, and contain information which is adequate for many purposes, there are evidently some things which can be obtained from the original data that cannot be obtained from a distribution. For instance, referring to the first of the above tables, we can find neither the exact size of the lowest and highest money incomes nor the exact average income of the 261 spending units in the lowest group. Nevertheless, frequency distributions present *raw* (unprocessed) data on which they are based in a more usable form, and the price which we must pay, the loss of certain information, is usually a fair exchange.

Data are sometimes grouped solely to facilitate the calculation of further statistical descriptions. We shall go into this briefly in Chapter 3, but it is worth noting that this function of frequency distributions is diminishing in importance in view of the ever increasing availability of high-speed computing equipment.

Frequency Distributions

The construction of a numerical distribution consists essentially of three steps: (1) we must choose the classes into which the data are to be grouped, (2) we must sort (or tally) the data into the appropriate classes, and (3) we must count the number of items in each class. Since the last two of these steps are purely mechanical, we shall concentrate on the first, namely, the problem of choosing suitable classifications. Note that if the data are recorded on punch-cards, a method that is nowadays widely used, the sorting and counting can be done automatically in a single step.

The two things we shall have to consider in the first step are those of determining the *number of classes* into which the data are to be grouped and the *range of values* each class is to cover, that is, "from where to where" each class is to go. Although both of these choices are essentially arbitrary (they depend largely on the ultimate purpose the distribution is to serve), the following are some rules which are generally observed:

(a) We seldom use fewer than 6 or more than 15 classes; the exact number used in a given situation will, of course, have to depend on the nature, magnitude, and range of the data.

(b) We *always* choose classes which are such that all of the data can be accommodated.

(c) We *always* make sure that each item belongs to only one class; in other words, we avoid overlapping classes, namely, successive classes having one or more values in common.

(d) Whenever possible, we make the class intervals of *equal length*, that is, we make them cover equal ranges of values. It is also generally desirable to make these ranges multiples of 5, 10, 100, etc. (or other numbers that are easy to work with), to facilitate the reading and the use of the resulting table.

Note that the first three, but not the fourth, of these rules were observed in the construction of the numerical distribution on page 11, assuming that the income figures were rounded to the nearest dollar. (Had these figures been given to the nearest cent, an income of, say, $1,999.45 could not have been accommodated, as it would have fallen between the second and the third class.) The fourth rule was violated in two ways: First, the intervals from $5,000 to $7,499 and from $7,500 to $9,999 cover considerably wider ranges of values than those of the second, third, fourth, and fifth classes of the distribution. Secondly, the first and last classes are *open;* for all we know, the first class might include a negative value indicating a deficit or a loss, and the last class might include incomes of a million dollars or more. If a set of data contains a few values that are much greater (or much smaller) than the rest, open classes can help to simplify the over-all picture by reducing the number of required classes; otherwise, open classes should be avoided as they can make it impossible (or at least difficult) to give certain further descriptions of the data.

As we have pointed out, the appropriateness of a classification may depend on whether the data are rounded to the nearest dollar or the nearest cent. Similarly, it may depend on whether data are given to the nearest inch or the nearest hundredth of an inch, whether they are given to the nearest per cent or the nearest tenth of a per cent, and so on. Thus, if we want to group the sizes of orders received by a mail-order house, it might be appropriate to use the classification

Size of Order
(in dollars)

5.00 – 9.99
10.00 – 14.99
15.00 – 19.99
20.00 – 24.99
etc.

assuming that the data are given to the nearest cent. Similarly, for bond yields given to the nearest tenth of a per cent, we might use the classification

Yield on Bonds
(per cent)

1.0 – 1.9
2.0 – 2.9
3.0 – 3.9
4.0 – 4.9
etc.

and for the number of defectives observed hourly in the inspection of some manufactured product we might use the classification

Number of Defectives

0 – 4
5 – 9
10 – 14
15 – 19
etc.

To give a concrete example of the construction of a frequency distribution, or frequency table, let us consider a set of data pertaining to the "downtimes" of a certain machine. A downtime is the time during working hours in which the machine is not operating due to such difficulties as breakage or failure. The following are the lengths of 100 consecutive downtimes of the machine, rounded to the nearest minute:

13	56	35	48	19	57	24	29	13	18
31	45	12	33	41	27	35	16	39	24
9	21	12	25	63	38	53	27	20	6
18	25	31	24	21	48	25	72	23	82
35	17	52	19	5	21	24	46	23	39
14	27	46	33	35	38	29	25	41	21
17	86	24	37	43	51	20	44	37	31
28	58	16	25	42	25	57	63	72	35
34	30	31	46	60	53	27	41	36	30
44	36	52	18	49	26	28	51	62	25

Since the smallest of these values is 5 and the largest is 86, it would seem reasonable (for most practical purposes) to choose the *nine* classes going from 0 to 9, from 10 to 19, from 20 to 29, . . . , and from 80 to 89. Performing the actual tally and counting the number of items in each class, we obtain the results shown in the following table:

Downtimes (minutes)	Tally	Frequencies
0 – 9	///	3
10 – 19	##### ##### ////	14
20 – 29	##### ##### ##### ##### ##### ////	29
30 – 39	##### ##### ##### ##### //	22
40 – 49	##### ##### ////	14
50 – 59	##### #####	10
60 – 69	////	4
70 – 79	//	2
80 – 89	//	2
		100

The numbers shown in the right-hand column of this table are called the *class frequencies;* they give the number of items falling into each class. Also, the smallest and the largest values that can go into any given class are referred to as its *class limits;* thus, the class limits of the above table are 0 and 9, 10 and 19, 20 and 29, and so on. More specifically, 0, 10, 20, . . . , and 80 are referred to as the *lower class limits*, while 9, 19, 29, . . . , and 89 are referred to as the *upper class limits* of the respective classes.

Further terms used in connection with frequency distributions are "class mark," "class interval," and "class boundary." *Class marks* are simply the midpoints of the classes, and they are easily obtained by averaging the class limits, that is, by adding the class limits and dividing by two. Thus, the class marks of the given "downtime" distribution are 4.5, 14.5, 24.5, . . . , and 84.5. A *class interval* is merely the length of a class, namely, the range of values it can contain; when dealing with *equal* class intervals, their length is given by the difference between any two successive class marks. Thus, the above distribution has class intervals of length 10 or, as it is customary to say, it has a class interval of 10. Note that the class interval is *not* given by the difference between the upper and lower class limits, which in our example would equal 9.

Using the terminology just introduced, we can now restate our comment on page 13 by saying that *the choice of the class limits depends on the extent to which the numbers we want to group are rounded off.* If we are dealing with prices rounded to the nearest dollar, the class which has the limits $10–$19 *actually* contains all prices between $9.50 and $19.50.

Similarly, if we are dealing with measurements rounded to the nearest tenth of an inch, the class which has the limits 1.5–1.9 *actually* contains all values between 1.45 and 1.95. Referring again to the "downtime" example, we might, thus, say that the first class contains all values less than 9.5 minutes, the second class contains all those falling between 9.5 and 19.5 minutes, the third contains all those falling between 19.5 and 29.5 minutes, and so forth. It is customary to refer to these values as the *class boundaries*, although they have also been referred to as the *"real" class limits*. Note that the difference between a class's two boundaries equals the class interval. In order to make this true also for the classes which are at the two extremes of the distribution in our example, we artificially give the first class a lower class boundary of −0.5 and the last one an upper class boundary of 89.5. It is important to remember that class boundaries are always "impossible" values inasmuch as they can never occur among the values which we want to group; we make sure of this by accounting for the extent to which the numbers are rounded when we choose the class limits of a distribution. For instance, the class boundaries of the "size of order" distribution on page 13 are the impossible values $4.995, $9.995, $14.995, and so on.

There are some situations in which it is preferable to present data in what is called a *cumulative frequency distribution*, or simply a *cumulative distribution*. In such a distribution we indicate directly how many of the items are *less than* or *greater than* various values. Successively adding the frequencies in the table we obtained for the downtime data, we get the following *"or less" distribution:*

Downtimes (minutes)	Cumulative Frequencies
9 or less	3
19 or less	17
29 or less	46
39 or less	68
49 or less	82
59 or less	92
69 or less	96
79 or less	98
89 or less	100

Note that in this table we could also have written "less than 10," "less than 20," ..., and "less than 90" to indicate the various classes. If we

successively add the frequencies starting at the other end of the distribution, we can similarly construct a *cumulative "or more" distribution*, which
shows how many of the downtimes were 80 minutes or more, how many
were 70 minutes or more, how many were 60 minutes or more, and so
forth.

Sometimes it is preferable to show what percentage of the items falls
into each class instead of the class frequencies. To convert a frequency
distribution (or a cumulative frequency distribution) into a corresponding
percentage distribution, we have only to divide each frequency by the total
number of cases and multiply by 100. Referring to the income distribution on page 11, we find, for example, that the first class contains
$\frac{261}{3,014} \cdot 100 = 8.7$ per cent of the data, that the second class contains
$\frac{331}{3,014} \cdot 100 = 11.0$ per cent of the data, and so on.

So far we have discussed only numerical distributions, but the general
problem of constructing categorical (or qualitative) distributions is very
much the same. Again we must decide how many classes (categories)
to use and what kind of items each category is to contain, making sure
that all of the items are accommodated and that there are no ambiguities.
Since the categories must often be selected before any data are actually
obtained, sound practice is to include a category labeled "others." This
was done, for instance, in the illustration on page 11.

When dealing with categorical distributions, we do not have to worry
about such mathematical details as class limits, class boundaries, class
marks, etc.; on the other hand, we now have a more serious problem
with ambiguities and we must be careful and explicit in defining what
each category is to contain. For this reason, it is often advisable to use
standard categories developed by the Bureau of the Census and other
government agencies. (For references to such lists see the book by
P. M. Hauser and W. R. Leonard in the Bibliography at the end of the
book.)

EXERCISES

1. Decide for each of the following quantities whether it can be determined on the basis of the income distribution on page 11 and, if
   possible, give a numerical answer:

    (a) The number of spending units with incomes of at least $5,000.

    (b) The number of spending units with incomes of more than $5,000.

    (c) The number of spending units with incomes over $20,000.

    (d) The number of spending units with incomes of less than $3,000.

    (e) The number of spending units with incomes of at most $3,000.

    (f) The number of spending units with incomes of at least $6,000.

2. If the sizes of the orders received by a mail-order house are grouped into a frequency table with the classes $5.00–$9.99, $10.00–$14.99, $15.00–$19.99, $20.00–$24.99 (which presumably accommodate all of the data), decide for each of the following quantities whether it can be determined on the basis of the resulting distribution:

    (a) The number of orders for less than $20.00.

    (b) The number of orders for $20.00 or less.

    (c) The number of orders for more than $5.00.

    (d) The number of orders for more than $25.00.

    (e) The number of orders for $5.00 or more.

3. A set of temperature readings, given to the nearest tenth of a degree Fahrenheit, are grouped into a table whose classes have the boundaries 69.95–89.95, 89.95–109.95, 109.95–129.95, 129.95–149.95, and 149.95–169.95. What are the corresponding class limits?

4. The class marks of a distribution of retail food prices (given to the nearest cent) are 20, 29, 38, 47, 56, and 65. Find the corresponding class limits.

5. The mileages obtained per gallon in test runs with a new automobile engine are rounded to the nearest mile and grouped into a table having the classes 5–9, 10–14, 15–19, 20–24, and 25–29. Find the corresponding class boundaries, the class marks, and the class interval.

6. The weights of the male employees of a certain firm are given to the nearest tenth of a pound, with the lowest being 152.4 and the highest being 224.9 pounds. Give the class limits of a table with eight equal classes into which these weights might be grouped.

7. The annual salaries of 400 executives are rounded to the nearest $100, with the smallest being $9,700 and the largest $36,200. Construct a table with six equal classes in which these figures might be grouped, giving the class limits as well as the class boundaries.

8. The following are the number of years the 100 cash registers owned by a chain of variety stores have been in service

```
7.1  3.5  4.2  5.6  6.0  5.8  3.3  5.4  6.1  6.7
2.6  9.1  5.0  9.3  4.7  6.5  5.2  5.8  5.0  2.3
6.9  5.8  6.1  4.0  5.7  5.3  6.4  4.8  2.0  7.7
8.5  5.4  6.9  6.3  9.8  8.6  7.5  6.0  8.2  3.1
5.2  4.0  7.5  8.6  5.5  3.7  5.1  5.6  10.6  9.2
9.4  5.8  5.6  7.2  6.8  4.3  2.5  7.4  3.8  6.3
3.0  6.5  8.2  9.7  7.5  8.1  8.4  4.5  5.2  5.9
4.2  8.8  2.6  3.7  9.2  5.0  6.1  6.6  6.8  5.4
7.8  5.1  6.2  6.9  5.0  6.3  5.8  5.8  10.4  7.5
5.5  6.7  5.3  5.2  7.8  5.6  4.1  3.9  5.7  6.8
```

Group these figures, which are rounded to the nearest tenth of a year, into a distribution having the classes 2.0–2.9, 3.0–3.9, 4.0–4.9, . . . , and 10.0–10.9. Also construct a cumulative "less than" distribution for the ages of these cash registers.

9. Automating its equipment, the chain of variety stores of Exercise 8 is offered by one firm a trade-in of $80 for each cash register which (rounded to the nearest tenth of a year) is less than 4 years old, $50 for each cash register which (rounded to the nearest tenth of a year) is at least 4 years but less than 8 years old, and $25 each for those that are older. Use the cumulative distribution obtained in Exercise 8 to decide whether this firm offers a higher total trade-in than another one which offers a flat $4,500 for the 100 cash registers.

10. The following are the number of replacement parts used in a mill in 50 consecutive weeks for a certain group of similar machines:

```
49  41  45  52  47  46  48  42  43  46
45  36  56  44  61  68  54  58  51  44
47  49  42  48  53  48  41  65  45  52
58  50  55  45  43  72  63  45  38  43
42  47  43  49  46  57  49  44  47  48
```

Group these figures into a table having the classes 35–39, 40–44, 45–49, . . . , and 70–74. Also construct the corresponding cumulative "or more" percentage distribution.

11. If the mill of Exercise 10 has a standing weekly order for 50 of the replacement parts, how often (what per cent of the time) will they find at the week's end that the inventory of replacement parts has actually increased?

12. To study the price increases of certain kinds of items it buys, a company's management considers a sample of 200 items, for which the following are the percentage increases over the past two years:

9.2	4.5	3.3	2.6	9.2	8.0	3.4	4.7	8.5	10.2
2.5	11.4	3.9	7.1	2.5	2.6	10.3	6.4	4.7	5.2
4.4	2.8	10.5	11.9	3.4	3.4	4.7	9.5	2.4	2.1
6.6	7.3	5.0	5.7	5.4	4.6	12.1	4.6	3.5	2.0
3.5	6.0	2.9	13.4	8.9	6.3	2.5	8.4	5.6	4.6
5.1	9.5	8.7	6.0	3.5	2.9	3.4	2.1	6.5	7.4
8.0	14.2	4.4	2.8	12.6	3.7	5.5	3.8	11.3	6.6
7.9	2.1	11.4	2.4	2.9	10.3	13.2	6.1	2.0	3.7
4.8	3.6	6.4	12.0	10.1	5.5	2.0	10.3	2.8	4.4
3.0	5.1	3.2	7.4	4.1	11.5	2.8	5.0	4.1	13.9
5.2	9.4	9.1	3.2	6.7	6.1	7.0	5.2	5.0	5.8
10.7	4.4	2.8	5.0	3.1	2.0	3.8	9.0	9.1	8.7
7.6	12.7	4.2	8.5	5.0	3.1	9.6	2.5	7.1	6.5
2.4	5.9	8.1	6.1	15.7	7.2	4.0	3.9	4.7	4.5
2.3	6.5	3.8	9.7	2.5	9.8	8.7	6.9	10.5	7.0
9.6	8.6	5.2	8.5	4.3	5.6	3.9	7.6	5.4	2.1
4.0	2.2	9.0	3.1	7.8	8.2	10.5	6.2	2.7	10.3
6.8	3.7	4.5	2.6	11.3	2.8	6.4	4.7	4.3	6.5
3.4	13.5	7.0	4.1	3.2	12.5	2.9	8.4	3.5	2.8
8.7	4.5	2.7	6.0	5.3	3.2	8.4	2.7	7.9	5.9

Group these percentage increases into a frequency distribution and construct the corresponding "or less" cumulative distribution.

13. Early in 1963, a stock brokerage firm sent out a report recommending 47 stocks as "good candidates" for 1963. The price-earnings ratios of these stocks, based on 1962 year-end prices and 1962 earnings, were

17.6	23.8	14.0	18.7	20.0	17.1	19.7	23.4
14.3	17.1	24.9	27.5	13.7	9.7	12.9	15.0
15.7	11.6	15.4	17.8	12.7	14.1	13.9	24.5
9.9	11.6	23.9	18.5	18.9	21.5	25.5	30.5
13.9	17.3	21.7	23.5	25.6	15.0	9.6	15.6
23.5	24.7	21.3	12.8	16.2	11.4	13.3	

Group these figures into six equal classes with an interval of 4.

14. In its training program for inspectors, a company uses sheets of paper with random arrays of the digits 0, 1, 2, 3, 4, 5, 6, 7, 8, and 9. There are 1,000 digits on each sheet, among which the fives and sixes, of

which there are altogether 60, are considered to be defective parts. To simulate the inspection of manufactured products, a trainee is given 120 "lots" of 1,000 "parts" to "inspect" in an allotted time. The following are the number of "defectives" one trainee recorded for each lot:

59	53	61	63	58	57	60	59	56	62	59	61
50	62	57	56	60	60	62	58	48	58	52	53
58	60	60	60	54	61	60	54	58	60	59	54
55	59	46	55	57	60	58	56	61	61	57	57
63	60	58	60	59	51	59	61	62	67	55	56
60	56	60	62	60	56	54	59	57	58	63	62
59	57	62	51	64	58	62	60	60	59	60	59
58	48	60	59	60	60	58	57	59	61	49	58
53	60	53	60	56	61	60	52	60	57	58	57
61	58	60	54	59	64	57	60	55	58	60	54

Group these figures into a frequency distribution and construct the corresponding "or more" cumulative percentage distribution.

15. The following are the direct labor costs (in dollars) incurred in the repair of a certain kind of machinery:

25.75	38.60	23.45	40.57	23.69	30.55	22.14	42.35
51.00	26.74	57.93	34.25	72.89	27.50	26.41	29.15
20.45	37.85	32.43	39.51	25.60	47.82	37.49	31.20
49.60	28.75	56.13	31.55	38.76	21.45	34.67	20.10
33.12	43.57	33.68	50.50	36.00	60.75	41.85	45.12
28.60	54.45	45.10	25.33	68.72	35.15	28.83	25.04
27.05	21.65	39.46	78.80	32.15	20.69	41.36	40.82
64.50	34.52	36.48	47.03	26.27	53.41	30.00	24.65
44.24	25.25	27.14	24.89	55.16	42.11	48.31	35.25
30.20	24.53	43.66	66.78	29.15	58.64	21.10	63.12

Group these figures into a distribution having the classes 15.00–24.99, 25.00–34.99, 35.00–44.99, 45.00–54.99, 55.00–64.99, 65.00–74.99, and 75.00–84.99.

16. To show how the choice of different classifications can alter the over-all shape of a distribution, regroup the figures of Exercise 15 into a table having the classes 20.00–29.99, 30.00–39.99, 40.00–49.99, 50.00–59.99, 60.00–69.99, and 70.00–79.99.

17. Construct a distribution showing the frequencies with which the letters a, e, i, o, and u appeared on page 8 of this book.

18. Use a daily newspaper listing prices on the New York Stock Exchange and construct a table showing how many of the *R*, *S*, and *T* stocks traded on a certain day showed a net increase, a net decrease, or no change in price.

19. Take that part of the classified ads of a large daily newspaper where individuals (not dealers) advertise cars for sale, and construct a distribution showing how many of these cars are station wagons, how many are sedans, how many are convertibles, and so on.

20. Choose a local television station and construct a table showing how many of the programs it broadcasts during one week are situation comedies, adventure stories, children's programs, educational programs, and so forth. (Disregard differences in the lengths of the programs.)

Graphical Presentations

When frequency distributions are constructed primarily to condense large sets of data and display them in an "easy to digest" form, it is

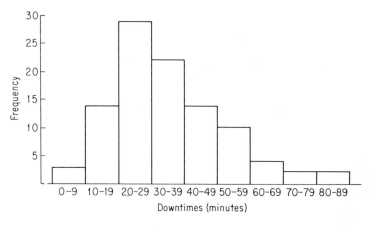

FIGURE 2.1

usually advisable to present them graphically, that is, in a form that appeals to the human power of visualization. The most common among all graphical presentations of statistical data is the *histogram*, an example of which is shown in Figure 2.1. A histogram is constructed by representing the measurements of observations that are grouped (in Figure 2.1 the downtimes in minutes) on a horizontal scale, the class frequencies on a vertical scale, and drawing rectangles whose bases equal the class interval and whose heights are determined by the corresponding class frequencies. The markings on the horizontal scale can be the class limits as in Figure 2.1, the class boundaries, the class marks, or arbitrary key values. For easy readability it is generally preferable to indicate the class limits, although the rectangles actually go from one class boundary to the next. Note that histograms cannot be used in connection with frequency distributions having open classes and that they must be used

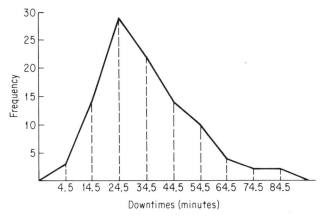

FIGURE 2.2

with extreme care (see discussion on page 27) if the classes are not all equal.

An alternate, though less widely used, form of graphical presentation is the *frequency polygon* (see Figure 2.2). Here the class frequencies are plotted at the class marks and the successive points are connected by means of straight lines. If we apply this same technique to a cumulative distribution, we obtain a so-called *ogive*. Note, however, that now the cumulative frequencies are *not* plotted at the class marks—it stands to reason that the frequency corresponding, say, to "29 or less" should be plotted at 29 or preferably at the class boundary of 29.5, since "29 or less" actually includes everything up to 29.5. Figure 2.3 shows an ogive corresponding to the "or less" distribution of the downtime data.

Although the visual appeal of histograms, frequency polygons, and ogives exceeds that of frequency tables, there are ways in which distributions can be presented even more dramatically and probably also more

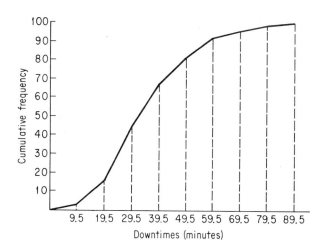

FIGURE 2.3

effectively. Two examples of such pictorial presentations are given in Figures 2.4 and 2.5, and the reader must surely be familiar with pictograms like these through newspapers and magazines.

Although whole books could be (and have been) written on the subject of the graphical presentation of statistical data, we shall not pursue this any further. Generally speaking, it is either mainly a matter of artistic ingenuity or a matter of obeying rules (concerning the kind of lettering to be used, the size of margins, and so forth).

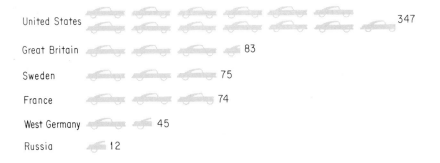

FIGURE 2.4. Motor vehicles per thousand persons in 1955. (*Source:* American Iron and Steel Institute.)

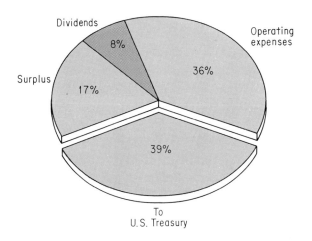

FIGURE 2.5. Disposition of Reserve Bank earnings 1914–1953. (*Source:* The Federal Reserve System, 1954.)

EXERCISES

1. Construct a histogram of the ages of the cash registers grouped in Exercise 8 on page 19. Also construct an ogive of the cumulative "less than" distribution obtained in the same exercise.

2. Construct a histogram of the distribution obtained in Exercise 10 on page 19 and an ogive of the corresponding "or more" percentage distribution.

3. Construct a histogram of the percentage increases grouped in Exercise 12 on page 20 and an ogive of the corresponding "or less" cumulative distribution.

4. Construct a frequency polygon for whichever data you grouped among those of Exercises 8, 10, and 12 on pages 19 and 20.

5. Construct a histogram and a frequency polygon for the price-earnings ratios grouped in Exercise 13 on page 20.

6. Construct a histogram of the distribution obtained in Exercise 14 on page 20 and an ogive of the corresponding "or more" distribution.

7. Draw histograms of the two distributions obtained in Exercises 15 and 16 on page 21 and compare their shapes.

8. The following are the scores which 80 job applicants obtained in a screening test given by a large manufacturer:

Score	Number of Applicants
45 – 49	3
50 – 54	5
55 – 59	11
60 – 64	15
65 – 69	20
70 – 74	8
75 – 79	7
80 – 84	5
85 – 89	4
90 – 94	2
	80

Construct a histogram of this distribution and also draw a histogram of the modified distribution obtained by combining all scores from 55 through 64 into one class (making the adjustment indicated on page 28).

9. Categorical distributions are often presented as pie charts like the one of Figure 2.5, where a circle is divided into sectors which are proportional in size to the frequencies of the corresponding categories. Construct a pie chart for the following percentage distribution, which shows how the different manufacturers split up the first half of 1961 retail sales of all U.S. made automobiles:

General Motors	49.6%
Ford	30.8%
Chrysler	11.5%
American Motors	6.8%
Studebaker-Packard	1.3%

(*Hint:* Note that in a pie chart 1 per cent is represented by a central angle of 3.6 degrees.)

10. Draw a pie chart for the distribution obtained in Exercise 18 on page 22.

11. Draw a pie chart for the distribution obtained in Exercise 20 on page 22.

A Word of Caution

Intentionally or unintentionally, frequency tables, histograms, and other pictorial presentations can be very misleading. Suppose, for instance, that in the downtime example we had combined the two classes going from 40 to 49 and 50 to 59 into one class. This new class has a frequency of 24, but in Figure 2.6, where we still use the heights of the rectangles to represent the class frequencies, we get the erroneous

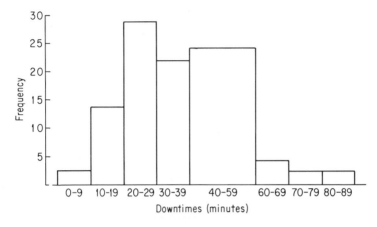

FIGURE 2.6

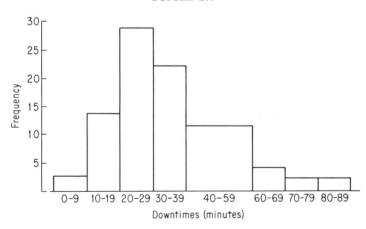

FIGURE 2.7

impression that this class contains almost half of the 100 items. This is due to the fact that when we compare the size of rectangles, triangles, and other plane figures, we instinctively compare their *areas,* and not their sides. In order to correct for this, we will have to draw the rectangles of histograms so that the class frequencies are represented by their areas.

All this does not matter when the classes are all equal, but since the class going from 40 to 59 in our example is *twice as wide* as any of the others, we must accordingly *divide the height of the rectangle by two*. This was done in Figure 2.7, and we now get the correct impression that the class going from 40 to 59 contains about as many items as the one going from

9 billion
dollars in 1950

27 billion
dollars in 1960

FIGURE 2.8. Value of industrial bonds held by U.S. life insurance companies. (*Source:* 1961 Life Insurance Fact Book.)

30 to 39. This is as it should be, since one contains 24 items while the other contains 22.

The same difficulty arises in the construction of so-called pictograms, where the sizes of various kinds of objects are supposed to illustrate and emphasize differences among the data. Suppose, for instance, we want to dramatize the fact that the value of industrial bonds held by U.S. life insurance companies has increased from about 9 billion dollars in 1950 to roughly 27 billion dollars in 1960. Since the amount has actually tripled, we might be tempted to draw a picture like the one of Figure 2.8, where the height as well as the width of the bond certificate is multiplied by three. Unfortunately, this gives the erroneous impression that the amount is multiplied by *nine;* to correct for this, we have to make the *area* of the second bond certificate three times that of the first, and we

9 billion
dollars in 1950

27 billion
dollars in 1960

FIGURE 2.9. Value of industrial bonds held by U.S. life insurance companies. (*Source:* 1961 Life Insurance Fact Book.)

accomplished this in Figure 2.9 by making each side of the second bond certificate $\sqrt{3} = 1.73$ times the corresponding side of the first.

There are many other ways in which tabular and graphical presentations can give misleading and erroneous impressions; some of these are treated in an amusing fashion in *How to Lie with Statistics*, the book by D. Huff referred to in the Bibliography at the end of the book.

THREE
SUMMARIZING
DATA:
STATISTICAL
DESCRIPTIONS

Samples and Populations

Descriptions of statistical data can be quite brief or quite elaborate, depending partly on the nature of the data themselves, and partly on the purpose for which they are to be used. In some instances we might even describe the same set of data in several different ways. To draw an analogy, a San Francisco department store might describe itself to the fire department by giving the number of exits, the total floor space, the number of sprinklers, and the number of employees; on the other hand, it might describe itself to a telephone caller as a "full-line department store with a fine men's department on the Post Street side." Both of these descriptions may serve the purposes for which they are designed, but they would hardly satisfy the New York Stock Exchange in passing on the department store's application for the listing of its stock. This would require detailed information on the nature of the store's business, its history, various kinds of financial statements, and so on.

Whether we describe things statistically or whether we simply describe them verbally, it is always desirable to say neither too little nor too much. Sometimes it may, thus, be satisfactory to present data simply as they are and let them "speak for themselves"; in other instances it may be satisfactory to group, classify, and present them using the methods discussed in Chapter 2. However, most of the time it is necessary to summarize them further by means of one or more well-chosen descriptions. In the next two sections we shall concentrate on two special kinds of descriptions, called *measures of location* and *measures of variation;* some others are mentioned very briefly in the section beginning on page 59.

When we said that the choice of a statistical description depends partly on the nature of the data themselves, we were referring among other things to the following distinction: *if a set of data consists of all conceivably possible (or hypothetically possible) observations of a certain phenomenon, we refer to it as a population; if it contains only part of these observations, we refer to it as a sample.* The qualification "hypothetically possible" was added to take care of such clearly hypothetical situations where, say, ten flips of a coin are looked upon as a *sample* from the *population* of all possible flips of the coin, or where we shall want to look upon the weights of eight 90-day-old heifers as a *sample* of the weights of all (past, present, and future) 90-day-old heifers. In fact, we often look upon the results obtained in an experiment as a sample of what we might obtain if the experiment were repeated over and over again.

In actual practice, whether a set of data is looked upon as a sample or as a population depends to some extent on what we intend to do with the data. Suppose, for example, we are offered a lot of 10,000 pieces of cord, which we may or may not buy depending on its strength. If we measure the breaking strength of five pieces of cord to estimate the average breaking strength of all the cord, these five measurements constitute a sample from the population which consists of the breaking strengths of all 10,000 pieces of cord. We thus have a sample of *size* five from a population of *size* 10,000. In another context, however, we might look on the 10,000 pieces of cord and their breaking strengths as only a sample of all the millions of pieces which the cord manufacturer produces throughout the years. To consider another illustration of this important distinction, suppose we are interested in the speed with which workmen's compensation benefits are paid to injured workmen. Suppose, also, that we have at our disposal figures on *all* compensation claims filed in Wisconsin during the years 1956–1959. If we do not generalize about the way in which such claims are paid in other states or in other years, including the future, we are justified in saying that the data (the time lapses between date of injury and date of payment) constitute a population; they contain all the information that is relevant to the phenomenon with which we are concerned. On the other hand, if we want to make generalizations about the speed with which such claims are paid, say, in the entire United States, the figures for Wisconsin are only a sample.

As we have defined it here, the word "sample" is used in very much the same way as it is used in everyday language. An employer considers the opinions of 50 of his 700 employees a sample of all their opinions on a given matter, and a consumer considers a box of Blum's candy a sample of the firm's product. (Later, in Chapters 7 through 12, we shall interpret the term "sample" in a somewhat narrower fashion, limiting it to data that can reasonably serve to make generalizations about the population from which they are obtained. Thus, the above mentioned sample of data pertaining to Wisconsin may not be acceptable as a sample if generalizations are to be made about the speed with which claims are paid in the entire United States.) The fact that the word "universe" is sometimes used instead of "population" makes it evident that neither term is used here in its colloquial sense. In statistics, both terms refer to the actual or hypothetical totality of measurements or observations with which we are concerned, and *not* to human beings or animals.

Measures of Location

It is often necessary to represent data by means of a single number which, in its way, is descriptive of the entire set; exactly what sort of number we use depends on what particular characteristic we wish to describe. Although we shall be concerned in this section mainly with ways of describing the "center" or "middle" of a set of data, that is, with so-called *measures of central location*, it should be noted that there are also instances where our interest is in such things as the total of the data, their extreme values, and others. For example, in order to determine why a bridge collapsed, we would have to know something about the total weight, rather than the average weight, of the cars and trucks which caused the collapse. Similarly, to vote on a proposed $792 million rapid transit system for the San Francisco Bay area, homeowners would be interested in the *maximum* added cost of the project in any year until the bonds are retired.

What is popularly called "the average" may not always be descriptive of what we need to know about a set of data, but it is without doubt the most widely used kind of statistical description. Inasmuch as the term "average" has a loose connotation and different meanings (for example, when we refer to a batting average, an average housewife, average taste, and so forth), we shall speak more formally of the *arithmetic mean*, or simply the *mean*.* The arithmetic mean of a set of n numbers is defined simply as their sum divided by n. To illustrate, let us refer to the following figures compiled by the SEC, which show the gross proceeds to issuers (in millions of dollars) of new securities issued by state and municipal governments during the years 1952 through 1956:

$$367 \quad 463 \quad 581 \quad 498 \quad 454$$

The mean of these numbers, that is, the "average" proceeds to the issuers over the given period of time, is

$$\frac{367 + 463 + 581 + 498 + 454}{5} = 472.6 \text{ million dollars}$$

Since we shall have occasion to calculate the mean of many different sets of data, it will be convenient to develop a simple formula that is applicable to any set of data. This requires that we represent the figures (measurements or observations) to which the formula is to be applied with some general symbols such as x, y, or z. In the above example, we could designate the gross proceeds to issuers by the letter x and refer to the five values as x_1 (x *sub-one*), x_2, x_3, x_4, and x_5. More generally, if we have n measurements which we designate x_1, x_2, ..., and x_n, we can write

$$\text{mean} = \frac{x_1 + x_2 + \ldots + x_n}{n}$$

This formula is perfectly general and it will take care of any set of data, but it is still somewhat cumbersome. To make it more compact, we introduce the symbol Σ (capital *sigma*, the Greek letter for S), which is simply a mathematical shorthand notation indicating the process of summation or addition. If we write Σx, this represents the "sum of the

---

* Since there are also a *geometric mean* and a *harmonic mean* (see Exercises 18 and 19 on page 45), it must be kept in mind that when we speak of *the mean*, we are referring to the arithmetic mean and not to the others.

x's", and we thus have

$$\text{mean} = \frac{\Sigma\, x}{n}$$

Using the sigma notation in this form, the number of terms to be added is not stated explicitly; it is tacitly understood to refer to all the x's with which we happen to be concerned. A more detailed discussion of the Σ notation may be found in Technical Note 1 on page 65.

To go one step further, we shall finish simplifying our notation by assigning a special symbol to the mean itself. If we look upon the x's as a sample, we write their mean as $\bar{x}$ (x-bar); if we look upon them as a population, we write their mean as μ (mu, the Greek letter for m). (Also, if we refer to sample data as y's or z's, we write their respective means as $\bar{y}$ and $\bar{z}$.) To emphasize the distinction, we denote the number of values in a sample, the *sample size*, with the letter n, and the number of values in a population, the *population size*, with the letter N. We thus have the formulas

MEAN
$$\bar{x} = \frac{\Sigma\, x}{n} \quad \text{or} \quad \mu = \frac{\Sigma\, x}{N} \qquad \star$$

depending on whether we are dealing with a sample or a population. In order to distinguish between descriptions of populations and descriptions of samples, statisticians not only use different symbols, but they refer to the first as *parameters* and the second as *statistics*. Hence, we say that μ is a parameter and that $\bar{x}$ is a statistic.

To illustrate this usage, let us consider the problem of a manufacturing company which annually uses in its work thousands of wooden panels which must have a certain impact strength. As it is obviously impossible to test all the panels it receives from a given supplier (the testing is destructive and shatters the panels beyond use), five panels are selected from a given shipment and their impact strengths (in pounds per square inch) are recorded as

$$3{,}000 \quad 3{,}210 \quad 3{,}150 \quad 3{,}400 \quad 3{,}290$$

These measurements constitute a sample, since we are actually interested in *all* the panels shipped by the given supplier. In other words, we are

---

★ Formulas marked with a star are actually used for practical computations. This will make it easier for the reader to distinguish between formulas used for calculations and those given primarily for definitions or as part of derivations.

interested in μ, the mean impact strength for the whole shipment, but we have only enough information to calculate $\bar{x}$. The value which we get for the mean is

$$\bar{x} = \frac{16{,}050}{5} = 3{,}210 \text{ psi}$$

and we can use this figure to *estimate* the unknown population mean μ, provided that sufficient care was taken in obtaining the sample. Note how our notation eliminates such confusing language as "we use a mean to estimate a mean"; the statement "we use $\bar{x}$ as an estimate of μ" makes it clear that we are using a statistic to estimate a parameter, namely, a sample mean to estimate the mean of a population.

The popularity of the mean as a measure describing the "middle" or "center" of a set of data is not just accidental. Anytime we use a single number to describe a set of data, there are certain desirable properties that must be kept in mind. Thus, some of the desirable features of the mean are: (1) it is familiar to most people, although they may not call it by this name; (2) it always exists, that is, it can be calculated for any kind of numerical data; (3) it is always unique, or in other words, a set of numerical data has one and only one mean; (4) it lends itself to further statistical manipulation (in Exercise 13 on page 44, for example, it will be shown how the means of several sets of data can be combined into an over-all mean descriptive of all the data); (5) it takes into account each individual item; and (6) it is relatively *reliable* in the sense that it does not vary too much when repeated samples are taken from one and the same population, at least not as much as some other kinds of statistical descriptions. This question of reliability is of fundamental importance when it comes to problems of estimation and testing hypotheses, and we shall have a good deal more to say about it in Chapters 7, 8, and 9.

Since the calculation of a mean is fairly easy and straightforward, involving only addition and one division, there is usually no need to look for short-cuts or simplifications. However, if the numbers are unwieldy or a set of data is very large, it may be advantageous to group the data first and then obtain the mean from the resulting distribution. Another reason why we shall have to look into the problem of calculating means of grouped data is that statistical information is often made public only in the form of distributions. In connection with this, it must be pointed out that when a set of data is grouped each item, so to speak, loses its identity, we know only how many items fall into the various classes, and the actual mean of the data cannot be obtained. However, we can get a good approximation by assigning the value of the class mark to each item falling into a given class; thus, the three values which fall into the first class of the downtime distribution on page 15 are treated as if they all equalled 4.5, the midpoint of the class going from 0 to 9. Similarly, the fourteen values falling into the second class are treated as if they all equalled 14.5, those falling into the third class are treated as if they all equalled 24.5, and so forth. This kind of approximation is usually excellent, since the errors that are introduced will more or less "average out."

To obtain a formula for the mean of a distribution, let us write the successive class marks as $x_1, x_2, \ldots, x_k$ (assuming that there are k classes) and the corresponding class frequencies as $f_1, f_2, \ldots, f_k$. The total that goes into the numerator of the formula for the mean is thus obtained by adding f_1 times the value x_1, f_2 times the value x_2, $\ldots$, and f_k times the value x_k; in other words, it is equal to $x_1f_1 + x_2f_2 + \ldots + x_kf_k$. Using again the Σ notation introduced on page 33, we can now write the formula for the mean of a distribution as

$$\bar{x} = \frac{\Sigma x \cdot f}{n} \qquad \bigstar$$

where $\Sigma x \cdot f$ represents, in words, the sum of the products obtained by multiplying each class mark by the corresponding class frequency. (When dealing with a population instead of a sample, we have only to substitute μ for $\bar{x}$ in this formula and N for n.)

To illustrate the calculation of the mean of a distribution, let us refer again to the downtime distribution on page 15. Writing the class marks in the second column, we get

Downtimes (minutes)	Class marks x	Frequencies f	Products x · f
0 – 9	4.5	3	13.5
10 – 19	14.5	14	203.0
20 – 29	24.5	29	710.5
30 – 39	34.5	22	759.0
40 – 49	44.5	14	623.0
50 – 59	54.5	10	545.0
60 – 69	64.5	4	258.0
70 – 79	74.5	2	149.0
80 – 89	84.5	2	169.0
		100	3430.0

and the mean of the distribution is

$$\bar{x} = \frac{3430.0}{100} = 34.3 \text{ minutes}$$

It is interesting to note that the mean of the actual ungrouped data on page 14 is $\bar{x} = \frac{3438}{100} = 34.38$ and that the difference between the two means is thus extremely small. In this particular example, the calculation of $\bar{x}$ was not very hard since the class marks were easy to work with and the frequencies were not very large. Otherwise, it might have saved time to use the *short-cut method* explained in Technical Note 2 on page 66.

Whether or not the fifth property of the mean listed on page 35 is actually desirable is open to some doubt; a single extreme (very large or very small) value can affect the mean to such an extent that it is debatable whether it is really "representative" or "typical" of the data. To illustrate this, let us consider the matter of changes in automobile insurance rates, which are established statistically to assure fair indemnification within policy limits. In general, rates have been rising steadily, and one reason for this has been the larger court awards in bodily injury suits. For instance, data from Creek County, Oklahoma, show that the mean award has recently increased by 3,500 per cent. However, closer inspection of the data shows that this figure is distorted by one unusually large verdict of $650,000, which affects both the mean and the percentage change. Omitting this one atypical value, the Insurance Information Institute showed that the increase reduced to 573 per cent, a figure which it considers much more representative of the data as a whole.

To avoid the difficulty pointed out in the preceding paragraph, we can describe the "middle," "center," or "average" of a set of data by means of some other kind of statistical description. One of these is the *median*, which is defined simply as the value of the middle item (or the mean of the values of the two middle items) when the data are arranged in an increasing or decreasing order of magnitude.

If we have an *odd* number of items, there is always a middle item whose value is the median. For example, the median of the five numbers

$$4 \quad 9 \quad 1 \quad 6 \quad 7$$

is 6, as can easily be verified by first arranging these numbers according to size, and the median of the nine numbers

$$1 \quad 3 \quad 4 \quad 7 \quad \textcircled{7} \quad 8 \quad 8 \quad 10 \quad 11$$

is 7. Note that there are two 7's in this last example and that we do not refer to either of them as *the* median. The median is a number and not an item, namely, the value of the middle item. Generally speaking, if there are n items and n is *odd*, the median is the value of the $\frac{n+1}{2}$ th largest item. Thus, the median of 15 numbers is given by the value of the $\frac{15+1}{2} = $ 8th largest, the median of 49 numbers is given by the value of the $\frac{49+1}{2} = $ 25th largest, and the median of 99 numbers is given by the value of the $\frac{99+1}{2} = $ 50th largest.

If we have an *even* number of items, there is never a middle item, and the median is defined as the mean (average) of the values of the two middle items. For instance, the median of the six numbers

$$2 \quad 5 \quad 7 \quad 9 \quad 12 \quad 14$$

(which are already ordered according to size) is $\frac{7+9}{2} = $ 8. It is halfway between the two middle values (here the 3rd and 4th) and, if we interpret it correctly, the formula $\frac{n+1}{2}$ again gives the *position* of the median. For the six given numbers the median is, thus, the value of the $\frac{6+1}{2} = $ 3.5th largest, and we interpret this as meaning "halfway between the values of the third and the fourth." Similarly, the median of 80 numbers is given by the value of the $\frac{80+1}{2} = $ 40.5th largest item, or halfway between the values of the 40th and the 41st. It is important to remember that the formula $\frac{n+1}{2}$ is *not* a formula for the median, itself; it merely tells us the *position* of the median, namely, the number of items we have to count until we reach the item whose value is the median (or the two items whose values have to be averaged to obtain the median).

It should not be surprising that the median and the mean of a set of data do not always coincide. Both of these measures describe the same thing, the center of a set of data, but they describe it in different ways. For the data directly above, the median is 8 and the mean is 8.2. The median is central in the sense that it splits the data so that the values of half the items are less than or equal to the median while the values of the other half are greater than or equal to the median. The mean is central in the sense that if all the values were the same size while their total remained unchanged, they would all have to be equal to the mean. Sometimes the mean and the median do coincide, though, and we interpret this as being indicative of a further property of the data, namely, their *symmetry*. We shall discuss this further on page 61.

The median has certain desirable properties, some of which it shares with the mean. Like the mean it always exists—that is, it may be found for any set of data—and it is always unique. Once the data are arranged according to size, the median is simple enough to find, but (unless the work is done automatically) ordering large sets of data can be a very tedious job. Unlike the mean, the median is *not* easily affected by extreme values, as is illustrated in Exercise 7 on page 43. Also unlike the mean, the median can be used to define the middle of a number of objects, properties, or qualities, which do not permit a quantitative description. It is possible, for instance, to rank a number of tasks according to their difficulty and then describe the middle one as being of "average" difficulty. Perhaps the most important distinction between the median and the mean is that in problems of inference (estimation, prediction, and so on) the mean is usually more reliable than the median. In other words, the median is usually subject to greater chance fluctuations than the mean, as is illustrated in Exercise 6 on page 193.

So far as symbolism is concerned, we shall write the median of a set of x's (looked upon as a sample) as $\tilde{x}$. Some statisticians correspondingly represent population medians with the symbol $\tilde{\mu}$, but there is no real need to introduce this notation. In most problems of estimation we assume that the population mean and median coincide; in fact, we shall be interested in the median mainly in connection with problems where sample medians are used to estimate population means.

If we want to determine the median of a set of data that has already been grouped, we find ourselves in a position similar to the one in which we found ourselves on page 35; we can no longer determine the *actual* value of the median, although we can find the class into which the median must fall. What we do in a situation like this is most easily understood with the aid of a diagram like that of Figure 3.1, showing again the histogram of the downtime distribution. The median of a distribution is defined as a number, a point, which is such that *half the total area of the rectangles of the histogram lies to its left and half lies to its right.* This means that the sum of the areas of the rectangles to the left of the dotted line of Figure 3.1 equals the sum of the areas to its right.

To find the median of a distribution containing n items, we first determine the class into which the median must fall by counting $n/2$ items starting at either end. In what follows, we shall start counting from the bottom (the smallest values) of the distribution. Having

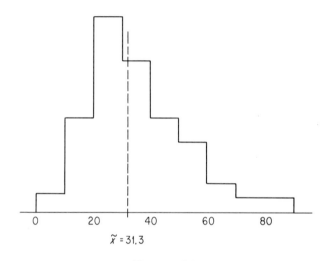

$\tilde{x} = 31.3$

FIGURE 3.1

$n = 100$ in the downtime example, we thus have to count $n/2 = 50$ items to find the class into which the median must fall. Since 46 of the values are 29 minutes or less while 68 are 39 minutes or less, it follows that the desired class is the one whose limits are 30–39. Now we must count another 4 items in addition to the 46 items falling below this class, and we accomplish this by adding $4/22$ of the class interval of 10 to 29.5, the lower boundary of the class. (We add $4/22$ of the class interval because we want to count 4 of the 22 values contained in this class.) We thus get

$$\tilde{x} = 29.5 + \frac{4}{22} \cdot 10 = 31.3 \text{ minutes}$$

Generally speaking, if L is the lower boundary of the class containing the median, f is its frequency, c the class interval, and j the number of items we still lack when reaching L, then the *median of the distribution* is given by the formula

$$\tilde{x} = L + \frac{j}{f} \cdot c \qquad\qquad ★$$

It is possible, of course, to arrive at the median of a distribution by starting at the other end and *subtracting* an appropriate fraction of the class interval from the upper boundary U of the class into which the median must fall. For the downtime distribution we thus obtain

$$\tilde{x} = 39.5 - \frac{18}{22} \cdot 10 = 31.3 \text{ minutes}$$

and the two answers are identical, as they should be. A general formula for the case where we start counting at the top of the distribution is given by

$$\tilde{x} = U - \frac{j'}{f} \cdot c \qquad\qquad ★$$

where j' is the number of items we still lack when reaching U.

The method we have just described can also be used to determine any other *fractile* of a distribution. The three *quartiles* Q_1, Q_2, and Q_3 are such that 25 per cent of the data fall below Q_1, 25 per cent fall between Q_1 and Q_2, 25 per cent fall between Q_2 and Q_3, and 25 per cent fall above Q_3. To find the first and third quartiles of a distribution (Q_2 actually *is* the median), we can use either of the two formulas given above. For Q_1 we count 25 per cent of the items starting at the bottom of the distribution, and for Q_3 we count 75 per cent of the items starting at the bottom or 25 per cent starting at the top. Referring again to the downtime distribution, we obtain

$$Q_1 = 19.5 + \frac{8}{29} \cdot 10 = 22.3 \text{ minutes}$$

and

$$Q_3 = 49.5 - \frac{7}{14} \cdot 10 = 44.5 \text{ minutes}$$

The *deciles* D_1, D_2, ..., and D_9 are such that 10 per cent of the data fall below D_1, 10 per cent fall between D_1 and D_2, 10 per cent fall between D_2 and D_3, ..., and 10 per cent fall above D_9. For example, counting 30 per cent of the items starting at the bottom of the downtime distribution, we find that

$$D_3 = 19.5 + \frac{13}{29} \cdot 10 = 24.0 \text{ minutes}$$

and counting 10 per cent of the items starting at the other end, we find that

$$D_9 = 59.5 - \frac{2}{10} \cdot 10 = 57.5 \text{ minutes}$$

The *percentiles* of a distribution, P_1, P_2, ..., and P_{99}, are such that 1 per cent of the data falls below P_1, 1 per cent falls between P_1 and P_2, ..., and 1 per cent falls above P_{99}. (Note that the fifth decile and the fiftieth percentile are both equal to the median, and that the twenty-fifth and seventy-fifth percentiles equal Q_1 and Q_3, respectively.)

Besides the median and the mean, there are numerous other ways in which we can describe the center, or "average," of a set of data. Some of these, the *geometric mean*, the *harmonic mean*, and the *weighted mean*, are explained in Exercises 18, 19, and 16 on pages 45 and 46. Another measure of "central" location worth mentioning is the *mode*, which is defined simply as the value which occurs with the highest frequency. Thus, if more applicants for a job are 23 years old than any other age, we say that 23 is their *modal age* (that is, the mode is 23). Similarly, in the downtime distribution the class which has the limits 20–29 is the *modal class* (it has the highest frequency), and if more savings banks pay $4\frac{1}{2}\%$ on savings accounts than any other rate, we say that $4\frac{1}{2}\%$ is the *modal rate*. An obvious advantage of the mode is that it requires no calculations, and its principal value lies in the fact that it can be used with qualitative as well as quantitative data. Dealing with qualitative data, we can say, for instance, that if most of the members of a sorority are blondes, then blond is the *modal color* of these girls' hair. A definite disadvantage of the mode is that it need not be unique, as is illustrated by the following data:

$$2 \quad 4 \quad 7 \quad 2 \quad 5 \quad 2 \quad 3 \quad 8 \quad 7 \quad 4 \quad 7$$

Here 2 and 7 both occur with the highest frequency of three. (The fact that there is more than one mode is sometimes indicative of a lack of homogeneity of the data, namely, that they are actually a combination of several sets of data.) A very definite disadvantage of the mode is that if no two values are alike, the mode does not exist.

EXERCISES

1. Suppose we are given complete information about the refunds residents of Arizona obtained on the federal income tax which was withheld from their paychecks in 1963. Give one illustration each of situations where we would consider this set of data to be (a) a population and (b) a sample.

2. Suppose we are given complete information about the mileages that police cars were driven in Los Angeles County during December, 1963. Give one example each of problems in which we would consider these data to constitute (a) a population and (b) a sample.

3. Twenty cans of cleansing powder are randomly selected from a large production lot and their net weights determined with the following results: 13.9, 14.1, 14.2, 13.9, 13.9, 14.0, 14.1, 14.0, 14.0, 13.9, 14.0, 14.0, 14.1, 13.9, 14.0, 13.9, 14.0, 14.1, 14.0, 14.0 ounces. What is the mean weight of these cans?

4. Fourteen business executives, asked to estimate the percentage change in the Gross National Product for a given period, came up with the following results: 1.0, 2.0, 1.5, 2.0, 4.0, 1.8, 2.0, 0.5, −0.5, 3.0, 1.2, 2.0, 5.0, and 4.6 per cent. Find the mean and the median of these estimates.

5. Twelve large banks reported the following three operating ratios for a given year:

   (a) Net profits as a percentage of total capital accounts: 6.2, 6.6, 6.3, 7.7, 7.8, 8.4, 8.0, 7.9, 8.7, 8.0, 7.9, 9.4.

   (b) Salaries and wages as a percentage of total earnings: 31.7, 29.9, 26.2, 27.0, 28.1, 31.2, 31.0, 30.8, 30.6, 35.2, 35.4, 32.1.

   (c) Real estate assets as a percentage of total assets: 1.3, 1.1, 1.1, 1.0, 1.2, 1.2, 0.7, 0.7, 0.8, 0.6, 1.1, 1.2.

   Find the means, the medians, and (if possible) the modes of these three sets of percentages.

6. A large company has decided to meet a competitive action by marketing a new product. Twenty members of its executive staff, asked whether the product should be marketed in 2, 3, or 4 different models, gave the following answers: 2, 3, 3, 4, 2, 2, 3, 3, 2, 3, 3, 2, 4, 3, 3, 2, 3, 3, 2, and 3. Find the mean, the median, and the mode, and comment on the suitability of each as a way of expressing the "average" preference of the group.

7. At the end of a year, an office machines company measures the performance of its 15 salesmen by expressing the respective total sales as percentages of quota. Obtaining 80, 94, 110, 100, 99, 98, 100, 420, 95,

98, 101, 90, 88, 75, and 80 per cent, find the mean, median, and mode and comment on the suitability of each as a way of expressing "average" performance of the group.

8. An elevator is designed to carry a maximum load of 5,500 pounds. If it is loaded with 30 passengers having an average (mean) weight of 150 pounds, is there any danger that it might fail?

9. It has been reported that "the typical embezzler is about 34, married and the father of two children, belongs to the middle income group, and works on the average five years before he begins to rob the till." Comment on the statistical aspects of this statement.

10. A bill was introduced in a state legislature to repeal the sales tax on prescription drugs. Comment on the argument of the state finance director that "the average per capita prescription bill for the past three years is a trifling $2.00, which is not really a burden to anyone."

11. A student took six readings on the direction from which the wind blew at a certain place, obtaining 10, 348, 355, 5, 12, and 350 degrees. (These angles are measured clockwise with $0°$ being due North.) Averaging these figures he obtains a mean of $180°$, which means that the wind blew from the South. Find the fallacy of this argument and a more appropriate way of averaging the six readings.

12. In 1949, automobile property damage claims for $100 or less averaged $33.91, those from $101 to $1,000 averaged $216.89, while those over $1,000 averaged $1,635.09. Taking the mean of these three figures, is it reasonable to claim that the over-all average of these insurance claims is $628.63?

13. Given k sets of data having the means $\bar{x}_1, \bar{x}_2, \ldots, \bar{x}_k$, and consisting, respectively, of $n_1, n_2, \ldots, n_k$ observations, the over-all mean of all the data may be obtained by means of the formula

$$\frac{n_1\bar{x}_1 + n_2\bar{x}_2 + \ldots + n_k\bar{x}_k}{n_1 + n_2 + \ldots + n_k} \qquad \bigstar$$

where the numerator represents the total of all the observations, while the denominator represents the total number of observations. Use this formula to find the correct over-all average of the insurance claims referred to in Exercise 12, if the number of claims in the three classifications are, respectively, 715,673, 157,879, and 1,707.

14. If an investor bought 50 shares of Central Valley National Bank at $35 a share, 10 shares at $31, and 40 more shares at $38, what was his average cost per share?

15. In three consecutive years 3.4, 4.2, and 4.0 million spending units spent an average of $280, $260, and $275, respectively, for refrigerators. What was the average cost per spending unit for the three years?

16. The formula of Exercise 13 is a special case of the following formula for the *weighted mean*

$$\bar{x}_w = \frac{w_1 x_1 + w_2 x_2 + \ldots + w_k x_k}{w_1 + w_2 + \ldots + w_k} \qquad \star$$

where the w's are weights which are indicative of the relative importance of the corresponding x's. (In Exercise 13, the quantities we wanted to average were the means, and the weights were the sizes of the respective sets of data.) Using this formula, show that if a person invests $1,000 at 2 per cent, $800 at 3 per cent, and $3,200 at 5 per cent, the average return on these investments is 4.08 per cent.

17. The following table shows a baseball player's batting average and the number of times he was at bat in four consecutive seasons:

Year	Batting Average	Times at Bat
1960	0.291	420
1961	0.276	380
1962	0.302	480
1963	0.265	320

What is his over-all batting average for these four seasons?

18. The *geometric mean* of a set of n numbers is the nth root of their product, and it is used mainly to average ratios, rates of change, index numbers (see Chapter 4), and the like. In practice, it is obtained by adding the logarithms of the n numbers, dividing by n, and then taking the antilogarithm. Verify that the geometric mean of 107, 132, 120, 116, 130, 126, 116, and 122, the 1954 Wholesale Price Indexes of eight major commodity groups, is approximately 121. Also find the geometric mean of 8 and 32, that of 4, 6, and 9, and that of 1, 1, 2, and 8.

19. The *harmonic mean* of n numbers is defined as n divided by the sum of the reciprocals of the n numbers, namely, as $n/\Sigma \dfrac{1}{x}$. Its use as an average is appropriate only in very special situations. For instance, if $12 is spent for replacement parts costing 40 cents a dozen and another $12 is spent for replacement parts costing 60 cents a dozen, the average

price per dozen is *not* $\dfrac{40 + 60}{2}$ = 50 cents. It is 48 cents, since a total of \$24 is spent on a total of 50 dozen parts. Verify that this average is, in fact, the harmonic mean of 40 and 60.

20. If a motorist travels the first 10 miles of a trip at 30 miles per hour and the next 10 miles at 60 miles per hour, what is his average speed for these 20 miles? Does the harmonic mean give the correct answer?

21. Find the median as well as Q_1 and Q_3 for the income distribution on page 11. Is it possible to find P_{95} on the basis of this distribution?

22. Find the mean of the ages of the cash registers of Exercise 8 on page 19 using (a) the ungrouped data and (b) the formula on page 36 and the distribution obtained in that exercise.

23. Find the mean of the weekly number of replacement parts of Exercise 10 on page 19 using (a) the ungrouped data and (b) the formula on page 36 and the distribution obtained in that exercise. Compare the two results.

24. Find the median of whichever data you grouped among those of Exercises 8, 10, 12, 13, 14, and 15 on pages 19 through 21. Also find Q_1 and Q_3 for this distribution.

(Exercises 25, 26, 27, and 28 are based in part on the material in Technical Note 2.)

25. Use the short-cut formula on page 66 to compute the mean of the distribution obtained in Exercise 12 on page 20.

26. Find the mean of the distribution of the price-earnings ratios obtained in Exercise 13 on page 20 using (a) the formula on page 36 and (b) the short-cut formula on page 66. Compare the results.

27. Find the mean of the distribution obtained in Exercise 14 on page 20, using the short-cut formula on page 66.

28. Find the mean of the distribution of the direct labor costs obtained in Exercise 15 on page 21, using the short-cut formula on page 66.

(The following exercises pertain to the material in Technical Note 1.)

29. Given $x_1 = 3$, $x_2 = 1$, $x_3 = 2$, $x_4 = 1$, and $x_5 = 2$, find

(a) $\Sigma\ x$.

(b) $\Sigma\ x^2$.

30. Given $x_1 = 2$, $x_2 = -3$, $x_3 = 4$, $f_1 = 5$, $f_2 = 7$, $f_3 = 13$, $y_1 = 2$, $y_2 = 3$, and $y_3 = 5$, find

(a) $\Sigma\ x \cdot f$.   (c) $\Sigma\ x \cdot y$.

(b) $\Sigma\ x^2 \cdot f$.   (d) $\Sigma\ (x - y)$.

31. Write each of the following in full, that is, without summation signs:

(a) $\displaystyle\sum_{i=1}^{5} x_i$.

(c) $\displaystyle\sum_{j=2}^{4} (x_j + y_j)$.

(b) $\displaystyle\sum_{i=1}^{4} w_i^2$.

(d) $\displaystyle\sum_{i=3}^{6} x_i^2 \cdot f_i$.

32. Write each of the following as a summation:

(a) $F_1 + F_2 + F_3 + \ldots + F_{40}$.

(b) $x_1y_1 + x_2y_2 + x_3y_3 + x_4y_4$.

(c) $x_1^2 + x_2^2 + x_3^2 + x_4^2 + x_5^2 + x_6^2 + x_7^2$.

(d) $y_1f_1 + y_2f_2 + \ldots + y_Nf_N$.

33. Prove that

(a) $\displaystyle\sum_{i=1}^{n} (x_i - k) = \sum_{i=1}^{n} x_i - nk$.

(b) $\displaystyle\sum_{i=1}^{n} (x_i - \bar{x}) = 0$, where $\bar{x}$ is the mean of the given x_i.

34. Is it true in general that

$$\left[\sum_{i=1}^{n} x_i \right]^2 = \sum_{i=1}^{n} x_i^2$$

(*Hint:* Check whether the equation holds for $n = 2$.)

Measures of Variation

One of the most important characteristics of a set of data is that the values are generally *not all alike;* indeed, the precise extent to which they are unalike, or vary among themselves, is of basic importance in statistics. The various measures of central location discussed in the preceding section describe one important property of a set of data, their middle or their "average," but they do not tell us anything about this other basic characteristic. Hence, we require ways of measuring the extent to which statistical data are dispersed, spread out, or bunched, and the statistical measures which provide us with this information are called *measures of variation.*

First, let us give a few examples to illustrate the importance of measuring variability. Suppose, for instance, that we are interested in buying a certain stock and we find that its latest closing price on the New York Stock Exchange is $51\frac{1}{8}$ (dollars per share). To decide whether this is a good buy, many things will have to be taken into account; among other things we may want to know how much the price of this stock *fluctuates* and we thus look for the year's High and Low. Supposing that these figures are $68\frac{1}{2}$ and 45, respectively, we now have some information about the *variation* in the price of the stock, and this may be critical in deciding whether or not it should be bought. Of course, an intelligent investor would want to compare the fluctuations of this stock with those of other stocks and, probably, also with those of the market as a whole.

Another example which demonstrates the need for measuring variability may be found in the following problem, dealing with the inspection of steel ordered for the construction of a bridge. Engineering specifications call for steel with a minimum compressive strength of 46,000 psi (pounds per square inch), and to play it safe, steel has been ordered with the specification that its mean strength must be 60,000 psi. When the first shipment is received, an inspector tests a sample of five pieces of the steel to determine the quality of the lot, and he obtains the following measurements:

$$71{,}000 \quad 45{,}250 \quad 70{,}400 \quad 81{,}350 \quad 42{,}000$$

The mean compressive strength of this sample is 62,000 psi, which is slightly above specifications, and from this it might appear that the steel is entirely satisfactory. However, if we look at the *variation* among the five measurements, we find that they vary considerably; in fact, two of the five pieces have a compressive strength *below* the minimum requirement of 46,000 psi, and a large portion of the shipment may well be unsatisfactory. In a problem like this it is important, therefore, to consider variability besides measuring average strength. As a matter of fact, the original specifications for the steel should have contained something about the permissible variability besides the specification about average strength.

The concept of variability or dispersion is of fundamental importance in statistical inference (estimation, testing hypotheses, making predictions, etc.), where key questions always involve the concept of *chance variation*. To illustrate what this means, suppose that a coin is flipped 100 times and that we obtain 29 heads and 71 tails. In order to decide whether this *supports or contradicts* the assumption that the coin is balanced (that heads and tails are equally likely), let us see for a moment what we might reasonably expect. Although we would, on the average, expect 50 heads and 50 tails, we would not be surprised if we got, say,

48 heads and 52 tails, 54 heads and 46 tails, or 43 heads and 57 tails, attributing the few extra heads or tails entirely to chance. To see whether 29 heads in 100 flips, a discrepancy of 21, might also be attributed to chance, let us investigate this kind of chance effect by repeatedly flipping a supposedly balanced coin 100 times and observing the results. Suppose, then, that we perform ten such "experiments" and that we obtain 51, 54, 48, 55, 41, 49, 58, 52, 46, and 51 heads. Of course, ten repetitions of such an experiment do not tell us too much, but they provide us with some idea about the magnitude of the fluctuations (variations) produced by chance in the number of heads we obtain in 100 flips of a coin. Judging from the above data, in which the number of heads varied from 41 to 58, we might feel that anything from 40 to 60 heads is "not unusual," but that 29 heads in 100 tosses is completely "out of line." We thus conclude that there must be something wrong with the coin; perhaps it is worn on one side or something like that. This whole argument has been presented on a rather intuitive basis, in order to illustrate the need for measuring chance variation; in later chapters we shall treat the same problem more rigorously and in more detail.

To consider a final example from inductive statistics (statistical inference) in which the concept of variability plays an important role, suppose we want to *estimate* the true average drained weight of all cans of fruit salad of a certain size put up by a large canner. Suppose, further- more, that a sample of three cans yielded the following drained weights (in ounces): 14.0, 13.8, 14.2. The mean drained weight of this sample is $\bar{x} = 14.0$ ounces, and we might conclude from this that μ, the true average weight of all such cans of fruit salad, equals 14.0 ounces, or at least that μ is very close to 14.0. Since the size of this sample is very small, any such conclusion constitutes quite a generalization; whether or not it is reasonable or justifiable depends on many factors, of which we are interested at the moment in just one: the *variability of the population* from which the sample came. To explain what this means, consider the follow- ing two possibilities:

Case 1: The true mean drained weight is 14.1 ounces, the filling process is *very consistent*, and all the cans of fruit salad under consider- ation have a drained weight somewhere between 13.8 and 14.4 ounces.

Case 2: The true mean drained weight is 14.1 ounces, but the filling process is *very inconsistent*, and the drained weights of all the cans of fruit salad under consideration vary considerably, all the way from 12.0 ounces to 16.2 ounces.

If the population whose mean we are estimating is the one described in Case 1, we can be *sure* that the sample mean will not differ from the true mean by much, no matter how small the sample. In fact, it could not possibly be off by more than 0.3 ounces, and off by this much only if the weights in the sample were all 13.8 ounces or all 14.4 ounces. The population described in Case 2 is an entirely different collection of weights, however, although it has the same mean as the first. If, by chance, we picked a sample in which the weights are all 12.0 ounces (or all 16.2 ounces), our estimate, the sample mean $\bar{x}$, would differ from the quantity it is supposed to estimate, the population mean μ, by as much as 2.1 ounces. This serves to illustrate that *in order to judge the "goodness" of a generalization or the "closeness" of an estimate, we must know something about the variability of the population from which the sample is obtained.*

The purpose of these four examples has been to demonstrate how the concept of variability plays an important role in practically all aspects of statistics. While giving the first example, we actually introduced one way of indicating (or measuring) variability, namely, by giving the two *extreme values* of a sample. More or less the same is accomplished by giving the *difference between the two extremes*, to which we refer as the sample *range*. Thus, for the first example of this section the *range* of the prices paid for a share of the given stock is $68\frac{1}{2} - 45 = 23\frac{1}{2}$ dollars, and for the last example the range of the weights obtained for the three cans of fruit salad is $14.2 - 13.8 = 0.4$ ounces.

In spite of the obvious advantages of the range that it is *easy to calculate* and *easy to understand*, it does not provide a very useful measure of variation in a wide variety of statistical problems. Being based only on the two extremes, its main shortcoming is that it does not tell us anything about the dispersion of the data which fall in between. Each of the following three sets of data

$$5 \quad 17 \quad 17 \quad 17 \quad 17 \quad 17 \quad 17 \quad 17 \quad 17 \quad 17$$
$$5 \quad 5 \quad 5 \quad 5 \quad 5 \quad 17 \quad 17 \quad 17 \quad 17 \quad 17$$
$$5 \quad 6 \quad 8 \quad 10 \quad 11 \quad 14 \quad 14 \quad 15 \quad 16 \quad 17$$

has a range of $17 - 5 = 12$, but the dispersions of the data are by no means the same. Thus, the range is used mainly in situations where it is desired to get a quick, though not necessarily a very accurate, picture of the variability of a set of data. In some cases, where the sample size is very small, the range is quite adequate as a measure of variation; it is thus used widely in *quality control*, where it is important to keep a continuous check on the variability of raw materials, machines, or manufactured products by regularly taking small samples.

To define the *standard deviation*, by far the most useful measure of variation, let us observe that the dispersion of a set of data is *small* if the numbers are bunched closely about their mean, and that it is *large* if the numbers are spread over considerable distances away from their mean. Hence, it would seem reasonable to measure the variation of a set of data in terms of the amounts (distances or deviations) by which the various numbers depart from their mean. If a set of numbers $x_1, x_2, \ldots, x_N$, looked upon as a population, has the mean μ, the differences $x_1 - \mu$, $x_2 - \mu, \ldots, x_N - \mu$ are called the *deviations from the mean*, and it suggests itself that we might use their average, namely, their mean, as a measure of the variation of the population. This would not be a bad idea, except for the fact that we would always get 0 for an answer, no matter how widely dispersed the data might be. Using the rules of Technical Note 1, it can easily be shown that $\Sigma (x - \mu)$, that is, the sum of the deviations from the mean, is always equal to zero—some of the deviations are positive, some are negative, and their sum as well as their mean are always equal to zero (see also Exercise 33 on page 47).

Since we are really interested in the *magnitude* of the deviations and not in their signs, we might simply "ignore" the signs and, thus, define a measure of variation in terms of the *absolute values* of the deviations from the mean. Indeed, adding the values of the deviations from the mean as if they were all positive and dividing by N, we obtain an intuitively appealing measure of variation called the *average deviation*. However, using precisely the same deviations from the mean, there is another way of eliminating their signs, which is preferable on theoretical grounds. The *squares* of the deviations from the mean cannot be negative; in fact, they are positive unless an x happens to coincide with the mean, in which case both $x - \mu$ and $(x - \mu)^2$ are equal to zero. It thus suggests itself that we measure the variability of a set of data in terms of the *squared deviations from the mean*, and this leads us to the following formula, defining what is called the *population variance:*

$$\sigma^2 = \frac{\Sigma (x - \mu)^2}{N}$$

This measure of variation, which is denoted by σ^2 (where σ, *sigma*, is the lower-case Greek letter for s), is simply the average of the squared deviations from the mean. One disadvantage of the variance is that *it is not in the same units of measurement* as the original data, but we can take care of this by simply taking its square root and thus defining the *population standard deviation*

$$\sigma = \sqrt{\frac{\Sigma (x - \mu)^2}{N}}$$

Having defined the standard deviation of a population, it may seem logical to use the same formula also for a sample, with n and $\bar{x}$ substituted for N and μ. This is almost, but not quite, what we do. Instead of dividing the sum of the squared deviations from the mean by n, we divide it by $n - 1$, and accordingly we define the *sample standard deviation* as

$$s = \sqrt{\frac{\Sigma (x - \bar{x})^2}{n - 1}}$$

and the *sample variance*, without the square root, as

$$s^2 = \frac{\Sigma (x - \bar{x})^2}{n - 1}$$

The following explains why we divide here by $n - 1$ and not by n: if we want to use a sample variance to *estimate* a population variance, we would obtain a value which is *on the average* too small if we divide by n instead of $n - 1$. As a matter of fact, it would be too small *on the average* by the factor $(n - 1)/n$, and this is why we divide by $n - 1$ instead of n. We cannot prove this theoretical fact at the level of this book, but since we shall frequently use sample variances as estimates of the variances of the corresponding populations, we prefer the above definition of s^2. Note, however, that this modification is of significance only when n is small; its effect is negligible when n is large, say, 100 or more.

To illustrate the calculation of a sample standard deviation, let us find s for the following six donations made to the United Fund (in dollars): 7, 14, 8, 5, 15, and 11. Substituting into the formula for s yields

x	$(x - \bar{x})$	$(x - \bar{x})^2$
7	-3	9
14	4	16
8	-2	4
5	-5	25
15	5	25
11	1	1
60		80

$$\bar{x} = \frac{60}{6} = 10$$

$$s = \sqrt{\frac{80}{5}} = \sqrt{16} = 4$$

Using 4 as an estimate of σ, the standard deviation of *all* gifts to the United Fund in the area where the sample was obtained, we will later be able to judge how close $\bar{x} = \$10.00$ might be to μ, the true mean of this population of gifts to the United Fund.

In the above example, the calculation of s was very simple, and this was due largely to the fact that the x's, their mean, and, hence, also the deviations from the mean, were all whole numbers. Had this not been the case, the calculations could have become fairly involved, and it might well have been preferable to use the following *short-cut formula for s*

$$s = \sqrt{\frac{n(\Sigma\ x^2) - (\Sigma\ x)^2}{n(n-1)}} \qquad \bigstar$$

This formula does *not* constitute an approximation and it can be derived from the other formula for s by using the rules for summations given in Technical Note 1 on page 65. The advantage of this short-cut formula is that we do not have to go through the process of actually finding the deviations from the mean; instead we calculate $\Sigma\ x$, the sum of the x's, $\Sigma\ x^2$, the sum of their squares, and substitute directly into the formula. Referring again to the United Fund data, we now have

x	x^2
7	49
14	196
8	64
5	25
15	225
11	121
60	680

$$s = \sqrt{\frac{6(680) - (60)^2}{6 \cdot 5}}$$

$$= \sqrt{\frac{480}{30}} = 4$$

In this particular example it may seem that the "short-cut" method is actually more involved; this may be the case, but in actual practice, when we are dealing with realistically complex data (and not merely a blackboard example), the short-cut formula usually provides considerable simplifications. Incidentally, the same short-cut formula can be used to find σ, provided we substitute n for the factor $n-1$ in the denominator before we replace s and n with σ and N. A further simplification in the calculation of s or σ consists of adding or subtracting a suitable constant (the *same* number) from each of the values for which we want to compute the standard deviation. The advantage of doing this is illustrated in Exercise 2 on page 57.

If we want to calculate the standard deviation of a distribution, that is, grouped data, we are faced with the same problem as on page 35. Again assigning the value of the class mark to each value falling into a given class, we obtain the formula

$$s = \sqrt{\frac{\Sigma (x - \bar{x})^2 \cdot f}{n - 1}}$$ ★

and if we substitute σ, μ, and N for s, $\bar{x}$, and $n - 1$, we obtain an analogous formula for a distribution that is looked upon as a population. Note that in this formula for the standard deviation of a distribution the x's are now the class marks and the f's are the corresponding class frequencies. Illustrating the use of the formula with reference to the downtime distribution (see page 15) whose mean was $\bar{x} = 34.3$, we obtain

Class marks x	Frequencies f	$(x - \bar{x})$	$(x - \bar{x})^2$	$(x - \bar{x})^2 \cdot f$
4.5	3	−29.8	888.04	2,664.12
14.5	14	−19.8	392.04	5,488.56
24.5	29	− 9.8	96.04	2,785.16
34.5	22	0.2	0.04	0.88
44.5	14	10.2	104.04	1,456.56
54.5	10	20.2	408.04	4,080.40
64.5	4	30.2	912.04	3,648.16
74.5	2	40.2	1,616.04	3,232.08
84.5	2	50.2	2,520.04	5,040.08
	100			28,396.00

$$s = \sqrt{\frac{28,396}{99}} = \sqrt{286.8} = 16.9 \text{ minutes}$$

This last square root was obtained from Table X at the end of the book, whose use is explained in Technical Note 3 on page 67.

It is apparent from the above example that the arithmetic required to find the standard deviation of a distribution can be quite involved. This is not serious, however, because there exists a short-cut method which will reduce the work considerably. This method, based on a prior "coding" of the data, is discussed in Technical Note 2 on page 66.

In the argument which led to the definition of the standard deviation, we observed that the dispersion of a set of data is small if the values are bunched closely about their mean and that it is large if the values are spread over considerable distances away from the mean. Correspondingly, we can now say that if the standard deviation of a set of data is small, the values are concentrated near the mean, and if the standard deviation is large the values are scattered widely about the mean. To present this argument on a less intuitive basis (after all, what is *small* and what is *large*?), let us briefly mention an important theorem, which will be taken up later in Technical Note 5. According to this theorem, called *Chebyshev's Theorem*, we can be *sure* for any kind of data (populations as well as samples) that, among other things, *at least 75 per cent of the data must fall within two standard deviations of the mean.* Thus, if a set of data has the mean $\bar{x} = 122$ and $s = 15$, we can be *certain* that at least 75 per cent of the data fall on the interval from 92 to 152. Had the standard deviation of this set of data been smaller, say, $s = 3$, we could have argued that at least 75 per cent of the data must fall on the much smaller interval from 116 to 128. According to Chebyshev's Theorem we can also assert that at least 88.8 per cent of the data must fall within *three* standard deviations of the mean and that at least 96 per cent must fall within *five* standard deviations of the mean. Thus, if two populations have the same mean of $\mu = 240$ while their standard deviations are, respectively, $\sigma = 50$ and $\sigma = 20$, we can assert for the first population that at least 75 per cent of the data must fall between 140 and 340, while for the second population we can make the much stronger statement that at least 96 per cent of the data must fall on the same interval. This illustrates how the magnitude of the standard deviation "controls" the concentration of a set of data about its mean.

An important feature of Chebyshev's Theorem is that it holds for any kind of data. However, if we *do* have some information about the over-all shape of a set of data, that is, the over-all shape of their distribution, we can often make much stronger statements. For instance, if a distribution is *bell-shaped* like the one shown in Figure 3.2, we can expect roughly 95 per cent (instead of *at least* 75 per cent) of the data to fall within two standard deviations of the mean and over 99 per cent (instead of *at least* 88.8 per cent) to fall within three standard deviations of the mean. The percentages given here pertain to the so-called *normal distribution*, which will be discussed in detail in Chapter 7.

In the beginning of this section we demonstrated that there are many ways in which knowledge of the variability of a set of data can be important. Another interesting application arises in the comparison of numbers belonging to *different sets of data*. Suppose, for instance, that in a given month Mr. Green, a salesman of industrial chemicals, made sales of $14,000, while Mr. Miller, a salesman of office supplies, made sales of only $7,250—from which the unwary might conclude that Mr. Green is almost twice as good a salesman as Mr. Miller. However, both men are members of large sales forces and in that month sales by salesmen of

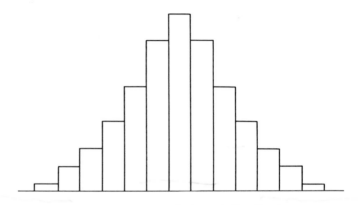

FIGURE 3.2. A bell-shaped distribution.

industrial chemicals had a mean of $12,000 and a standard deviation of $2,000, while those of salesmen of office supplies had a mean of $6,000 and a standard deviation of $500. Thus, Mr. Green's sales were

$$\frac{14,000 - 12,000}{2,000} = 1 \text{ standard deviation}$$

above the mean of his group, while Mr. Miller's sales were

$$\frac{7,250 - 6,000}{500} = 2\tfrac{1}{2} \text{ standard deviations}$$

above the mean of his group. These figures can now be meaningfully compared, and we can say that Mr. Miller's performance for the given month was actually better than Mr. Green's. Mr. Miller rated much higher among salesmen of office supplies than Mr. Green rated among salesmen of industrial chemicals.

What we did here was to convert the two sales figures from dollars into so-called *standard units*. If x is a measurement belonging to a set of data having the mean $\bar{x}$ (or μ) and the standard deviation s (or σ), then its value in *standard units*, denoted by the letter z, is given by

$$z = \frac{x - \bar{x}}{s} \qquad \text{or} \qquad z = \frac{x - \mu}{\sigma}$$

[handwritten: standard unit / normal unit]

In these units, z tells us how many standard deviations an item is above or below the mean of the set of data to which it belongs. Another example showing the importance of converting to standard units will be discussed in Chapter 7, in connection with the problem of tabulating the so-called normal distribution.

EXERCISES

1. Using the basic formula defining s on page 52, calculate the standard deviation of the twenty weights of Exercise 3 on page 43.

2. Repeat Exercise 1 after subtracting 14.0 from each of the twenty weights. Compare the results.

3. Find the standard deviation of the percentages of part (c) of Exercise 5 on page 43, using the basic formula defining s on page 52.

4. Calculate the *average deviation* (the mean of the absolute values of the deviations from the mean) of the 15 percentages of Exercise 7 on page 43.

5. Use the short-cut formula on page 53 to calculate the standard deviation of the ages of the 100 cash registers of Exercise 8 on page 19.

6. Find the ranges of the three sets of percentages of Exercise 5 on page 43.

7. Find the standard deviation of the impact strengths of the five wooden panels given on page 34.

8. Use the formula on page 54 to find the standard deviation of the distribution of Exercise 8 on page 25.

(Exercises 9, 10, 11, and 12 require use of the short-cut formulas discussed in Technical Note 2 on page 66.)

9. Use the short-cut formula on page 66 to find the standard deviation of the distribution of Exercise 8 on page 25.

10. Use the short-cut formula on page 66 to find the standard deviation of whichever data you grouped among those of Exercises 8, 10, and 12 on pages 19 and 20. Referring back to the original data, determine

what percentage of the data falls (a) within one standard deviation of the mean, and (b) within two standard deviations of the mean.

11. Use the short-cut formula on page 66 to find the standard deviation of whichever data you grouped among those of Exercises 13, 14, and 15 on pages 20 and 21. Referring back to the original data, also determine what percentage of the data falls (a) within one standard deviation of the mean, (b) within two standard deviations of the mean, and (c) within three standard deviations of the mean.

12. The following is the distribution of the number of defective pieces found in 200 samples taken from large shipments of a certain kind of shaft:

Number of Defective Pieces	Frequency
0	53
1	38
2	27
3	22
4	16
5	14
6	10
7	8
8	5
9	3
10	2
11	1
12	1

Find the mean and the standard deviation of this distribution, and then determine what percentage of the data falls within two standard deviations of the mean.

13. If a distribution of the heights of certain individuals has a mean of 68.2 inches and a standard deviation of 4.1 inches, at least what percentage of these heights must fall (a) between 60.0 and 76.4 inches, and (b) between 55.9 and 80.5 inches?

14. Having kept a record for many years, Mr. Jones knows that it takes him on the average 27.4 minutes to drive to work and that the standard deviation of these figures is 2.52 minutes. If Mr. Jones starts out 40 minutes before he has to be at work, *at most* what percentage of the time can he expect to arrive late?

15. A buyer for a department store knows that the daily sales of women's stockings form a distribution having a mean of 420 pairs and a standard deviation of 45 pairs. If he plans his inventory so that each morning

there are 500 pairs, at most what proportion of the time can he expect to finish a day with 305 or more pairs of these stockings?

16. Chebyshev's Theorem states that $1 - 1/k^2$ is the *minimum fraction* of a set of data that must fall within k standard deviations of its mean. Use this expression to verify the three percentages given in the text. Also, *at least* what percentage of the time can Mr. Jones of Exercise 14 expect to arrive on time if he leaves his home 35 minutes before he has to be at work?

17. An investment service reports for each stock that it lists the price at which it is currently selling, its average price over a certain period of time, and a measure of its variability. Stock A, it reports, has a normal (average) price of $76 with a standard deviation of $22 and it is currently selling at $109. Stock B sells normally for $26, has a standard deviation of $4, and is currently selling at $38. If an investor owns both kinds of stock and wants to dispose of one, which one might he sell and why?

18. Mr. Brown's house costs $23,500 and he lives in a development where prices have a mean of $22,000 and a standard deviation of $2,000. Mr. Black's house costs $16,400 and he lives in a development where prices have a mean of $14,800 and a standard deviation of $800. How do the costs of Brown's and Black's houses compare to those of their respective developments?

19. One disadvantage of the standard deviation as a measure of variation is that it depends on the units of measurement. Thus, if a set of measurements, say, of the diameter of a shaft, have a standard deviation of 0.45 mm, we cannot say whether these measurements are very precise unless we know something about the size of the diameter of the shaft. What we need here is a measure of *relative variation* like the *coefficient of variation*, which is given by the formula $\frac{s}{\bar{x}} \cdot 100 \left(\text{or } \frac{\sigma}{\mu} \cdot 100 \right)$, expressing the standard deviation as a percentage of the mean. Using the results of Exercise 3 on page 43 and Exercise 1 on page 57, find the coefficient of variation of the 20 weights.

20. Using the coefficient of variation (see Exercise 19) it is possible to compare the relative dispersions of two or more sets of data. Referring to the two stocks of Exercise 17, which is, relatively speaking, less variable?

Further Descriptions

So far we have discussed statistical descriptions coming under the general headings of "measures of location" and "measures of variation."

Actually, there is no limit to the number of ways in which statistical data can be described, and statisticians are continually developing new methods of describing characteristics of numerical data that happen to be of interest in particular problems. In this section we shall investigate the general problem of describing the *over-all shape* of a distribution.

Although frequency distributions can assume almost any shape or form, there are certain standard types which fit most distributions we

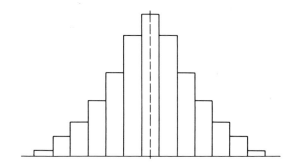

FIGURE 3.3. A bell-shaped distribution.

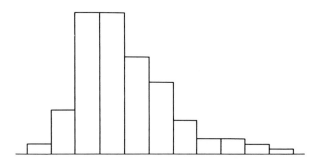

FIGURE 3.4. A skewed distribution.

meet in actual practice. Foremost among these is the aptly described *bell-shaped* distribution, which is illustrated by the histogram of Figure 3.3. We repeatedly run into this kind of distribution when dealing with actual data, and there exist certain theoretical reasons why, in many problems, we can actually expect to get bell-shaped distributions. Although the distribution of Figure 3.4 is also more or less bell-shaped, it differs from the one of Figure 3.3 inasmuch as the latter is *symmetrical* while the former is *skewed*. We say that a distribution is symmetrical if we can picture its histogram folded (say, along the dotted line of

Figure 3.3) so that the two halves will more or less coincide. If a distribution has a more pronounced "tail" on one side than on the other (or a "tail" on one side and none on the other), such as the distribution of Figure 3.4, we say that the distribution is *skewed*. Note that the downtime distribution, whose histogram is shown in Figure 2.1 on page 22, is slightly skewed with a modest "tail" on the right. We say that it has *positive skewness* or that it is *positively skewed*. If the "tail" is on the left, we correspondingly say that the distribution has *negative skewness* or that it is *negatively skewed*.

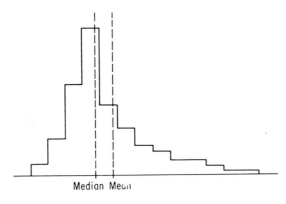

Median Mean

FIGURE 3.5

There are several ways in which we can measure the extent to which a distribution is skewed. One of these, a relatively easy one, is based on the fact illustrated in Figure 3.5, namely, that if a distribution has a "tail" on the right, its median will generally be exceeded by the mean. (If the "tail" is on the left, this order will be reversed, and the median will generally exceed the mean.) Based on this difference, the so-called *Pearsonian coefficient of skewness* measures the skewness of a distribution by means of the formula

$$\frac{3(\text{mean} - \text{median})}{\text{standard deviation}} \qquad \star$$

Here the difference between the mean and the median is divided by the standard deviation, to make this description of the shape of the distribution independent of the units of measurement we happen to use. Substituting the values obtained for the mean, median, and standard deviation of the downtime distribution on pages 37, 40, and 54, we find that for this distribution the Pearsonian coefficient of skewness equals

$$\frac{3(34.3 - 31.3)}{16.9} = 0.53$$

The fact that this value is a small positive number implies that the distribution is slightly skewed with the tail on the right. (Had the tail been on the left, the value of the Pearsonian coefficient of skewness

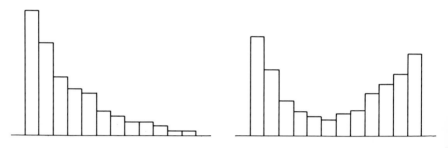

FIGURE 3.6. J-shaped and U-shaped distributions.

would have been negative; at least, this would have been the case had the median exceeded the mean.)

Besides bell-shaped distributions, two other kinds—*J-shaped and U-shaped distributions*—are sometimes, though less frequently, met in actual practice. As is illustrated in Figure 3.6, the names of these distributions literally describe their shapes; examples of J-shaped and U-shaped distributions may be found in Exercises 5 and 6 below.

EXERCISES

1. Use the mean, median, and standard deviation previously calculated for whichever data you grouped among those of Exercises 8, 10, 12, 13, 14, or 15 on pages 19 through 21, to determine the distribution's Pearsonian coefficient of skewness.

2. Find the Pearsonian coefficient of skewness for the distribution of the scores of the 80 job applicants of Exercise 8 on page 25.

3. Find the Pearsonian coefficient of skewness for the distribution of Exercise 12 on page 58.

4. Give one example each of actual data whose distribution might reasonably be expected to be

   (a) bell-shaped and symmetrical.

   (b) bell-shaped but not symmetrical.

   (c) negatively skewed.

   (d) positively skewed.

   (e) J-shaped.

5. If we roll a pair of dice, the number of sixes we obtain is either 0, 1, or 2. Rolling a pair of dice 100 times, construct a distribution showing how often 0, 1, and 2 sixes were obtained, and draw a histogram of this distribution, which should be *J-shaped* with its tail on the right.

6. If a coin is flipped five times, the result may be represented by means of a sequence of H's and T's (for example, HHTTH), where H stands for *heads* and T for *tails*. Having obtained such a sequence of H's and T's, we can then check after each successive flip whether the number of heads exceeds the number of tails. For example, for the sequence HHTTH, heads is ahead after the first flip, after the second flip, after the third flip, *not* after the fourth flip, but again after the fifth flip; altogether, it is ahead *four times*. Repeating this experiment 50 times, construct a histogram showing in how many cases heads was ahead 0 times, 1 time, 2 times, . . ., and 5 times. The resulting distribution should be *U-shaped;* can you explain why?

A Word of Caution

The fact that there is a certain amount of arbitrariness in the selection of statistical descriptions has led some persons to believe that they can take a set of data, apply the magic of statistics, and prove almost anything they want. To put it more bluntly, a nineteenth century British statesman once said that there are three kinds of lies: lies, damned lies, and statistics. To give an example where such a criticism might be justified, suppose that a paint manufacturer asks his research department to "prove" that on the average a gallon of his paint covers more square feet than that of his two principal competitors. Suppose, furthermore, that the research department tests five cans of each brand, getting the following results (in square feet per gallon can):

Brand A:	505,	516,	478,	513,	503
Brand B:	512,	486,	511,	486,	510
Brand C:	496,	485,	490,	520,	484

If the manufacturer's own brand is Brand A, the person who is doing this analysis will find to his delight that the means of the three samples are, respectively, 503, 501, and 495. He can, thus, claim that in actual tests a can of his employer's product covered on the average more square feet than those of his competitors.

Now suppose, for the sake of argument, that the manufacturer's own brand is Brand B. Clearly, the person who is doing the analysis can no longer base the comparison on the sample means; *this would not prove his point*. Trying instead the sample medians, he finds that they are, respectively 505, 510, and 490, and this provides him with exactly the kind of ammunition he wants. The median is a perfectly respectable measure of the "average" or "center" of a set of data, and using the medians he can claim that his employer's product came out best in the test.

Finally, suppose that the manufacturer's own brand is Brand C. After going down the list of various measures of central location, the analyst comes upon one that does the trick. The *mid-range* is defined as the mean of the smallest and largest values in a sample, and for the given data, the mid-ranges of the three samples are, respectively, 497, 499, and 502. Gleefully, he thus points out that Brand C, his employer's product, scored on the average highest in the test. The moral of this example is that *if data are to be compared, the method of comparison should be decided on beforehand, or at least without looking at the actual data.* All this is aside from the fact that comparisons based on samples are often far from conclusive. It is quite possible that whatever differences there may be among the three means (or three other descriptions) can be attributed entirely to chance (see Exercise 4 on page 390).

Another point which must be remembered is that a statistical measure always describes a particular characteristic of a set of data and that it, furthermore, describes this characteristic in a special way. Whether this "special way" is appropriate for a given situation, is something which will have to be examined individually in each case. Suppose, for instance, that we want to buy a house and that we are shown a house in a neighborhood where, according to the broker, average family income is in excess of $24,000. This gives the impression of a relatively prosperous neighborhood, but it could well be a neighborhood where most families have incomes of less than $4,000 while one very wealthy family has an income of several hundred thousand dollars a year. This is the kind of situation we warned about on page 37, namely, a situation where the mean is greatly affected by one extreme value. It would be much more informative to say in this case that the median family income is less than $4,000, mentioning, perhaps, the special situation created by the one wealthy family. Further examples of this kind may be found in *How to Lie with Statistics*, the book by D. Huff referred to in the Bibliography at the end of this book.

Technical Note 1 (Summations)

When we introduced the Σ notation on page 33, we referred to it as a kind of mathematical shorthand. In fact, it is an abbreviated sort of shorthand, as it does not tell us explicitly what x's, or how many of them, we are supposed to add. This is taken care of in the more explicit notation

$$\sum_{i=1}^{n} x_i = x_1 + x_2 + \ldots + x_n$$

where it is made clear that we are adding the x's whose subscripts i are 1, 2, ..., and n. We did not use this notation in the text, in order to simplify the over-all appearance of the various formulas, assuming that it is clear in each case what x's we are referring to and how many there are.

To verify some of the formulas involving summations that are stated but not proved in the text, the reader will find it convenient to use the following rules:

$$Rule\ A: \quad \sum_{i=1}^{n} (x_i \pm y_i) = \sum_{i=1}^{n} x_i \pm \sum_{i=1}^{n} y_i$$

$$Rule\ B: \quad \sum_{i=1}^{n} k \cdot x_i = k \cdot \sum_{i=1}^{n} x_i$$

$$Rule\ C: \quad \sum_{i=1}^{n} k = k \cdot n$$

The first of these rules states that the summation of the sum (or difference) of two terms equals the sum (or difference) of the individual summations, and it can be extended to the sum or difference of more than two terms. The second rule states that we can, so to speak, factor a constant out of a summation, and the third rule states that the summation of a constant is simply n times that constant. All of these rules can be proved by actually writing out in full what each of the summations represents.

Technical Note 2 (Short-cut Formulas for the Mean and the Standard Deviation of Grouped Data)

The calculation of the mean and the standard deviation of a distribution can be quite tedious when the frequencies are high and the class marks involve many digits, that is, if they are numbers such as 25,349.5 or 1.3465. To simplify these calculations, we often perform a "change of scale"; in other words, we replace the class marks with numbers that are easier to handle. Referring to this process also as "coding," we might replace the class marks of the downtime distribution on page 15 with the consecutive integers $-3, -2, -1, 0, 1, 2, 3, 4,$ and 5 (originally, they were $4.5, 14.5, 24.5, \ldots,$ and 84.5). Of course, when we do something like this, we also have to account for it in the formulas we use to calculate the mean and the standard deviation. Referring to the new (coded) class marks as u's, the formula for the mean of a distribution becomes

$$\bar{x} = x_0 + \frac{\Sigma u \cdot f}{n} \cdot c$$

where x_0 is the class mark (in the original scale) to which we assign 0 in the new scale, c is the class interval, n is the number of items grouped, and $\Sigma u \cdot f$ is the sum of the products obtained by multiplying each of the new class marks by the corresponding class frequency. Similarly, the formula for the standard deviation becomes

$$s = c \sqrt{\frac{n(\Sigma u^2 \cdot f) - (\Sigma u \cdot f)^2}{n(n-1)}}$$

where $\Sigma u^2 \cdot f$ is the sum of the products obtained by multiplying the *squares* of the new class marks by the corresponding class frequencies. Note that this kind of coding of the class marks can be used only if the class intervals are all equal. If that is the case, *we assign consecutive integers to the class marks, preferably with 0 near the center of the distribution.*

To illustrate the use of these short-cut formulas for the mean and the standard deviation of a distribution, let us recalculate $\bar{x}$ and s for the downtime distribution on page 15. Using the coding indicated above, we get

x	u	f	$u \cdot f$	$u^2 \cdot f$
4.5	-3	3	-9	27
14.5	-2	14	-28	56
24.5	-1	29.	-29	29
34.5	0	22	0	0
44.5	1.	14	14	14
54.5	2	10	20	40
64.5	3	4	12	36
74.5	4	2	8	32
84.5	5	2	10	50
		100	-2	284

$$\bar{x} = 34.5 + \frac{(-2)}{100} \cdot 10 = 34.5 - 0.2 = 34.3 \text{ minutes}$$

$$s = 10 \sqrt{\frac{100(284) - (-2)^2}{100 \cdot 99}} = 10 \sqrt{2.868} = 16.9 \text{ minutes}$$

and it should be noted that these results are identical with the ones obtained earlier. The short-cut formulas given here will *always* yield the same results as the corresponding formulas on pages 36 and 54. Incidentally, these short-cut formulas can also be used to find the mean and the standard deviation of a population, provided we substitute μ, σ, and N for $\bar{x}$, s, and n, after replacing $n - 1$ with n in the formula for the standard deviation.

Technical Note 3 (The Use of Square Root Tables)

Although square root tables are relatively easy to use, most beginners seem to have some difficulty in choosing the right column and in placing the decimal point correctly in the answer. Table X, in addition to containing the *squares* of the numbers from 1.00 to 9.99 spaced at intervals of 0.01, gives the *square roots* of these numbers rounded to 6 decimals. To find the square root of any positive number rounded to 3 significant digits, we have only to use the following rule in deciding whether to take the entry of the $\sqrt{n}$ or the $\sqrt{10n}$ column:

Move the decimal point an even number of places to the right or to the left until a number greater than or equal to 1 but less than 100 is reached. If the resulting number is less than 10 go to the $\sqrt{n}$ column; if it is 10 or more go to the $\sqrt{10n}$ column.

Thus, to find the square roots of 12,800, 379, and 0.0812 we go to the $\sqrt{n}$ column since the decimal point has to be moved, respectively, 4 places to the left, 2 places to the left, and 2 places to the right, to give 1.28, 3.79, and 8.12. Similarly, to find the square roots of 5248, 0.281, and 0.0000259 we go to the $\sqrt{10n}$ column since the decimal point has to be moved, respectively, 2 places to the left, 2 places to the right, and 6 places to the right, to give 52.48, 28.1, and 25.9.

Having found the entry in the appropriate column of Table X, the only thing that remains to be done is to put the decimal point in the right position in the answer. Here it will help to use the following rule:

Having previously moved the decimal point an even number of places to the left or right to get a number greater than or equal to 1 but less than 100, the decimal point of the entry of the appropriate column in Table X is moved half as many places in the opposite direction.

For example, to determine the square root of 12,800 we first note that the decimal point has to be moved *four places to the left* to give 1.28. We thus take the entry of the $\sqrt{n}$ column corresponding to 1.28, move its decimal point *two places to the right*, and get $\sqrt{12,800} = 113.1371$. Similarly, to find the square root of 0.0000259, we note that the decimal point has to be moved *six places to the right* to give 25.9. We thus take the entry of the $\sqrt{10n}$ column corresponding to 2.59, move the decimal point *three places to the left*, and get $\sqrt{0.0000259} = 0.005089204$. In actual practice, if a number whose square root we want to find is rounded, the square root will have to be rounded to as many significant digits as the original number.

FOUR
SUMMARIZING
DATA:
INDEX
NUMBERS

Basic Problems

High on the list of statistical measures that are most important in everyday use are the ones called *index numbers*. As their name implies, these measures are numbers which *indicate* something, usually how much things have changed or how they compare with one another. For instance, if we compare the 575,000 trucks made by U.S. manufacturers in the first six months of 1961 with the 725,000 trucks produced during the first six months of 1960, we find that the 1961 figure is only 79.3 per cent of what it was the year before. In the same way, a comparison of North American Aviation's nonaircraft sales of $606 million in 1960 with corresponding sales of $93 million in 1953 shows that the 1960 sales were 651.6 per cent of those in 1953. Further comparisons show that 105.8 per cent as much steel was used for appliances in 1961 as was used on the average in the years 1957–1959, that 702.8 per cent as much steel was used for appliances in 1961 as was used for utensils and cookery, and so on. These percentages, each of which compares two things, are *simple* examples of index numbers; we stressed the word "simple" because there are also numbers of this sort which are intended to indicate changes in such complicated phenomena as consumer prices, total industrial production, business cycles, and the stock market. In fact, there are many different indicators for each of these phenomena; for instance, we determine "how the market is doing" by means of a confidence index, a breadth-of-the-market index, an odd lot transactions indicator, a short interest trend indicator, a disparity indicator, a quarterly turn indicator, and several other measures coming under the general heading of "index numbers."

Although index numbers are commonly associated with business and economics, they are also widely used in other fields. Psychologists measure intelligence quotients, which are essentially index numbers comparing a person's intelligence with that of an average for his or her age. Health authorities prepare indexes to display changes in the adequacy of hospital facilities, educational research organizations devise indexes to measure the effectiveness of school systems, sociologists construct indexes measuring population changes, the Weather Bureau has devised a so-called "Discomfort Index" to measure the combined effect of heat and humidity on individuals, and so on. In practice, index numbers are used mainly to make comparisons between two different periods of time, but they can serve equally well to indicate comparisons between different locations, different industries, different nationalities, and the like.

In recent years, the use of index numbers has extended to so many fields of human activity that some knowledge of index numbers really belongs under the heading of "general education." Index numbers are now of vital interest to millions of workers whose wages automatically go up or down with the level of the *Consumer Price Index* of the Bureau of Labor Statistics; they are of great concern to farmers whose subsidies depend on the *Parity Index* of the federal government; and they are no less important to business firms and individuals for whom they provide actual insurance against changing prices. Index numbers have also found their way into alimony agreements, trust fund payments, and legacies, which can be made to vary with an index of the purchasing power of the dollar.

Like other statistical measures, index numbers are usually constructed to serve definite purposes. Sometimes, the stated purpose of an index is such that the only problem which might arise in its construction is that of locating the necessary data. For instance, in studying the over-all problem of the uninsured driver, it may be required to construct an index showing the change from 1957 to 1960 in the number of drivers actually detected operating an automobile without insurance in New York State. Comparable figures available from Motor Vehicle Bureau records show that there were 163 such cases in 1957 and 4,300 in 1960. Thus, we have

$$\text{index} = \frac{4,300}{163} = 26.38 \text{ (or 2638 per cent)}$$

and the problem is solved. In contrast, there are many situations in which some very complex problems arise as soon as the purpose of an index has been stated. The most basic among these are: (1) the availability and comparability of data, (2) the selection of items to be included in the comparison, (3) the choice of time periods (localities, etc.) that are to be compared, (4) the selection of appropriate weights measuring the relative importance of various items which are to be compared, and (5) the choice of a suitable index number formula by means of which the data are to be combined. Some of these critical problems will now be discussed in detail.

The availability and comparability of data. It would hardly seem necessary to point out that comparisons cannot be made and index numbers cannot be constructed unless the required statistical data can be obtained. Many research workers have been frustrated by the fact that essential information needed by townships was tabulated by counties, sales data needed by brand were available only by type of merchandise, insurance losses were given per risk and not per claim, and so on. Unfortunately, there often is a considerable lack of uniformity in the methods used in reporting statistical data, and this can lead to serious difficulties in index number construction.

The question of availability also enters the picture if we want to make a comparison, say, of the cost of living in 1962 with that of the year 1914. Nowadays television sets, frozen foods, and appliances of all sorts are widely used, but none of them were sold commercially in 1914. We may thus be forced to invent fictitious prices for what such items might have cost had they been available in 1914.

The question of comparability can also be quite troublesome. In congressional hearings some labor organizations have complained that, to some extent, the *Consumer Price Index* reflects deterioration in quality rather than an actual change in prices. It does not matter to us here whether this criticism is valid, but it serves to indicate that it can be very difficult to make sure that prices are actually comparable, namely, that they refer to goods and services which are identical in quality.

The comparability of statistical data may also be questioned if parts of the data are obtained from different sources. It is very confusing, for example, to note that the Bureau of the Census reports that the 1939 production of nonferrous minerals in the United States had a total value of $350 million, while the Bureau of Mines reports a corresponding figure of $434 million. (This discrepancy arises from the fact that the Bureau of the Census figures are those given by producers while the Bureau of Mines figures are those given by purchasers and transportation companies.) The situation with regard to import-export data supplied by the partners in trade is sometimes so bad that one wonders whether any confidence at all can be placed in international trade statistics. For example, the following table, based on figures published by the United Nations in *Commodity Trade Statistics*, shows the importer's and exporter's versions of how many metric tons of certain commodities the second country received from the first in 1960:

Commodity	Exporter's Data		Importer's Data	
Butter	France	5,005	United Kingdom	3,787
Eggs	Denmark	63,534	West Germany	51,273
Coffee	El Salvador	38,153	United States	27,693
Wheat	Canada	288,535	Netherlands	164,578

These figures were deliberately selected to illustrate our point, and although similar difficulties arise, say, with employment and production figures quoted by different sources or sickness and accident data supplied by different agencies, they are the exception rather than the rule. Nevertheless, they stress the seriousness of the problem of obtaining reliable and comparable data.

The selection of items to be included in the comparison. If an index is designed for the special purpose of comparing the price of a commodity at two different times, there is no question as to what figures should be included. However, the situation is entirely different in the construction of so-called *general purpose indexes*, for instance, those designed to measure general changes in wholesale or consumer prices. It must be clear that it is physically impossible, or at least highly impractical, to include in such a comparison all commodities from alum to zircons and to include, furthermore, all prices at which these commodities are traded in every single transaction throughout the entire country. The only reasonable alternative is to take samples in such a way that the items and transactions included adequately reflect the over-all situation. For example, the *Consumer Price Index* is based on about 300 items (goods and services) playing a significant role in the average budget of persons belonging to a certain population group. The prices included in this index are samples with respect to the goods and services that are included and also with respect to the stores and cities that are canvassed in the necessary surveys. The sampling methods used in selecting commodities for an index often come under the heading of what we shall later refer to as "judgment sampling"; it means that the selection is not left to chance, but to the professional judgment of the person (or persons) responsible for the construction of the index.

The choice of time periods that are to be compared. If an index number is designed for the specific purpose of comparing 1962 figures with those of some other year, say, 1959, it is customary to refer to 1962 as the *given year*, to 1959 as the *base year*, and the latter is usually indicated by writing 1959 = 100. In general, the year or period we want to compare is called the *given year* or *given period*, while the year or period relative to which the comparison is made is called the *base year* or *base period*.

The choice of the base year or base period does not present any problems if an index is constructed for a specific comparison. So far as general purpose indexes describing complex phenomena are concerned, it is generally desirable to base the comparison on a period of *relative economic stability* as well as a period that is *not too distant in the past*. The reason for the first stipulation is that during a time of abnormal economic conditions (for example, during a war) there may be no free trading of some commodities, there may be black markets, and the buying habits of the public may be irregular due to shortages of products that would otherwise figure in the average person's budget.

One reason for choosing a relatively recent base period is that some newly developed items must usually be incorporated in an index; the farther back the base period, the more difficult (if not actually impossible) it becomes to find comparative data relating both to the present and to the earlier period. Base periods that are too far in the past also raise problems not unlike those faced by an art critic who, instead of judging two paintings by holding them next to one another, is forced to compare them individually with a third, and then relate the individual comparisons.

The federal government has made it a practice to establish a standard reference base for use by federal agencies. About every ten years, this base period has been brought forward. In 1940, for example, a reference base of 1935–1939 was established; in 1951 a new base of 1947–1949 was designated, and in 1960 a new three-year period, 1957–1959, was established by the Bureau of the Budget for all general purpose government indexes. Where feasible, conversion to the new base commenced with the January 1962 indexes. It is worth noting that the 1957–1959 period is probably as stable a period as can be found in the post-World War II era. But, as the government has pointed out, the selection of a base period does not imply "normality" in any real sense; a base period is merely a necessary and convenient reference point if comparisons are to be made. Various government indexes now refer to the new 1957–1959 base, but some (the indexes of prices received and prices paid by farmers, for example) are still tied by law to the pre-World War I period from 1910 to 1914. Until Congress sees fit to change the law, it is infeasible to calculate these indexes with a more recent base.

The selection of appropriate weights. As illustrated by the exercises on page 45, there are many situations in which figures cannot be averaged without paying due attention to the relative importance of each item; this applies particularly to index numbers. Suppose, for example, that we want to construct an index comparing the 1949 and 1962 prices of wood products used in the home, and that we arbitrarily decide to include the two items: toothpicks and furniture. Let us suppose, furthermore, that for furniture alone the index is 160 per cent, while for toothpicks alone it is 110. We could go ahead and claim on the basis of these figures that the price of wood products used in the home in 1962 is $\frac{160 + 110}{2}$ = 135 per cent of what it was in 1949, but it must be clear that this average is of very little use. To get a more meaningful result, we would have to *weight* the items in some way to account for their relative significance in the over-all situation we are trying to describe. This is precisely the problem we discussed in Exercise 12 on page 44.

The problem of choosing suitable weights in the construction of an index is not an easy one. It depends on whether we want to average prices, quantities, or (as in the above illustration) indexes of individual commodities. As it is virtually impossible to treat this problem without referring to specific index number formulas, let us defer discussion of this matter until later, when we shall study weighted index number formulas.

The choice of a suitable formula. In the same way in which the average of a set of data can be described by using the mean, median, mode, and other measures of central location, relative changes can be described by employing any one of a great number of formulas, all of which by defini-tion yield index numbers. In the next two sections, we shall treat some of the simpler among these formulas and we shall also go into the factors that must be taken into account when choosing an appropriate one for a given problem. After reading these sections, it will be clear that any such choice will ultimately have to depend on practical considerations as well as on some of the mathematical niceties of the formulas.

The symbolism we shall use in the remainder of this chapter consists of referring to index numbers as I, base-year prices as p_0, given-year prices as p_n, base-year quantities as q_0, and given-year quantities as q_n.

Unweighted Index Numbers

To illustrate some of the simplest methods used in index number construction, let us compare the February 1961 retail prices of six kinds of meat with their average retail prices in 1950. The following prices, taken from data supplied by the Bureau of Labor Statistics, are all in cents per pound:

	February 1961	*1950*
Round steak	106.2	93.6
Chuck roast	62.7	61.6
Pork chops	87.7	75.4
Bacon, sliced	70.8	63.7
Ham, whole	62.8	62.0
Lamb, leg	71.8	74.4

Adding the February 1961 prices and dividing their sum by that of the corresponding 1950 prices, we get

$$\frac{106.2 + 62.7 + 87.7 + 70.8 + 62.8 + 71.8}{93.6 + 61.6 + 75.4 + 63.7 + 62.0 + 74.4} = \frac{462.0}{430.7} = 1.073$$

and this tells us that the combined February 1961 prices are 107.3 per cent of those of 1950. We say that in February 1961 with 1950 = 100 *this food price index stands at 107.3.* The method which we employed here is called the *simple aggregative method* and the resulting index is accordingly called a *simple aggregative index.* In general, the formula for a simple aggregative index is

$$I = \frac{\Sigma\, p_n}{\Sigma\, p_0} \cdot 100$$

★

where $\Sigma\, p_n$ is the sum of the given-year prices, $\Sigma\, p_0$ is the sum of the base-year prices, and the ratio of the two is multiplied by 100 to express the index as a percentage.

A simple aggregative index is easy to compute and easy to understand, but it does not meet a criterion of adequacy called the *units test.* The index can yield widely divergent results depending on the units for which the prices of the various commodities are quoted. If we had combined, say, the prices of a ton of round steak, a pound of chuck roast, five pork chops, a rasher of bacon, a ten pound ham, and a seven pound leg of lamb, we would have gotten an entirely different indicator of the way in which the prices of these foods have changed. Largely for this reason, simple aggregative indexes are nowadays rarely used and very few of them appear in publications.

An alternate way of comparing the two sets of food prices would be to calculate first a separate index for each of the six kinds of meat, and then average these so-called *price relatives* with some measure of central location. Writing the individual price relatives as percentages, we obtain

Price Relatives

Round steak	$\dfrac{106.2}{93.6} \cdot 100 = 113$ per cent
Chuck roast	$\dfrac{62.7}{61.6} \cdot 100 = 102$ per cent
Pork chops	$\dfrac{87.7}{75.4} \cdot 100 = 116$ per cent
Bacon, sliced	$\dfrac{70.8}{63.7} \cdot 100 = 111$ per cent
Ham, whole	$\dfrac{62.8}{62.0} \cdot 100 = 101$ per cent
Lamb, leg	$\dfrac{71.8}{74.4} \cdot 100 = 97$ per cent

To construct an over-all index comparing the prices of these different kinds of meat, we can now take the mean, median, or some other "average" of the six price relatives. Choosing the mean, we get

$$\frac{113 + 102 + 116 + 111 + 101 + 97}{6} = 106.7$$

and this index is appropriately called an *arithmetic mean of price relatives.* Symbolically, the formula for this kind of index is

$$I = \frac{\sum \frac{p_n}{p_0} \cdot 100}{k} \qquad \qquad \bigstar$$

where k is the number of items (commodities) whose price relatives are being combined.

Had we used the median of the price relatives in this example, we would have obtained an index of 106.5, and had we computed the geometric mean (see Exercise 18 on page 45) we would have obtained 106.4. Although, in principle, any measure of central location can be used, price relatives are usually averaged with either the arithmetic mean or the geometric mean.

It is a matter of historical interest that the earliest index number on record is an arithmetic mean of price relatives. In the middle of the eighteenth century, G. R. Carli, an Italian, calculated the effect of the import of silver on the value of money, using a formula like the one given above to compare the 1750 prices of oil, grain, and wine with those of the year 1500.

Today the need for employing weights has been almost universally accepted and very few indexes are actually computed in this simple way. Prior to 1914, the *Wholesale Price Index* of the Bureau of Labor Statistics was computed as an arithmetic mean of the price relatives of about 250 commodities. As a result of an important study by W. C. Mitchell in 1915, which has affected index number construction since that time, the index was changed to a weighted index. Among the important government indexes only the daily *Index of Spot Market Prices* is still calculated as a simple (unweighted) geometric mean of price relatives.

The formulas we have given in this section are all price index formulas. However, if we want to compare quantities rather than prices, we have only to replace the p's with q's and use the same formulas for *quantity indexes*.

Weighted Index Numbers

To show how an index number can be made to account for differences in importance, let us consider the following data on the prices of five major crops in cents per bushel and their production in millions of bushels:

| | Prices | | Quantities | |
	1949–1951	1960	1949–1951	1960
Wheat	200	175	1,035	1,357
Corn	148	96	2,780	3,908
Oats	84	68	1,289	1,155
Rye	134	84	20	33
Barley	115	84	266	431

As it is customary and appropriate to average prices by using as weights the corresponding quantities sold, consumed, or produced, let us use the average production figures for the three-year period 1949–1951 as weights, calculate a *weighted mean* of the 1960 prices, another of the 1949–1951 prices, and define an index in terms of the ratio of the two. Ignoring the denominators of the two weighted means, which cancel, and multiplying by 100, we thus get

$$\frac{175(1,035) + 96(2,780) + 68(1,289) + 84(20) + 84(266)}{200(1,035) + 148(2,780) + 84(1,289) + 134(20) + 115(266)} \cdot 100$$

$$= 73.6 \text{ per cent}$$

The index which we have constructed here is called a *weighted aggregative index with base-year weights*. It is also known as a Laspeyres Index, named after the statistician who first suggested its use. In general, the formula for this index is

$$I = \frac{\Sigma \, p_n q_0}{\Sigma \, p_0 q_0} \cdot 100 \qquad \bigstar$$

where the numerator contains the sum of the products of the respective given-year prices and base-year quantities, whereas the denominator contains the sum of the products of the respective base-year prices and base-year quantities.

In case the reader is curious why we did not weight the base-year prices with base-year quantities and the given-year prices with given-year quantities, let us point out that this would have given us a *value index* rather than a price index. It would have compared the *total values* of the five crops and not comparable averages of their prices.

Instead of using base-year quantities as weights, we could also use given-year quantities or, for that matter, quantities referring to any other year or period. Employing given-year weights, we obtain a second *weighted aggregative index*, sometimes called a Paasche Index, whose formula is

$$I = \frac{\Sigma\ p_n q_n}{\Sigma\ p_0 q_n} \cdot 100 \qquad\qquad ★$$

Using the 1960 production totals given in the above table for the five crops, the reader can easily verify that this formula gives an index of 73.0 per cent (see also Exercise 6 on page 83).

Most of the important index numbers constructed by the federal government are published *in series*, that is, regularly every day, every week, every month, or every year. For these it would be highly impractical to use the Paasche formula since this formula would continually require new quantity weights. An index that is currently in great favor is the *fixed-weight aggregative index*, whose formula is

$$I = \frac{\Sigma\ p_n q_a}{\Sigma\ p_0 q_a} \cdot 100 \qquad\qquad ★$$

where the weights are quantities referring to some period other than the base year 0 or the given year n. Although it is actually calculated somewhat differently, one of the most important fixed-weight aggregative indexes is the *Wholesale Price Index* of the Bureau of Labor Statistics. Its current base period is the three-year period 1957–1959 and the q_a are quantities marketed in 1958 (see also Exercise 13 on page 84). We shall not illustrate the use of this last formula, since the calculations required are identical with those needed for the other weighted aggregative indexes.

Until now we have discussed two kinds of index numbers, those of the aggregative type and those that are averages of individual price relatives.

Having treated weighted aggregative indexes, let us now present in a parallel fashion *weighted averages of price relatives*. For example, we can write the formula for a *weighted arithmetic mean of price relatives* as

$$I = \frac{\sum \frac{p_n}{p_0} \cdot w}{\sum w} \cdot 100 \qquad\qquad ★$$

where the w's are suitable weights assigned to the individual price relatives, which are now written as proportions.

Since the importance of relative change in the price of a commodity is most adequately reflected by the *total amount of money* that is spent on it, it is customary to use *value weights* for the w's of this last formula. This raises the question whether to use the values (prices times quantities) of the base year, those of the given year, or perhaps some other fixed-value weights. It will be left to the reader to show in Exercise 7 on page 83 that base-year value weights $p_0 q_0$ would not yield a new index; with these weights, the last formula reduces to that of the Laspeyres Index given on page 78. To give an example in which we use *given-year weights*, let us refer again to the prices and the 1960 quantities on page 78. Calculating first the necessary price relatives and value weights, we obtain

	Price Relatives p_n/p_0	*Values** $p_n \cdot q_n$
Wheat	0.88	237,475
Corn	0.65	375,168
Oats	0.81	78,540
Rye	0.63	2,772
Barley	0.73	36,204

and the value of the index then becomes

$$\frac{0.88(237,475) + 0.65(375,168) + 0.81(78,540) + 0.63(2,772) + 0.73(36,204)}{237,475 + 375,168 + 78,540 + 2,772 + 36,204} \cdot 100$$

$$= 74.6 \text{ per cent}$$

Having compared the prices of the five crops in three different ways, we obtained indexes of 73.6, 73.0, and 74.6. The differences are evidently not very large, but if millions of dollars ride on an increase or decrease

---

* Since the prices were given in cents per bushel and the quantities in millions of bushels, the units of these value weights are $10,000.

of one point (as in some labor-management agreements containing escalator clauses), the question of choosing an appropriate index is a very serious matter.

EXERCISES

1. In 1959, the annual amount a family of four spends on five major food items was estimated for 1959, 1960, 1961, and 1962 as

Beef:	244, 238, 230, 224
Pork:	160, 143, 148, 154
Chicken:	54, 52, 51, 51
Eggs:	65, 62, 58, 54
Milk:	171, 171, 171, 171

   the figures being given chronologically in dollars.

   (a) Construct a simple aggregative price index for the given four-year period with 1959 = 100, that is, calculate the 1959, 1960, 1961, and 1962 values of such an index.

   (b) Comment on the applicability of these results to the changing food costs of an elderly couple and of a family of eight.

   (c) What accounts for the constancy of the milk cost?

   (d) Find the arithmetic mean of the relatives comparing the 1962 estimates with those for 1959.

2. The total June 1960 and 1961 output of selected appliances (in thousands of units) was

	June 1960	*June 1961*
Refrigerators	315	353
Freezers	102	109
Ranges	127	145
Water heaters	62	72
Dishwashers	41	50
Disposers	62	75
Dehumidifiers	82	55
Air conditioners	237	234

   (a) Calculate a simple aggregative index comparing the June 1961 production of these goods with that of June 1960.

   (b) Find the arithmetic mean of the relatives comparing the June 1961 production of these goods with that of 1960.

3. The following are the annual average wholesale prices (in dollars per gallon) of three selected chemicals and allied products:

	1957	1958	1959	1960	1961
Benzene	0.360	0.335	0.310	0.340	0.328
Paint, outside	4.758	4.815	4.799	4.806	4.953
Turpentine	0.662	0.633	0.535	0.489	0.332

(a) Find the 1958, 1959, 1960, and 1961 values of a simple aggregative index with 1957 = 100.

(b) Find a simple aggregative index comparing the 1961 prices with those of 1959.

(c) Find for 1960 and 1961 the arithmetic mean of the price relatives using 1957 = 100.

(d) Find the arithmetic mean of the relatives comparing the 1961 prices with those of 1959.

(e) Calculate the geometric mean of the relatives comparing the 1961 prices of benzene and paint with those of 1959.

4. The number of tourists visiting Hong Kong during the years 1955 through 1960 were (in thousands): 49.0, 50.3, 59.4, 70.4, 94.7, and 113.7. Construct an index number series for tourism in Hong Kong for the years 1955 through 1960 with 1958 = 100.

5. The following are figures on the 1959/60 consumption of fertilizers (in thousand metric tons) for the United Kingdom and the Common Market nations:

	Phosphatic Fertilizers	Nitrogenous Fertilizers	Potash Fertilizers
Belgium-Luxemburg	90.4	103.6	155.5
France	783.0	504.8	685.9
Germany (Fed. Rep.)	707.0	624.6	1046.6
Italy	389.3	350.8	108.2
Netherlands	110.9	212.1	152.6
United Kingdom	436.5	421.2	434.0

(a) Construct a simple aggregative index for each of the Common Market nations, comparing its total fertilizer consumption with that of the United Kingdom.

(b) Construct a simple aggregative index comparing the consumption of fertilizers in the United Kingdom with the corresponding *average* figures for the Common Market nations.

(c) Find the arithmetic mean of the relatives comparing the consumption figures for France with those for Germany.

6. Verify that the Paasche Index for the data on page 79 equals 73.0.

7. Show that if we substitute base-year value weights into the formula for a weighted arithmetic mean of price relatives, we obtain the formula for the Laspeyres Index.

8. It is interesting to note that the Laspeyres formula can generally be expected to *overestimate* price changes, while the Paasche formula will generally do just the opposite. Explain why this is so.

9. In the so-called "Ideal Index" (which has never been widely used for practical reasons) the biases referred to in Exercise 8 are compensated for by taking the geometric mean of the Laspeyres Index and the Paasche Index computed from the same data. Use the results obtained in the text to compute the "Ideal Index" for the data on page 78. Also write out a general formula for the "Ideal Index."

10. The following table contains prices and production totals of three metals, prices being given in cents per pound and production figures in thousands of short tons:

	Prices			Quantities		
	1952	*1955*	*1961*	*1952*	*1955*	*1961*
Copper	24.4	37.4	30.2	1,024	1,107	1,200
Lead	16.3	14.9	10.7	473	479	480
Zinc	16.2	12.3	11.5	905	964	844

(a) Using 1952 quantities as weights and 1952 = 100, find weighted aggregative indexes for the 1955 and 1961 prices of these metals.

(b) Calculate a weighted aggregative index comparing the 1961 prices of the three metals with those of 1952, using the 1961 quantities as weights.

(c) Calculate a weighted aggregative index comparing the 1961 prices of the three metals with those of 1952, using the *averages* of the 1955 and 1961 quantities as weights.

(d) With 1952 = 100, calculate for 1961 the weighted arithmetic mean of price relatives, using base year values as weights.

(e) With 1952 = 100, calculate for 1961 the weighted arithmetic mean of price relatives, using given year values as weights. Comment on the practical aspects of this index number.

(f) Interchanging the p's and q's in the formula used in part (e), construct an index comparing the 1961 production of the three metals with that of 1952.

11. The following are the 1954, 1958, and 1961 prices (in cents per pound) and production totals (in millions of pounds) of three food items:

	Prices			Quantities		
	1954	*1958*	*1961*	*1954*	*1958*	*1961*
Cheese	37.9	38.9	41.5	1383	1399	1629
Butter	59.7	58.7	60.5	1449	1390	1494
Margarine	26.6	26.5	25.5	1364	1573	1724

(a) Using the 1954 quantities as weights, construct aggregative indexes comparing the 1958 and 1961 prices, respectively, with those of 1954.

(b) Using the 1958 quantities as weights, construct aggregative indexes comparing the 1958 and 1961 prices, respectively, with those of 1954.

(c) Using 1961 quantities as weights, construct an aggregative index comparing the 1961 prices with those of 1954.

(d) Using the means of the 1954 and 1961 quantities as weights, construct an aggregative index comparing the 1961 prices with those of 1954.

(e) With 1954 = 100, calculate for 1961 the weighted arithmetic mean of the price relatives, using base year values as weights. Compare this result with the 1961 index number calculated in part (a).

(f) With 1954 = 100, calculate for 1961 the weighted arithmetic mean of the price relatives, using the given year values as weights.

12. Compare the 1961 prices of the three foods in Exercise 11 with those of 1954 by means of the "Ideal Index" (see Exercise 9).

13. Show that the formula for the weighted arithmetic mean of price relatives with value weights of the form $w = p_0 q_a$ reduces to the formula for a fixed-weight aggregative index.

Three Important Indexes

Among the many important indexes intended to describe assorted phenomena, some are prepared by private organizations. Financial institutions and utility companies, for example, often prepare indexes of such activities as employment, factory hours and wages, retail sales, etc., for the regions they serve; trade associations prepare indexes of price and quantity changes vital to their particular interests; and so on. Many of these indexes are widely used and highly regarded indicators of the phenomena they are aimed to describe. The most widely used and the most widely circulated indexes, however, are those prepared by the federal government. Of the many important government indexes, we shall briefly describe three, two price indexes and one quantity index; they are the *Consumer Price Index*, the *Wholesale Price Index*, and the *Index of Industrial Production*.

The *Consumer Price Index*, constructed by the Bureau of Labor Statistics, is designed to measure the change in prices of a collection of goods and services, called a "market basket," bought by city wage-earner and clerical-worker families. This market basket consists of fixed quantities of some 300 items, described by detailed specifications to insure comparability in successive periods. Included among these items are meats, dairy products, residential rents, clothing, appliances, used cars, gasoline and oil, physicians' services, drugs, haircuts, razor blades, TV sets, newspapers, cigarettes, beer, and the like, which are of major importance in family purchases and which, in fact, represent the greater part of family spending.

The items which comprise the market basket are periodically priced in a sample of 46 cities varying in size from small towns to the nation's largest cities. The prices that enter the index relate to *eight major groups*, namely, food, housing, apparel, medical care, personal care, reading and recreation, transportation, and other goods and services. Group indexes are regularly calculated for the 20 largest cities, and they are then combined into over-all city indexes, group indexes for all cities combined, and one index covering all groups and all cities. When the data for the individual groups are combined into a city index, each group is assigned a weight (differing from city to city) which is intended to represent the "relative importance" of the group in the average budget, or family expenditure, of families covered by the index. The combined index for the whole country, the Consumer Price Index, is calculated from the data obtained for the various cities, giving those for each city a weight in proportion to the part of the total wage-earner and clerical-worker population it represents in the over-all index. The current base period for the index is 1957–1959.

In calculating the Consumer Price Index and its various group and subindexes, the Bureau of Labor Statistics uses two formulas which differ in the mechanics of calculation, but which are mathematically the same. Both formulas represent fixed-weight aggregative indexes of the sort now commonly in use. Looking at the index as a weighted average of price relatives, the value (price times quantity) weights used vary from time to time, but this is due entirely to changes in prices, since the quantities making up the market basket are held fixed. In this way, the index measures the change in the prices of fixed quantities of goods and services.

A crucial factor in an index such as this is establishing as part of the value weights the "relative importance" of the different groups of goods and services in the index families' expenditures. The original value weights were established on the basis of a survey conducted in 1950 of the consumer expenditure patterns of 7,000 wage-earner and clerical-worker families in 91 cities, with the data of that year being adjusted to 1952 prices and consumption levels. Under normal conditions, the relative importance of the various categories of goods and services changes fairly slowly, so that these weights need only infrequent revision. Nevertheless, it must be understood that the relative importance weights are only (more or less good) approximations to the actual distribution of family expenditures at any time other than the point when revised weights are introduced into the index.

To account for the major social and economic developments that have taken place in this country in recent years, the Bureau of Labor Statistics initiated a major revision program for the index in 1958, with the January 1964 index scheduled as the first in the new series. Immediate steps consisted of increasing the number of prices collected by a fifth, increasing the sample of discount houses, suburban stores, and physicians, adding surgical insurance, and giving broader coverage to such categories as apparel, house furnishings, automobiles, and restaurant meals. In addition, a number of new items such as precooked foods and so-called "miracle" fabrics were priced for the first time.

The basic, and most time-consuming, factor of any major revision of this index is the necessary survey of consumer expenditures, incomes, and savings. Based upon such a survey, the Bureau of Labor Statistics has analyzed about 10,000 usable schedules from 70 sample cities to determine the current content of the market basket and, thus, obtain new weights for the revised Consumer Price Index. It is hoped that the new weights will serve for the remainder of this decade and that the new index will adequately reflect changes in the prices paid by urban families of two or more persons headed by a wage earner or clerical worker.

Also constructed by the Bureau of Labor Statistics, the *Wholesale Price Index* is intended to measure changes in the prices of commodities at their first important commercial transaction. Thus, the word "wholesale" does not refer to prices received by wholesalers, jobbers, and distributors, but to prices of large lots in primary markets. Most of the prices used are those quoted on organized exchanges or markets, or received by manufacturers and other producers. Like other comprehensive indexes, the Wholesale Price Index is based on a sample, not only of commodities, but also of specifications, reporters, and primary-market levels of transaction. Because of the importance of price movements in the many subdivisions of the economy, about 2,200 commodities are priced and more than 6,300 quotations are obtained. The commodities included in the index are not randomly selected; instead they are carefully chosen because in the opinion of experts they are the most important ones in the various categories. This is the sort of *judgment sample* we shall refer to again later on.

Making up the total index are fifteen major subgroups including farm products; processed foods; textile products and apparel; hides, skins, leather, and leather products; fuel, power and lighting materials; chemical and allied products; and nine others. Each of these major subdivisions is itself further subdivided; the processed-foods category, for example, includes cereal and bakery products, dairy products and ice cream, packaged beverage materials, and eight others.

Basically, though not strictly, the Wholesale Price Index is calculated as a fixed-weight aggregative index. As can easily be shown, however, this type of index is identical with one in which price relatives, p_n/p_0, are weighted with value weights $p_0 q_a$ (see Exercise 13 on page 84). At present, the weights used in calculating the index represent the values of sales (or shipments) made in primary markets in 1958. For technical reasons, the formula that is used in practice to calculate the index is a variation of the one on page 80, with $w = p_0 q_a$, and currently 1957–1959 = 100.

Unlike indexes measuring changes in prices, the Federal Reserve Board's *Index of Industrial Production* measures changes in volume or quantity. Since its origin in the 1920's with data based on 60 series relating to manufacturing and mining, the index has been periodically revised in an effort to keep pace with the output of a rapidly expanding economy. At present, the index is intended to measure changes in the physical volume or quantity of output of the nation's factories, mines, and electric and gas utilities. (The output of the latter was added to the index in a 1959 revision aimed at giving broader coverage and also permitting better comparisons with production indexes of other countries.) Directly, the index thus accounts for about 35 per cent of the country's total production, but indirectly it reflects an additional 25 per cent or so of total activity, namely, the distribution of industrial products and their use in construction. Production in the construction industry itself, however, on farms, in transportation, and in various trade and service industries is not covered by the index.

The monthly composite index showing changes in the nation's total industrial production is arrived at by combining 207 individual monthly series into a number of different groups and then combining the corresponding group indicators into an over-all figure. One such grouping of individual series is the so-called "industry grouping," which has the three main components: manufacturing, mining, and utilities. In this classification, manufacturing, for instance, is separated into durable and nondurable manufactures. Making up the durable goods group are primary and fabricated metals; machinery and related products; clay, glass, and lumber; and furniture and miscellaneous goods. The machinery and related products group, for example, includes in turn machinery (electrical and nonelectrical); transportation equipment (motor vehicles and parts, aircraft and other equipment); instruments and related products; and ordnance and accessories. Nondurable manufactures include textiles, apparel, and leather products; paper and printing; chemical, petroleum, and rubber products; and foods, beverages, and tobacco (all of which are, themselves, groups of further industry subdivisions). For their part, mining and utilities are also groupings (utilities of electricity and gas, for instance).

In addition to the industry groupings, the 1959 revision added another combination of production series called "market groupings." In this rearrangement the 207 monthly series are grouped broadly according to three major market sectors (consumer goods, equipment including defense, and materials), with further divisions and subdivisions as in the industry groupings. Consumer goods, for example, consists of automotive products; home goods and apparel; and consumer staples, with the latter including processed foods, beverages and tobacco, reading matter, and so on. One major advantage of the new market groupings is that they make possible careful studies of the relationships between changes in production and changes in dollar expenditures. Somewhat more broadly, it is hoped that the improved physical volume measures in the revised index will permit penetrating analyses of economic developments in the 1960's.

We shall not describe in detail the fairly complicated way in which the individual series are combined into group indexes and eventually into the over-all production index. Let us point out, however, that for the *total index* the calculations actually performed lead to a fixed-weight aggregative index which is the ratio of total value added in a given month to the corresponding value added in 1957–1959 (using in both cases 1957 unit prices); that is

$$I = \frac{\Sigma\, q_n p_{57}}{\Sigma\, q_{57-59} p_{57}} \cdot 100$$

For a while the index was published in two forms, one with 1947–49 = 100 and the other with 1957 = 100; these forms have now been dropped, however, and currently the published index relates to the base 1957–1959.

Unlike the Consumer Price Index, the Index of Industrial Production is intended to be a measure of current business conditions. Along with such other indicators of business activity as personal income, new plant and equipment expenditures, new businesses and business failures, and business sales and inventories—called "business indicators"—the production index is carefully watched by all whose current activities and future plans are in some way affected by the ever-changing over-all business conditions.

Some Special Applications

One of the most widely discussed of economic phenomena is what is often called the "shrinking value of the dollar." Of course, there are all sorts of "dollars," money spent for construction, money spent for food or rent, money spent for medical care, and so on, and what happens to a particular "dollar" is not of equal concern to everyone. Referring to these different dollars, we often hear such statements as "compared to 1947–49 the construction dollar is worth only 70 cents," "compared to 1940 the food dollar is worth only 41 cents," "compared to 1947–49 the rent dollar is worth only 71 cents," and so forth. This is another way of saying that what once bought a certain amount of construction now buys only 70 per cent of it, the amount of money that used to feed a family for 100 days now feeds it for only 41 days, and what once used to pay a year's rent now pays a little less than nine months'. In each of these examples, a change in price is expressed in terms of a so-called change in the value of the dollar.

It is easy to illustrate how the value of some single-commodity dollar is obtained. If a furniture manufacturer bought a certain amount of glue for $3.50 in 1947 and he had to pay $7.00 for the same amount of the identical glue in 1962, the value of this "glue dollar" in 1962 was only 50 cents compared to 1947. This simply means that the price has doubled and that the value or the *purchasing power* of the "glue dollar" has been cut in half. Generally speaking, the purchasing power of a dollar is simply the reciprocal of an appropriate price index, written as a proportion. If prices have doubled from some reference period, the price index is 2.00 (200 per cent), and what a dollar will buy is only $\frac{1}{2.00} = 1/2$ of what it used to buy. In other words, the purchasing power is 1/2 of what it was, or 50 cents. Similarly, if the price had risen by 50 per cent, the price index would stand at 1.50 and the purchasing power of the dollar would be $\frac{1}{1.50} = 2/3$ of what it was, or about 67 cents.

The same argument applies also when we speak of the purchasing power of a construction dollar, a food dollar, a rent dollar, a medical care dollar, etc., none of which obviously refers to a single commodity. Presuming that comprehensive indexes of construction, food, rent, medical care, and similar prices are available, we have only to take their reciprocals to arrive at the purchasing powers of the respective dollars. Thus, in the beginning of this section we arrived at a purchasing power of 70 cents for the construction dollar by taking the reciprocal of 1.43, the current value of an appropriate construction index. To obtain an estimate of the purchasing power of what is the nearest thing to "*the* dollar," an omnibus dollar used to buy the full range of goods and services available in the economy, we might take the reciprocal of such comprehensive indexes as the Consumer Price Index or the Wholesale Price Index. Referring to the 1961 edition of *Business Statistics*, a government publication where such series are actually published, we find that in that year the purchasing power of the dollar was $\frac{1}{1.265} = 0.791$ (or 79.1 cents) based on the index of consumer prices, and that it was $\frac{1}{1.196} = 0.836$ (or 83.6 cents) based on the index of wholesale prices, where in both cases 1947–49 = 100.

Another important application of price indexes is in the calculation of so-called "real wages." Since money is not an end in itself, wage earners are usually interested in what their wages will buy, and this depends on two things: how much they earn and the prices of the things they wish to buy. Clearly, a person would be worse off than before if his wages *doubled* while, at the same time, the prices of the things he wants to buy *tripled*.

To calculate "real wages," we can either multiply actual money wages by a quantity measuring the purchasing power of the dollar, or better, divide actual wages by an appropriate price index. This process is referred to as *deflating* and the price index used as a divisor is called a *deflator*. As an illustration, let us investigate the change in real wages of manufacturing employees from 1950 to 1960, using data from *Business Statistics 1961*. The first column of the following table shows the average weekly gross earnings in manufacturing establishments, while the second column shows corresponding values of an index of consumer prices, with its base *shifted* from 1947–49 = 100 to 1950 = 100 (see Exercise 10 on page 93). The values of the third column are the real wages obtained by dividing the index numbers (expressed as proportions) into the corresponding actual earnings:

	Average Weekly Wages	Consumer Prices 1950 = 100	Real Wages
1950	$59.33	100.0	$59.33
1960	$90.91	123.1	$73.85

As can easily be seen, the actual wages increased from 1950 to 1960 by 53.2 per cent, and if prices had remained unchanged, real wages would have increased by precisely the same amount. However, prices have increased by 23.1 per cent, there has been a decrease in what a dollar will buy, and real wages have increased only by 24 per cent since $\frac{73.85}{59.33} = 1.24$. Expressed in another way, a market basket of goods and services which could have been bought for $73.85 in 1950 cost $90.91 in 1960.

The method we have illustrated here is frequently used to deflate individual values, value series, or value indexes. It is applied in problems dealing with such diversified things as dollar sales, dollar inventories of manufacturers, wholesalers, and retailers, total values of construction contracts, incomes, wages, and so forth. The only real difficulty in applying this method is finding appropriate indexes, or as we have called them here, appropriate *deflators*.

EXERCISES

1. Explain why an economist might have been justified in saying that he was not surprised that the Consumer Price Index reached a (then)

record high in February 1958 when the country was in a recession phase and unemployment was increasing.

2. An elderly retired couple, planning to move from Baltimore to either San Francisco or Detroit, finds from a government publication that the most recent value of the Consumer Price Index for San Francisco stands at 107.5, while that for Detroit is only 102.8. Comment on their "deduction" from these figures that it would cost them 4.7 per cent more to live in San Francisco than in Detroit.

3. Comment on the following statements, wrong on both counts, which appeared in a "popular" article on index numbers:

   (a) "Probably the most important use of the Wholesale Price Index is in forecasting later movements in the Consumer Price Index."

   (b) "A direct comparison of the Wholesale Price Index and the Consumer Price Index gives a very close estimate of the profit margins between primary markets and other distributive levels."

4. A business magazine reported that in May 1961 the Index of Industrial Production was up 3 per cent and that the Federal Reserve Board had hinted that for June the index would likely return to its "pre-recession" level. Commenting on this, the magazine said, "In weighing these figures it is worth noting that, in a dynamic economy, such indexes always understate production." Why is a bias of this sort inherent in production indexes?

5. For one week in January 1963 relative to the same January 1962 week, department store sales were up 16 per cent in San Francisco and down 2 per cent in Cincinnati. Is it reasonable to conclude that for the given week department store sales in San Francisco were 18 per cent higher than in Cincinnati?

6. For January through July 1962, the gross average weekly earnings (in dollars) in manufacturing were 94.88, 95.20, 95.91, 96.56, 96.80. 97.27, and 96.80, respectively, and the corresponding values of the Consumer Price Index (1957–1959 = 100) were 104.5, 104.8, 105.0, 105.2, 105.2, 105.3, and 105.5.

   (a) Use the values of the Consumer Price Index to express the weekly earnings in constant 1957–59 dollars, that is, use them to deflate the given weekly earnings.

   (b) Use the results obtained in part (a) to compare the actual percentage increase in earnings from January to July 1962 with the corresponding percentage change in the "real" earnings.

   (c) Using the data of this exercise, calculate the January through July 1962 values of an index of the purchasing power of the dollar with 1957–59 = 100.

7. Given that the spendable average weekly earnings for workers with no dependents for the same months as in Exercise 6 were 76.51, 76.77, 77.34, 77.86, 78.05, 78.43, and 78.05 dollars, deflate these 1962 figures to constant 1957–59 dollars. Comment on the use of the Consumer Price Index in connection with this problem.

8. The following table contains the average monthly earnings of wage earners in manufacturing industries in Mexico and values of an index of consumer prices for Mexico with 1953 = 100 (published by the International Labor Office):

	Average Monthly Earnings in Pesos	Index of Consumer Prices (1953 = 100)
1953	443	100
1954	488	105
1955	559	122
1956	608	128
1957	633	135
1958	696	150
1959	773	154
1960	849	162

Deflate this series of average monthly earnings to constant 1953 pesos. Also calculate the actual percentage increase in these earnings from 1953 to 1960 and compare it with the corresponding percentage change in the "real" earnings.

9. When we deflate the 1962 value of a single commodity to, say, 1958 prices, we divide its value by an index expressing the 1962 price of the commodity as a relative of the 1958 price. Show symbolically that this process leads to the value of the commodity in 1962 at 1958 prices. (Although this argument does not apply strictly when we deflate an aggregate of the values of several commodities, we are in a sense estimating the total of the *same* goods at base year prices.)

10. It is often desirable (or necessary) to change the point of reference, or *shift the base*, of an index number series from one period to another. Ordinarily, this is done by simply dividing each value by the original index number for the period which is to be the new base (and multiplying by 100). For instance, if we wanted to shift the base of the Consumer Price Index for the years 1950 through 1960 from 1947–49 = 100 to 1950 = 100, we would divide each of the 11 yearly values by 102.8, the original value of the index for 1950. (This is how we obtained the 1950 and 1960 values of the index on page 91.) Given the following values of an index of payrolls in mining for the months of January through July 1962 with 1957–59 = 100, shift the base to January 1962: 87.8, 88.4, 88.7, 89.7, 90.3, 92.0, 88.8.

11. Shift the base of the index of consumer prices in Mexico of Exercise 8 to 1957 = 100, that is, calculate the values of the index for the given years so that the base year is 1957 instead of 1953.

12. In 1955 the average weekly earnings of a laborer in a certain region were $61.50 and in 1962 the corresponding earnings were $80.00. A regional "cost of living" index stands at 125 for 1955 and 175 for 1962 with 1947 = 100. Express the 1962 dollar earnings of these laborers in terms of constant 1955 dollars.

13. Since index numbers are designed to compare two sets of figures, it seems reasonable that if an index for 1962 with the base year 1957 stands at 200, the same index for 1957 with the base year 1962 should be equal to 50. (If one thing is twice as big as another, the second should be half as big as the first.) To test whether an index meets this criterion, called the *time reversal test*, we need only interchange the subscripts 0 and n wherever they appear in the formula, and then see whether the resulting index (written as a proportion) is the reciprocal of the first. Determine which indexes among the simple aggregative index, the weighted aggregative index, the arithmetic mean of price relatives, the geometric mean of price relatives, and the Ideal Index (see Exercise 9 on page 83) satisfy this criterion.

14. As has been suggested in the text, price index formulas can be changed into quantity index formulas simply by replacing the p's with q's and the q's with p's. Using this relationship between the formula for a price index and the corresponding formula for a quantity index, the *factor reversal test* requires that the product of the two (written as proportions) equal the value index $\Sigma\ p_n q_n / \Sigma\ p_0 q_0$. Show that this criterion is satisfied if we compare the prices, quantities, and values of a single commodity and for the Ideal Index (see Exercise 9 on page 83), but not for any of the other index number formulas given in this chapter.

A Word of Caution

Having already discussed some of the problems encountered in index number construction, let us now add a word of caution about their use and their interpretation. Difficulties always arise when attempts are made to generalize beyond the stated purpose of an index to phenomena it was never intended to describe. The word "general" serves well enough to distinguish general purpose indexes from those that are deliberately "special" in scope, but it is quite misleading in another sense: most "general purpose" indexes are strictly limited in purpose and in scope.

Perhaps the most widely misunderstood index of all is the Consumer Price Index of the Bureau of Labor Statistics. For various reasons, a change of half a point in this index almost causes a panic in the streets. One reason for this is that the Consumer Price Index is widely thought of as measuring not only the "cost of living" in different places, but current business conditions as well—neither of which it does. In view of the government's many careful explanations of just what the Consumer Price Index is and is not intended to measure, it is hard to account for the feeling that the index measures current business conditions. Whatever remote and indirect connection there may exist between the limited phenomenon described by the index and business conditions in general, is unintended. Thus, there is really nothing surprising about the fact that in February 1958, when the country was in a strong recession and unemployment was growing, the Consumer Price Index reached a (then) record high of 122.5. Also, there is very little basis for thinking of the Consumer Price Index as a general measure of the "cost of living," even though this was once its official name. Actually, as the government is careful to point out, the index does not measure the cost of living even of the families to which it applies. Clearly, a person's cost of living depends to some extent on his *level of living*, and changes in the level of living are not reflected in the index as it refers to a fixed market basket of goods. Moreover, the index does not take into account taxes paid to federal and state governments, nor does it (usually) account for price reductions on sale and discount items. What the index sets out to do, it does fairly well—it does estimate the "change in the prices of goods and services purchased by city wage-earner and clerical-worker families to maintain their level of living." It is not good practice to claim much beyond that.

There are some persons who would like to see the government develop bigger, better, and more general indexes, say, a truly "general" consumer price index (or even a cost of living index) covering *all* families and *all* goods and services. Others feel that the value of an index decreases more or less in proportion to the increase in its scope. From this latter point of view, such phenomena as changing retail prices, wholesale prices, industrial production, and so on, are far too broad ever to be described in terms of a single number. No matter how one feels about this problem, it is difficult to get away from the fact that the reduction of a large set of data to a single number entails the loss of such a tremendous amount of information that the whole procedure may have little practical value, if any. There are, indeed, some formidable difficulties connected both with the construction of index numbers by the professional and their interpretation by the layman. As one economist has pointed out:

> *"It ought to be conceded that index numbers are essentially arbitrary. Being at best rearrangements of data wrenched out of original market and technological contexts, they strictly have no economic meaning. Changes in tastes, technology, population composition, etc., over time increase their arbitrariness. But, of course, there is no bar to the use of indexes 'as if' they did have some unequivocal meaning provided that users remember that they themselves made up the game and do not threaten to 'kill the umpire' when the figures contradict expectations."**

* I. H. Siegel, in a letter to the editor, *The American Statistician*, February 1952.

FIVE
PROBABILITY

Mathematical Preliminary: Counting

In contrast to the complexity of many of the modern methods used in business and economics, the simple process of counting still plays an important role. One still has to count 1, 2, 3, 4, ..., say, when taking inventory, when counting cars passing a given spot, or when preparing a report showing how many rainy days there were during a given month. Sometimes the actual process of counting can be simplified by the use of mechanical devices, by performing the count indirectly (say, when determining the total number of sales from the serial numbers of invoices), or by using some of the mathematical theory which we shall discuss below.

To perform an actual count, it is always necessary to list, align, or otherwise arrange the objects to be counted in some way. Although this may sound easy, the following example will illustrate that sometimes it may not be. Suppose that a merchant wants to "unload" two pens and that he decides to try and sell them on Monday for $2.00 each; if necessary, he will lower the price to $1.00 on Tuesday and, if they are still unsold, he will give them away on Wednesday. What we would like to know is—in how many different ways can all this be done? One possibility is that he will sell both pens on Monday, another possibility is that he will sell them both on Tuesday, and a third possibility is that he will give them both away on Wednesday. A fourth possibility is that he will sell one on Monday and one on Tuesday, and a fifth possibility is that he will sell one on Monday and give the other away on Wednesday. Are there any other possibilities?

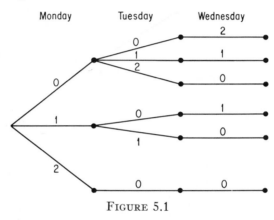

FIGURE 5.1

In order to handle problems of this kind systematically, it is often helpful (or necessary) to use a *tree diagram* like that of Figure 5.1. This diagram shows that there are three possibilities (three branches) for Monday depending on whether he sells 0, 1, or 2 pens; for Tuesday there are again three branches growing out of the first branch, but only two out of the second and one out of the third. Clearly, there are three possibilities for Tuesday if he did not sell any of the pens on Monday, two possibilities if he sold one, and one possibility if he sold two. Since what happens on Monday and Tuesday automatically determines what must happen on Wednesday, there is no need to go any further, and it can be seen that six different things can happen. Trying to list them without the tree diagram, we forgot to count the case where the merchant sells one pen on Tuesday and gives the other away on Wednesday.

To consider another example where a tree diagram can be of some aid, suppose that the Board of Directors of a company consists of Mr. Jones, Mr. Green, Mrs. Brown, and Mr. Smith. One of them is to be elected chairman, one is to be elected vice-chairman, and we would like to know in how many ways this can be done. Looking at the tree diagram of Figure 5.2, it is apparent that the selection can be made in 12 different ways, corresponding to the 12 distinct paths along the branches of the tree. Starting at the top, the first represents the election of Mr. Jones as vice-chairman and Mr. Green as chairman, the second represents the

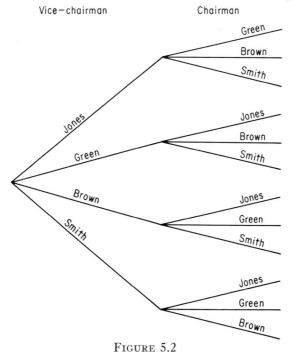

FIGURE 5.2

election of Mr. Jones as vice-chairman and Mrs. Brown as chairman, and so forth. Note that the answer which we obtained is the *product* of the number of ways in which they can first elect a vice-chairman and the number of ways in which they can then elect a chairman from among the three board members who remain after the vice-chairman has been elected. Generalizing from this example, we have the following theorem:

THEOREM A. *If an operation consists of two steps, of which the first can be performed in m ways and the second can then be performed in n ways, the whole operation can be performed in m · n ways.*

Thus, if a person has to buy one of eight different items on a list from one of five different department stores, he can do his shopping in $8 \cdot 5 = 40$ different ways.

Using appropriate tree diagrams, it is easy to generalize the above theorem so that it will apply also to operations involving more than two steps. If there are k steps we have

THEOREM B. *If an operation consists of k steps, of which the first can be performed in n_1 ways, the second can then be performed in n_2 ways, ..., and the kth can finally be performed in n_k ways, then the whole operation can be performed in $n_1 \cdot n_2 \cdot \ldots \cdot n_k$ ways.*

Thus, if a menu provides the choice of 15 different sandwiches, 8 kinds of drinks, and 6 different desserts, there are altogether $15 \cdot 8 \cdot 6 = 720$ ways in which a person can order a sandwich, a drink, and a dessert. Also, if the manager of a firm has the choice of buying his raw materials from any one of 6 vendors, processing them on any one of 3 machines, packaging the finished product in one of 4 different ways, and advertising it in one of 2 different media, he can plan the total operation in $6 \cdot 3 \cdot 4 \cdot 2 = 144$ different ways.

Theorem B is often applied to problems in which several selections are made from one set of objects and where the order in which they are made is of relevance. This was *not* the case in the examples immediately following Theorems A and B, but it was the case in the illustration on page 99, where it was shown that there are 12 ways in which a vice-chairman and a chairman can be chosen from among the four persons comprising the Board of Directors of a company. Generally speaking, if r objects are selected from a set of n objects, any particular arrangement of these r objects is referred to as a *permutation*. Thus, 32415 is a permutation of the first five positive integers, and ADE might be looked upon as a permutation of three letters selected from among the first five letters of the alphabet. As an immediate application of Theorem B we now have *Permutations*

THEOREM C. *The number of permutations of r distinct objects selected from a set of n objects is $n(n-1) \cdot \ldots \cdot (n-r+1)$.*   ★

To prove this we have only to note that in Theorem B (with $k = r$) we now have $n_1 = n$, $n_2 = n - 1$, ..., and $n_r = n - r + 1$. (The rth, and final, selection is made from the $n - (r - 1) = n - r + 1$ objects which remain after the first $r - 1$ selections have been made.) Thus, the number of ways in which a union with 20 members can elect a president, a vice-president, a secretary, and a treasurer is $20 \cdot 19 \cdot 18 \cdot 17 = 116{,}280$, and the number of ways in which 3 new territories can be assigned to 3 of 7 salesmen employed by a firm is $7 \cdot 6 \cdot 5 = 210$. (When using Theorem C it is always assumed that the objects are all distinct; how the theorem must be modified to find, say, the number of ways in which one can arrange the letters in the word "book," is indicated in Exercise 19 on page 105.) Note also that in the special case where $r = n$ we have

Combinations Permutations

THEOREM D. *The number of permutations of n distinct objects taken all together is* $n(n - 1) \cdot \ldots \cdot 2 \cdot 1$. ★

Thus, the number of ways in which 5 drivers can be assigned to 5 trucks is $5 \cdot 4 \cdot 3 \cdot 2 \cdot 1 = 120$, and the number of ways in which 7 different books can be arranged on a shelf is $7 \cdot 6 \cdot 5 \cdot 4 \cdot 3 \cdot 2 \cdot 1 = 5{,}040$.

Using the so-called *factorial notation*, we write the number of permutations of n distinct objects taken all together as $n! = n(n - 1) \cdot \ldots \cdot 2 \cdot 1$, so that $2! = 2$, $3! = 6$, $4! = 24$, $5! = 120$, $6! = 720$, and so on. In this notation it is also customary to let, by definition, $0! = 1$. It will be left to the reader to verify in Exercise 18 on page 105 that the formula of Theorem C, the one giving the number of permutations of r distinct objects selected from a set of n objects, can be written as $n!/(n - r)!$.

There are many problems in which we are interested in the number of ways in which r objects can be selected from a set of n objects, but where we do not care about the order in which the selection is made. We may thus want to know in how many ways a committee of 5 can be selected from among the 100 employees of a company, or the number of ways in which 10 stocks can be selected from a list of 24. To obtain an appropriate formula, let us first consider the following 24 permutations of three of the first four letters of the alphabet:

abc	acb	bac	bca	cab	cba
abd	adb	bad	bda	dab	dba
acd	adc	cad	cda	dac	dca
bcd	bdc	cbd	cdb	dbc	dcb

If we are interested only in the number of ways in which three of these four letters can be selected, and not in the order in which they are selected, it should be noted that each row in the above table contains $3 \cdot 2 \cdot 1 = 6$ permutations of the same three letters selected from among the first four letters of the alphabet. In fact, there are only four ways in which three letters can be selected from among the first four letters of the alphabet if we are not interested in the order in which the selection is made; they are a, b, and c; a, b, and d; a, c, and d; and b, c, and d. In general, there are $r!$ permutations of r specific objects selected from a set of n objects and, hence, the $n(n-1) \cdot \ldots \cdot (n-r+1)$ permutations of r objects selected from a set of n objects contain each set of r objects $r!$ times. (In our example, the 24 permutations of 3 letters selected from among the first 4 letters of the alphabet contained each set of 3 letters $3! = 6$ times.) Dividing $n(n-1) \cdot \ldots \cdot (n-r+1)$ by $r!$, we thus have

THEOREM E. *The number of ways in which r objects can be selected from a set of n distinct objects is*

$$\frac{n(n-1) \cdot \ldots \cdot (n-r+1)}{r!} \qquad \bigstar$$

Symbolically, we write the number of ways in which r objects can be selected from a set of n as $\binom{n}{r}$ and we refer to it as "the number of *combinations* of n objects taken r at a time." In Exercise 18 on page 105, the reader will be asked to verify that in the factorial notation

$$\binom{n}{r} = \frac{n!}{(n-r)!\,r!} \qquad \bigstar$$

for $r = 0, 1, 2, \ldots,$ and n.

Applying Theorem E we find, for example, that a person can invite 5 of his 8 friends to a party in $\dfrac{8 \cdot 7 \cdot 6 \cdot 5 \cdot 4}{5 \cdot 4 \cdot 3 \cdot 2 \cdot 1} = 56$ ways, an employer can fire 3 of his 10 salesmen in $\dfrac{10!}{7! \cdot 3!} = 120$ ways, and that a light fixture with 5 bulbs can have 2 bulbs burn out in 10 different ways. An easy way of calculating the quantities $\binom{n}{r}$, also called binomial coefficients, is illustrated in Exercise 15 below.

EXERCISES*

1. A sales agency for home air purifiers wants to dismiss one of two of its door-to-door salesmen, whose records have been equally poor. It is the agency's practice to have each salesman immediately call in each

---

* Many beginners seem to have some difficulties with combinatorial problems like these. Although they provide a foundation for much work in probability theory, they are not absolutely essential for the study of elementary statistics.

sale, and it is decided to retain the salesman who beats the other to calling in his *second* sale. (Thus, referring to the two salesmen as A and B, the sequence ABA represents the outcome where first a sale is called in by A, then a sale is called in by B, and then another sale is called in by A.)

(a) Construct a tree diagram showing the 6 possible outcomes for this "experiment," indicating in each case whether it is A or B who will keep his job.

(b) Given that the first sale is called in by Salesman A, how many possible outcomes are there now and how many of them are favorable to Salesman A?

2. A department store classifies its delinquent customers (1) according to whether the number of times the account has previously been delinquent is 0, 1, or 2 or more; (2) according to whether the amount owed is less than $40 or $40 or more; and (3) according to whether the amount owed is overdue by less than 2 months or by 2 months or more.

(a) Construct a tree diagram showing the different ways in which the department store classifies its delinquent customers.

(b) If there are 25 customers in each of the categories listed in part (a) and a courteous reminder is sent to all those whose account is delinquent for the first time or who owe less than $40, how many of these customers will receive a courteous reminder?

(c) If a warning is sent to each customer whose account is overdue by 2 months or more, how many customers will receive such a warning [assuming again that there are 25 customers in each of the categories obtained in part (a)]?

(d) How many of these delinquent customers receive a courteous reminder as well as a warning?

3. The manager of a store stocks *one each* of two different models of a TV set, reordering at the end of each day (for delivery early the next morning) if and only if both sets have been sold. Construct a tree diagram to show that if he starts on a Monday with both models, there are altogether 12 ways in which he can make sales on the Monday and Tuesday of that week.

4. The Standard and Poor's Corporation regularly rates common stocks, assigning them the ratings A+, A, A−, B+, B, B−, and C.

(a) In how many ways can they rate two different common stocks?

(b) In how many ways can they rate three different stocks, all of which rate B+ or higher?

(c) In how many ways can they rate two different stocks, if one of the stocks (but not both) has a rating of A or A+?

5. If a firm has 5 warehouses and 12 retail outlets, in how many different ways can an item be shipped from one of the warehouses to one of the stores?

6. A building contractor offers 2-, 3-, and 4-bedroom houses, which may be had in 6 different exterior finishes, with a carport or a garage, and with or without air-conditioning. How many distinct choices can a customer make?

7. Given that there are 6 main routes by which trucks travel from Denver to New Orleans, in how many different ways can a trucker plan a trip from Denver to New Orleans and back, if

   (a) he must travel both ways by the same route?
   (b) he can but need not travel both ways by the same route?
   (c) he cannot travel both ways by the same route?

8. If license plates are to have 3 letters followed by 3 digits, the first of which cannot be 0, how many distinct plates can be made?

9. If 10 books are being considered for a literary award, in how many ways can the first, second, and third prizes be awarded?

10. Repeat Exercise 9 if a cash award of $1,000 is given to each of the three authors whose books are selected, without there being any distinction as to who is first, second, and third.

11. If four executives are seated around a table for a business conference, how many possible arrangements are there if it matters only who is to whose left and who is to whose right?

12. A business is looking for two locations, one for a manufacturing plant and one for a distribution center. If 15 locations are being considered, in how many ways can the selection be made?

13. How many 5-man basketball teams can be chosen from a squad of 12, if one disregards the positions played by the members of the squad?

14. A shipment of 10 television sets contains one that is defective. In how many ways can two of the sets be selected so that

   (a) the defective set is not included?
   (b) the defective set is included?

15. The number of combinations of n objects taken r at a time can easily be determined by means of the following arrangement called *Pascal's triangle:*

$$
\begin{array}{ccccccc}
 & & & 1 & & 1 & & \\
 & & 1 & & 2 & & 1 & \\
 & 1 & & 3 & & 3 & & 1 \\
1 & & 4 & & 6 & & 4 & & 1 \\
1 & & 5 & & 10 & & 10 & & 5 & & 1 \\
\end{array}
$$

. . . .

where each row begins with a 1, ends with a 1, and each other entry is given by the sum of the nearest two entries in the row immediately above. Verify that the *third* row of this triangle contains the values of $\binom{3}{0}$, $\binom{3}{1}$, $\binom{3}{2}$, and $\binom{3}{3}$, and that the *fourth* row contains the values of $\binom{4}{0}$, $\binom{4}{1}$, $\binom{4}{2}$, $\binom{4}{3}$, and $\binom{4}{4}$. [It can be shown in general that the nth row of Pascal's triangle contains the values of $\binom{n}{0}$, $\binom{n}{1}$, $\binom{n}{2}$, $\ldots$, and $\binom{n}{n}$.]

16. Find the number of ways in which a person working for the Bureau of the Census can select 3 from among the 8 families living in an apartment house by using

    (a) the formula for computing $\binom{n}{r}$ on page 102.

    (b) the method suggested in the preceding exercise.

17. A private testing concern has 7 Brand X radios of which 2 have poor insulation against shock and are definitely unsafe. Using Pascal's triangle (see Exercise 15) to find the necessary quantities, indicate in how many ways the concern can select 2 of the radios at random so that

    (a) none of the unsafe ones are included in the sample.

    (b) exactly one unsafe one is included in the sample.

    (c) both of the unsafe ones are included in the sample.

    (*Hint:* the number of ways in which a good objects and b bad objects can be selected from a set containing A good ones and B bad ones, is the *product* of the number of ways in which we can select a objects from a set of A objects and the number of ways in which we can select b objects from a set of B objects.)

18. Verify symbolically that the number of permutations of n objects taken r at a time can be written $n!/(n - r)!$ and, hence, that the number of combinations of n objects taken r at a time can be written
    $$\frac{n!}{(n - r)!\,r!}.$$

19. If among n objects r are alike while the others are all distinct, the number of permutations of these n objects taken all together is $n!/r!$.

    (*a*) Use this formula to find the number of permutations of the letters in the word "book."

(b) Use this formula to find the number of ways in which five cars can place in a race by makes if three of the cars are Corvettes, one is a Jaguar, and one is a Ferrari.

(c) Justify the formula given in this example.

20. If among n objects r_1 are identical and another r_2 are identical, while the others are all distinct, the number of permutations of these n objects taken all together is $\dfrac{n!}{r_1!r_2!}$.

(a) Use this formula to find the number of permutations of the letters in the word "success."

(b) In its "How to Play Golf" section, a bookstore has 3 copies of a book by Sam Snead, 4 copies of a book by Ben Hogan, and 1 copy each of books by five other golfers. If these books are sold one at a time, in how many different ways (orders) can they be sold?

(c) Justify the formula given in this example and, if possible, make it more general.

Mathematical Preliminary: Sets and Events

In the application of probability and statistics to problems of business and economics, it is customary to refer to any process of observation as an *experiment*. Thus, using this term in a very wide sense, the simple process of determining the number of mistakes a typist makes on a page and the much more complicated process of obtaining and evaluating data to predict gross national product are both regarded as experiments. The results which one obtains from an experiment, whether they be instrument readings, counts, "yes" or "no" answers, or other kinds of measurements, are called the *outcomes* of the experiment, and the set (totality) of all possible outcomes of an experiment is called the *sample space*. (Other terms used instead of "sample space" are "possibilities space," "universal set," and "universe of discourse.")

In most cases it is convenient to think of the outcomes of an experiment, the elements of the sample space, as a set of points. Thus, if an experiment consists of determining whether on a certain day the price of a given stock goes down, remains unchanged, or goes up, the sample space may be thought of as consisting of three points, say, the three points of Figure 5.3, to which we arbitrarily assigned the numbers 1, 2, and 3. (Instead, we could have used any other configuration of three points and we could have assigned to them any arbitrary numbers.)

Had we been interested in the behavior of two stocks, the sample space could have been given as in Figure 5.4, where 1, 2, and 3 again stand

Down   Unchanged   Up

1   2   3

FIGURE 5.3

for a stock's price going down, remaining unchanged, and going up, while the two coordinates refer to the respective stocks. Thus, the point $(2, 3)$ represents the outcome that the price of the first stock remains unchanged while that of the second stock goes up. Note that if we had been interested in n stocks in this experiment, the corresponding sample space would have consisted of 3^n points. For instance, for 5 stocks there would have been $3^5 = 3 \cdot 3 \cdot 3 \cdot 3 \cdot 3 = 243$ points, that is, 243 different outcomes, among which $(1, 2, 1, 1, 3)$ represents the case where the prices of the first, third, and fourth stocks go down, that of the second stock remains unchanged, while that of the fifth stock goes up. (Since this sample space has more than three dimensions, that is, each point has more than three coordinates, it cannot readily be pictured geometrically like the sample spaces of Figures 5.3 and 5.4.)

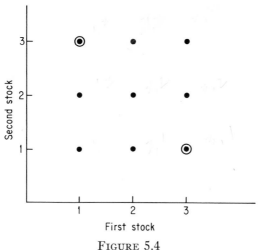

First stock

FIGURE 5.4

What kind of a sample space is actually appropriate for a given experiment will have to depend on what we look upon as an individual outcome. If in the two-stock example we had been interested only in the total number of stocks whose prices go down, remain unchanged, or go up, we could have used the three-dimensional sample space of Figure 5.5 instead of the one of Figure 5.4. Here the first coordinate gives the number of stocks whose prices go down, the second coordinate gives the number of stocks whose prices remain unchanged, while the third coordinate gives the number of stocks whose prices go up. Thus $(0, 2, 0)$ represents the outcome that the prices of both stocks remain unchanged, while $(0, 1, 1)$ represents the outcome that the price of one stock remains unchanged while the price of the other goes up. Note that the two points circled in Figure 5.4 correspond to the single point circled in Figure 5.5. It will be

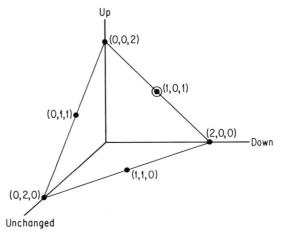

FIGURE 5.5

left to the reader to check what point or points of Figure 5.4 correspond to the other points of Figure 5.5. (It is interesting to note that the sample space of Figure 5.5 could also be used to represent the experiment described on page 98, the one which dealt with the merchant and his two pens. Letting the first coordinate stand for the number of pens sold on Monday, the second coordinate for the number of pens sold on Tuesday, and the third coordinate for the number of pens given away on Wednesday, the six points of Figure 5.5 could be used to represent the individual outcomes shown in the tree diagram of Figure 5.1.)

Generally speaking, it is desirable to use sample spaces whose elements cannot be further subdivided; that is, the individual points should not represent two or more outcomes which are distinguishable in some fashion. Thus, in the example dealing with the two stocks, it would in most instances be preferable to use the sample space of Figure 5.4 rather than that of Figure 5.5.

Having defined a sample space as the set of all possible outcomes of an

xperiment, let us now explain what we mean by an *event*. This is impor-
ant because probabilities invariably refer to the occurrence or non-
·ccurrence of some event. We assign a probability to the *event* that a
andidate will be elected to office, to the *event* that a shipment will arrive
·n time, to the *event* that someone who is 50 will live to be 75, and so
orth. Hence, let us state formally that *when we speak of an event, we
·re speaking of an appropriate subset of a sample space* (by *subset* we mean
·ny part of a set including the set as a whole and, trivially, the empty
·et which has no elements at all). Thus, in Figure 5.4 the subset which
·onsists only of the point (1, 1) represents the *event* that the prices of
·oth stocks go down; the subset which consists of the two points circled
·n Figure 5.4 represents the *event* that the price of one stock goes up
·vhile that of the other goes down; and the subset of the sample space of
·'igure 5.4 which consists of the five points (3, 1), (1, 3), (3, 2), (2, 3), and
·3, 3) represents the event that the price of *at least one* of the stocks goes
·p.

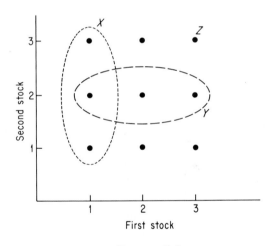

FIGURE 5.6

Still referring to the example of the two stocks, let us now suppose
·hat X stands for the event that the price of the first stock goes down
·egardless of what happens to the price of the second, Y stands for the
·vent that the price of the second stock remains unchanged regardless
·f what happens to the price of the first, and that Z stands for the event
·hat the prices of both stocks go up. Referring to Figure 5.6, giving the
·ame sample space as Figure 5.4, it can be seen that X consists of the three
·oints inside the dotted line, Y consists of the three points inside the

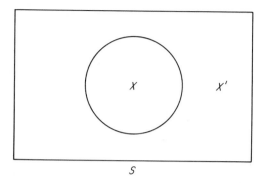

FIGURE 5.7

dashed line, while Z consists of the point $(3, 3)$. Note that X and Z have n‹ points in common; they are referred to as *mutually exclusive events*, whicł means that they cannot both occur in the same experiment. On the othe‹ hand, X and Y are *not* mutually exclusive, since these two events botł occur when the price of the first stock goes down while that of the secon‹ stock remains unchanged.

There are many problems of probability in which we are interested iⁱ events that can be expressed in terms of two or more other events. Fo instance, in our example we might be interested in the event that *eithe; the price of the first stock goes down or the prices of both stocks go up*, or w‹ might be interested in the event that *the price of the first stock goes dow* *and the price of the second stock remains unchanged*. In the first case w‹ are interested in the event that *either X or Z* occurs and in the secon‹ case we are interested in the event that X *and Y both* occur.

In general, if A and B are any two events we define their *union* $A \cup I$ as the event which consists of all the individual outcomes contained eitheɪ in A, in B, or in both. It is customary to read $A \cup B$ as "A cup B" oɪ simply as "A or B." With reference to the above example, we find thaʈ $X \cup Y$ consists of the five points $(1, 1)$, $(1, 2)$, $(1, 3)$, $(2, 2)$, and $(3, 2)$ while $X \cup Z$ consists of the four points $(1, 1)$, $(1, 2)$, $(1, 3)$, and $(3, 3)$ Also, if A and B are any two events we define their *intersection* $A \cap I$ as the event which consists of all the individual outcomes contained iⁱ both A and B. We read $A \cap B$ as "A cap B" or simply as "A and B." With reference to the above example we thus find that $X \cap Y$ consists of the point $(1, 2)$ and that $X \cap Z$ has no elements at all, it is empty Denoting the empty set by the Greek letter ϕ (phi), we can thus write $X \cap Z = \phi$.

Cap – and
cup – or

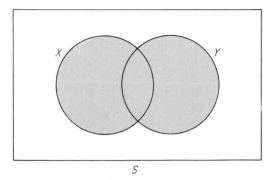

S

FIGURE 5.8

To complete our notation, let us define the *complement A'* of an event A with respect to a sample space S as the event which consists of all the individual outcomes of S that are not contained in A. Thus, with reference to our example X' stands for the event that the price of the first stock does not go down and it consists of the six points $(2, 1)$, $(2, 2)$, $(2, 3)$, $(3, 1)$, $(3, 2)$, and $(3, 3)$. Also, $(X \cup Y)'$, the complement of the event $X \cup Y$, consists of the points $(2, 1)$, $(3, 1)$, $(2, 3)$, and $(3, 3)$; it represents the event that the price of the first stock will not go down while that of the second stock will not remain unchanged.

When dealing with sample spaces, subsets, and events, it is often helpful to represent the entire sample space S by means of a rectangle and events by means of regions within the rectangle (usually circles or pieces of circles). Such representations are called *Venn diagrams* and some examples are shown in Figures 5.7, 5.8, and 5.9. Looking upon the rec-

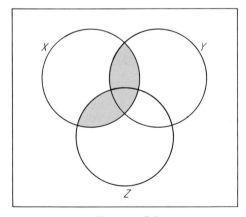

FIGURE 5.9

tangle of Figure 5.7 as representing the sample space for the experiment with the two stocks, event X could be represented by the circle, in which case its complement X' would be represented by the remainder of S. Similarly, the two circles of Figure 5.8 could be used to represent the events X and Y, in which case the region common to the two circles would represent the event $X \cap Y$, while the entire shaded region would represent the event $X \cup Y$. When dealing with three events, it is customary to draw the respective circles as in Figure 5.9. Note that the shaded region represents the event $X \cap (Y \cup Z)$, namely, the event which consists of all outcomes belonging to X and also to either Y or Z. As indicated in the exercises below, Venn diagrams are often used to verify various kinds of relationships among sets, subsets, or events, without requiring rigorous proofs based on a formal Algebra of Sets.

EXERCISES

1. A discount house advertises a sale on a certain kind of TV set which is no longer made. It has five of these sets, and we are interested in how many of these sets are sold during the special sale by each of the two salesmen working in its television department. Using the point $(3, 2)$ to represent the outcome that the first salesman sells 3 and the other sells 2, the point $(0, 4)$ to represent the outcome that the first salesman sells none while the other sells 4, and so on, draw a figure showing the 21 points constituting the sample space, that is, the set of all possible outcomes.

2. Referring to Exercise 1, let U be the event that all of the sets are sold, V the event that the first salesman sells at least two of the sets, and W the event that the two salesmen sell the same number of sets. List the outcomes belonging to event

   (a) U.   (e) $U \cap V$.
   (b) V.   (f) $U \cap W$.
   (c) W.   (g) $(V \cap W)'$.
   (d) $U \cup V$.   (h) $V' \cup W'$.

   Also check whether U and V are mutually exclusive, whether U and W are mutually exclusive, and whether V and W are mutually exclusive.

3. A taxicab company has two cabs, each of which can carry at most four passengers. Using the point $(0, 3)$ to indicate that the first cab is empty while the second has three passengers, the point $(2, 1)$ to indi-

cate that the first cab has 2 passengers while the second cab has 1 passenger, and so on, draw a figure showing the 25 points which correspond to the different ways in which the two cabs can be occupied.

4. Referring to Exercise 3, let P be the event that the total number of passengers carried by the two cabs is at least 5, Q be the event that at least one of the two cabs is empty, and R be the event that at least one of the two cabs carries exactly two passengers. List the outcomes belonging to

(a) P.

(b) Q.

(c) R.

(d) $Q \cap R$.

(e) $P \cap Q$.

(f) $P \cap R$.

(g) $P \cap Q'$.

(h) $Q \cap (P' \cap R')$.

(i) $Q \cap (P \cup R)$.

(j) $(Q \cap P) \cup (Q \cap R)$.

5. A coin is tossed three times in succession and the result is recorded as HHT if there are first two heads and then a tail, THT if there is first a tail, then a head, and then another tail, and so on. List the eight possible outcomes of this "experiment."

6. Referring to Exercise 5, let E represent the event that the first two tosses are heads, and let F represent the event that at least one of the tosses is tails. List the outcomes belonging to

(a) E.

(b) F.

(c) $E \cap F$.

(d) $E \cup F'$.

(e) $E' \cap F'$.

(f) $(E \cap F') \cup (E \cap F)$.

(g) $E \cap (E \cup F)$.

(h) $E \cup (E \cap F)$.

7. If in Exercise 5 we let 0 stand for "tail" and 1 for "head," we can let the point $(1, 1, 0)$ represent HHT, $(0, 1, 0)$ represent THT, and so on. Draw a figure showing the 8 possible outcomes in a three-dimensional sample space.

8. In a survey of newly constructed houses, each house is classified according to whether it has 1, 2, 3, or 4 bedrooms and according to whether it has 1, 2, or 3 baths. Letting $(2, 1)$ represent a house which has 2 bedrooms and 1 bath, $(4, 2)$ represent a house which has 4 bedrooms and 2 baths, and so on, draw a figure showing the 9 points which correspond to the different ways in which one of these houses can be classified, assuming that none of the houses has fewer bedrooms than baths.

9. Referring to Exercise 8, let K be the event that the sum of the number of bedrooms and the number of baths is 5, let L be the event that there are more bedrooms than baths, and let M be the event that there are

2 bedrooms. List the possibilities belonging to

(a) K.

(b) L'.

(c) M.

(d) $L \cap M$.

(e) $L \cup M$.

(f) $K \cap L'$.

(g) $L \cup (K \cap M)$.

(h) $(L \cup K) \cap (L \cup M)$.

Also check whether K and L are mutually exclusive, whether K and M are mutually exclusive, and whether L and M are mutually exclusive.

10. It was pointed out in the text that the points $(1, 3)$ and $(3, 1)$ of Figure 5.4 together represent the same event as the point $(1, 0, 1)$ of Figure 5.5. Indicate what point or points of Figure 5.4 correspond to each of the other points of Figure 5.5.

11. If the reader did not make any mistakes in parts (g) and (h) of Exercise 2, he obtained identical answers. Use a Venn diagram to verify in general that $(A \cap B)' = A' \cup B'$, where the equality is meant to imply that $(A \cap B)'$ has the same elements (or members) as $A' \cup B'$.

12. If the reader has done parts (i) and (j) of Exercise 4 correctly, he will find that the answers are the same. Use Venn diagrams to verify in general that $A \cap (B \cup C) = (A \cap B) \cup (A \cap C)$, which is one of the *distributive laws* in the Algebra of Sets.

13. In Exercise 6, the reader should have obtained the same answer for parts (a), (f), (g), and (h). Verify by means of Venn diagrams that in general $(E \cap F') \cup (E \cap F)$, $E \cap (E \cup F)$, and $E \cup (E \cap F)$ are all equal to E.

14. In Exercise 9, the reader should have obtained the same answer for parts (g) and (h). Verify by means of Venn diagrams that in general $A \cup (B \cap C) = (A \cup B) \cap (A \cup C)$, which is another of the *distributive laws* of the Algebra of Sets. (Compare with Exercise 12 and note that in ordinary algebra there is only one distributive law.)

15. If A and B are mutually exclusive and A and C are mutually exclusive, are B and C necessarily also mutually exclusive?

The Concept of Probability

Directly or indirectly, probabilities play important parts in all problems of business and economics which somehow involve an element of uncertainty. A business man may want to know the probability that a new venture will succeed, a production manager may want to know the probability that a shipment will arrive on time, a quality control inspector may want to know the probability that an item will meet specifications, a broker may want to know the probability that the market will rise, and so forth. In view of its wide usage, it is unfortunate that the term "probability" itself is not easy to define; in fact, it is quite controversial.

In the study of probability there are essentially three kinds of problems. First there is the question of *what we mean* when we say that the probability for rain is 0.25, that the probability for a new product's acceptance is 0.40, or that the probability of a door-to-door salesman's making a sale is 0.08. Then there is the question of *how to obtain* numerical values for such probabilities and, finally, there is the question of *how to calculate* the probabilities of relatively complex events in terms of the probabilities of other (simpler) events.

About one thing there is general agreement, and that is that a probability should be a real number which we assign to an event (the outcome of an experiment) and that this number is to fall on the interval from 0 to 1, inclusive. A *zero* probability means that the event cannot happen or, at least, that it is so unlikely or rare that we might as well act as if it could not happen at all; a probability of *one* means that the event must happen or, at least, that it is so likely or certain that we might as well act as if it had to happen. We thus assign zero probabilities to the impossible event of getting *both* heads and tails on one flip of an ordinary coin and the event that a monkey, set loose on a typewriter, will reproduce the complete works of Shakespeare without a mistake. Similarly, we assign probabilities of one to the certain event that a card drawn from an ordinary deck of playing cards is either red or black and the event that at least one New Yorker will not spend the winter in Florida, a practical certainty.

When we say "the probability that a man of 50 will live to be 80 is 0.20," we mean that if present conditions prevail, 20 per cent of all men aged 50 will live to be 80. Similarly, when we say "the probability of getting heads with a balanced coin is 0.50," we mean that in the long run we will get about 50 per cent heads and 50 per cent tails. The following is another way of looking at these probabilities: if the probability that a man of 50 will live to be 80 is 0.20, an actuary might say that it is reasonable (or fair) to bet $4.00 to $1.00 that a man of 50 will *not* live to be 80 (or $1.00 to $4.00 that he will); similarly, in connection with the toss of a balanced coin, we might say that the two possible outcomes are even-money bets. This whole idea will be discussed further in Chapter 6.

Interpreting the probability of an event as the proportion of the time (or relative frequency) with which it will occur in the long run, it would seem reasonable to *estimate* such a probability in terms of the proportion of the time it has taken place in the past (or similar events have taken place in the past). Thus, if in the past 92 per cent of all patients who received a certain treatment were cured of a given disease, we *estimate* the probability that any one patient with this disease will be cured with the given treatment as 0.92; similarly, if in the past 78 per cent of all shipments from a given firm have arrived on time, we *estimate* the probability that any one shipment will arrive on time as 0.78. When there is not enough information available as to how often some kind of event or similar events have occurred in the past, there may be no choice but to *estimate* probabilities *subjectively*, that is, at least partly in terms of personal judgment, collateral information, "educated" guesses, perhaps intuition and other factors. A businessman may, thus, *estimate* the probability for the success of a new venture as 0.60 (or, more loosely, as better than an even chance) on the basis of an analysis of business conditions in general, the opinions of several experts, and his own subjective evaluation of the whole situation.

There are also many problems where one has no choice but to specify probabilities by *making assumptions* which, one hopes, are appropriate for the situation at hand. For instance, when starting a new business which has no precedent, it may seem reasonable to assume that a customer is just as likely to buy Brand A as Brand B. Later on, if this assumption is not borne out by experience, adjustments in the assumption (and corresponding changes in production or inventory) will have to be made.

In the remainder of this chapter we shall be concerned mainly with the third kind of question mentioned in the beginning of this section, namely, that of determining the probabilities of relatively complex events in terms of known (estimated or assumed) values of the probabilities of simpler kinds of events. We shall thus go into some of the simpler rules of what is usually called the *Calculus of Probability*.

Some Rules of Probability

The symbol which we shall use for the probability of an event A is $P(A)$. Thus, referring to the example of the two stocks (see page 107), $P(X)$ represents the probability that the price of the first stock will go down, and $P(X \cap Y)$ represents the probability that the price of the first stock will go down and that of the second stock will remain unchanged.

As is customary in modern mathematics, we shall begin our study of probability with a set of basic rules, called the *postulates* (or *axioms*). The first two of these postulates are merely precise formulations of what we pointed out informally on page 115, namely, that a probability is a real number on the interval from 0 to 1, inclusive, and that the probability of a certain event is equal to 1. It is assumed here (and throughout this chapter) that the events we are referring to belong to a sample space which has only a *finite number* of possible outcomes. (For examples where this assumption of finiteness is dropped, see Exercise 9 on page 135 and the discussion of the continuous case in Chapter 7.)

POSTULATE 1. $0 \leq P(A) \leq 1$ *for each event* A.

POSTULATE 2. $P(S) = 1$, *where* S *is a sample space.*

The second of these postulates states the fact that one of the outcomes constituting a sample space S is certain to happen. The third and last postulate pertains to the union of mutually exclusive events (see page 110) and it is usually referred to as the *Special Rule of Addition:*

POSTULATE 3. *If* A *and* B *are mutually exclusive events, then*

$$P(A \cup B) = P(A) + P(B) \qquad \bigstar$$

To justify Postulate 3 consider an event A that the switchboard of a company will have at most 200 incoming calls on a given day and an event B that it will have more than 200 incoming calls but at most 400. Then if $P(A) = 0.60$ and $P(B) = 0.30$, this means that 60 per cent of the time the daily number of incoming calls is at most 200, while 30 per cent of the time the daily number of incoming calls is more than 200 but at most 400. Hence, $60 + 30 = 90$ per cent of the time the daily number of incoming calls is at most 400, that is, $P(A \cup B) = 0.60 + 0.30 = 0.90$. Note that the events A and B are mutually exclusive in this example; otherwise Postulate 3 could not have been applied. For instance, if C is the event that a person entering a given men's store will buy a shirt, D is the event that he will buy a tie, $P(C) = 0.15$, and $P(D) = 0.08$, then $P(C \cup D)$, the probability that he will buy a shirt or a tie (or both) is not necessarily equal to $0.15 + 0.08 = 0.23$. In fact, the answer is incorrect, since there must surely be many customers who buy a shirt as well as a tie. We shall return to this example later to illustrate Theorem J, the *General Rule of Addition.*

Starting with the three postulates, we can obtain various other rules of probability which have many useful applications. Some of the simpler ones will be given below and two others, which are of special interest, will be taken up in the section beginning on page 129.

First, there is a theorem to the effect that (as we have pointed out earlier) an event which cannot possibly happen has probability 0. Formally, we express this by writing $P(\phi) = 0$, where ϕ again denotes the empty set which has no elements at all. Clearly, if one of the outcomes must happen, the probability that none of them will happen is equal to zero. (To give a rigorous proof of this, we have only to make use of Postulates 2 and 3 and the fact that ϕ and S are mutually exclusive; see Exercise 13 on page 125.)

To introduce a second theorem, consider the fact that if 32 per cent of the executives of a large corporation belong to a certain club, it follows that 68 per cent do not belong to the club; also, if 25 per cent of the students in a class get A's then 75 per cent do not get A's, and if 88 per cent of the shipments made by a firm arrive without a mishap then 12 per cent do not. This leads to the following theorem:

THEOREM F. $P(A') = 1 - P(A)$ *for any event A.*   ★

(To prove this rigorously, we have only to use Postulates 2 and 3, the fact that A and A' are by definition mutually exclusive, and the fact that between them A and A' contain all the elements of the sample space S, namely, that $A \cup A' = S$.) Thus, if the probability that the price of a stock will go up is 0.40, the probability that it will not go up is 0.60; if the probability that a business venture will succeed is 0.45, the probability that it will not succeed is 0.55; and if the probability that Mr. Smith will be elected president of his company is 0.80, the probability that he will not be elected is 0.20.

The Special Rule of Addition, Postulate 3, can easily be generalized to apply to more than two mutually exclusive events. [We say that k events are mutually exclusive if they are all pairwise mutually exclusive.] Repeatedly applying Postulate 3, it immediately follows that

THEOREM G.   *If A_1, A_2, ..., and A_k are mutually exclusive events, then*   ★

$$P(A_1 \cup A_2 \cup \ldots \cup A_k) = P(A_1) + P(A_2) + \ldots + P(A_k)$$

With this theorem we have a formula for calculating the probability that one or another of a set of mutually exclusive events will occur. For instance, if the probabilities that a person who immigrated to the United States in 1955 came from England, Germany, or Italy are, respectively, 0.06, 0.12, and 0.13, then the probability that he came from one of these countries is $0.06 + 0.12 + 0.13 = 0.31$. Also, if the probabilities that a person eating in a given restaurant will order steak, pork chops, chicken, or lobster are, respectively, 0.28, 0.09, 0.32, and 0.16, then the probability that he will order one or another of these dishes is $0.28 + 0.09 + 0.32 + 0.16 = 0.85$; the probability that he will order something else instead is $1 - 0.85 = 0.15$.

The problem of determining the probabilities of the various events in which one might be interested in a given "experiment" is greatly simplified by the following theorem. (Note that for a sample space with as few as 20 individual outcomes there are already over a million different subsets or events, 1,048,576 to be exact.)

THEOREM H. *The probability of an event A equals the sum of the probabilities of the individual outcomes comprising A.*

(To prove this result we have only to refer to Theorem G; the individual outcomes are by definition mutually exclusive.)

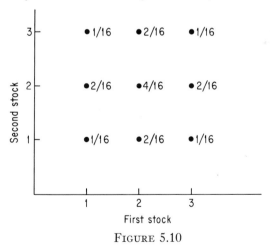

FIGURE 5.10

To illustrate the use of Theorem H, let us refer again to the example of the two stocks on page 107 and let us suppose that the nine possible outcomes have the probabilities shown in Figure 5.10. Then, the probability that the price of the first stock will go down is 4/16, namely, the sum of the probabilities assigned to the points $(1, 1)$, $(1, 2)$, and $(1, 3)$; similarly, the probability that the price of at least one of the stocks will go up is $7/16$, namely, the sum of the probabilities assigned to the points $(3, 1)$, $(3, 2)$, $(3, 3)$, $(2, 3)$, and $(1, 3)$.

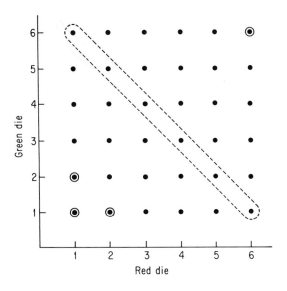

FIGURE 5.11

To consider another example, suppose we are interested in the roll of a pair of dice, one red and one green, and that each of the 36 possible outcomes (see Figure 5.11) is assigned a probability of $1/36$. Then, the probability of rolling a total of 7 is the *sum* of the probabilities of the points inside the dotted line and it is equal to $1/6$; also, the probability of rolling a total of 2, 3, or 12 is the sum of the probabilities assigned to the four points which are circled in Figure 5.11 and it is equal to $1/9$. Note that in this example, where the 36 possible outcomes have *equal* probabilities, the probability of any event is given by $1/36$ *times* the number of individual outcomes comprising the event. More generally, when dealing with "experiments" where the individual outcomes are *equiprobable* we have the following useful theorem:

THEOREM I. *If an experiment has n equiprobable outcomes and if s of these outcomes constitute event A, then $P(A) = s/n$.*   ★

This theorem is sometimes given as a "definition" of probability in elementary texts, claiming that if there are n equally likely outcomes among which s are labeled "success," then the probability of a success is s/n. We advisedly wrote the word "definition" in quotes in view of the obvious *circularity* of defining probability in terms of equally likely, that is, equiprobable events. As it is stated here, Theorem I is an immediate consequence of Theorem H.

Theorem I is of particular value in games of chance where it is assumed, for example, that heads and tails are equiprobable, that in a deck of 52 playing cards each card has an equal chance of being drawn, that each face of a die has the same probability of turning up, and so on. Thus, the probability of drawing an ace from an ordinary deck of 52 playing cards is 4/52 (there are 4 aces) and the probability of rolling 5 or 6 with a die is 2/6. Of course, Theorem I also applies, say, when each household in a given area has an equal chance of being included in a survey, when each ball bearing in a lot of some manufacturer's product has an equal chance of being chosen for inspection, and when each customer entering a supermarket has an equal chance of being asked certain questions.

In order to find a general formula for $P(A \cup B)$ when A and B need not be mutually exclusive, let us refer again to the example on page 117, where C was the event that a person entering a given store will buy a shirt, D was the event that he will buy a tie, while $P(C)$ and $P(D)$ equalled 0.15 and 0.08, respectively. Let us now add the information that $P(C \cap D) = 0.03$, namely, that 3 per cent of the customers buy a shirt as well as a tie. The situation with which we are now faced is described in Figure 5.12 and we find that $P(C \cup D)$ equals $0.12 + 0.03 + 0.05 = 0.20$,

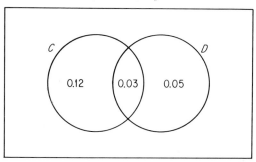

FIGURE 5.12

namely, the sum of the probabilities that a customer will buy a shirt but not a tie, the probability that he will buy a shirt as well as a tie, and the probability that he will buy a tie but not a shirt. (These probabilities can be added, since they obviously refer to mutually exclusive events.)

We could also have obtained this result by *subtracting* $P(C \cap D)$ from $P(C) + P(D)$, namely, by writing $P(C \cup D) = 0.15 + 0.08 - 0.03 = 0.20$. Accounting thus for the outcomes which are included *twice* when we add $P(C)$ and $P(D)$, we arrive at the following theorem, called the *General Rule of Addition:*

THEOREM J. $P(A \cup B) = P(A) + P(B) - P(A \cap B)$ ★

To illustrate this rule, let us refer again to the example of the two stocks and Figure 5.10. If, as before, X is the event that the price of the first stock will go down while Y is the event that the price of the second stock will remain unchanged, it can be seen from Figure 5.10 that $P(X)$ $= \frac{1}{16} + \frac{2}{16} + \frac{1}{16} = \frac{1}{4}$, that $P(Y) = \frac{2}{16} + \frac{4}{16} + \frac{2}{16} = \frac{1}{2}$, and that $P(X \cap Y) = \frac{2}{16} = \frac{1}{8}$. Hence, the probability that at least one of these two events will occur is

$$P(X \cup Y) = P(X) + P(Y) - P(X \cap Y) = \tfrac{1}{4} + \tfrac{1}{2} - \tfrac{1}{8} = \tfrac{5}{8}$$

It is interesting to note that this result can be verified by calculating $P(X \cup Y)$ directly; since $X \cup Y$ consists of the five points $(1, 1)$, $(1, 2)$, $(1, 3)$, $(2, 2)$, and $(3, 2)$, we obtain $\frac{1}{16} + \frac{2}{16} + \frac{1}{16} + \frac{4}{16} + \frac{2}{16} = \frac{10}{16} = \frac{5}{8}$.

To consider another example, suppose we want to determine the probability of getting either a red card (event A) or a queen (event B) when drawing a card from an ordinary deck of 52 playing cards. Assuming that each card has a probability of $\frac{1}{52}$ of being drawn, we obtain

$$P(A \cup B) = \tfrac{26}{52} + \tfrac{4}{52} - \tfrac{2}{52} = \tfrac{28}{52}$$

since there are 26 red cards, 4 queens, and 2 red queens. This result can also be verified by observing that the number of "successes" in this case is 28, there being 26 red cards and 2 black queens.

EXERCISES

1. Analyzing a certain stock, three different brokers made the following claims: The first broker claims that the probabilities for the stock's price going up, remaining unchanged, and going down are, respectively, 0.57, 0.26, and 0.14; the second broker claims that the corresponding

probabilities are 0.49, 0.33, and 0.18; and the third broker claims that the probabilities are 0.51, 0.38, and 0.13. Comment on these claims.

2. Explain why there must be a mistake in each of the following claims:

   (a) A quality control engineer claims that the probabilities that a large shipment of glass bricks contains 0, 1, 2, 3, 4, or 5 defectives are 0.11, 0.24, 0.37, 0.16, 0.09, and 0.05, respectively.

   (b) The probabilities that there will be 0, 1, 2, or 3 or more fires in a company's warehouse during 1963 are 0.47, 0.25, 0.13, and 0.05, respectively.

   (c) The probability that a driver will have one accident during a policy year is 0.17 and the probability that he will have one or more accidents during a policy year is 0.11.

   (d) The probability that Mr. Black's income tax return will be audited in detail by the Internal Revenue Service is 0.25, and the probability that Mr. Black's return as well as that of his neighbor, Mr. Smith, will both be audited in detail by the Internal Revenue Service is 0.35.

3. Given the mutually exclusive events A and B for which $P(A) = 0.30$ and $P(B) = 0.45$, find

   (a) $P(A')$.   (c) $P(A \cup B)$.   (e) $P(A' \cap B')$.

   (b) $P(B')$.   (d) $P(A \cap B)$.

   [*Hint:* For part (e) the reader may find it convenient to draw a Venn diagram and fill in the probabilities which are associated with the various regions.]

4. Given $P(A) = 0.60$, $P(B) = 0.30$, and $P(A \cap B) = 0.15$, find

   (a) $P(A')$.   (c) $P(A \cup B)$.   (e) $P(A' \cap B)$.

   (b) $P(B')$.   (d) $P(A \cap B')$.   (f) $P(A' \cap B')$.

   [*Hint:* For parts (d), (e), and (f) the reader may find it convenient to draw a Venn diagram and fill in the probabilities which are associated with the various regions.]

5. If G is the event that a firm offers for public sale an unregistered new stock and H is the event that the SEC issues a stop order, state in words what events are referred to by each of the following probabilities:

   (a) $P(G')$.   (c) $P(G \cap H')$.

   (b) $P(G \cap H)$.   (d) $P(G' \cap H')$.

6. Referring to Exercise 3 on page 112, suppose that each of the 25 possible outcomes has the same probability of $1/25$. If P, Q, and R

are as defined in Exercise 4 on page 113, find each of the following probabilities:

(a) $P(P)$.   (d) $P(P \cap Q)$.   (g) $P(Q \cap R)$.

(b) $P(Q)$.   (e) $P(P \cup R)$.   (h) $P(Q' \cap P)$.

(c) $P(R)$.   (f) $P(P \cap R)$.

7. Referring to Exercise 8 on page 113, suppose that the 9 possible outcomes are assigned probabilities in the following way: Each outcome in which there are as many bedrooms as baths is assigned a probability of 1/10, each outcome in which there is one more bedroom than there are baths is assigned a probability of 3/20, each outcome in which there are two more bedrooms than there are baths is assigned a probability of 1/10, and each outcome in which there are three more bedrooms than there are baths is assigned a probability of 1/20. Verify that this is a permissible way of assigning probabilities to the 9 possible outcomes. Also, if the events K, L, and M are defined as in Exercise 9 on page 113, find each of the following probabilities:

(a) $P(K)$.   (d) $P(K \cup L)$.   (g) $P(K \cap L')$.

(b) $P(L)$.   (e) $P(K \cap M)$.   (h) $P(L' \cap M')$.

(c) $P(M)$.   (f) $P(L \cup M)$.

(*Hint:* Use Theorem H.)

8. A student is chosen at random from a class of 30 students, 15 of whom are marketing majors, 5 of whom are on the Dean's list; and of those who are on the Dean's list, 3 are also marketing majors.

(a) What is the probability that the person chosen is either a marketing major or is on the Dean's list?

(b) What is the probability that the person chosen is neither a marketing major nor on the Dean's list?

(c) What is the probability that the person chosen is a marketing major who is not on the Dean's list?

9. Assuming that each of the 52 cards of an ordinary deck of playing cards has a probability of 1/52 of being drawn, what is the probability of drawing

(a) a black king?   (c) a red jack or a black king?

(b) a queen, king, or ace?   (d) a card which is either a club or an ace?

10. Referring to Exercise 5 on page 113, what is the probability of getting 2 heads and 1 tail (not necessarily in that order), if each of the possible outcomes is assigned a probability of 1/8?

11. The probability that Mr. Jones drives his own car to work is 0.21, the probability that he rides to work with his neighbor is 0.14, the probability that he takes a bus is 0.48, the probability that he takes a taxi is 0.12, and the probability that he walks to work is 0.05.

    (a) What is the probability that he will either take his own car, ride with his neighbor, or take a taxi?
    (b) What is the probability that he will take a taxi or go by bus?
    (c) What is the probability that he will not walk to work?

12. The probabilities that a company's switchboard will receive 0, 1, 2, 3, 4, 5, 6, 7, 8, 9, or 10 incoming calls during an afternoon are, respectively, 0.01, 0.03, 0.08, 0.14, 0.18, 0.18, 0.15, 0.11, 0.06, 0.04, and 0.02.

    (a) What is the probability that there will be fewer than 5 incoming calls?
    (b) What is the probability that there will be at least 7 incoming calls?
    (c) What is the probability that there will be anywhere from 3 to 7 incoming calls, inclusive?

13. Following the suggestions on page 118, prove that $P(\phi) = 0$.

14. Following the suggestions on page 118, prove Theorem F.

Conditional Probability

To speak of the probability of an event is meaningful only if we specify a sample space to which the event belongs. Thus, to ask for the probability that an executive (selected in some fashion) has an annual salary of $10,000 or more is meaningless unless we specify whether we are referring to a given company, a certain industry, the entire United States, and so forth.

Since there are many problems in which we are interested in probabilities relative to several different sample spaces, let us introduce the symbol $P(A \mid S)$ to indicate that we are referring to a specific sample space S and let us call $P(A \mid S)$ the *conditional probability of event A relative to S*. In this sense, every probability is a conditional probability, although (whenever possible) we use the simplified notation $P(A)$ with the tacit understanding that we are referring to some specific sample space S.

To discuss the concept of a conditional probability somewhat more deeply, let us consider the following problem: Suppose that there are 100 male applicants for a position, with each having a probability of 0.01

of being selected for the job. Some of these applicants are married, some are single, some are college graduates, some are not, with the exact breakdown as given in the following table:

	Married	Single
College Graduate	52	26
Not a College Graduate	15	7

If we let M represent the event that the person selected is married and C the event that he is a college graduate, we have

$$P(M) = \frac{52 + 15}{100} = 0.67 \quad \text{and} \quad P(C) = \frac{52 + 26}{100} = 0.78$$

by virtue of the assumption that each applicant has an equal chance of being selected. It follows that $P(M') = 1 - 0.67 = 0.33$ and $P(C') = 1 - 0.78 = 0.22$, where these are the respective probabilities that the person selected is single and that he is not a college graduate.

Now suppose that for some reason the selection is restricted to college graduates and that we would like to know the probability $P(M \mid C)$ that the person selected is married *given that he is a college graduate.* The reduced sample space in which we are now interested has 78 possible outcomes and, assuming that these 78 outcomes are still equally likely, we obtain

$$P(M \mid C) = \frac{52}{78} = \frac{2}{3}$$

Note that this conditional probability can also be written

$$P(M \mid C) = \frac{52/100}{78/100} \quad \text{or} \quad P(M \mid C) = \frac{P(M \cap C)}{P(C)}$$

namely, as the *ratio* of the probability that the person selected is a married college graduate to the probability that he is a college graduate.

Had the selection been restricted to persons who are single and had we been interested in $P(C' \mid M')$, the probability that the person selected is not a college graduate given that he is single, we would similarly have obtained $P(C' \mid M') = \frac{7}{33}$, assuming that the 33 possible outcomes in the reduced sample space are still equally likely. This result can also be written in the form $P(C' \mid M') = \dfrac{P(C' \cap M')}{P(M')}$, namely, as the ratio of the probability that the person selected is single and not a college graduate to the probability that he is single. Using these examples as an intuitive justification, let us now make the following definition:

If A and B are events belonging to some sample space S and $P(B) \neq 0$, then the conditional probability of A relative to B is given by

$$P(A \mid B) = \frac{P(A \cap B)}{P(B)} \qquad \bigstar$$

$$P_h(A) = P_h(A) \times P_h(B/A)$$

This definition is quite general; it does not depend on the assumption of equal probabilities which we used in the example.

To illustrate this further, suppose that a manufacturer knows from past experience that (1) the probability that an order will be ready for shipment on time is 0.75 and (2) the probability that an order will be ready for shipment on time *and* that it will also be delivered on time is 0.60. What we would like to know is the probability that such an order will be delivered on time *given* that it was ready for shipment on time. Letting R stand for the event that an order is ready for shipment on time and D for the event that it is delivered on time, we have $P(R) = 0.75$, $P(D \cap R) = 0.60$, and hence

$$P(D \mid R) = \frac{P(D \cap R)}{P(R)} = \frac{0.60}{0.75} = 0.80$$

Thus, 80 per cent of these shipments are delivered on time provided that they are ready for shipment on time.

An immediate consequence of our definition of conditional probability, called the *General Rule of Multiplication*, is expressed by the following theorem:

THEOREM K. $P(A \cap B) = P(B) \cdot P(A \mid B)$

$$P(A \cap B) = P(A) \cdot P(B \mid A) \qquad \bigstar$$

In words, this theorem states that the probability that events A and B *both* occur is the product of the probability that one of them will occur and the probability that the other will occur given that the first has occurred, occurs, or will occur. [The first part of this theorem is proved by simply multiplying $P(A \mid B)$ by $P(B)$; the second part is proved by interchanging A and B and making use of the fact that $A \cap B$ equals $B \cap A$.]

Referring again to the example on page 126, it can easily be verified that the conditional probability that the person selected is a college graduate given that he is married is $P(C \mid M) = 52/67$; there are 52 college graduates among the 67 married applicants. Multiplying this probability by $P(M) = 67/100$, the previously obtained probability that the person selected is married, we get

$$P(C \cap M) = P(M) \cdot P(C \mid M) = \frac{67}{100} \cdot \frac{52}{67} = \frac{52}{100}$$

for the probability that the person selected is a married college graduate. Note that this result could have been obtained directly from the table on page 126, which shows that among the 100 applicants 52 are married college graduates.

To give another illustration, let us determine the probability of drawing two kings in succession from an ordinary deck of 52 playing cards, without the first card being replaced before the second is drawn. Since there are four kings, the probability of getting a king on the first draw is $4/52$, assuming that each card has the same probability of being drawn. Given that the first card drawn is a king, the probability of getting a king on the second draw is $3/51$, since only three kings are left among the 51 cards which remain. Hence, according to Theorem K the probability of getting two kings in a row is $\frac{4}{52} \cdot \frac{3}{51} = \frac{1}{221}$.

Had the first card been replaced before the second was drawn in this example, the probability of getting a king on the second draw would have been $4/52$ (the same as that of getting a king on the first draw) and the answer would have been $1/169$. Since the probability of getting a king on the second draw is *now* $4/52$ regardless of what happened on the first draw, we refer to these draws as *independent*. Generally speaking, *two or more events are said to be independent if the occurrence of one in no way affects the probability of the occurrence of any of the others*. Symbolically, the independence of events A and B asserts, among other things, that $P(A) = P(A \mid B)$, and substituting $P(A)$ for $P(A \mid B)$ into the first equation of Theorem K, we obtain the following theorem, called the *Special Rule of Multiplication:*

THEOREM L. *If A and B are independent, then*

$$P(A \cap B) = P(A) \cdot P(B) \qquad \star$$

In words, if two events are independent, the probability that they will both occur equals the product of their respective probabilities. Thus, assuming independence, the probability of getting heads in two flips of a balanced coin is $\frac{1}{2} \cdot \frac{1}{2} = \frac{1}{4}$. Also, if the probability that a person interviewed in a survey has completed four years of college is 0.08 and the probability that he has blue eyes is 0.15, then the probability that he has completed four years of college *and* also has blue eyes is $(0.08)(0.15) = 0.012$.

The Special Rule of Multiplication can easily be extended to more than two independent events. Given k independent events $A_1, A_2, \ldots,$ and A_k, the probability that these events will all occur is

$$P(A_1 \cap A_2 \cap \ldots \cap A_k) = P(A_1) \cdot P(A_2) \cdot \ldots \cdot P(A_k) \qquad \star$$

For instance, the probability of getting four heads in a row with a balanced coin is $\frac{1}{2} \cdot \frac{1}{2} \cdot \frac{1}{2} \cdot \frac{1}{2} = \frac{1}{16}$; also, if a missile has three components, the probability that the first will fail is $1/500$, the probability that the second will fail is $1/1,000$, and the probability that the third will fail is $1/200$, then *assuming independence* the probability that none of the components will fail is $\dfrac{499}{500} \cdot \dfrac{999}{1,000} \cdot \dfrac{199}{200} = 0.992$ approximately.

In actual practice, it is more common to meet events that are dependent (not independent) than events that are independent. For instance, if A and B represent, respectively, a husband and his wife's having been born in Vermont, these events are not independent; and if they represent a person's being a secondary school teacher and his having an income of over \$10,000 a year, these events are also dependent.

Some Further Rules of Probability

There are many problems in which the ultimate outcome depends on what happens in various intermediate stages. Suppose, for instance, that two slates of candidates are competing for positions on the Board of Directors of a company, the probability for the first slate's winning being 0.70 and that for the second slate's winning being 0.30. Furthermore, if the first slate of candidates is elected the probability for a stock split is 0.90, and if the second slate of candidates is elected the probability for a stock split is only 0.40. What we would like to know is the probability for a stock split as things are right now, that is, prior to the election of the new members of the board.

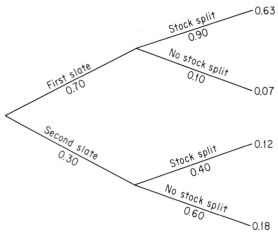

FIGURE 5.13

Referring to the tree diagram of Figure 5.13, it can be seen that the probability that the first slate will be elected and that subsequently there will be a stock split is $(0.70)(0.90) = 0.63$, multiplying the two probabilities in accordance with Theorem K. Similarly, the probabilities for the paths leading to the other three outcomes are $(0.70)(0.10) = 0.07$, $(0.30)(0.40) = 0.12$, and $(0.30)(0.60) = 0.18$. Since the four outcomes are mutually exclusive and the first and third together represent the event that the stock will split, we find that the desired probability for a stock split is $0.63 + 0.12 = 0.75$.

Symbolically, if A stands for the event that there will be a stock split, B_1 for the election of the first slate, and B_2 for the election of the second slate, the probabilities we were originally given are $P(B_1) = 0.70$, $P(B_2) = 0.30$, $P(A \mid B_1) = 0.90$ and $P(A \mid B_2) = 0.40$. Our subsequent calculations can be written as

$$P(A) = P(B_1) \cdot P(A \mid B_1) + P(B_2) \cdot P(A \mid B_2)$$
$$= (0.70)(0.90) + (0.30)(0.40)$$
$$= 0.75$$

More generally, if B_1, B_2, ..., and B_k constitute a set of mutually exclusive events, none of which has zero probability and one of which has to happen, we have the following theorem, often called the *Rule of Elimination:*

THEOREM M.

$$P(A) = P(B_1) \cdot P(A \mid B_1) + P(B_2) \cdot P(A \mid B_2) + \ldots \qquad \bigstar$$
$$+ P(B_k) \cdot P(A \mid B_k)$$

Note that in this formula each term represents a path along the branches of a tree which leads to an outcome included in event A. The first leads to A via B_1, the second leads to A via B_2, ..., and the last leads to A via B_k.

To illustrate the use of this theorem, suppose that a company makes machine parts in three different plants with daily production figures of 1,000, 1,200, and 1,800 parts. Suppose, furthermore, that the probability that a part produced by Plant 1 is defective is 0.004, while the corresponding probabilities for the other two plants are 0.010 and 0.008, respectively. What we would like to know is the probability of event A that a part selected at random (with equal probabilities) from a day's total production is defective. Since the probability that a part is produced by Plant 1 is $P(B_1) = \dfrac{1000}{1000 + 1200 + 1800} = 1/4$, while the corresponding probabilities for the other two plants are $P(B_2) = 3/10$ and $P(B_3) = 9/20$, substitution into the formula of Theorem M yields

$$P(A) = (1/4)(0.004) + (3/10)(0.010) + (9/20)(0.008)$$
$$= 0.001 + 0.003 + 0.0036$$
$$= 0.0076$$

This situation is also described by the tree diagram of Figure 5.14, which shows only the three branches leading to defective parts and not those leading to elements of A'.

Still referring to this same example, suppose now that we are interested in an entirely different question: One part is selected at random (with equal probabilities) from a day's total production, it is found to be defective, and we would like to know the probability that it came from Plant 1. To answer this kind of question, we use the famous *Rule of Bayes* given by the following theorem, where as before B_1, B_2, ..., and B_k constitute a set of mutually exclusive events, none of which has zero probability and one of which must happen:

THEOREM N.

$$P(B_i \mid A) = \frac{P(B_i) \cdot P(A \mid B_i)}{P(B_1) \cdot P(A \mid B_1) + P(B_2) \cdot P(A \mid B_2) + \ldots + P(B_k) \cdot P(A \mid B_k)}$$

for $i = 1, 2, \ldots,$ *or* k.   ★

This theorem gives the probability that event A is reached along a *particular* path of a tree like the ones of Figures 5.13 and 5.14, given that A

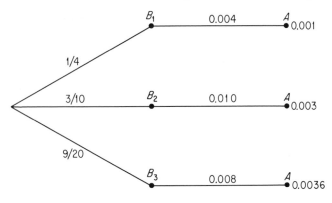

FIGURE 5.14

has been (or must be) reached along one of these paths. In words, the formula of Theorem N states that the probability $P(B_i \mid A)$ equals the ratio of the probability of the path leading to A via B_i to the *sum* of the probabilities of all the paths (branches) leading to event A. Referring back to our numerical example, we obtain by direct substitution

$$P(B_1 \mid A) = \frac{(1/4)(0.004)}{(1/4)(0.004) + (3/10)(0.010) + (9/20)(0.008)}$$

$$= 5/38$$

for the probability that the defective part came from Plant 1. The reader will be asked to verify in Exercise 12 below that the corresponding probabilities for Plants 2 and 3 are, respectively, 15/38 and 18/38. [Incidentally, to prove Theorem N we have only to write

$$P(B_i \mid A) = \frac{P(B_i \cap A)}{P(A)}$$

n accordance with the definition of a conditional probability. Then we substitute in the numerator $P(B_i \cap A) = P(B_i) \cdot P(A \mid B_i)$ in accordance with Theorem K, and in the denominator we substitute for $P(A)$ the expression given by the formula of Theorem M.]

Although Theorem N follows readily from the postulates of probability, t has been the subject of extensive controversy. A good deal of the mysticism surrounding the Rule of Bayes is due to the fact that it entails a "backward" or "inverse" sort of reasoning, that is, *reasoning from effect to cause.* In our numerical example we thus asked for the probability that the defective part was "caused" in Plant 1. To illustrate this idea further, consider the following example, taken from Hans Reichenbach's *The Theory of Probability,* University of California Press, 1949:

"Mr. Smith's gardener is not dependable; the probability that he will forget to water the rosebush during Smith's absence is 2/3. The rosebush is in questionable condition anyhow; if watered, the probability for its withering is 1/2; if it is not watered, the probability for its withering is 3/4. Upon returning Smith finds that the rosebush has withered. *What is the probability that the gardener did not water the rosebush?*"

Letting W represent the event that the rosebush is watered and D the event that it withers, we are asked to find $P(W' \mid D)$ and according to the Rule of Bayes we have

$$P(W' \mid D) = \frac{(2/3)(3/4)}{(1/3)(1/2) + (2/3)(3/4)} = 0.75$$

Another interesting problem whose solution is based on the Rule of Bayes will be given on page 138.

EXERCISES

1. Referring to the example on page 126, find $P(C \mid M)$ and $P(M \mid C')$.

2. If K is the event that Mr. Miller will take a job in Arizona, L is the event that he will work for a utility company, and M is the event that he will be satisfied with his salary, state in words what probability is expressed by each of the following:

(a) $P(L \mid K)$.   (d) $P(L \cap M \mid K)$.

(b) $P(M \mid K')$.   (e) $P(M \mid K \cap L)$.

(c) $P(M \mid L)$.   (f) $P(M' \cap K \mid L')$.

3. If A and B are independent events, $P(A) = 0.25$, and $P(B) = 0.40$ find

(a) $P(A \mid B)$.   (c) $P(A \cup B)$.

(b) $P(A \cap B)$.   (d) $P(A' \cap B')$.

4. Referring to Exercise 6 on page 123, find $P(P \mid R)$ and $P(R \mid P)$; also express in words what probabilities are referred to by these symbols.

5. Referring to Exercise 7 on page 124, find

(a) $P(K \mid M)$.   (c) $P(K \mid L)$.

(b) $P(L \mid M)$.   (d) $P(M \mid K')$.

6. In giving away a door prize, the owner of a gas station randomly (with equal probabilities) selects one of 1,000 slips filled in by his customers. There is only one slip per customer and their breakdown into those who paid cash and those who used their credit card, and also into those who are regular customers and those who are not, is as follows:

	Credit-card Customers	Cash Customers
Regular Customers	130	270
Not Regular Customers	120	480

Letting R represent the event that the prize is won by a regular customer and C the event that the prize is won by a credit-card customer, find each of the following probabilities:

(a) $P(R)$.   (d) $P(R \cap C)$.   (g) $P(C \mid R)$.

(b) $P(C)$.   (e) $P(R' \cap C')$.   (h) $P(C \mid R')$.

(c) $P(R \cup C)$.   (f) $P(R \mid C)$.   (i) $P(R' \mid C')$.

7. Suppose that in Exercise 6 the owner of the gas station arranges things so that each of his regular customers has a probability of $3/1,800$ while each of the other customers has a probability of $1/1,800$ of winning the prize. Recalculate the nine probabilities asked for in Exercise 6.

8. Given $P(A) = 0.40$, $P(B) = 0.60$, and $P(A \cap B) = 0.24$, verify that

(a) $P(A) = P(A \mid B)$.   (c) $P(B) = P(B \mid A)$.

(b) $P(A) = P(A \mid B')$.   (d) $P(B) = P(B \mid A')$.

(It is interesting to note that if any one of these four relations is satisfied, the other three must also be satisfied and the events A and B are independent.)

9. One critical operation in assembling a delicate electronic device requires that a skilled operator fit one part to another precisely. If the operator succeeds in matching the parts on his first attempt he moves on to the next assembly, otherwise he repeats his (independent) attempts until he gets a match. What is the probability that an operator with a constant match probability of $1/2$ will succeed in matching the parts in a given assembly within 3 attempts? (Note that in this example the set of all possible outcomes is *not* finite; nevertheless, it is possible to solve this problem with the methods discussed so far in this chapter.)

10. Two firms consider bidding for a construction job which may or may not be awarded depending on the amounts of the bids. Firm Q submits a bid and the probability is $3/4$ that it will get the job provided Firm R does not submit a bid. If R submits a bid, the probability that Firm Q will get the job is only $1/3$. What is the probability that Firm Q will get the job, if there is a fifty-fifty chance that R will bid?

11. Bin A contains 2 defective and 4 good tubes, while Bin B contains 2 defective and 1 good tube. If a man chooses a bin at random (with equal probabilities) and then randomly selects 1 tube from this bin what is the probability that the tube selected is good?

12. Verify for the example on page 132 that the probabilities that the defective part came from Plants 2 and 3 are, respectively, $15/38$ and $18/38$.

13. A distributor of phonograph records employs two stock clerks, Bill and John, who pull records from bins and stack them for subsequent packaging. Bill makes a mistake (gets the wrong record or the wrong quantity) 1 time in 100, while John makes a mistake 1 time in 10. Bill also works much faster than John; he fills 75 per cent of the orders that are delivered for verification, leaving the remaining 25 per cent to John. Given that a mistake is found in a particular order, what is the probability that the order was filled by Bill?

14. In-basket Q contains 2 "routine" and 3 "action" letters while in-basket R contains 5 "routine" and 2 "action" letters. One letter is randomly selected from Q and put into R, then a letter is randomly drawn from R. If the letter drawn from R is an "action" letter, what is the probability that the letter moved from Q to R was also an "action" letter?

15. Suppose that if a person with tuberculosis is given a chest X-ray the probability that his condition will be detected is 0.98 and that if a person without tuberculosis is given a chest X-ray the probability

that he will erroneously be diagnosed as having tuberculosis is 0.001. Suppose, furthermore, that 0.1 per cent of the adult residents of a certain town have tuberculosis. If one of these persons (selected at random, that is, with equal probabilities) is diagnosed as having tuberculosis, what is the probability that he actually has tuberculosis?

Probability Distributions

The two tables which follow give the probabilities that are associated with two very simple experiments, one consisting of the roll of a die and the other of three flips of a balanced coin. They illustrate what we mean by a *probability distribution*, namely, a correspondence which assigns probabilities to numerical descriptions of an experiment. The first of these tables was easily obtained on the basis of the assumption that each

Number of Points Rolled with a Die	Probability	Number of Heads Obtained in Three Flips of a Coin	Probability
1	1/6	0	1/8
2	1/6	1	3/8
3	1/6	2	3/8
4	1/6	3	1/8
5	1/6		
6	1/6		

face of the die has a probability of 1/6 of turning up; the second was obtained by considering the eight possible outcomes

$$TTT \quad HTT \quad THT \quad TTH$$
$$THH \quad HTH \quad HHT \quad HHH$$

where H stands for "head" and T for "tail," as equally likely.

Whenever possible, we try to give probability distributions by means of formulas with which we can calculate the probabilities that are associated with the various outcomes. With the usual functional notation, we can thus write

$$f(x) = 1/6 \qquad \text{for } x = 1, 2, 3, 4, 5, 6$$

for the first of the above examples, with $f(1)$ representing the probability of rolling a 1, $f(2)$ representing the probability of rolling a 2, and so on.

'or the second example we can similarly write

$$f(x) = \binom{3}{x} \cdot \frac{1}{8} \qquad \text{for } x = 0, 1, 2, 3$$

/here $\binom{3}{x}$ is the number of combinations of 3 objects taken x at a time.
t will be left to the reader to verify that

$$\binom{3}{0} = 1, \binom{3}{1} = 3, \binom{3}{2} = 3, \binom{3}{3} = 1$$

nd, hence, that the formula yields the probabilities given in the
bove table. The formula itself is a special case of the one treated in
.heorem O below.

There are many applied problems in which we are interested in the
·robability that an event will take place x times in n "trials," or in other
·ords, x times out of n, while the probability that it will take place in
ny one trial is some number p and the trials are independent. We may
hus be interested in the probability of obtaining 18 responses to 80 mail
uestionnaires, the probability that 7 of 30 new bowling alleys will go
ankrupt within three years, the probability of getting 3 defective television
ubes in a sample of 50, and so forth. Referring to the occurrence of any
·ne of these events as a "success" (which is a holdover from the days when
·robabilities were studied almost exclusively with reference to games of
hance), we are thus interested in each case in the probability of getting
·x successes in n trials." To handle problems of this kind we use the
pecial distribution given in the following theorem (its formula is actually
.erived in Technical Note 4 on page 145):

THEOREM O. *The probability of getting x successes in n independent
trials is given by*

$$f(x) = \binom{n}{x} p^x (1 - p)^{n-x} \qquad for \; x = 0, 1, 2, \ldots, n \qquad \bigstar$$

*where p is the constant probability of a success for each individual
trial.*

·his probability distribution is called the *binomial distribution*. To illus-
rate its use let us first calculate the probability of getting 5 heads and
tails in 12 flips of a balanced coin. Substituting $x = 5, n = 12, p = 1/2$,

and $\binom{12}{5} = \dfrac{12 \cdot 11 \cdot 10 \cdot 9 \cdot 8}{5 \cdot 4 \cdot 3 \cdot 2 \cdot 1} = 792$, we get

$$f(5) = 792 \left(\frac{1}{2}\right)^5 \left(1 - \frac{1}{2}\right)^7 = \frac{99}{512}$$

or approximately 0.19. Similarly, to find the probability of gettin 3 responses to 10 mail questionnaires, let us suppose that the probabilit of any one person's answering the questionnaire is $1/5$. Then substitutin

$x = 3$, $n = 10$, $p = 1/5$, and $\binom{10}{3} = \dfrac{10 \cdot 9 \cdot 8}{3 \cdot 2 \cdot 1} = 120$, we get

$$f(3) = 120 \left(\frac{1}{5}\right)^3 \left(1 - \frac{1}{5}\right)^7 = \frac{393,216}{1,953,125}$$

or approximately 0.20.

In actual practice, problems involving the binomial distribution ar often solved by referring to special tables (see Bibliography) or by usin approximations, among others the ones discussed in Exercise 11 belo and in Chapter 7. The direct application of the formula of Theorem would be much too involved, for instance, to calculate the probabilit that 120 of 500 patients will be helped by a new drug, the probabilit that at least 350 of 750 customers entering a store will make a purchas or the probability that fewer than 250 of 1,000 persons drafted by th army have an I.Q. of over 105.

Before we give another example, let us remind the reader that th formula for the binomial distribution applies only when the probabilit of a "success" remains constant from trial to trial and if, furthermore the trials are independent. It cannot be used, therefore, to find the prob ability that it will rain, say, on 30 out of 120 consecutive days (at a certai resort). Not only does the probability for rain vary over such a length period of time, but the "trials" are not even independent. Clearly, th probability that it will rain on any given day will depend to some exten on whether it did or did not rain on the day before.

The following is an interesting example involving the binomial distr bution as well as the Rule of Bayes: Mr. Adam and Mr. Brown inten to form a partnership to operate a number of gas stations; according t Mr. Adam the probability that any new gas station will show a prof during the first year is $1/2$ and according to Mr. Brown this probabilit is $2/3$. An expert whom they consult feels (on the basis of a subjectiv evaluation of the situation) that Mr. Adam is *three times more likely* to b right than Mr. Brown. Referring to the event that the *correct value* of this probability is $1/2$ as B_1 and to the event that the *correct value* is $2/3$ as B_2, we thus have $P(B_1) = 3/4$ and $P(B_2) = 1/4$; this makes the probability of B_1 three times that of B_2. Now suppose that the partnership opens six gas stations and that five of them show a profit during the first year—*How does this affect the merits of the two partners' original claims?* Letting A represent the event that 5 of 6 of these gas stations will show a profit during the first year, we have according to Theorem O

$$P(A \mid B_1) = \binom{6}{5}\left(\frac{1}{2}\right)^5 \left(1 - \frac{1}{2}\right)^1 = \frac{3}{32}$$

and

$$P(A \mid B_2) = \binom{6}{5}\left(\frac{2}{3}\right)^5 \left(1 - \frac{2}{3}\right)^1 = \frac{64}{243}$$

since B_1 and B_2 represent the respective claims that the quantity p in the formula for the binomial distribution equals $1/2$ and $2/3$. If we now substitute all these probabilities into the formula for the Rule of Bayes, we obtain

$$P(B_1 \mid A) = \frac{P(B_1) \cdot P(A \mid B_1)}{P(B_1) \cdot P(A \mid B_1) + P(B_2) \cdot P(A \mid B_2)}$$

$$= \frac{(3/4)(3/32)}{(3/4)(3/32) + (1/4)(64/243)}$$

$$= 0.51$$

and it follows that $P(B_2 \mid A) = 1 - 0.51 = 0.49$. *This makes Mr. Brown's claim almost as likely as Mr. Adam's.* It is interesting to note how we have combined the direct evidence (5 of the 6 gas stations showed a profit during the first year) with the subjective evaluation of the expert, and how the weight of the direct evidence has given increasing merit to Mr. Brown's claim. Reasoning of this kind is referred to as a *Bayesian inference*, a method of inference which is currently gaining in favor among some statisticians [see also Exercise 7(a) on page 153].

EXERCISES

1. Using the formula for the binomial distribution, find

    (a) the probability of rolling 2 sixes in 5 rolls of a balanced die.

    (b) the probability of rolling at most 2 sixes in 5 rolls of a balanced die.

(c) the probability of getting 6 heads in 8 flips of a balanced coin.

(d) the probability of getting at least 6 heads in 8 flips of a balanced coin.

2. A multiple-choice test consists of 10 questions and 4 answers to each question. If each question is answered by rolling a die until 1, 2, 3, or 4 appears and scoring the question accordingly,

(a) What is the probability of getting exactly 3 correct answers?

(b) What is the probability of getting exactly 0 correct answers?

(c) If each question is worth 10 points, no partial credit is given, and 70 is passing, what is the probability of passing the test?

3. It is known from experience that 50 per cent of the persons who admit a door-to-door dictionary salesman into their homes will buy a dictionary. What is the probability that among 8 persons who admit such salesmen into their homes at most 2 will buy the book?

4. What is the probability that a tank will _not_ be knocked out by five shots from an antitank gun which has a constant kill probability of p? What will p have to be so that the probability asked for equals $1/1,024$?

5. It is known that in a very large city 75 per cent of the families belonging to a certain low-income class own television sets. If 12 families are selected at random for intensive sociological and economic study, what is the probability that exactly 10 of the families will own television sets? (Assume that the number of families under consideration is so large that the conditions underlying the binomial distribution are approximately met.)

6. It is known that 40 per cent of the defective parts produced in a certain operation can be made satisfactory by rework. What is the probability that in a batch of 6 such defective parts at least 3 can be satisfactorily reworked?

7. If 5 cards are drawn in succession from an ordinary deck of 52 playing cards, what is the probability of getting exactly one ace _if each card is replaced and the deck is reshuffled before the next card is drawn?_ Can this problem be solved with the use of the binomial distribution if the cards are not replaced?

8. If n elements are selected from a set containing a elements of one kind and b elements of another kind,

(a) find an expression for the total number of ways in which n elements can be selected from this set.

(b) find expressions for the number of ways in which x elements of the first kind can be selected from this set and for the number of ways in which $n - x$ elements of the second kind can be selected from this set.

(c) use the results of parts (a) and (b) to show that the probability that n elements randomly selected from this set contain x elements of the first kind and $n - x$ elements of the second kind is given by

$$ f(x) = \frac{\binom{a}{x}\binom{b}{n-x}}{\binom{a+b}{n}} \qquad \text{for } x = 0, 1, 2, \ldots, a \qquad \bigstar $$

(d) this probability distribution, called the *hypergeometric distribution*, applies to so-called *sampling without replacement;* use it to work Exercise 7 for the case where the cards are not replaced.

9. It is known that two-thirds of the 120 employees of a company are qualified to operate company-owned cars by reason of having passed a safe-driver course. What is the probability that among 5 randomly selected employees exactly 3 are qualified to operate company-owned cars? What result would we have obtained if we erroneously had used a binomial distribution with $p = 2/3$ in this example?

10. In a file of 1000 freight bills 5 per cent contain errors. If an auditor randomly selects 3 bills from this file, what is the probability that none of them contains an error? How much would we be off in this example, if we approximated the desired probability by using a binomial distribution with $p = 0.05$?

11. If n is large and p is small, the binomial distribution is often approximated by means of the *Poisson distribution*, whose formula is given by

$$ f(x) = \frac{(np)^x \cdot e^{-np}}{x!} \qquad \text{for } x = 0, 1, 2, \ldots \qquad \bigstar $$

[Note that for this distribution the set of all values assumed by x is infinite; this is merely a matter of mathematical convenience and in actual practice the probabilities become negligible (very close to 0) after a fairly small set of values of x.] In this formula e is the number 2.71828 ... used in connection with natural logarithms, and values of e^{-np} may be obtained from Table IX on page 450. Use the Poisson distribution to find an approximate value for the probability of getting 3 successes in 100 (binomial) trials with $p = 0.05$.

12. The Poisson distribution has many important applications which have no direct connection with the binomial distribution. In that case np is replaced by the parameter λ (*lambda*) and we calculate the probability

for getting x successes by means of the formula

$$f(x) = \frac{\lambda^x e^{-\lambda}}{x!} \quad \text{for } x = 0, 1, 2, \ldots$$

(As we shall see in Chapter 6, λ can be interpreted as the *average* number of successes that we might expect.) Use the above formula to solve each of the following problems:

(a) Assuming that the number of calls arriving at a company's switch board during a 5-minute span has a Poisson distribution with $\lambda = 5.2$, what is the probability that there will be exactly 4 incoming calls during such a 5-minute span?

(b) In the inspection of cloth produced in continuous rolls, the probability of spotting x defects in 10 minutes may be calculated by means of the formula for the Poisson distribution with $\lambda = 2$. What is the probability that an inspector will find exactly one defect during 10 minutes of inspection?

(c) The probability that there will be x accidents at a busy intersection during a week can be calculated by means of the formula for the Poisson distribution with $\lambda = 3.5$. What is the probability that there will be exactly 2 accidents at this intersection during a given week?

13. Suppose that in the example on page 139 only two of the six gas stations showed a profit during the first year. Recalculate the values of $P(B_1 \mid A)$ and $P(B_2 \mid A)$ and interpret the results, that is, indicate how the direct evidence has affected the weights given to Mr. Adam's and Mr. Brown's claims.

14. In planning the operations of a new restaurant, one expert claims that only 1 out of 4 waitresses can be expected to stay with the establishment for more than a year, while a second expert claims that it would be more correct to say 1 out of 3. In the past, the two experts have been about equally reliable, so that in the absence of direct information we would assign their judgments equal weights. What probabilities would we assign to their claims if it were found that among 8 waitresses actually hired for the restaurant only 1 stayed for more than a year?

15. Asked about the sale of a large estate, one broker feels that a newspaper ad should produce 3 serious inquiries about the estate, a second broker feels that it should produce 5 serious inquiries, and a third broker feels that it should produce 8. In the past, the first broker has been about twice as reliable as the second while the second has been about twice as reliable as the third; in the absence of any further knowledge, we thus assign to their "educated guesses" the respective

probabilities of 4/7, 2/7, and 1/7. How would these probabilities be affected if the ad actually produced 6 inquiries about the estate, assuming that probabilities concerning the number of inquiries are given by a Poisson distribution for which $\lambda = 3$, $\lambda = 5$, or $\lambda = 8$ according to the three claims? [See also Exercise 7 (b) on page 153.]

A Word of Caution

One law of probability which is very often misunderstood is the so-called *law of large numbers*, which in everyday language is commonly referred to as the *law of averages*. This law states that if we increase the number of trials, that is, if we repeat whatever we are doing a great number of times, it is practically certain or at least highly probable that the *proportion* of successes will come close to the actual probability of success. Many people are under the erroneous impression that this law of averages somehow compensates for the discrepancies which they might find in the results obtained in a relatively short series of events. They are inclined to bet on tails after a long run of heads, claiming that thanks to the law of averages "tails is due to come up." Such reasoning is entirely incorrect—*a coin has neither a memory nor a conscience to which such a law could possibly appeal.*

Perhaps it will be best to illustrate this fallacy concerning the law of averages with an example. Suppose that a coin has been tossed 100 times and that we observed only 30 heads, which is considerably less than the 50 we might expect. Then, the coin is flipped another 100 times yielding 44 heads, again less than expected, and it might seem that the law of averages is letting us down. Actually, this is not the case; after the first 100 flips of the coin the proportion of heads was $\frac{30}{100} = 0.30$, while after the 200 flips it was $\frac{30 + 44}{200} = 0.37$. In spite of the fact that the discrepancy between the observed number of heads and the number which we might have expected has become worse, the *proportion* of heads has come closer to the probability of 0.50, and this is entirely in accordance with the law of large numbers.

Many fallacies involving probabilities are due to the incorrect use of the special Rule of Multiplication, that is, the multiplication of probabilities of events which are *not* independent, to inappropriate assumptions concerning the equal-likelihood of events, and to confusion concerning the

terms "probability" and "odds." If the probability that some event wil
occur is 4/5, then the probability that it will not occur is 1/5 and we
say that the *odds* in favor of its occurrence are 4 to 1. Similarly, i
$P(A) = 0.05$ and, hence, $P(A') = 0.95$, we say that the odds are 1 to 19
for the occurrence of event A or 19 to 1 against it. Generally speaking
by "odds" we mean the ratio of the probability that a given event wil
occur to the probability that it will not occur.

The following is a good example of the difficulties in which we may find
ourselves by carelessly assuming that certain events are equally likely:

"Among three indistinguishable boxes one contains 2 pennies, one
contains a penny and a dime, and one contains 2 dimes. Selecting
one of these boxes at random (each box has a probability of 1/3),
one coin is taken out at random (each coin has a probability of 1/2)
without looking at the other. If the coin that is taken out is a
penny, what is the probability that the other coin in this box is
also a penny?"

Without giving the matter too much thought, it may seem reasonable t
say that this probability is 1/2. After all, the penny must have com
either from the box with the penny and the dime or from the box with
the two pennies. In the first case the other coin is a dime, in the second
case it is a penny, and it would seem reasonable to say that these two
possibilities are equally likely. Actually, this is not the case; the correc
value of the probability is 2/3, as the reader can verify by drawing ai
appropriate tree diagram or by applying the Rule of Bayes. (When
drawing a tree diagram showing the six possible outcomes corresponding
to which of the six coins is actually taken out of its box, the reader wil
find it convenient to label the two pennies in the box with two pennie
P_1 and P_2, and the two dimes in the box with two dimes D_1 and D_2.)

Another point we should mention is that the three postulates of prob
ability given in this chapter apply to sample spaces that are *finite*. The
will have to be modified, for instance, for the situation described i
Exercise 9 on page 135, where (logically speaking) it might take ti
doomsday until the operator finally matches two parts, and for the
situation described in Exercise 11 on page 141, where (as a matter o
mathematical convenience) we use a sample space with infinitely man
outcomes. The postulates will also have to be modified, say, if we ar
interested in the distance a missile hits from its target, since such mis

distances are measured on a *continuous* scale. Since this matter is rather technical, we shall not discuss it in this book in any detail.

Technical Note 4   (The Binomial Distribution)

To derive the formula for the binomial distribution, let us first observe that the probability of getting x successes in n trials and, hence, x successes and $n - x$ failures, *in some specific order* is $p^x(1 - p)^{n-x}$. There is one factor p for each success, one factor $1 - p$ for each failure, and the x factors p and $n - x$ factors $1 - p$ are all multiplied together by virtue of the assumption that the n trials are independent. Since this probability is evidently the same for each individual outcome representing x successes and $n - x$ failures (it does not depend on the order in which the successes and failures are obtained), the desired probability for x successes in n trials *in any order* is obtained by multiplying $p^x(1 - p)^{n-x}$ by the number of ways in which the x successes can be distributed among the n trials. In other words, $p^x(1 - p)^{n-x}$ is multiplied by the number of points (individual outcomes) of the sample space, each of which corresponds to the event of getting x successes and $n - x$ failures in some order. Hence, $p^x(1 - p)^{n-x}$ is multiplied by $\binom{n}{x}$, the number of ways in which x objects can be selected from a set of n objects (see Theorem E), and this completes the proof of Theorem O.

SIX

EXPECTATIONS, GAMES, AND DECISIONS

Mathematical Expectation

The 1958 Commissioners Standard Ordinary Table is based on the mortality experience of 15 life insurance companies for the years 1950 through 1954. According to these statistics, of 9,241,359 persons living at age 40, on the average 32,622 will die within a year. Thus, the probability of death is 32,622/9,241,359 = 0.00353. If a life insurance company insures 100,000 persons of age 40 for $1,000 for one year, on the average it will have to pay claims on 0.353 per cent, or 353, of these policies. The sum of these payments is $353,000 and the company will have to charge each of the 100,000 insured a natural premium of 353,000/100,000 = $3.53 to meet the *expected* claims. (Plus, of course, loading if the company is to meet operating expenses and, if a stock company, make a profit.)* This illustrates what we mean by a *mathematical*

---

* We are also ignoring the interest earned on the premiums during the policy year.

expectation; the company's management does not expect 353 of the policy holders to die in the sense of "wishful thinking" or on the basis of its actuary's horoscope or his personal convictions. To give another example, consider the game of "heads or tails," and suppose that we win $1.00 each time a coin comes up heads and lose $1.00 each time it comes up tails. We can *expect* to break even in this game, even though in a long series of flips of the coin it is very unlikely that this will actually occur. A mathematical expectation is really an average, or to be more exact an "average in the long run." To be specific,

if the probabilities of obtaining the amounts A_1, A_2, ..., and A_k are, respectively, $P(A_1)$, $P(A_2)$, ..., and $P(A_k)$, and the events of getting these amounts are mutually exclusive, then the mathematical expectation is

$$A_1 \cdot P(A_1) + A_2 \cdot P(A_2) + \ldots + A_k \cdot P(A_k) \qquad \bigstar$$

Each amount is multiplied by the corresponding probability and the mathematical expectation is the sum of the products thus obtained. In the first of the above examples we have $A_1 = \$1{,}000$, $P(A_1) = 0.00353$, and an *expected* cost of $3.53 per policy; in the second example $A_1 = 1.00$, $A_2 = -1.00$, $P(A_1) = 1/2$, $P(A_2) = 1/2$, and the mathematical expectation is $1.00(1/2) + (-1.00)(1/2) = 0$. Note that this defines what we mean by an *equitable* game; the mathematical expectation is 0, or in other words we expect neither to win nor lose. Also note that the amounts A_1, A_2, ..., and A_k are positive or negative depending on whether they are won or lost, spent or received.

To consider another example, suppose that an importer is offered a shipment of bananas for $20,000 and that the probabilities that he will be able to sell them for $24,000, $22,000, $20,000, or $18,000 are, respectively, 0.28, 0.43, 0.17, and 0.12. Whether or not this transaction is worthwhile will depend among other things on the amount of money the importer can *expect* to receive. Substituting into the formula for a mathematical expectation, we get

$$24{,}000(0.28) + 22{,}000(0.43) + 20{,}000(0.17) + 18{,}000(0.12) = 21{,}740$$

so that the *expected gross profit* is $1,740. Whether this makes the transaction worthwhile is another matter; that would have to depend on the importer's overhead, the length of time that his money will be tied up, and other factors.

Originally, the concept of a mathematical expectation was designed for games of chance, lotteries and the like, and the A's were the amounts of money one stood to win or lose. Nowadays, mathematical expectations are used in connection with any kinds of numbers and we find such statements as "a married couple in Hawaii can *expect* to have 2.29 children," "a person living in the United States can *expect* to be fed 6.3 pounds of turkey a year," and "a family in the United States can *expect* to move into a different house about once every five years." Expectations like these, which will be discussed further below, must, of course, always be interpreted as averages.

The Mean of a Probability Distribution

Let us now use the concept of a mathematical expectation in connection with the two probability distributions on page 136. The first dealt with the number of points rolled with a die, and if we multiply 1, 2, 3, 4, 5, and 6 by their respective probabilities, which all equalled $1/6$, we find that the *expected* number of points is

$$1\left(\frac{1}{6}\right) + 2\left(\frac{1}{6}\right) + 3\left(\frac{1}{6}\right) + 4\left(\frac{1}{6}\right) + 5\left(\frac{1}{6}\right) + 6\left(\frac{1}{6}\right) = 3\tfrac{1}{2}$$

Of course, we cannot get $3\tfrac{1}{2}$ in any one roll of a die, but this is the *average* value we should get if we rolled the die a great many times. Considering now the second probability distribution on page 136, the one which dealt with the number of heads obtained in 3 flips of a balanced coin, we find that the *expected* number of heads is $1\tfrac{1}{2}$. This value, which must again be interpreted as an average, is the sum of the products obtained by multiplying 0, 1, 2, and 3 by their respective probabilities of $1/8$, $3/8$, $3/8$, and $1/8$.

The expected values which we have calculated in these two examples are referred to as the *means* of the respective probability distributions, using this term in very much the same sense as in Chapter 3. In general, if we are given a probability distribution, that is, the probabilities $f(x)$ which are associated with the various values of x (the numerical descriptions of an experiment), *we define the mean of this probability distribution as*

$$\mu = \Sigma \, x \cdot f(x) \qquad\qquad \bigstar$$

with the summation extending over all values of x. This average, which is denoted by the Greek letter μ (*mu*) to distinguish it from the mean of an actual set of data, is, in fact, the value which we can *expect* for the particular numerical description of the experiment.

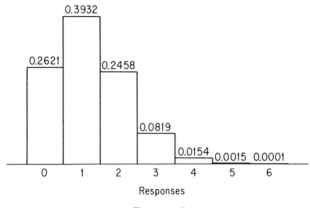

FIGURE 6.1

To study another example, let us consider the probability distribution whose histogram is shown in Figure 6.1. It gives the probabilities (rounded to four decimals) of getting 0, 1, 2, 3, 4, 5, or 6 responses to a mail-order solicitation sent to 6 families, when the probability that any one family will respond is 0.20. Multiplying 0, 1, 2, . . . , and 6 by the corresponding probabilities and adding the products thus obtained, it can easily be verified that the mean is $\mu = 1.2002$ or approximately 1.2. Under the stated conditions one can, therefore, *expect* that many responses to the mail-order solicitation sent to 6 families.

When x, the numerical description with which we are concerned, assumes a very large set of values, the calculation of μ can be fairly tedious. To illustrate, consider the following two examples: (1) we want to know how many among 400 customers entering a department store can be expected to make a purchase, when the probability that any one of them will make a purchase is 0.30; and (2) we are interested in the number of heads one can expect in 200 tosses of a balanced coin. If we followed the procedure used so far, we would have to calculate 401 probabilities in the first example and then use the formula on page 148; in the second example we would similarly have to begin by calculating 201 probabilities (corresponding to 0, 1, 2, . . . , and 200 heads). However, if we think for a moment, we might argue that in the long run 30 per cent of the customers make a purchase, 30 per cent of 400 is 120, and it would seem reasonable to say that we *expect* 120 of the 400 customers to make a purchase.* Similarly, it stands to reason that in the coin-tossing example we might *expect* as many heads as tails, that is, 50 per cent heads and 50 per cent tails, and that we might, therefore, *expect* 200(0.50) = 100 heads in the 200 flips of a balanced coin. These two values are, indeed, correct and we were able to find them so easily because there exists the special formula

$$\mu = n \cdot p \qquad \qquad \bigstar$$

for the mean of a *binomial distribution*, that is, the distribution of the number of successes in n trials, when the probability of success is p for each trial and the trials are independent (see page 138). In words, the mean of a binomial distribution is, simply, the product of the number of trials and the probability of success for an individual trial.

Using this special formula, we can now verify the value obtained for the mean of the second distribution on page 136 and the value obtained for the mean of the probability distribution of Figure 6.1. For the number of heads obtained in 3 flips of a balanced coin we have $n = 3$, $p = 1/2$, $\mu = 3(1/2) = 1\frac{1}{2}$, and this agrees with the value obtained before; for the probability distribution of Figure 6.1 we have $n = 6$, $p = 0.20$, $\mu = 6(0.20) = 1.20$, and the difference between this result and the one obtained before is the small rounding error of 0.0002. It is important to remember that the special formula $\mu = np$ applies only to binomial distributions; there exist other special formulas for other special kinds of probability distributions (see Exercise 14 on page 154), but we shall not go into them at this time.

The Variance of a Probability Distribution

In Chapter 3 we saw that there are many problems in which we must describe the *variability* of a distribution (that is, its spread or dispersion) as well as its mean or some other measure of central location. This argument applies also to probability distributions, as was illustrated by means of the example on page 48. As we pointed out in Chapter 3, the most widely used measure of variability is the *variance*, or its square

---

* It is assumed that we are referring here to customers shopping alone and not to shopping parties of two or more.

root the *standard deviation*, which measures the spread of a set of data by averaging the *squared deviations from the mean*. When dealing with probability distributions, we measure variability in almost the same way —instead of averaging the squared deviations from the mean, we use their *expected* value. If x is some numerical description of an experiment and the mean of the corresponding probability distribution is μ, then the deviation from the mean is $x - \mu$, and *we define the variance of the probability distribution as the value which we expect for the squared deviation from the mean*, namely, we define it as

$$\sigma^2 = \Sigma \ (x - \mu)^2 \cdot f(x) \qquad \qquad \star$$

The summation extends over all values of x and, as in Chapter 3, the square root of the variance defines the standard deviation σ of the probability distribution.

To illustrate the calculation of the variance of a probability distribution, let us refer again to the second of the two probability distributions on page 136, namely, the one dealing with the number of heads obtained in 3 flips of a balanced coin. Since the mean of this distribution was shown to be $\mu = 3(1/2) = 1.50$, we can arrange the calculations as in the following table:

Number of Heads, x	Probability	Deviation from Mean	Square of Deviation from Mean	$(x - \mu)^2 \cdot f(x)$
0	1/8	−1.50	2.25	0.28125
1	3/8	−0.50	0.25	0.09375
2	3/8	0.50	0.25	0.09375
3	1/8	1.50	2.25	0.28125
				$\sigma^2 = 0.75000$

The values in the last column are obtained by multiplying each squared deviation from the mean by the corresponding probability, and their sum equals the variance of the distribution. Thus, the standard deviation of this probability distribution is $\sigma = \sqrt{0.75}$, which equals approximately 0.87. Following these same steps, the reader will be asked to show in Exercise 12 below that the variance of the first probability distribution on page 136 is $\sigma^2 = 35/12$, and that the one for the probability distribution of Figure 6.1 equals approximately 0.96.

As in the case of the mean, the calculation of the variance or the standard deviation of a probability distribution can often be simplified when dealing with special kinds of probability distributions. For instance, for the *binomial distribution* we have the formula

$$\sigma^2 = n \cdot p \cdot (1 - p) \qquad\qquad \star$$

which we shall not prove, but which can easily be verified for our various examples. For the distribution of the number of heads obtained in 3 flips of a balanced coin we have $n = 3$, $p = 0.50$,

$$\sigma^2 = 3(0.50)(0.50) = 0.75$$

and this agrees with the value we obtained before. Similarly, for the probability distribution of Figure 6.1 we have $n = 6$, $p = 0.20$, and

$$\sigma^2 = 6(0.20)(0.80) = 0.96$$

namely, the value the reader is asked to verify by the long method in Exercise 12 below.

Intuitively speaking, the variance and the standard deviation of a probability distribution measure its spread or its dispersion: when σ is small the probability is high that we will get a value close to the mean, and when σ is large we are more likely to get a value far away from the mean. This important idea is expressed rigorously in a theorem called *Chebyshev's Theorem*, which is discussed briefly in Technical Note 5 on page 177. Several of the exercises which follow require the use of this theorem and they are marked accordingly.

EXERCISES

1. A builder is bidding on a construction job which promises a profit of $36,000 with a probability of 4/5 or a loss (from rework, late performance penalties, etc.) of $12,000 with a probability of 1/5. What is the builder's expected profit if he gets the job?

2. A lot of 10 parts among which 3 are defective is put on sale "as is" at $10 per part with no inspection possible. If a defective part represents a complete loss of $10 to the buyer and good parts can be resold for $15 each, is it worthwhile to buy one of these parts and select it at random?

3. An urn contains 7 red beads and 3 white beads, and a player is to draw 2 beads at random but without replacement.

(a) What are the probabilities that he will draw 0, 1, or 2 red beads?

(b) If he wins $10 for each red bead and $5 for each white bead, what is his expectation?

(c) If the player receives $3 for each red bead he draws, how much should he be "penalized" for each white bead he draws to make the game equitable?

4. A grab-bag contains 5 packages worth $1.00 apiece, 5 packages worth $3.00 apiece, and 10 packages worth $5.00 apiece. Is it worthwhile to pay $4.00 for the privilege of selecting one of these packages at random?

5. The probability that Mr. Jones will sell his house at a loss of $1,000 is 3/18, the probability that he will break even is 5/18, the probability that he will sell it at a profit of $1,000 is 7/18, and the probability that he will sell it at a profit of $2,000 is 3/18. What is his expected profit?

6. If the two teams are evenly matched, the probabilities that the World Series will end in 4, 5, 6, or 7 games are, respectively, 1/8, 1/4, 5/16, and 5/16. Under this condition, how many games can we *expect* a World Series to last?

7. (a) In the example on page 139, we actually obtained the following probability distribution for p (the probability that any new gas station will show a profit during the first year):

p	Probability
1/2	0.51
2/3	0.49

Calculate the mean of this probability distribution to obtain a *Bayesian estimate* of the true value of the probability that a new gas station will show a profit during the first year.

(b) Looking upon the probabilities obtained in Exercise 15 on page 142 as the values of a probability distribution for λ, the average number of inquiries about the estate produced by the ad, calculate the mean of this probability distribution to obtain a *Bayesian estimate* of the true average number of inquiries produced by such an ad.

8. If in shooting dice a person bets $1.00 on the "Field," he wins $1.00 on the roll of 3, 4, 9, 10, or 11, he wins double on 2, triple on 12, and otherwise he loses. What is the expectation of such a "Field" bet?

9. An urn contains 2 black beads and 3 red beads. If two players, A and B, take turns drawing one bead without replacement, with A going

first, what is Player A's expectation if whoever draws a red bead first wins $10.00? (*Hint:* Draw a tree diagram showing the various possible outcomes.)

10. The probabilities of getting 0, 1, 2, 3, or 4 heads in 4 tosses of a balanced coin are, respectively, 1/16, 4/16, 6/16, 4/16, and 1/16. Use the basic definitions of μ and σ^2 to compute the mean and the variance of this probability distribution. Verify the results using the special formulas for the mean and the variance of the binomial distribution.

11. Use the probabilities obtained in part (a) of Exercise 3 to find the mean and the standard deviation of the probability distribution for the number of red beads drawn from the urn.

12. Use the definition of σ^2 to calculate (a) the variance of the probability distribution given in Figure 6.1, and (b) the variance of the first probability distribution given on page 136.

13. Find the mean and the standard deviation of each of the following binomial distributions:

(a) the number of heads obtained in 400 tosses of a balanced coin.

(b) the number of defectives in a sample of 100 parts made with a certain machine, if the probability that any one of the parts is defective is 0.03.

(c) the number of cars with faulty brakes among 1,000 cars stopped at a road-block, if the probability that any one of the cars has faulty brakes is 0.10.

14. The probabilities of catching 0, 1, 2, 3, or 4 trout while fishing for an hour in Horton Creek are, respectively, 0.37, 0.37, 0.18, 0.06, and 0.02. Compute the mean and the variance of this probability distribution. The probabilities in this exercise were chosen so that the distribution is approximately a *Poisson distribution* (see Exercise 12 on page 141), with $\lambda = 1$. Use your results to verify the formulas $\mu = \lambda$ and $\sigma^2 = \lambda$, which hold for any Poisson distribution.

(The exercises which follow are based on the material in Technical Note 5 on page 177.)

15. Referring to part (a) of Exercise 13, what can we say (according to Chebyshev's Theorem) about the probability of getting more than 230 or fewer than 170 heads?

16. Referring to part (b) of Exercise 13, what can we say (according to Chebyshev's Theorem) about the probability that the sample will contain fewer than 10 defective parts? (Round to the nearest multiple of σ.)

17. Referring to part (c) of Exercise 13, what can we assert (according to Chebyshev's Theorem) with a probability of at least 8/9?

18. Referring to Exercise 14, what can we say (according to Chebyshev's Theorem) about the probability of catching more than 3 trout? Compare this value with the actual value of catching more than 3 trout as given in that exercise.

A Decision Problem

Philosophers and social scientists have suggested that a person's behavior might be called *rational* if in situations involving uncertainties and risks he always chooses the alternative which has the highest mathematical expectation. Although this may look like a fairly reasonable criterion for rational behavior, it involves a number of difficulties. To illustrate, let us consider an example. Suppose that Mr. Jones has the choice of spending a summer operating either a soft drink concession or a hot coffee and donut stand at a seaside resort. If the summer turns out to be very hot he will make more money selling soft drinks, if it turns out to be relatively cool he will make more money selling hot coffee and donuts. To be more specific, suppose that on the basis of past experience he has the following information: *if the summer turns out to be very hot* the soft drink concession will yield a profit of \$3,000 whereas the hot coffee and donut stand will yield only a profit of \$1,800. On the other hand, *if the summer turns out to be relatively cool* the soft drink concession will yield a profit of \$1,500 whereas the hot coffee and donut stand will yield a profit of \$2,400. Schematically, this information can be arranged as follows:

	Very Hot Summer	*Relatively Cool Summer*
Soft Drink Concession	\$3,000	\$1,500
Hot Coffee and Donut Stand	\$1,800	\$2,400

To make an intelligent choice, it will help Mr. Jones to know something about the probability that it will be a very hot summer. Let us suppose (again based on past experience) that the probability for a very hot summer is 1/3 and the probability for a relatively cool summer is 2/3.

Mr. Jones might then argue as follows: if he runs the soft drink concession, the *expected profit* is

$$3{,}000 \left(\frac{1}{3}\right) + 1{,}500 \left(\frac{2}{3}\right) = \$2{,}000$$

and if he runs the hot coffee and donut stand, the *expected profit* is

$$1{,}800 \left(\frac{1}{3}\right) + 2{,}400 \left(\frac{2}{3}\right) = \$2{,}200$$

Being *rational* in the sense of choosing the alternative which has the
highest expectation, Mr. Jones will decide to operate the hot coffee and
donut stand, perhaps keeping his fingers crossed that the weather will
not get too hot.

If mathematical expectations are to serve as criteria for making rational
decisions, it is essential to know the correct values of all relevant probabilities. Had the probabilities for a very hot summer and a relatively
cool summer both equaled 1/2 in our example, the *expected profit* for
the soft drink concession would have been

$$3{,}000 \left(\frac{1}{2}\right) + 1{,}500 \left(\frac{1}{2}\right) = \$2{,}250$$

the *expected profit* for the hot coffee and donut stand would have been

$$1{,}800 \left(\frac{1}{2}\right) + 2{,}400 \left(\frac{1}{2}\right) = \$2{,}100$$

and it would have been rational for Mr. Jones to choose the soft drink
concession.

Having shown in this example how mathematical expectations might
be used as a basis for rational decisions, let us examine briefly what
Mr. Jones might have done if he had no idea whatsoever about the
probabilities of having a very hot or a relatively cool summer. To
introduce one possible approach, suppose that Mr. Jones is a *confirmed
optimist;* looking at the situation through rose-colored glasses, he sees
that if he operates the soft drink stand he might make as much as $3,000,
whereas the hot coffee and donut stand would at best yield $2,400.
Always expecting the best (in the sense of wishful thinking), he thus
decides to sell soft drinks. On the other hand, if Mr. Jones were a *con-*

firmed pessimist, he would note that the soft drink concession might yield only $1,500, whereas the hot coffee and donut stand might yield only $1,800. Always expecting the worst (in the sense of resignation or fear), he would thus decide to sell hot coffee and donuts and make at least $1,800.

Since decisions based on optimism or pessimism alone can hardly be called very rational, let us consider another way in which Mr. Jones' problem might be resolved. Let us suppose that in desperation he decides to leave the decision to *chance*, writing "soft drink concession" on a number of slips of paper, "hot coffee and donut stand" on a number of others, mixing them up thoroughly, and then making his decision according to which kind is drawn. Suppose, furthermore, that the numbers of slips marked "soft drink concession" and "hot coffee and donut stand" are such that the probability for drawing one of the first kind is some number p and, hence, the probability for drawing one of the second kind is $1 - p$. Letting E represent Mr. Jones' *expected profit*, we then have

$$E = 3,000p + 1,800(1 - p)$$

for a summer which is very hot and

$$E = 1,500p + 2,400(1 - p)$$

for a summer which is relatively cool. Graphically, this situation is described in Figure 6.2, where we have plotted the two lines whose equations are

$$E = 3,000p + 1,800(1 - p) \quad \text{and} \quad E = 1,500p + 2,400(1 - p)$$

for values of p from 0 to 1. (Actually, these lines were obtained by connecting the respective values obtained for $p = 0$ and $p = 1$, namely, 1,800 and 3,000 for the line giving Mr. Jones' expected profit for a summer which is very hot, and 2,400 and 1,500 for the line giving Mr. Jones' expected profit for a summer which is relatively cool.) Note also that by putting $3,000p + 1,800(1 - p)$ equal to $1,500p + 2,400(1 - p)$ and solving for p, we find that the two lines intersect at $p = 2/7$.

Let us now see how the lines of Figure 6.2 might be used to help Mr. Jones choose a value of p. If he labeled 2 slips of paper "soft drink concession" and 5 slips of paper "hot coffee and donut stand," p would actually equal $2/7$, provided that each slip of paper has the same prob-

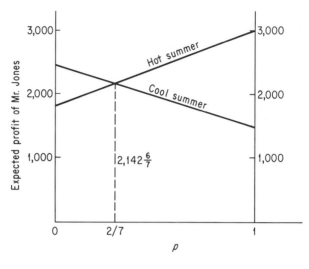

FIGURE 6.2

ability of being drawn. He would then have an expected profit of

$$3{,}000 \left(\frac{2}{7}\right) + 1{,}800 \left(\frac{5}{7}\right) = 2142\tfrac{6}{7}$$

or \$2142.86 rounded to the nearest cent. (Note that the identical result would have been obtained if we had substituted $p = 2/7$ into the other equation; that is, $1500(2/7) + 2400(5/7)$ also equals $2142\tfrac{6}{7}$.) Now observe from Figure 6.2 that for any other value of p there are always two distinct expected profits, one for very hot summers and one for relatively cool summers, and that one or the other is always less than \$2,142.86. For values of p less than $2/7$ the expected profit for hot summers is the one which is less, and for values of p greater than $2/7$ the expected profit for cool summers is the one which is less. Mr. Jones might thus argue that $p = 2/7$ is the best value to use—*his expected profit is \$2,142.86 regardless of the weather, while for any other value of p one or the other of the two expected profits is less.*

Choosing a probability of $2/7$, that is, labeling 2 slips of paper "soft drink concession" and 5 slips of paper "hot coffee and donut stand," and acting according to which kind is drawn, Mr. Jones is basing his decision on the so-called *maximin criterion.* He *maximizes* the *minimum* expected profit or, in other words, he chooses the value of p for which the smaller of the two expected profits is as large as possible. (This criterion is also referred to as the *minimax criterion*, since minimizing the maximum expected losses is equivalent to maximizing the minimum expected gains.)

This kind of decision procedure, in which the ultimate decision is left to chance, is called *randomized* or *mixed*. Although it may seem strange that a "rational" decision should be left to chance, there are situations in which randomized decision procedures actually provide the most desirable results. This is true, particularly, in games of strategy, such as the ones which we shall discuss in the next section. It should be mentioned, perhaps, that instead of drawing slips of paper out of a hat, any other kind of gambling device providing the correct odds can also be used.

Earlier in this section, we pointed out that optimism and pessimism *alone* can hardly be looked upon as rational criteria for making decisions. Nevertheless, there are situations where questions of optimism or pessimism might outweigh all other factors. Suppose, for example, that a builder is given a choice between Contracts 1 and 2 which he appraises as follows: Contract 1 will result in a profit of $48,000 with a probability of 3/4 or a loss of $12,000 (from rework, late-performance penalties, etc.) with a probability of 1/4; Contract 2 will result in a profit of $120,000 with a probability of 6/10 or a loss of $50,000 with a probability of 4/10. As can easily be verified, the expected profits corresponding to the two contracts are $33,000 and $52,000, so that (according to the criterion that it is rational to maximize one's expected profit) it would seem that the builder should undertake Contract 2.

Now suppose, however, that the financial condition of the builder is such that a loss of $50,000 would put him out of business, whereas a loss of $12,000, though unfortunate, would be something he could bear. Under these conditions it would seem entirely reasonable for the builder to *protect himself against the worst that can happen* and undertake Contract 1. A parallel example, where questions of optimism might outweigh the principle of maximizing one's expected profit, is given in Exercise 6 on page 161. It is hoped that these additional examples will serve to stress the point that there is no omnibus rule or criterion which will invariably lead to the "best" decisions.

EXERCISES

1. A wildcatter drilling for oil is faced with the problem of whether to stop or to continue drilling. It is not possible to place monetary values

on either the loss from stopping the drilling when oil in fact lies below, or the gain from continuing to drill and striking oil. However, the driller measures the relative values involved in the situation in terms of crude "satisfaction" units as follows

	No Oil	Oil
Stop Drilling	100	−500
Continue Drilling	−300	1,000

Thus, his satisfaction in stopping now if no oil will be found is 100 units, in continuing to drill when no oil will be found it is −300 units, and so on.

(a) What action should the driller take if he wishes to maximize his expected satisfaction and he feels that the probability of striking oil is 2/3?

(b) What action should the driller take if he wishes to maximize his expected satisfaction and he feels that the probability of striking oil is 1/10?

(c) What action should the driller take if he wanted to maximize his minimum expected satisfaction?

(d) What action would the driller take if he were a confirmed optimist?

(e) What action would the driller take if he were a confirmed pessimist?

2. A fraternity raises money each year by selling pennants outside the stadium after the Big Game. They can buy the pennants from a supplier in either of two batches: Batch 1, which contains more of Team A's pennants and less of Team B's pennants, or Batch 2, which contains just the reverse. Previous experience shows that if they buy Batch 1 and Team A wins they will make a profit of $1,000, but if Team A loses they will make only $200. On the other hand, if they buy Batch 2 and Team A wins they will make a profit of $300, but if Team A loses they will make $800.

(a) Which batch should they buy so as to maximize their expected profit if the teams are about evenly matched?

(b) Which batch should they buy so as to maximize their expected profit if the odds are 3 to 1 against Team A?

(c) What should they do if they had no information about the odds on the game and they wanted to maximize their minimum expected profit?

3. At one point in a generally bad winter season, snow conditions are very poor in the Sierras and the operator of a ski resort is considering whether to continue operating the resort or accept an offer of another person to lease the facilities for the rest of the season for $20,000. The operator of the resort estimates that if no new snow fell he would lose $30,000 in salaries, operation of the lift, and so on, but that if the area did get new snow he would make a profit of $35,000 before the season ends.

   (a) What action would the operator of the resort take if he wanted to maximize his expected profit and he felt that the probability for new snow was $1/2$?

   (b) What action would he take if he wanted to maximize his expected profit and he felt that the probability for new snow was $4/5$?

   (c) What action would the operator of the resort take if he were the kind of person who always visualizes the worst?

   (d) What action might the operator of the resort be inclined to take if he owed a bank $25,000 and the mortgage on the resort would be foreclosed unless he could pay the bank before the season ends?

4. Suppose that the Mr. Jones referred to in the example of the text is the kind of person who always worries about "what might have happened if." Looking at the table on page 155, he finds that if he decides to run the soft drink concession and the summer turns out to be relatively cool, he will lose out on $900 (what he could have made with the hot coffee and donut stand *minus* what he will make with the soft drink concession). Referring to this figure as the *"regret"* associated with this situation, he also finds that if he decides to run the hot coffee and donut stand and the summer turns out to be very hot, his *regret* will be $1,200. In the other two cases the regret is 0. What action should Mr. Jones take so as to *minimize the maximum regret?*

5. Using the concept of regret introduced in the preceding exercise, what action should the oil driller of Exercise 1 take so as to *minimize the maximum regret?*

6. A contractor has to choose between two jobs. The first promises a profit of $80,000 with a probability of $3/4$ or a loss of $20,000 (due to strikes and other delays) with a probability of $1/4$; the second promises a profit of $120,000 with a probability of $1/2$ or a loss of $30,000 with a probability of $1/2$.

   (a) Which job should the contractor choose so as to maximize his expected profit?

   (b) What job might the contractor choose if his business is in fairly bad shape and he will go broke unless he can make a profit of at least $100,000 on his next job?

7. A manufacturer has produced for sale a large lot of items among which an unknown proportion p are defective. He can decide (1) not to put the lot on the market at all, or (2) sell the lot with a double-your-money back guarantee on all defective items.

   (a) What should the manufacturer do if he has no information whatsoever about p and he wants to minimize his maximum losses?

   (b) Discuss the reasonableness of using the minimax criterion in this kind of situation.

8. A retailer has shelf space for 4 highly perishable items which are destroyed at the end of the day if they are not sold. The unit cost of the item is $2.00, the selling price is $4.00, and the profit is thus $2.00 per item sold.

   (a) If nothing is known about the possible demand for the item, how many should the retailer stock so as to minimize the maximum possible losses? Comment on the appropriateness of this criterion in the given problem.

   (b) How many items should the retailer stock so as to maximize his expected profit, if it is known that the probabilities of the demand for 0, 1, 2, 3, or 4 items are, respectively, 0.10, 0.30, 0.40, 0.10 and 0.10?

Games of Strategy

The example which we discussed in the preceding section may have given the impression that Mr. Jones is playing some sort of game with *Nature* as his opponent, and that in this game each of the two players tries to outwit the other. Mr. Jones selects one of two "moves," taking the soft drink concession or the stand for selling hot coffee and donuts, while Nature also selects one of two "moves," making the summer very hot or making it reasonably cool. Depending on which strategy is chosen by each player, there is a certain *payoff*, namely, the corresponding profit made by Mr. Jones.

This analogy to a game is not at all far-fetched; in fact, the problem we have discussed is typical of the kind of situation treated in a branch of mathematics called the *Theory of Games*, which has become increasingly important in recent years. Although we are using the word "game," this theory is not limited to parlor games or sports; it is applied to any kind of competitive situation as one might find in economic planning, in business management, in war, in the study of social behavior, and in many other areas.

To begin with, let us consider what is called a *2-by-2 zero-sum two-person game*. As its name implies, there are two players (two persons or two sets of interests which for convenience are called "players") opposing each other in this kind of game. The "2-by-2" means that each player has the choice of two possible strategies (or alternatives), and the "zero-sum" means that whatever amount is won by one player is lost by the other; that is, there is no "cut for the house" as there is in professional gambling and there is also no capital created during the course of play.

Suppose, then, that there are two players A and B, with the strategies of Player A labeled I and II and those of Player B labeled 1 and 2. Depending on the strategies chosen by the two players, the *payoff* to Player B, the amount Player A has to pay Player B, is a, b, c, or d, as shown in the following table:

		Player A	
		I	II
	1	a	b
Player B			
	2	c	d

It will be assumed that these payoff amounts are in terms of money (dollars), although in actual practice they could be in terms of any goods or services, or units of satisfaction or utility; they could even mean life or death.

Thus, if Player A chooses Strategy I and Player B chooses Strategy 1, Player A pays Player B the amount a; if Player A chooses Strategy II and Player B chooses Strategy 1, Player A pays Player B the amount b; and so forth. Since most games will have to allow for payments from Player A to Player B as well as payments from Player B to Player A, we shall adopt the following practice: if a payoff amount a, b, c, or d is *positive*, this means that it is paid by Player A to Player B; if it is *negative*, this means that the amount is paid by Player B to Player A. Thus, if $a = 2$, Player A has to pay \$2.00 to Player B when their respective strategies are I and 1; if $c = -3$, Player B has to pay \$3.00 to Player A when their respective strategies are 2 and I. Using this convention, it is natural to call Player B the *maximizing* player and Player A the *minimizing* player; Player B's winnings are Player A's losses, and the direct conflict of interests arises from the fact that one player is trying to make large what the other is trying to make small. It should also be pointed out that in all of the games considered in this section each player has to choose his strategy *without* knowledge of the choice made by the other.

In actual practice, we are accustomed to describe a game by listing the rules by which it is played, we describe the pieces or other kinds of equip- ment that are being used, and we might state what penalties or rewards there are involved. All this is important if we actually want to play the game, but its analysis in the Theory of Games requires only that we list the moves (strategies) available to each player and the corresponding payoff amounts. This information is sufficient to determine what choice of strategies or moves is most profitable for each player, and this is the foremost objective of the Theory of Games. In the examples which follow we shall thus ignore the question of whether the game is played with cards, dice, or ping-pong balls, whether it involves physical activity, whether it pertains to a fight between a battleship and a submarine or the competition between two department stores.

To illustrate some of the problems involved in selecting a "best" strategy for each player in some simple games, let us consider a few examples, where the strategies of Players A and B and the payoff amounts are given as indicated on page 163. First, let us consider the game which is represented by the following scheme:

Player A

		I	II
	1	1	−6
Player B			
	2	2	4

As can easily be seen, it would be foolish of Player B to choose Strategy 1 regardless of the choice made by his opponent, Player B will make more if he chooses Strategy 2 and this strategy is thus said to *dominate* Strategy 1. Having eliminated the first line in the above table of payoff values, usually called a *payoff matrix*, the best strategy for Player A also becomes readily apparent. Since he would rather lose $2.00 than $4.00 his best choice is obviously Strategy I. The payoff of $2.00 correspond- ing to Strategies I and 2 is said to be the *value* of the game. If the value of a game is positive it favors Player B, if it is negative the game favors Player A, and if it is zero, the game is said to be *equitable* (in other

vords, it does not favor either player). We thus find that in this first
;ame the "cards are stacked" against Player A and he can hardly be
›lamed for not wanting to play. Unfortunately, people sometimes find
hemselves forced against their will into games (conflict situations) where
hey cannot possibly win. We presume, however, that if one must lose,
ne should behave in such a way so as to lose as little as possible.

To consider a second example, suppose the payoff values for a 2-by-2
ero-sum two-person game are given by

Player A

		I	II
	1	4	−3
Player B			
	2	3	1

'his time there is no *dominance* among the strategies of Player B, but
t can easily be seen that for Player A Strategy II dominates Strategy I;
›o matter what choice is made by Player B, it is advantageous to Player A
o choose Strategy II in preference to Strategy I. Crossing out the
olumn of values corresponding to Strategy I, it follows that Player B
hould choose Strategy 2 since this would make him win $1.00 rather
han lose $3.00. The *value* of this game is $1.00, the payoff corresponding
o Strategies II and 2, and this game is also biased favoring Player B.
ks the reader will be asked to demonstrate in Exercise 6 on page 173,
iowever, this can easily be changed by subtracting an appropriate
iumber from each payoff amount.

To introduce another concept which is important in the Theory of
;ames, let us consider the following 3-by-3 zero-sum two-person game,
vhere the amounts are, as before, the payments made by Player A to
'layer B:

Player A

		I	II	III
	1	−2	5	−3
Player B	2	1	3	5
	3	−3	−7	11

Inspecting this table, it can be seen that there are no dominances among the strategies of either player, and we will, therefore, have to find some other way of obtaining the best strategies. Considering first the strategies of Player A, we find that if he uses Strategy I the worst that can happen is that he will lose $1.00, if he uses Strategy II the worst that can happen is that he will lose $5.00, and if he uses Strategy III the worst that can happen is that he will lose $11.00. Looking at it from this point of view, it would seem advantageous for Player A to choose Strategy I, as he would thus *minimize his maximum losses.* Considering now the strategies of Player B, we find that if he uses Strategy 1 the worst that can happen is that he will lose $3.00, if he uses Strategy 2 the worst that can happen is that he will win $1.00, and if he uses Strategy 3 the worst that can happen is that he will lose $7.00. Looking at it from this point of view, it would seem advantageous for Player B to choose Strategy 2; he would thus *maximize the minimum amount he stands to win.*

The selection of Strategies I and 2, called *minimax strategies,* is really quite reasonable. By playing Strategy I, Player A makes sure that his opponent can win at most $1.00, and by choosing Strategy 2, Player B makes sure that he actually does win this amount. The value of this game is the payoff which corresponds to Strategies I and 2, and it is equal to $1.00. The game thus favors Player B, although this could again be changed by subtracting an appropriate number from each value of the payoff matrix. Another important aspect of the game is that it is completely "spyproof" in the sense that neither player can profit from knowledge of the other's strategy. Even though Player B announced publicly that he would use Strategy 2, Player A would still use Strategy I; similarly, the information that Player A is planning to use Strategy I would be worth nothing to Player B, since changing to either of his other strategies would hurt rather than help.

The payoff amount which gives the value of the game in this last example (that is, the entry in the second row and the first column of the payoff matrix) is called a *saddle point.* In practice, if a saddle point exists, it can easily be found by making use of its definition as being *the smallest value of its row and the largest value of its column.* To facilitate this, we write the row minima and the column maxima, respectively, alongside and at the bottom of the payoff table. Then, if the largest among the row minima (indicated below by means of an arrow) equals the smallest among the column maxima (also indicated by means of an arrow), they correspond to a saddle point. For the game discussed directly above, we can show this as follows:

		Player A			Row
		I	II	III	Minima
	1	−2	5	−3	−3
Player B	2	1	3	5	1 ←
	3	−3	−7	11	−7
Column Maxima		1 ↑	5	11	

and, as can be seen, the saddle point corresponds to Strategies I and 2.

Note that in the first two examples of this section the value of the game was in each case given by a saddle point; in the first example 2 is less than 4 but greater than 1, and in the second example 1 is less than 3 but greater than −3. It is also of interest to note that if a game has more than one saddle point, it can be shown that the corresponding amounts must all be equal and that it does not matter which of the saddle points is used to determine the best strategies for the two players. Thus, in the game

		Player A			Row
		I	II	III	Minima
	1	−2	2	−1	−2
Player B	2	6	3	5	3 ←
	3	4	3	4	3 ←
Column Maxima		6	3 ↑	5	

there are two saddle points, one corresponding to Strategies II and 2 and one corresponding to Strategies II and 3. Note that it does not matter here whether Player B chooses Strategy 2 or 3 when Player A chooses Strategy II.

Games which have a saddle point are said to be *strictly determined*. If every game were strictly determined, the above analysis would provide a satisfactory solution to the problem of finding the best strategy for each player; unfortunately, this is not the case, as is illustrated by the following example:

| | | Player A | | Row |
		I	II	Minima
Player B	1	4	8	4 ←
	2	15	2	2
Column Maxima		15	8	

↑

As can be seen by inspection, the largest of the row minima is 4, the smallest of the column maxima is 8, the two are not equal, and, hence, there is no saddle point. Analyzing this game like the last one, however, we find that if Player A uses Strategy I the worst that can happen is that he will lose $15.00, and if he uses Strategy II the worst that can happen is that he will lose $8.00. Player B, on the other hand, will win at least $4.00 if he chooses Strategy 1 and at least $2.00 if he chooses Strategy 2. By playing Strategy II, Player A can thus make sure that he will not lose more than $8.00, and by playing Strategy 1, Player B can make sure that he will win at least $4.00.

If A and B actually played these strategies, the payoff would be $8.00, and this should be a pleasant surprise to Player B; it is more than the $4.00 minimum he tried to assure for himself by selecting Strategy 1. On the other hand, this situation is not very satisfactory so far as Player A is concerned, and he might try to improve things by reasoning as follows: if Player B is the kind of player who always tries to make the minimum he stands to win as large as possible, he will choose Strategy 1; hence, Player A can hold his losses down to $4.00 by playing Strategy I. This would work nicely, unless Player B reasons that this is precisely what A is going to do and that it would, therefore, be smart for him to play Strategy 2 and win $15.00. *We can continue this argument ad infinitum.* If Player A thinks that Player B will try to outsmart him by playing Strategy 2, he can in turn try to outfox Player B by choosing Strategy II, thus holding his losses down to $2.00. If Player B thinks that this is what Player A is going to do, he will switch to Strategy 1, trying to assure for himself a payoff of $8.00, and so on, and so on.

An interesting feature of this situation is that one player can outsmart the other if he knows how his opponent will react under certain conditions.

'or instance, if Player A knows that Player B is an *incurable optimist,* he
an figure that Player B will select Strategy 2 hoping to make $15.00,
nd he can take advantage of this by playing Strategy II. In view of all
his it would seem reasonable to suggest that each player should somehow

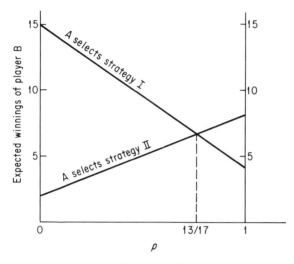

FIGURE 6.3

nix up his strategies, so that he cannot be outfoxed by his opponent's
se of psychology or of outside information arrived at in any way—by
spionage, experience, or otherwise. Since each player will always have
o choose one strategy or another, this can only be done by somehow
eaving the ultimate choice to chance. As in the example on page 157, we
hall, therefore, have to determine what probabilities each player should
se in the selection of his strategy; the criterion on which this is usually
ased is that of *maximizing the least a player can expect to win,* or which
s the same, *minimizing the greatest amount he can expect to lose.*

Referring again to the last example, suppose now that Player B assigns
o his two strategies the respective probabilities p and $1 - p$. Then,
'layer B can *expect* to win

$$E = 4p + 15(1 - p)$$

f Player A selects Strategy I, and he can *expect* to win

$$E = 8p + 2(1 - p)$$

f Player A selects Strategy II. Analyzing Figure 6.3 as we did Figure 6.2,
ve find that the *least* amount Player B can expect to win is *greatest* for the

value of p for which the two lines intersect. Equating $4p + 15(1 - p)$ and $8p + 2(1 - p)$ and solving for p, we thus get

$$4p + 15(1 - p) = 8p + 2(1 - p)$$

and
$$p = 13/17$$

Labeling 13 slips of paper "Strategy 1," 4 slips of paper "Strategy 2," shuffling them thoroughly and drawing one, Player B can thus assure for himself *expected winnings* of

$$4(\tfrac{13}{17}) + 15(\tfrac{4}{17}) = 6\tfrac{10}{17}$$

or $6.59 rounded to the nearest cent. Leaving the ultimate choice to chance, this over-all strategy of Player B is referred to as a *mixed strategy*. Note that this mixed strategy assures Player B expected winnings of $6.59, whereas the direct choice of one of his *pure strategies*, Strategy or Strategy 2, could assure him only minimum winnings of $4.00.

So far as Player A is concerned, the analysis is very much the same. If he assigns his two strategies the respective probabilities r and $1 - r$, his *expected losses* are

$$E = 4r + 8(1 - r)$$

when Player B chooses Strategy 1 and they are

$$E = 15r + 2(1 - r)$$

when Player B chooses Strategy 2. Drawing a diagram like those of Figures 6.2 and 6.3, it can be seen that the *greatest* amount Player A can expect to lose is *least* where the two lines intersect. Equating the two expected losses and solving for r, we thus get

$$4r + 8(1 - r) = 15r + 2(1 - r)$$

and
$$r = 6/17$$

Labeling 6 slips of paper "Strategy I," 11 slips of paper "Strategy II," shuffling them thoroughly and drawing one, Player A can thus hold his *expected losses* down to

$$4(\tfrac{6}{17}) + 8(\tfrac{11}{17}) = 6\tfrac{10}{17}$$

or approximately $6.59. Note that this is less than the $8.00 to which he could be sure to hold down his losses by playing directly one of his *pure strategies*, Strategy I or Strategy II. Incidentally, the amount of $6.59

to which Player A can hold down his expected losses and to which Player B can push up his expected winnings, is called the *value* of this (random-ized) game.

The examples of this section were designed to introduce the reader to some of the basic concepts of the Theory of Games: Dominating strategies, saddle points, and mixed strategies which serve to minimize maximum losses. These concepts are also used in the analysis of more complicated kinds of games, although the mathematical detail may then get quite involved. Most games that are of any practical significance have to allow for more than two strategies for each player, there are often more than two players, and many important applications are not even *zero-sum* (that is, they involve the creation or destruction of capital of some form). For instance, game theory might be used in connection with a competitive situation arising among five men's clothing stores. So long as each manager acts strictly in his own interest and against all others, this is a five-person game.* The manager of each store has to decide (among other things) whether to advertise in newspapers, on the radio, or on television, and he may have to decide whether or not to have a special sale, whether or not to remain open an additional evening each week, and so on. Also, the situation is *not zero-sum*, since each store could make a profit, with the actual size of the profit depending on which strategies are employed.

The numerical examples of this section were all stated without giving them any "real" physical interpretation, but this did not matter since we were interested only in the mathematical structure of the problem. Indeed, the great contribution of Game Theory is not in solving trivial problems with intuitively obvious solutions, but rather in dealing with complex problems which do not yield at all to conventional analysis. Even in fairly simple situations, however, the Game Theory approach has the positive advantage of forcing one to formulate problems clearly, to anticipate the various consequences of one's actions, to retain the relevant and eliminate the irrelevant, to place "cash values" on the differ-ent consequences, and so on. No matter how far it is pursued, this kind of systematic approach can hardly fail to be of tremendous help.

---

* We would have an entirely different kind of game if, say, four of the managers formed a coalition aimed at driving the fifth out of business, shared information, and, in general, acted differently in the interest of the coalition than they would if they were acting only in their own interests.

EXERCISES

1. Each of the following is the payoff matrix (the payments made by Player A to Player B) for a zero-sum two-person game. Eliminate all dominated strategies and determine the best strategies for the two players as well as the value of the game.

(a)

-2	3
7	5

(b)

8	-10
6	3

(c)

-2	4	5
-3	1	8
-11	0	2

2. Find the saddle point of each of the games of Exercise 1.

3. Each of the following is the payoff matrix (the payments made by Player A to Player B) for a zero-sum two-person game. Find the saddle point (or saddle points) of each of the games.

(a)

7	0	1
5	3	2
-2	7	0

(b)

2	0	7	1
2	2	1	2
3	4	4	3
3	5	7	3

Also find the value of each of these games.

4. The following is the payoff matrix of a zero-sum two-person game:

3	-1
-2	4

(a) What mixed strategy should Player A use so as to minimize his maximum expected losses?

(b) What mixed strategy should Player B use so as to maximize his minimum expected gain?

(c) What is the value of this game?

5. Find the best strategies and the value of each of the following games:*

(a)

−1	−2	8
7	5	−1
6	0	12

(b)

2	−2	3	7
6	5	1	4

(*Hint:* First eliminate all dominated strategies.)

6. Referring to the 2-by-2 game on page 165, show that nothing is changed insofar as the choice of strategies is concerned, if we subtract 1 from each entry in the payoff matrix. What will this do to the value of the game?

7. Referring to the 2-by-2 game on page 168, show that if Player B uses the probabilities 13/17 and 4/17 to choose between Strategies 1 and 2 while Player A uses the probabilities r and $1 - r$ to choose between Strategies I and II, the expected profit of Player B does not depend on r. (*Hint:* The probability that the players will choose Strategies 1 and I is $(13/17) \cdot r$, the probability that they will choose Strategies 1 and II is $(13/17)(1 - r)$, and so on.)

8. Suppose that in the area and under the snow conditions referred to in Exercise 3 on page 161 there are two resorts whose business is highly competitive. The operators of both resorts prefer to shut down for the season rather than face the loss which might accrue if there is no new snow. Both are worried, however, over a loss of prestige if one closes and the other does not and the possible adverse effect of this on later seasons. Each figures that if he closes early and the other remains open, this will be a "point" (a gain of 1 unit) in the other's favor; if both close early or both remain open, the status quo will be maintained and there is a 0 gain in either case. What actions should the two operators take under these conditions?

9. A certain type of computer is made by only two companies who share the market for the machine equally. Both would prefer not to introduce a new model at this time, but both suspect that the other is readying a new model and that if it is introduced some sales will be lost to the competitor. If neither brings out a new model or if both bring out new models, the status quo will be maintained and both will continue to get their same relative share of the market. If, however, one brings out a new model and the other does not, there will be a loss of 10 per cent in share of the market to the competitor with the new

* Note that in the game of part (b) Player A has the choice of 4 strategies while Player B has the choice of only 2.

machine. What is the best strategy for the two companies to use with respect to the introduction of a new model?

10. Country B has two island bases with installations worth $100,000 and $500,000, respectively. Of these bases it can defend only one against an attack by Country A. Country A, on the other hand, can attack only one of these islands and take it successfully only if it is left undefended. Considering the "payoff" to Country B to be the total value of the installations held by Country B after the attack, find optimum strategies for both countries and the value of this "game." Why wouldn't it be best for Country B simply to defend the island with the more valuable installation?

11. Two people agree to play the following game: The first writes either or 4 on a slip of paper and at the same time the second writes either . or 5 on another slip of paper. If the sum of the two numbers is odd the first wins this amount (in dollars), otherwise the second wins $2.00.

    (a) What are the best strategies for the two players?

    (b) How much should the first player pay the second for the "privilege" of playing the game, so as to make the game equitable?

12. A New York florist decides each Monday morning whether to sell his roses during the week for $3.00 a dozen with a discount of 20 per cent for an order of 3 dozen (or more), or whether to sell them at $2.70 a dozen with no special discount for large orders. There is a delivery charge of 30 cents for flowers delivered to any one person. Each Sunday a gentleman living in a suburb mails in an order for either 3 dozen roses to be delivered to *one* of his lady friends or 1 dozen roses to be delivered to each of *three* of his lady friends. The order is received on Monday after the florist has set the price for the week, and the 20 per cent discount applies only if the whole order goes to one person.

    (a) Considering only this one transaction, how should the florist price the roses so as to maximize his minimum receipts?

    (b) How should the suburban gentleman decide upon his order so as to minimize his maximum cost?

13. Because of various difficulties, the supplier of glue used in the manufacture of a laminated fibreboard product can guarantee the manufacturer only that it will deliver on schedule the required quantity of either Glue Q or Glue R (but not some of both). Because of time requirements, however, the manufacturer must set up his production process prior to knowledge of which glue will be available with no later change possible if he is to meet contractual obligations. Both glues can be used with any one of six production methods open to the company, but for technical reasons the profit per piece differs substantially from one method to another for the same glue. The estimated unit

profits (in cents) for methods 1–6 using Glue Q are 96, 146, 135, 160, 125, and 154, respectively, while the corresponding figures for Glue R are 255, 116, 175, 195, 235, and 202 cents. Which production method should the manufacturer use if he wants to maximize his minimum unit profit? Is this a reasonable criterion to use in this kind of situation? (*Hint:* Eliminate all dominated "strategies" and then look for a saddle point.)

14. Suppose that in Exercise 13 the manufacturer has the choice of only three production methods for which the unit profits (in cents) using Glue Q are, respectively, 120, 100, and 190. If the corresponding figures for Glue R are 205, 180, and 165 cents, what production method should the manufacturer use so as to maximize his minimum expected unit profit?

15. Suppose that in Exercise 13 there are three glues, Q, R, and S, and that the manufacturer has the choice of only two production methods for which the unit profits (in cents) using Glue Q are, respectively, 70 and 150. If the corresponding figures for Glue R are 100 and 80 cents, while those for Glue S are 140 and 60 cents, how should the manufacturer decide which method to use so as to maximize his minimum expected unit profit? (*Hint:* Suppose that the manufacturer chooses the first method with probability p and draw 3 lines like those of Figure 6.3, giving his expected profit using, respectively, Glues Q, R, and S; then find the value of p for which the smallest of the corresponding values on the lines is as large as possible.)

16. There are two gas stations in a certain block and the owner of the first station knows that if neither station lowers its prices, he can expect a net profit of $100 on any given day. If he lowers his prices while the other station does not, he can expect a net profit of $140; if he does not lower his prices but the other station does, he can expect a net profit of $70; and if both stations participate in this "price war," he can expect a net profit of $80. The owners of the two gas stations decide independently what prices to charge on any given day, and it is assumed that they cannot change their prices after they discover those charged by the other.

    (a) Should the owner of the first gas station charge his regular prices or should he lower them, if he wanted to maximize his minimum net profit?

    (b) Assuming that the above profit figures apply also to the second gas station, how might the owners of the gas stations collude so that each could expect a net profit of $105? (Note that this "game" is *not* zero-sum, so that the possibility of collusion opens entirely new possibilities.)

A Word of Caution

One of the greatest difficulties in applying the methods of this chapter (and more general methods) to realistic problems in statistics, business management, and economics in general, is that *we seldom know the exact values of all risks that are involved*. That is, we seldom know the exact values of the payoffs corresponding to the various eventualities, and we seldom have sufficient information about the values of all relevant probabilities. For instance, if a manufacturer has to decide whether to market a new drug right away, how can he put a cash value on the damage that might be caused by not waiting for a more thorough evaluation of the side effects of the drug, or the lives that might be lost by not marketing the drug? Similarly, if a management consultant has to decide whether to recommend the marketing of a new detergent, how can he possibly take into account all the effects which this advice (good or bad) might have on himself, on the company which produces the detergent, and ultimately on the consumer of the product?

The fact that we seldom have adequate information about all pertinent probabilities provides considerable obstacles in finding suitable decision criteria. For instance, in the example which dealt with Mr. Jones' decision whether to operate the soft drink concession or the hot coffee and donut stand, is it reasonable to base the decision on optimism, pessimism, or the principle of maximizing minimum expected profits? This last criterion we borrowed from the Theory of Games, where it is reasonable because the theory applies to conflicts between players who, so to speak, are out to cut each other's throat. However, if we look at Mr. Jones' problem as a game between him and Nature, with Nature having control of the weather, is it reasonable to look upon Nature as a *malevolent opponent*, trying to make Mr. Jones' life as difficult and unprofitable as possible?

The difficulties we have just pointed out present serious obstacles to the application of the methods of this chapter, but they are nevertheless important because they tend to clarify the logic which underlies statistical thinking and decision making in general. The problems of statistical decision making which we shall introduce in later chapters will indeed, be easier to grasp if we formulate them (at least tacitly) as games in which all sorts of things can happen, in which each interested party including Nature has various moves, and in which there are all sorts of consequences on which we may or may not be able to put appropriate values.

Technical Note 5 (Chebyshev's Theorem)

When the standard deviation of a frequency distribution is small, this means that most values are concentrated closely about the mean. So far as probability distributions are concerned, it implies that we are very likely to get a value that is close to the mean. When the standard deviation of a frequency distribution is large, this means that the values are scattered widely about the mean. So far as probability distributions are concerned, it implies that we are less likely to get a value that is close to the mean. Intuitively, this is what we mean when we say that the standard deviation is a measure of spread or dispersion. Formally, this idea is expressed by the following theorem, called *Chebyshev's Theorem* in honor of the Russian mathematician P. L. Chebyshev (1821–1894):

THEOREM P. *Given a probability distribution with the mean μ and the standard deviation σ, the probability of obtaining a value within k standard deviations of the mean is at least $1 - 1/k^2$.*

Thus, the probability of getting a value within *two* standard deviations of the mean (a value on the interval from $\mu - 2\sigma$ to $\mu + 2\sigma$) is at least $3/4$, the probability of getting a value within *five* standard deviations of the mean is at least $24/25$, and the probability of getting a value within *ten* standard deviations of the mean is at least $99/100$. (The quantity k in Theorem P can be any positive number, although the theorem becomes trivial when k is 1 or less.)

If in some actual problem we have $\mu = 25$ and $\sigma = 1$, we can thus say that the probability of getting a value between 20 and 30 is at least 0.96 (corresponding to $k = 5$); had σ been larger, say, $\sigma = 2.5$, we would have been able to assert only that the probability of getting a value between 20 and 30 is at least 0.75 (corresponding to $k = 2$).

Changing around the argument in Theorem P, we can also say that *the probability of getting a value which differs from the mean by more than k standard deviations is less than $1/k^2$.* We thus have a probability less than 0.25 of getting a value which differs from the mean by more than *two* standard deviations, and a probability less than 0.04 of getting a value which differs from the mean by more than *five* standard deviations

To give a concrete application, suppose we obtained 146 heads and 254 tails in 400 flips of a coin and we are wondering whether this is sufficient evidence to raise the question whether the coin is really balanced If the coin is balanced we are dealing with a binomial distribution having $n = 400$ and $p = 1/2$, and substitution into the special formulas on pages 150 and 152 yields

$$\mu = n \cdot p = 400(1/2) = 200$$

and $$\sigma = \sqrt{np(1 - p)} = \sqrt{400(1/2)(1/2)} = 10$$

Using $k = 5$, Chebyshev's Theorem asserts that the probability of getting anywhere from 150 to 250 heads is at least 0.96 *or* that the probability of being off by more than 50 heads from the expected 200 is less than 0.04. Since this probability is quite small, it would seem reasonable to go ahead and question the "honesty" of the coin.

It is of interest to note that Chebyshev's Theorem applies also to frequency distributions, that is, distributions of actual data. In that case we can assert that *the proportion of the total number of cases (values or items) which fall within k standard deviations of the mean is at least $1 - 1/k^2$* Thus, at least 75 per cent of all the items must fall within *two* standard deviations of the mean, and at least 96 per cent must fall within *five* standard deviations of the mean.

SEVEN
SAMPLING
AND SAMPLING
DISTRIBUTIONS

Random Sampling

Earlier in this book we distinguished between *populations* and *samples*, stating that a population consists of all conceivably or hypothetically possible instances (or observations) of a given phenomenon, while a sample is simply a part (subset) of a population. Now let us distinguish further between populations that are *finite* and those that are *infinite*. A population is said to be *finite* if it consists of a finite number, or fixed number, of elements (items, objects, measurements, or observations). In statistics, we are interested mainly in populations whose elements are numbers, and we might thus consider the finite population consisting of the total automobile registration figures for all counties in the United States, the finite population consisting of the serial numbers of all home wall safes manufactured in the United States in 1963, or the finite population consisting of the ages of all the employees of a given firm at a given date.

In contrast to finite populations, a population is said to be *infinite* if there is (at least hypothetically) no limit to the number of elements it can contain. For instance, the population consisting of the results obtained in all hypothetically possible rolls of a pair of dice is an infinite population, and so is the one consisting of all hypothetically possible additions that could be made by a digital computer. Also, we may want to look at the weights of 5 cows as a sample from the hypothetically infinite population consisting of the weights of all past, present, and future cows, and we may want to look at the number of mistakes 3 secretaries made in copying a certain report as a sample from the hypothetically infinite population consisting of the number of mistakes these secretaries (and, perhaps, other secretaries) might make while copying similar reports.

The purpose of most statistical investigations is to generalize from samples about both finite and infinite populations, and there are certain rules that must be observed to avoid obviously poor, irrelevant, or invalid results. Suppose, for instance, we want to determine how much money the average person spends on his vacation. It seems unlikely that we would arrive at anything even remotely accurate, if we based our conclusions only on information supplied by Deluxe Class passengers on a 45-day ocean cruise. Similarly, we can hardly expect to obtain reasonable generalizations about personal income in general in the United States from data reporting only on the incomes of doctors, and we can hardly expect to infer much about wholesale prices of farm products in general on the basis of figures pertaining only to wholesale prices of winter pears. These examples are, of course, extreme, but they serve to emphasize the point that sound generalizations (that is, sound inferences) do not come easily.

The whole problem of when and under what conditions samples permit reasonable generalizations is not easily answered. In the theory we shall develop in the next four chapters we shall always assume that we are dealing with a particular kind of sample called a *random sample*. (Other kinds of sampling procedures will be discussed briefly in Chapter 12.) To illustrate the notion of a *random sample from a finite population*, let us consider a finite population consisting of 5 elements which we shall label a, b, c, d, and e. (These might be the incomes of the 5 vice-presidents of a publishing house, the I.Q.'s of 5 students, the prices of 5 kinds of tires, and so on.) The problems we shall investigate are (1) how many distinct samples of, say, size 3 we might be able to take from this finite population, (2) how a random sample is to be defined, and (3) how such a sample might be obtained in actual practice. To answer the first of these questions, we have only to refer to Theorem E on page 102. According to his theorem, there are $\dfrac{n!}{(n-r)!\,r!}$ ways in which r objects can be selected from a set of n objects, where $n! = n(n-1)(n-2)\cdot\ \ldots\ \cdot 2\cdot 1$. In our example we have $n = 5$, $r = 3$, and there are therefore $\dfrac{5!}{2!3!} = 10$ ways of selecting a sample of size 3 from a finite population of size 5. One of these contains the elements a, b, c, another contains the elements a, d, e, another contains the elements b, c, e, and so on.

If we select one of the 10 possible samples in such a way that each has the same probability of being chosen, we say that we have a *simple random sample*, or more briefly, a *random sample*. One way in which this might be done is by writing each combination on a slip of paper, mixing the slips thoroughly, and then drawing one without looking. It would seem reasonable to say that with this method of selection each sample has a probability of $1/10$ of being drawn. This clearly conveys the idea that the selection of a random sample must, in some way, be left to chance; in fact, it is common practice to use various kinds of gambling devices as sampling aids.

In most realistic problems it is impossible, or at least impractical, to proceed as we suggested in our example; if a random sample of size 3 had to be drawn from a finite population of size 100, we would need 161,700 slips of paper to accommodate all possible samples (see Exercise 2 on page 183). Fortunately, such an elaborate and tedious procedure is unnecessary, since we can achieve the identical results by simply choosing our sample in such a way that each element of the finite population has the same chance of being included. As a matter of fact, when sampling from finite populations we often define a random sample in the following way: *a sample from a finite population is random if every element has an equal chance of being included in the sample*. To obtain a random sample of size 3 from a population of size 100, we might thus list each element on a slip of paper, mix the 100 slips of paper thoroughly, and then draw 3 without looking. Similarly, if we wanted to investigate the attitudes of 540 members of a city's restaurant association toward a proposed uniform closing hour, we could select a random sample of, say, 10 by writing the name of each member on a slip of paper, mixing them thoroughly, and drawing 10 without looking, and then interview the corresponding members.

As we have indicated earlier, the use of a gambling device can become impractical when the number of items (the size of the population) is very large, but there exists a device which, so to speak, does most of the work for us. It is a table of *random numbers* (or *random digits*) which consist of many pages on which the digits 0, 1, 2, 3, . . . , and 9 are set down in "random" fashion, much as they would appear if they had been generated by a gambling device giving each digit an equal probability of being selected. In fact, we could construct such a table ourselves by using a perfectly constructed spinner like the one shown in Figure 7.1. In actual

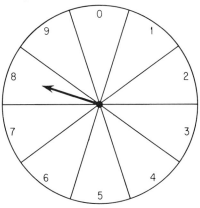

FIGURE 7.1

practice, tables of random numbers like Table VIII on pages 446 through 449 are usually generated by means of electronic computers; several commercially published tables of random numbers are listed in the Bibliography at the end of the book.

Working with prepared tables of random numbers, it is simple to select a random sample from a finite population. Referring again to the problem of selecting 10 of the 540 members of a restaurant association, we might number them 000, 001, 002, 003, . . . , and 539, arbitrarily pick a page in a table of random numbers, a row and three columns from which to start and then move down the page reading off 3-digit numbers. For instance, if we arbitrarily use the table on page 446 and the 5th, 6th, and 7th columns starting with the 6th row, our sample will consist of the association's members whose numbers are

080   051   420   162   246   305   350   402   177   146

Note that in this selection we ignored numbers exceeding 539 and we also ignored each number after it had occurred for the first time.

Having defined random sampling from finite populations and having indicated how random samples may be obtained with the use of gambling devices or random numbers, we should add that in actual practice this is often easier said than done. For example, if we wanted to estimate (on the basis of a sample) the average outside diameter of a lot of 500,000 ball bearings packed in 100 cases of 5,000 each, it would hardly be practical to number the bearings 000,001, 000,002, 000,003, . . . , 500,000, choose 6-digit numbers from a table of random numbers, and locate the corresponding bearings as their numbers appeared. In a situation like this there is really very little choice but to proceed according to the dictionary definition of the word "randomness," that is, "haphazardly without definite aim or purpose," hoping that this will produce a sample which can be treated by statistical theory ordinarily reserved for random samples.

To this point we have been discussing only random sampling from finite populations. The concept of a random sample from an *infinite* population is somewhat more difficult to define. To give a simple illustration, let us consider 10 tosses of a balanced coin as a sample from the (hypothetically) infinite population which consists of all possible tosses of the coin. We shall consider these 10 tosses a random sample provided the probability of getting heads is the same for each toss and if, furthermore, the 10 tosses are independent. In general, we shall similarly assert that *the selection of each item in a random sample from an infinite population must be controlled by the same probabilities, and successive selections must be independent of one another.*

EXERCISES

1. How many different samples of size 2 can be selected

   (a) from a finite population of size 6?
   (b) from a finite population of size 10?
   (c) from a finite population of size 50?

2. How many different samples of size 3 can be selected

   (a) from a finite population of size 6?
   (b) from a finite population of size 25?
   (c) from a finite population of size 100?

3. Referring to the example on page 180, list the 10 possible samples of size 3 which can be drawn from the finite population consisting of the elements a, b, c, d, and e. Then, assigning each of the 10 possible samples a probability of $1/10$, show that the probability that element a will be included in the sample is $3/5$. Does the same probability apply to elements b, c, d, and e?

4. List all possible samples of size 2 that can be drawn from the finite population whose elements are the numbers 1, 2, 3, 4, 5, and 6. Assigning each of these samples the same probability, show that the probability that any particular element of the population will be included in the sample is $1/3$.

5. Use random numbers to select a restaurant from among those listed in the yellow pages of your telephone directory (or that of a neighboring city).

• 6. Suppose you want three building contractors to bid on a construction job. Use random numbers to select the three building contractors from among those listed in the yellow pages of your telephone directory (or that of a neighboring city).

7. The employees of a company have badges numbered serially from 1 to 946. Use random numbers to select a random sample of 25 of the employees.

8. Explain why each of the following samples does not qualify as a random sample from the required population or might fail to give the desired information:

(a) In order to predict a city election, a research organization telephones people randomly selected from the city's telephone directory.

(b) To estimate the average length of logs fed into a mill by a constant-speed conveyor belt, measurements are made of the length of the logs which pass a given point exactly every five minutes.

(c) To study the religious affiliations of its subscribers, a magazine sends a questionnaire to each 25th subscriber on its alphabetically arranged mailing list.

(d) To estimate the average annual income of Harvard graduates ten years after graduation, questionnaires are sent in 1964 to all members of the Class of '54, and the estimate is based on the ones returned.

(e) To ascertain facts about bathing habits, a random sample of the residents of a community are asked whether they take a bath each day.

(f) To study consumer reaction to its product, the manufacturer of Frigidaire refrigerators hires a research organization to ask people the question, "How do you like your Frigidaire?"

(g) A house-to-house survey is made to study consumer reaction to a new product, with no provisions for return visits in case no one is at home.

Sampling Distributions

Let us now introduce what is probably the most fundamental concept of statistical inference, that of the *sampling distribution* of a statistic. This ties in closely with the idea of chance variation, which we discussed earlier to emphasize the need for measuring the variability of a set of data. Suppose, for instance, that a fairly large financial concern wants to determine the average number of incoming calls arriving at its switchboard over a ten-minute span. It needs this information to determine the adequacy of its present equipment, whether it has enough lines, and so forth. Suppose, furthermore, that the number of incoming calls is recorded for 5 such ten-minute intervals and that the figures obtained are 14, 9, 11, 7, and 8. The mean of this sample is $\dfrac{14 + 9 + 11 + 7 + 8}{5}$ = 9.8, and in the absence of any other information it would seem reasonable to use this value as an *estimate* of the true average number of calls arriving at the switchboard over a ten-minute span. However, at the same time we must acknowledge the fact that if the experiment were repeated, if data were obtained for 5 other ten-minute intervals, the mean would probably be some number other than 9.8. Indeed, if we repeated the experiment over and over again, we might get such divergent values as 7.4, 11.6, 13.2, 8.2, 10.4, . . . , for the means of the respective samples. It will be assumed that these differences are due to chance (and not due to differences in the time of day or other possible factors), so that by studying the distribution of the $\bar{x}$'s we can learn something about the actual size of chance fluctuations. In other words, we can learn how the $\bar{x}$'s are scattered about the true mean they are intended to estimate, and, hence, we can learn something about the *error* to which we might be exposed when using a sample mean to estimate the mean of the population. It is customary to refer to this kind of distribution of $\bar{x}$'s as a *sampling distribution of the mean*. If it is based on values obtained from repeated random samples as indicated above, we call it an *experimental sampling distribution;* if it is based on appropriate mathematical theory, we call it a *theoretical sampling distribution.* In what follows, we shall first consider a theoretical sampling distribution of the mean for random samples from a very small finite population. After that we shall actually construct an experimental sampling distribution of the mean with reference to the above switchboard example.

For our first example, let us refer to the finite population with 5 elements mentioned on page 180, and let us suppose that its elements are the numbers 1, 2, 3, 4, and 5. Referring to the formulas on pages 34 and 51, we find that the mean of this finite population is $\mu = 3$ and that its standard deviation is $\sigma = \sqrt{2}$ (see also Exercise 1 on page 192). If we take a random sample of size 3 from this population, its mean can be as small as 2 or as large as 4. Listing the 10 possible samples, we obtain the results shown in the following table, where the middle column contains the probabilities of obtaining the different samples (based on the assumption of randomness), and the right-hand column contains the corresponding sample means:

Sample Values	Probability	$\bar{x}$
1, 2, 3	1/10	2
1, 2, 4	1/10	$2\frac{1}{3}$
1, 2, 5	1/10	$2\frac{2}{3}$
1, 3, 4	1/10	$2\frac{2}{3}$
1, 3, 5	1/10	3
1, 4, 5	1/10	$3\frac{1}{3}$
2, 3, 4	1/10	3
2, 3, 5	1/10	$3\frac{1}{3}$
2, 4, 5	1/10	$3\frac{2}{3}$
3, 4, 5	1/10	4

Using this table, we can now construct a distribution which shows the probabilities of getting the different values of $\bar{x}$ for random samples of size 3 from the given finite population. As can easily be verified, the values of this *theoretical sampling distribution of the mean*, whose histogram is shown in Figure 7.2, are

$\bar{x}$	Probability
2	1/10
$2\frac{1}{3}$	1/10
$2\frac{2}{3}$	2/10
3	2/10
$3\frac{1}{3}$	2/10
$3\frac{2}{3}$	1/10
4	1/10

This sampling distribution tells us that if a random sample of size 3 is taken from the finite population which consists of the numbers 1, 2, 3, 4, and 5, the probability that $\bar{x}$ will equal 2 is $1/10$, the probability that $\bar{x}$

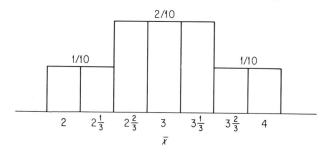

2/10

1/10 1/10

| 2 | $2\frac{1}{3}$ | $2\frac{2}{3}$ | 3 | $3\frac{1}{3}$ | $3\frac{2}{3}$ | 4 |

$\bar{x}$

FIGURE 7.2

will equal $2\frac{1}{3}$ is $1/10$, the probability that it will equal $2\frac{2}{3}$ is $2/10$, and so on. In particular, the distribution tells us that (in this example) the probability that a sample mean is "off" by $1/3$ *or less* is equal to $6/10$, while the probability that it is "off" by as much as 1 is equal to $2/10$.

Further useful descriptions of this (and other) sampling distributions are given by the mean $\mu_{\bar{x}}$ and the standard deviation $\sigma_{\bar{x}}$, where we are using the subscript $\bar{x}$ to indicate that we are referring to the mean and the standard deviation of the sampling distribution of the mean. In accordance with the definitions on pages 148 and 151 we have

$$\mu_{\bar{x}} = 2(\tfrac{1}{10}) + 2\tfrac{1}{3}(\tfrac{1}{10}) + 2\tfrac{2}{3}(\tfrac{2}{10}) + 3(\tfrac{2}{10}) + 3\tfrac{1}{3}(\tfrac{2}{10}) + 3\tfrac{2}{3}(\tfrac{1}{10}) + 4(\tfrac{1}{10})$$
$$= 3$$

and

$$\sigma_{\bar{x}}^2 = (2-3)^2(\tfrac{1}{10}) + (2\tfrac{1}{3}-3)^2(\tfrac{1}{10}) + (2\tfrac{2}{3}-3)^2(\tfrac{2}{10}) + (3-3)^2(\tfrac{2}{10})$$
$$+ (3\tfrac{1}{3}-3)^2(\tfrac{2}{10}) + (3\tfrac{2}{3}-3)^2(\tfrac{1}{10}) + (4-3)^2(\tfrac{1}{10})$$
$$= \tfrac{1}{3}$$

so that $\sigma_{\bar{x}}$ equals approximately 0.577. Note that the mean of this sampling distribution equals the mean of the population. The standard deviation of this sampling distribution will be discussed further on page 191.

To give an example of an *experimental sampling distribution* of the mean, let us return to the problem of estimating the true average number of calls arriving at a company's switchboard over a ten-minute span, and let us suppose that 40 repetitions of the experiment yielded the results shown in the following table:

Sample	No. of Calls	Sample	No. of Calls
1	14, 9, 11, 7, 8	21	10, 11, 8, 6, 15
2	4, 10, 10, 13, 8	22	8, 11, 9, 7, 13
3	6, 12, 9, 9, 12	23	13, 8, 9, 6, 11
4	8, 6, 6, 8, 9	24	4, 11, 9, 5, 5
5	12, 5, 8, 9, 20	25	9, 9, 11, 7, 4
6	8, 12, 9, 8, 4	26	8, 12, 11, 7, 8
7	9, 17, 11, 11, 8	27	8, 14, 8, 10, 7
8	5, 7, 9, 7, 7	28	4, 10, 11, 10, 5
9	11, 9, 5, 12, 10	29	10, 11, 7, 11, 10
10	12, 11, 9, 11, 8	30	10, 7, 10, 5, 10
11	5, 15, 10, 9, 8	31	12, 13, 6, 12, 8
12	13, 10, 9, 13, 16	32	11, 12, 7, 10, 6
13	4, 14, 8, 5, 10	33	15, 12, 7, 10, 17
14	12, 9, 11, 10, 15	34	12, 5, 6, 12, 15
15	11, 10, 7, 13, 13	35	10, 15, 9, 14, 6
16	9, 7, 13, 7, 17	36	6, 8, 10, 11, 8
17	17, 7, 9, 9, 9	37	8, 7, 12, 9, 7
18	13, 8, 5, 6, 14	38	11, 13, 7, 4, 12
19	9, 11, 10, 13, 8	39	8, 8, 8, 6, 9
20	9, 10, 10, 7, 6	40	12, 10, 9, 12, 11

Each of these samples contains 5 values, namely, the number of incoming calls recorded over 5 different ten-minute intervals of time. Calculating the means of these 40 samples, we obtain

9.8	9.0	9.6	7.4	10.8	8.2	11.2	7.0	9.4	10.2
9.4	12.2	8.2	11.4	10.8	10.6	10.2	9.2	10.2	8.4
10.0	9.6	9.4	6.8	8.0	9.2	9.4	8.0	9.8	8.4
10.2	9.2	12.2	10.0	10.8	8.6	8.6	9.4	7.8	10.8

and an over-all picture of their distribution is given by the histogram of Figure 7.3. Inspection of this distribution provides us with quite some information about the scattering (that is, the chance fluctuations) of these means. For instance, we find that 28 out of 40 (or 70 per cent) of the means fall on the interval from 7.5 to 10.5, and that 38 out of 40 (or 95 per cent) of the means fall on the interval from 6.5 to 11.5.

This information becomes more meaningful and easier to interpret if we reveal the fact that the 40 samples were obtained with the use of random numbers, *simulating* a population for which the probabilities of getting the values 0, 1, 2, 3, . . . , are given by a Poisson distribution (see Exercise 12 on page 140) with the mean $\mu = 9$ and the standard deviation $\sigma = 3$.

How this was actually done is explained in Technical Note 6. Using the fact that the mean of the population is $\mu = 9$, we can restate our description of the distribution of Figure 7.3 by saying that 70 per cent of the sample means were "off" by at most 1.5, and that 95 per cent of the

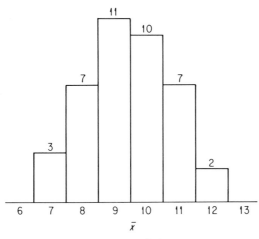

FIGURE 7.3

sample means were "off" by at most 2.5. This kind of information is important, inasmuch as it tells us how close we can expect a sample mean to be to the mean of the population, namely, the quantity it is supposed to estimate.

The two examples of this section were designed to introduce the concept of a sampling distribution, and it must be remembered that in actual practice we usually have only one sample, not 40, and we seldom can afford to go to the extreme of enumerating all possible samples from a finite population and thus construct a theoretical sampling distribution. In most practical situations we have no choice but to use special theorems concerning sampling distributions; fortunately, this generally provides us with all the information we need. The following is the first of these theorems:

THEOREM Q. *If random samples of size n are taken from a finite population of size N with the mean μ and the standard deviation σ, the theoretical sampling distribution of x̄ has the mean μ and the standard deviation*

$$\sigma_{\bar{x}} = \frac{\sigma}{\sqrt{n}} \cdot \sqrt{\frac{N-n}{N-1}}$$ ★

One aspect of this theorem should not be surprising, and that is the fact that the mean of the sampling distribution of $\bar{x}$ equals the mean of the population. We already saw this in our first example, where the mean of the population as well as the mean of the sampling distribution of $\bar{x}$ equalled 3. The reader will be asked to verify this fact also for the distribution of $\bar{x}$ for random samples of size 2 and 3 from a given finite population of size 6 (see Exercises 2 and 3 on page 193).

It is customary to refer to $\sigma_{\bar{x}}$, the standard deviation of the sampling distribution of the mean, as the *standard error of the mean*. Its role in statistics is fundamental, as it measures the extent to which means fluctuate, or vary, due to chance. Regarding the above formula for $\sigma_{\bar{x}}$, note that it consists of the product of $\dfrac{\sigma}{\sqrt{n}}$ and $\sqrt{\dfrac{N-n}{N-1}}$. The first of these two factors displays the following two important pieces of information:

1. *If σ is large and there is considerable variation in the population from which the sample is obtained, we can expect proportionately large fluctuations in the distribution of the means.*

2. *The larger the sample size n, the smaller is the variation among the means and the closer we can expect a sample mean to be to the mean of the population.*

Both of these arguments should seem plausible on intuitive grounds. After all, if there is considerable variability in the values from which the sample is obtained, this is apt to reflect also in the sample; so far as the second point is concerned, it stands to reason that if we have more information, we should also get better, that is, more reliable, estimates.

The second factor in the formula for $\sigma_{\bar{x}}$ is often omitted unless the sample constitutes a substantial portion of the population. For instance, if $n = 100$ and $N = 10,000$ (and the sample constitutes but 1 per cent of the population),

$$\sqrt{\frac{N-n}{N-1}} = \sqrt{\frac{10,000 - 100}{10,000 - 1}} = 0.995$$

which is so close to 1 that this factor can be ignored (for most practical purposes) in calculating the standard error of the mean.

Returning for a moment to the example where we constructed the sampling distribution of the mean for random samples of size 3 from a given finite population of size 5, we had $\sigma = \sqrt{2}$ (see page 186), and substituting this value together with $n = 3$ and $N = 5$ into the formula for $\sigma_{\bar{x}}$ yields

$$\sigma_{\bar{x}} = \frac{\sqrt{2}}{\sqrt{3}} \cdot \sqrt{\frac{5-3}{5-1}} = \frac{1}{\sqrt{3}}$$

This agrees with the calculations on page 187, where we showed that the variance of this theoretical sampling distribution of $\bar{x}$ is $1/3$. In Exercises 2 and 3 on page 193, the reader will be asked to verify this formula for $\sigma_{\bar{x}}$ also for the sampling distributions of $\bar{x}$ for random samples of size 2 and 3 from a given finite population of size 6.

Since the factor $\sqrt{\dfrac{N-n}{N-1}}$ approaches 1 when n is fixed and N becomes large, it suggests itself that this factor might be omitted altogether for random samples from *infinite populations*. That this is actually the case is expressed in the following theorem:

THEOREM R. *If random samples of size n are taken from an infinite population with the mean μ and the standard deviation σ, the theoretical sampling distribution of $\bar{x}$ has the mean μ and the standard deviation*

$$\sigma_{\bar{x}} = \frac{\sigma}{\sqrt{n}} \qquad \bigstar$$

In the light of this theorem, let us now take another look at the experimental sampling distribution which we constructed for the switchboard example, namely, the one where we took 40 random samples of size 5 and grouped their means into the distribution shown in Figure 7.3. As we pointed out on page 188, the mean and the standard deviation of the population from which these samples were obtained are $\mu = 9$ and $\sigma = 3$, so that according to Theorem R we would expect $\mu_{\bar{x}} = 9$ and $\sigma_{\bar{x}} = \dfrac{3}{\sqrt{5}} = 1.34$. Actually calculating the mean and the standard deviation of the distribution whose histogram is shown in Figure 7.3, we obtain 9.4 and 1.32, respectively, and although these experimental values are not *identical* with the ones we might expect according to Theorem R, they are sufficiently close to provide some sort of experimental verification of the formulas of Theorem R. In Exercise 4 on page 193, the reader will be asked to verify the formulas *exactly* for random samples of size 2 from a special kind of infinite population.

To illustrate how the results of Theorems Q and R are actually applied, we require another theorem, called the *Central Limit Theorem*, which provides some general information about the over-all shape of sampling distributions of $\bar{x}$. In fact, it tells us that for reasonably large samples such sampling distributions can be approximated very closely with certain *continuous* distribution curves called *normal* curves. Since this requires the introduction of several new concepts, we shall defer discussion of this matter until the following section. However, applying *Chebyshev's Theorem* (Theorem P on page 177) to the sampling distribution of $\bar{x}$, we can assert with a probability of *at least* $1 - 1/k^2$ that the mean of a random sample of size n will differ from the mean of the population from which it was obtained by at most $k \cdot \sigma_{\bar{x}}$. Thus, if we take a random sample of size 64 from an infinite population with $\sigma = 20$, we can assert with a probability of at least $1 - 1/2^2 = 0.75$ that the sample mean, used as an estimate of the mean of the population, is "off" by not more than

$$2 \cdot \frac{20}{\sqrt{64}} = 5.$$ Similarly, if we take a random sample of size 100 from an infinite population with $\sigma = 4$, we can assert with a probability of at least $1 - 1/5^2 = 0.96$ that the sample mean, used as an estimate of the mean of the population, is "off" by not more than $5 \cdot \dfrac{4}{\sqrt{100}} = 2$. Note that we are thus able to make probability statements about the mean of *one* sample without having to go through the tedious process of constructing an actual sampling distribution.

The main purpose of the preceding discussion has been to introduce the concept of a sampling distribution, and we chose for this purpose the sampling distribution of the mean. We could continue our study of sampling distributions by calculating the medians, the ranges, the standard deviations, or other statistics for the 40 samples on page 188 and grouping them into corresponding sampling distributions (see Exercises 6 and 7 below). Then we could also check how closely the standard deviations of these sampling distributions agree with the corresponding *standard errors* (obtained according to appropriate statistical theory), or otherwise compare the shape or other features of these distributions with theoretical expectations.

EXERCISES

1. Verify that the mean and the standard deviation of the finite population whose elements are 1, 2, 3, 4, and 5 are $\mu = 3$ and $\sigma = \sqrt{2}$.

2. Random samples of size 2 are taken from the finite population which consists of the numbers 1, 2, 3, 4, 5, and 6.

   (a) Show that the mean of the population is $\mu = 3.5$ and its standard deviation is $\sigma = \sqrt{35/12}$.

   (b) List the 15 possible random samples of size 2 that can be taken from this finite population and calculate their respective means.

   (c) Using the results of part (b) and assigning each of the possible samples a probability of $1/15$, construct the sampling distribution of the mean for random samples of size 2 from the given finite population.

   (d) Calculate the mean and the variance of the probability distribution obtained in part (c) and compare with the corresponding values expected according to Theorem Q.

3. Repeat parts (b), (c), and (d) of Exercise 2 for random samples of size 3 from the given population.

4. The finite population of Exercise 2 can be converted into an infinite population if we *sample with replacement*, that is, if we obtain the random sample of size 2 by first drawing one value and replacing it before drawing the second value.

   (a) List the 36 possible samples of size 2 that can be drawn with replacement from the given population.

   (b) Calculate the means of the 36 samples obtained in part (a) and, assigning each of the samples a probability of $1/36$, construct the sampling distribution of the mean for random samples of size 2 from this infinite population.

   (c) Calculate the mean and the standard deviation of the probability distribution obtained in part (b) and compare with the corresponding values expected according to Theorem R.

5. Convert the 40 samples on page 188 into 20 samples of size 10 by combining Samples 1 and 2, Samples 3 and 4, . . . , and Samples 39 and 40. Averaging the respective means of the original samples given on page 188, find the means of the 20 new samples, calculate their mean and their standard deviation, and compare with the corresponding values expected according to Theorem R.

6. Find the medians of the 40 samples on page 188 and calculate their mean and their standard deviation. Comparing the standard deviation of this experimental sampling distribution of the median with that of the corresponding experimental sampling distribution of the mean (which was 1.32), what do we learn about the relative "reliability" of the median and the mean in estimating the mean of the given population?

7. The variances of the 40 samples on page 188 are, respectively, 7.7, 11.0, 6.3, 1.8, 32.7, 8.2, 12.2, 2.0, 7.3, 2.7, 13.3, 7.7, 16.2, 5.3, 6.2, 18.8, 15.2, 16.7, 3.7, 3.3, 11.5, 5.8, 7.3, 9.2, 7.0, 4.7, 7.8, 10.5, 2.7, 5.3, 9.2, 6.7, 15.7, 18.5, 13.7, 3.8, 4.3, 14.3, 1.2, and 1.7.

   (a) Group these sample variances into a distribution having the classes 0–5, 5–10, 10–15, ... (Note that there will be no ambiguities since none of values actually equals 5, 10, 15, ...)

   (b) Calculate the mean of this sampling distribution of s^2 obtained in part (a) and compare the result with the population variance $\sigma^2 = 9$.

8. What happens to the standard error of the mean (and, hence, to the size of the errors to which we are exposed when we use an $\bar{x}$ to estimate a μ) when the sample size is increased from 50 to 200? (Assume you are dealing with an infinite population.)

9. What happens to the standard error of the mean for random samples from an infinite population, when the sample size is changed from 64 to 576?

(The exercises which follow are based on the material discussed in Technical Note 6.)

10. Using four random digits to represent the result obtained when tossing four balanced coins (0, 2, 4, 6, and 8 represent *head* while 1, 3, 5, 7, and 9 represent *tail*), simulate an experiment consisting of 160 tosses of four coins. Compare the observed number of times that 0, 1, 2, 3, and 4 heads occurred with the corresponding expected frequencies which are 10, 40, 60, 40, and 10.

11. The infinite population for which $x = 1, 2, 3, \ldots, 10,$ and 11 with respective probabilities of 0.01, 0.03, 0.07, 0.12, 0.17, 0.20, 0.17, 0.12, 0.07, 0.03, and 0.01, has the mean $\mu = 6$ and the standard deviation $\sigma = 2$.

   (a) Use the two-digit random numbers 00 through 99 to simulate an experiment which consists of taking 100 random samples of size 5 from the given population.

   (b) Calculate the means of the 100 samples obtained in part (a) and group them into a suitable frequency table.

   (c) Calculate the mean and the standard deviation of the experimental sampling distribution of the mean obtained in part (b) and compare with the corresponding values expected according to Theorem R.

12. Use random numbers and the scheme on page 214 to simulate an experiment in which 50 random samples of size 4 are taken from a population having the Poisson distribution with $\mu = 9$ and $\sigma = 3$. Group the

means of the 50 samples into a suitable distribution and compare the
mean and the standard deviation of this sampling distribution with
the corresponding values expected according to Theorem R.

13. Referring to Exercise 2, label the 15 possible samples listed in part (b)
1, 2, 3, ..., 14, and 15, and then use random numbers to simulate an
experiment in which 100 random samples of size 2 are taken from the
given finite population. Calculate the means of these 100 samples and
compare their distribution (converting the frequencies into proportions) with the corresponding theoretical sampling distribution
obtained in part (c) of that exercise.

14. Assign the numbers 1, 2, 3, ..., 35, and 36 to the 36 samples listed in
part (a) of Exercise 4, and then use random numbers to simulate an
experiment in which 100 random samples of size 2 are taken from the
given infinite population. Calculate the means of these 100 samples
and compare their distribution (converting the frequencies into proportions) with the corresponding theoretical sampling distribution
obtained in part (b) of that exercise. Is there an easier way of using
random numbers to simulate this experiment?

The Normal Distribution

When we first discussed histograms in Chapter 2, we pointed out that
the frequencies, percentages, or proportions (and we might now add

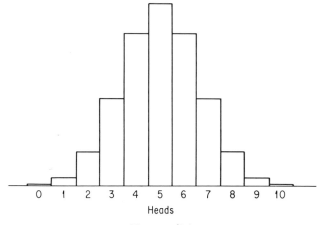

Heads

FIGURE 7.4

probabilities) that are associated with the various classes are represented
by the *areas* of the rectangles. For example, the areas of the rectangles
of Figure 7.4 represent the probabilities of getting 0, 1, 2, ..., and

10 heads in 10 tosses of a balanced coin or, better, they are equal or proportional to these probabilities. If we now look carefully at Figure 7.5, which is an enlargement of a portion of Figure 7.4, it is apparent that the

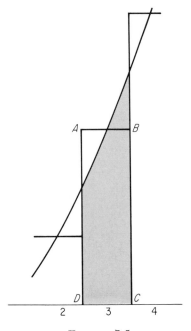

FIGURE 7.5

area of rectangle $ABCD$ is nearly equal to the shaded area under the continuous curve which we have drawn to approximate the histogram. Since the area of rectangle $ABCD$ is equal to (or proportional to) the probability of getting 3 heads in 10 tosses of a balanced coin, we can say that this probability is also given by the shaded area under the continuous curve. More generally, *if a histogram is approximated by means of a smooth curve, the frequency, percentage, or probability associated with any given class (or interval) is represented by the corresponding area under the curve.*

If we approximate the distribution of 1960 family incomes in the United States with a smooth curve, as we did in Figure 7.6, we can determine what proportion of the incomes falls into any given interval by looking at the corresponding area under the curve. By comparing the shaded area of Figure 7.6 with the total area under the curve (representing 100 per cent), we can judge that roughly 16 or 17 per cent of the families ad incomes of $10,000 or more. It can similarly be seen from Figure 7.6 that about 44 per cent of the families had incomes under $5,000. We obtained these percentages by (mentally) dividing the corresponding areas under the curve by the total area under the curve.

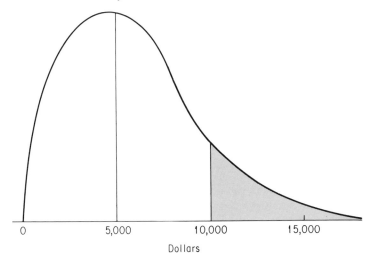

FIGURE 7.6. 1960 family incomes in the United States. (*Source:* 1962 Statistical Abstract of the United States.)

Had we drawn Figure 7.6 so that the total area under the curve actually equaled 1, the proportion of the families belonging to any income group would have been given directly by the corresponding area under the curve. Indeed, we shall refer to a curve as a *distribution curve* or as a *continuous distribution* if the area under the curve between any two values a and b (see Figure 7.7) *equals* the proportion of the cases falling between a and b. It follows that for a continuous distribution the total

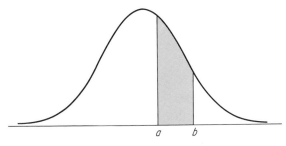

FIGURE 7.7

area under the curve must always be equal to 1. Repeating this definition in terms of probabilities, *we refer to a curve as a continuous distribution curve if the area under the curve between any two values a and b equals the probability of getting a value between a and b.*

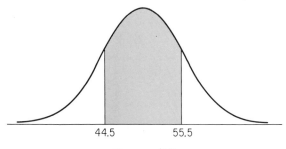

44.5   55.5

FIGURE 7.8

For instance, if the curve of Figure 7.8 approximates the probability distribution of the number of housewives who prefer Package A to Package B in a random sample of 100 housewives (drawn from a very large population in which 50 per cent of the housewives prefer Package A and 50 per cent prefer Package B), the probability of getting anywhere from 45 to 55 housewives preferring Package A is given by the shaded area of Figure 7.8. Note that we shaded the area between 44.5 and 55.5 and *not* the area between 45 and 55. The number of housewives favoring Package A can only be a whole number, and in order to approximate the probability distribution with a continuous curve we must make the *continuity correction* of letting each integer k be represented by the interval from $k - 1/2$ to $k + 1/2$. Thus, 45 is represented by the interval from 44.5 to 45.5, . . . , 55 is represented by the interval from 54.5 to 55.5; and "45 to 55 housewives" is represented by the interval from 44.5 to 55.5.

Since continuous distribution curves can always be looked upon as close approximations to histograms, we can define the mean and the standard deviation of continuous distributions (informally) in the following way: if a continuous distribution is approximated with a sequence of histograms having narrower and narrower classes, the means of the distributions represented by these histograms will approach a value which defines the mean of the continuous distribution. Similarly, the standard deviations of these distributions will approach a value which defines the standard deviation of the continuous distribution. Intuitively speaking, the mean and the standard deviation of a continuous distribution measure the identical features as the mean and the standard deviation

on of an ordinary frequency distribution (or a probability distribution),
amely, its center and its spread. More rigorous definitions of these
ɔncepts cannot be given without the use of calculus.

Among the many continuous distributions used in statistics, the *normal*
urve, or the *normal distribution*, is by far the most important. Its study
ates back to the eighteenth century and investigations into the nature
f experimental errors. It was observed that discrepancies between
ɛpeated measurements of the same physical quantity displayed a sur-
rising degree of regularity; their patterns (distribution), it was found,
ɔuld be closely approximated by a certain kind of continuous distribution
urve, referred to as the "normal curve of errors" and attributed to the
ɪws of chance. The mathematical properties of this kind of continuous
istribution curve and its theoretical basis were first investigated by
ʲierre Laplace (1749–1827), Abraham de Moivre (1667–1745), and Carl
ɟauss (1777–1855).

The normal curve is a bell-shaped curve that extends indefinitely in
ɔth directions. Although this may not be apparent from a small drawing
ke the one of Figure 7.9, the curve comes closer and closer to the

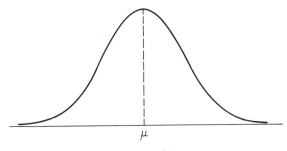

FIGURE 7.9

orizontal axis without ever reaching it, no matter how far we might go
ɪ either direction away from the mean. Fortunately, it is seldom neces-
ary to extend the tails of the normal curve very far because the area
ɪnder that part of the curve lying more than 4 or 5 standard deviations
way from the mean is for most practical purposes negligible.

An important property of a normal curve is that it is completely deter-
ɲined by its mean and its standard deviation. In other words, the mathe-
ɲatical equation for the normal curve is such that we can determine the
ɹrea under the curve between any two points on the horizontal scale if we
ɹre given its mean and its standard deviation. In practice, we obtain
ɹreas under a normal curve by means of special tables, such as Table I

on page 437. To be able to use this table, we shall first have to explain what is meant by the normal curve in its *standard form*. Since the equation of the normal curve depends on μ and σ, we get different curves and, hence, different areas, for different values of μ and σ. For instance Figure 7.10 shows the superimposed graphs of two normal curves, one having $\mu = 10$ and $\sigma = 5$, and the other having $\mu = 20$ and $\sigma = 10$

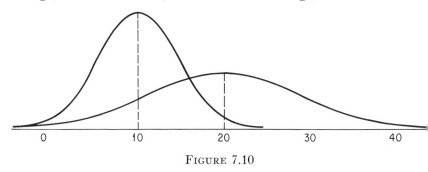

FIGURE 7.10

As can be seen from this diagram, the area under the curve, say, between 10 and 12, is *not* the same for the two distributions.

As it would be impossible to construct separate tables of normal curve areas for each conceivable pair of values of μ and σ, we tabulate these areas only for the so-called *standard normal distribution* which has $\mu = 0$ and $\sigma = 1$. Then, we obtain areas under *any* normal distribution by performing

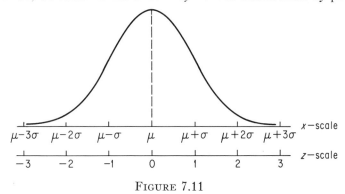

FIGURE 7.11

ing the change of scale shown in Figure 7.11. All that is really necessary is to convert the units of measurement into *standard units* (see page 57 by means of the formula

$$z = \frac{x - \mu}{\sigma}$$

To find areas under normal curves whose mean and standard deviation are *not* 0 and 1, we have only to convert the *x*'s (the values to the left of which, to the right of which, or between which we want to determine areas under the curve) into *z*'s and then use Table I on page 437. *The entries in this table are the areas under the standard normal distribution between the mean ($z = 0$) and $z = 0.00, 0.01, 0.02. \ldots, 3.08$, and 3.09.* In other words, the entries in Table I are areas under the standard normal distribution like the one shaded in Figure 7.12. Note that Table I has

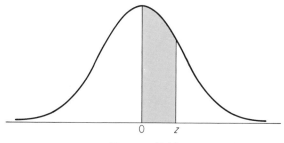

FIGURE 7.12

no entries corresponding to negative values of *z*, but these are not needed by virtue of the *symmetry* of a normal curve about its mean. We can thus find the area under the standard normal distribution, say, between $z = -1.25$ and $z = 0$, by looking up the area between $z = 0$ and $z = 1.25$. As can be checked in Table I, the answer is 0.3944.

Questions concerning areas under normal distributions arise in various ways, and the ability to find any desired area quickly can be a big help. For instance, although the table gives only the areas between the mean and selected values of *z*, we often have to find areas to the right of a given *z*, to the right or left of $-z$, between $-z$ and *z*, and so forth. Finding any one of these areas is easy, provided we remember exactly what part of the curve is referred to by a tabular value and the following property of the normal curve: since the curve is symmetrical about its mean, the area to the right of the mean as well as the area to the left of the mean is 0.5000. With this knowledge we find, for example, that the probability of getting a *z* less than 1.64 (the area to the left of $z = 1.64$) is $0.5000 + 0.4495 = 0.9495$, and that the probability of getting a *z* greater than -0.47 (the area to the right of $z = -0.47$) is $0.5000 + 0.1808 = 0.6808$ (see also Figure 7.13). Similarly, we find that the probability of getting a *z* greater than 0.76 is $0.5000 - 0.2764 = 0.2236$, and that the probability of getting a *z* less than -1.35 is $0.5000 - 0.4115$

= 0.0885 (see Figure 7.14). The probability of getting a z between 0.95 and 1.36 is $0.4131 - 0.3289 = 0.0842$, and the probability of getting a z between -0.45 and 0.65 is $0.1736 + 0.2422 = 0.4158$ (see Figure 7.15).

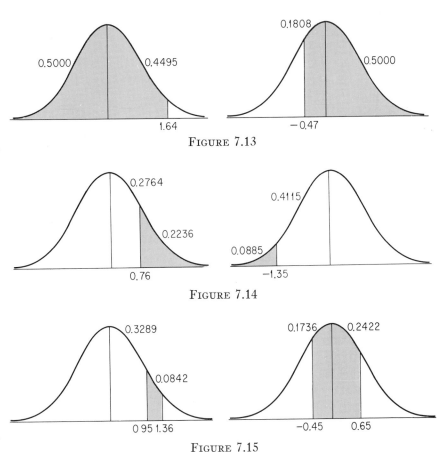

FIGURE 7.13

FIGURE 7.14

FIGURE 7.15

There are also problems in which we are given areas under the normal curve and we are asked to find corresponding values of z. For instance, if we want to find a z which is such that the area to its right is 0.1000, it is apparent from Figure 7.16 that this z will have to correspond to an entry of 0.4000 in Table I. Referring to this table, we find that the closest value is $z = 1.28$.

We are now in the position to verify the remark made on page 55, namely, that for reasonably symmetrical bell-shaped distributions we can expect about 68 per cent of the data to fall within one standard deviation of the mean, about 95 per cent of the data to fall within two standard deviations of the mean, and over 99 per cent of the data to fall within three standard deviations of the mean. These figures apply to normal distributions, and it will be left to the reader to verify that 0.6826 of the area under the standard normal curve falls between $z = -1$

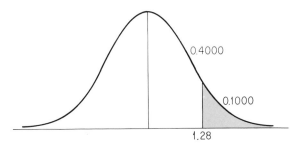

0.4000

0.1000

1.28

FIGURE 7.16

and $z = 1$, that 0.9544 of the area falls between $z = -2$ and $z = 2$, and that 0.9974 of the area falls between $z = -3$ and $z = 3$ (see Exercise 3 on page 208). This last result also provides a basis for our earlier remark that (although the tails extend indefinitely) the area under a normal curve lying more than 4 or 5 standard deviations from the mean is negligible.

To illustrate the use of Table I in connection with normal curves not given in the standard form, let us consider the following two applied examples:

The weights of a very large lot of packages of soap powder are approximately normally distributed with a mean of 3.5 ounces and a standard deviation of 0.25 ounces. (a) What is the probability that a package drawn at random from the lot weighs more than 3 ounces? (b) Above what weight can we expect to find the heaviest 2 per cent of the packages?

In part (a) of this problem we must find the area to the right of 3, or in standard units the area to the right of

$$z = \frac{3 - 3.5}{0.25} = -2$$

Looking up $z = 2$ in Table I we obtain 0.4772, and the desired probability is $0.5000 + 0.4772 = 0.9772$ (see also Figure 7.17). To solve part (b), we will first have to determine what z corresponds to a tabular entry of

0.4800 (see Figure 7.18), and then convert this value into the corresponding weight in ounces by means of the formula $z = \dfrac{x - \mu}{\sigma}$. Getting $z = 2.05$ from Table I, we obtain

$$2.05 = \frac{x - 3.5}{0.25}$$

and upon solving for x this yields $x = 2.05(0.25) + 3.5 = 4.01$. Expressed

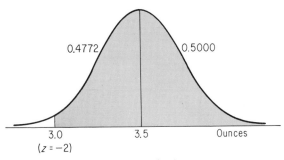

0.4772   0.5000

3.0   3.5   Ounces
$(z = -2)$

FIGURE 7.17

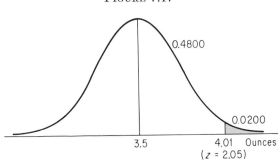

0.4800

0.0200

3.5   4.01   Ounces
              $(z = 2.05)$

FIGURE 7.18

in another way, this tells us that if we randomly selected a single package from the lot, the probability that its weight exceeds 4.01 ounces is 0.02.

A brass polish manufacturer wants to set his filling equipment so that in the long run only 3 cans in 1,000 will contain less than a desired minimum net fill of 31.4 ounces. It is known from experience that the filled weights are approximately normally distributed with a standard deviation of 0.2 ounces. At what level will the mean fill have to be set in order to meet this requirement?

n this problem we are given x, σ, and a percentage (a normal curve area), nd we are asked to find μ. As can be seen from Figure 7.19, we will first ave to find the z which is such that the normal curve area to its left quals 0.0030. Getting $z = -2.75$, we have

$$-2.75 = \frac{31.4 - \mu}{0.2}$$

nd upon solving for μ we finally obtain $\mu = 32.0$. Thus, if the equipment set to fill the cans on the average with 32.0 ounces (and if the distribu-

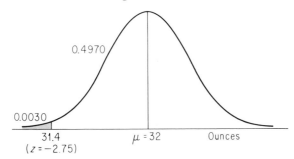

FIGURE 7.19

on of the fills is approximately normal with a standard deviation of .2 ounces), then in the long run only 3 cans in 1,000 will be below the esired minimum.

The normal distribution has many other important applications; it is sed, for instance, in the approximation of other probability distributions. Iow it serves to approximate the *binomial distribution* is discussed in 'echnical Note 7, and this is of special importance as it forms the basis or some of the methods treated in Chapters 8 and 9.

Since we must often assume that a set of data (perhaps, a population) as a distribution which can be approximated closely with a normal curve, would also seem desirable to have some way of checking whether this ssumption is at all reasonable. One such method, based on a special ind of probability graph paper, is discussed in Technical Note 8 on age 217.

We introduced the normal distribution in this chapter because of its asic role in the theory of sampling distributions. As we indicated on age 192, there exists a theorem, called the *Central Limit Theorem*, which ermits the use of normal curve theory in connection with the sampling istribution of $\bar{x}$. Formally, we have

THEOREM S. *If n is large, the theoretical sampling distribution of x̄ can be approximated closely with a normal curve having the mean μ and the standard deviation σ/√n, where μ and σ are the mean and the standard deviation of the infinite population from which the sample is obtained.*

This theorem applies also to samples from finite populations, provide that n (though large) constitutes but a very small portion of the popul tion. It is difficult to say precisely how large n must be so that th theorem applies; unless the distribution of the population has a ver unusual shape, the approximation will be good even if n is relativel small, say, $n = 30$. Note that the distribution of Figure 7.3 is fairl symmetrical and bell-shaped even though the sample size on which eac mean was based was only $n = 5$.

To illustrate the use of the Central Limit Theorem, let us refer to th first of the numerical examples on page 192, where we applied Cheb shev's Theorem to the sampling distribution of the mean. Taking random sample of size 64 from a population for which $σ = 20$, we aske for the probability that the mean of this sample will differ from the mea of the population by not more than 5. Referring to Figure 7.20, it ca

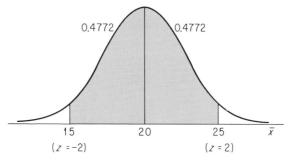

FIGURE 7.20

be seen that this probability is given by the normal curve area betwee $z = -2$ and $z = 2$ since $σ_x̄ = 20/√64 = 2.5$; Table I thus yields th result that the desired probability is $0.4772 + 0.4772 = 0.9544$. Not that without the Central Limit Theorem we were only able to asse that this probability is "at least" 0.75.

Although a sample of size 5 is ordinarily too small to apply the Centr Limit Theorem unless the distribution of the population itself follow closely the pattern of a normal curve, let us check briefly how the exper mental sampling distribution of $\bar{x}$ on page 189, the one based on the 40 means, agrees with what we might expect according to Theorem S. On page 188 we pointed out that 28 of the 40 means (or 70 per cent) fell on the interval from 7.5 to 10.5, namely, within 1.5 of the population mean $\mu = 9$. Since the standard deviation of the population equalled $\sigma = 3$, we had $\sigma_{\bar{x}} = 3/\sqrt{5} = 1.34$, and the probability of getting an $\bar{x}$ on the interval from 7.5 to 10.5 is given by the normal curve area between

$$z = \frac{7.5 - 9}{1.34} = -1.12 \quad \text{and} \quad z = \frac{10.5 - 9}{1.34} = 1.12$$

(see also Figure 7.21). It follows from Table I that the desired probability is $0.3686 + 0.3686 = 0.7372$, or in other words that we can expect

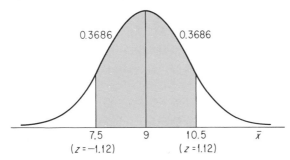

FIGURE 7.21

about 74 per cent of the sample means to fall on the interval from 7.5 to 10.5. This agrees quite well with the actual 70 per cent we obtained in the sampling experiment. In Exercise 11 below, the reader will be asked to show that for this sampling experiment the Central Limit Theorem would, similarly, lead us to expect about 94 per cent of the means to fall on the interval from 6.5 to 11.5, and this is very close to the 95 per cent we actually obtained.

EXERCISES

1. Find the normal curve area which lies

    (a) to the right of $z = 1.89$.

    (b) to the left of $z = 1.55$.

    (c) to the right of $z = -0.86$.

    (d) to the left of $z = -1.25$.

    (e) between $z = 1.05$ and $z = 1.45$.

(f) between $z = -0.85$ and $z = -0.65$.

(g) between $z = -1.78$ and $z = 0.84$.

2. Find z if

(a) the normal curve area between 0 and z is 0.4525.

(b) the normal curve area to the right of z is 0.2061.

(c) the normal curve area to the right of z is 0.8289.

(d) the normal curve area to the left of z is 0.6443.

(e) the normal curve area to the left of z is 0.0059.

(f) the normal curve area between $-z$ and z is 0.5034.

3. Find the normal curve area between $-z$ and z if

(a) $z = 1$.   (c) $z = 3$.   (e) $z = 2.33$.

(b) $z = 2$.   (d) $z = 1.96$.   (f) $z = 2.58$.

4. Assuming that the monthly food expenditures of families of a certain size in one income group are approximately normally distributed with a mean of $130 and a standard deviation of $20,

(a) What proportion of the expenditures are less than $70?

(b) What percentage of the expenditures are between $100 and $120?

(c) What percentage of the expenditures are either less than $120 or more than $150?

(d) Above what value does the top 10 per cent of the expenditures lie?

5. For a group of 1,800 employees of a national manufacturer, I.Q. is approximately normally distributed with mean 110 and standard deviation 12. It is known from experience that for a particular job only persons with I.Q.'s of at least 95 are intelligent enough for the work, but that those with I.Q.'s above 120 soon become bored and unhappy with it. On the basis of I.Q. alone, how many of the employees would you expect to be suitable for the work?

6. A manufacturer of household bleaches wants to set up his equipment so that on the average only 1 bottle in 100 will contain more than a desired maximum net weight of 12.3 ounces. Assuming that the fills can be closely approximated by a normal curve with a standard deviation of 0.1 ounces, what must the mean fill be in order to meet this requirement?

7. The mean time required to perform Job Q is 80 minutes with standard deviation 15 minutes, and the mean time required to perform Job R is 100 minutes with standard deviation 10 minutes. Assuming that both distributions of times can be closely approximated by normal curves, what percentage of Jobs Q take longer to perform than the average

Job R, and what percentage of Jobs R take less time to perform than the average Job Q?

8. A manufacturer guarantees chromium strips in this way: "Widths approximately normally distributed; on the average 3 strips in 1,000 wider than 2 inches; product relative variation 10 per cent." Assuming the correctness of the claim and that relative variation is measured by the *coefficient of variation*, show that the mean of the widths is 1.57 inches.

9. A manufacturer must buy coil springs which will stand at least a 15-lb load. Supplier A guarantees that his springs stand an average load of 20.5 pounds with a standard deviation of 2.1 pounds, Supplier B guarantees that his springs stand an average load of 19.9 pounds with a standard deviation of 1.5 pounds, and Supplier C guarantees that his springs stand an average load of 18.2 pounds with a standard deviation of 1.1 pounds. All distributions are assumed to be approximately normal. On the basis of the guarantees, which springs seem preferable to the manufacturer, and why?

10. A machine is set to fill "one-pound net" coffee cans with 16.2 ounces on the average. It is known from experience that the distribution of the weights is approximately normal with a standard deviation of 0.20 ounces.

    (a) If the filling process is "in control," how many of a lot of 100,000 cans may be expected to contain less than the desired one-pound net?

    (b) If the manufacturer wants on the average only 1 can in 500 to weigh less than a pound, at what level must the mean fill be set?

11. Show that if the Central Limit Theorem is applied to the illustration on page 188 (even though n is only 5), we can expect 94 per cent of the sample means to fall on the interval from 6.5 to 11.5. Compare this figure with the percentage actually observed.

12. A sample of 256 employees is chosen at random from among the employees of a very large company whose mean I.Q. is 100 with a standard deviation of 18.2.

    (a) What is the probability that the mean of the I.Q.'s in the sample will exceed 101.0?

    (b) What is the probability that the mean of the I.Q.'s in the sample will be less than 99.4?

    (c) What is the probability that the mean of the I.Q.'s in the sample will be less than 99.2 or more than 102.6?

    (d) What is the probability that the mean of the I.Q.'s in the sample will fall between 101.5 and 102.5?

13. In a large city the delinquent charge accounts in the three largest department stores are approximately normally distributed with a mean of $131.25 and a standard deviation of $20.25. If a sample of 100 accounts is taken at random from the population, what is the probability that the mean delinquency is (a) greater than $140.50, (b) less than $134.50, (c) between $127.00 and $129.00, and (d) less than $132.15 or more than $133.75?

14. If the weights of all men traveling by air from a large city have a mean of 162 pounds and a standard deviation of 20 pounds, what is the probability that the combined gross weight of 49 men on a plane departing from this city is more than 8,330 pounds?

(*Exercises 15 through 20 are based on the material discussed in Technical Note 7.*)

15. Find the probability of getting exactly 7 heads in 12 tosses of a balanced coin by using (a) the formula of Theorem O on page 137, and (b) the normal curve approximation to the binomial distribution.

16. Find the approximate probability of getting fewer than 40 or more than 60 heads in 100 flips of a balanced coin.

17. A manufacturer knows that on the average 3 per cent of his product is defective. Use the normal curve approximation to find the probability that there will be 15 or more defectives in a lot of 400.

18. If 60 per cent of the charge-account customers of a large department store make at least one purchase a week, what is the probability that in a random sample of size 100 selected from among the charge-account customers of the store at least 68 make at least one purchase a week?

19. If 45 per cent of the voters in a large school district are for a new bond issue while 55 per cent are against it, what is the probability that the bond issue will nevertheless be passed if a random sample of only 400 of the voters actually goes to the polls?

20. If the probability that a shipment from a large mail-order house gets lost or damaged in transit is 0.08, what is the probability that among 1,000 such shipments anywhere from 70 to 90, inclusive, get lost or damaged in transit?

(*The exercises which follow are based on the material discussed in Technical Note 8.*)

21. Use probability graph paper to check whether a normal curve provides a reasonably good approximation to the downtime distribution on page 15.

22. Plot the cumulative percentages of whichever data you grouped among those of the exercises on pages 19 through 21 on probability graph

paper and decide whether a normal curve provides a reasonably good fit.

23. Use probability graph paper to check whether a normal curve provides a reasonably good fit to the distribution of Exercise 8 on page 25.

24. Use probability graph paper to check whether a normal curve provides a good fit to the probability distribution of Exercise 11 on page 194. Also use this graph to estimate σ and compare with the actual value of 2.

25. Use the graph obtained in Exercise 21 to estimate the standard deviation of the downtime distribution and compare with the result obtained on page 54.

A Word of Caution

Having devoted most of our attention to the sampling distribution of $\bar{x}$ and the normal distribution, let us emphasize the point that we could parallel the discussion of the preceding sections by considering, say, the sampling distribution of s^2, the sample variance, and an appropriate theoretical distribution. We used the sampling distribution of $\bar{x}$ and the normal distribution because questions concerning the distribution of $\bar{x}$ arise more often in practice than questions concerning any other statistic. We might also add that the normal distribution provides the basis for many other theoretical sampling distributions, particularly if we are dealing with large samples. Indeed, even though the distribution of the sample variances in Exercise 7 on page 194 was highly skewed and very much *unlike* the normal distribution, it can be shown that if each sample had contained, say, 30 or 40 observations, the resulting distribution would probably have been close to the over-all pattern of a normal distribution.

A point worth repeating is that the experimental sampling distribution based on the 40 means and the theoretical sampling distribution for which we had to list all possible samples were meant to be *teaching aids*, designed to convey the concept of a sampling distribution. These examples do not reflect what we do in actual practice, where we must base an inference on *one* sample and not 40, and where there is seldom any need (or any advantage) to enumerate all possible samples. In Chapters 8 and 9 we shall delve more deeply into the problem of translating theory concerning sampling distributions into methods of evaluating the goodness of an estimate or the merits and disadvantages of a statistical decision procedure.

Another fact worth noting concerns the $\sqrt{n}$ appearing in the denominator of the formulas for the standard error of the mean. As we pointed out on page 190, it reflects the idea that if we get a larger sample and, hence, more information, the resulting generalizations should be subject to smaller errors and, in general, our methods should be more reliable and more precise. On the other hand, the formulas for $\sigma_{\bar{x}}$ also illustrate the fact that *gains in precision or reliability are not proportional to increases in the size of the sample*. That is, doubling the size of the sample does *not* double the reliability of $\bar{x}$ as an estimate of the mean of a population, and so on. As is apparent from the formula $\sigma_{\bar{x}} = \sigma/\sqrt{n}$ for samples from infinite populations, we must take 4 times as large a sample to cut the standard error in half, and 9 times as large a sample to triple the reliability, namely, to divide the standard error by 3. This clearly illustrates the fact that *it seldom pays to take excessively large samples*. For instance, if we increase the sample size from 100 to 10,000 (probably at a considerable expense), the size of the errors to which we are exposed is reduced only by a factor of 10. Similarly, if we increase the sample size from 50 to, say, 20,000, the chance fluctuations to which we are exposed are reduced only by a factor of 20, and this is seldom worth the cost of taking 19,950 additional observations. Note that this argument is not limited to the distribution of means; this "law of diminishing returns" concerning the information gained from samples applies also to most other statistics.

Technical Note 6 (Simulating Sampling Experiments)

Although we introduced random numbers originally to select random samples from finite populations, they are used for many other purposes. They serve to *simulate* almost any kind of gambling device; in fact, they can be used to simulate almost any situation involving an element of uncertainty or chance. For example, we can play the game of "Heads or Tails" without ever flipping a coin by letting the digits 0, 2, 4, 6, and 8 represent *heads* while the digits 1, 3, 5, 7, and 9 represent *tails*. Then, using, for instance, the 4th column of the table on page 447, we get 1, 5, 2, 0, 7, 5, 1, 0, 2, 5, ..., and we interpret this as *tail, tail, head, head, tail, tail, tail, head, head, tail, ...*

We can similarly simulate the simultaneous flips of 3 coins by using, say, the first three columns of the table on page 448. Getting 550, 325, 467, 354, 352, 557, 747, 333, 550, 638, ..., we interpret these results as getting, respectively, 1, 1, 2, 1, 1, 0, 1, 0, 1, 2, ... heads. If we did not want to use three columns of random numbers for this "experiment," we could make use of the results obtained on page 136, where we showed that the probabilities of getting 0, 1, 2, or 3 heads are, respectively, 1/8, 3/8, 3/8, and 1/8. Using the coding

Number of Heads	Random Digit
0	0
1	1, 2, 3
2	4, 5, 6
3	7

where the digits 8 and 9 are ignored whenever they occur), we interpret the random numbers 1, 5, 2, 0, 7, 5, 1, 0, 2, 5, ... in the fourth column of page 447 as representing, respectively, 1, 2, 1, 0, 3, 2, 1, 0, 1, 2, ... heads in three flips of a balanced coin. Note that if we did not want to "waste" any digits, we could have performed this experiment also with three columns of random numbers and the coding shown in the following table:

Number of Heads	Random Digits
0	000–124
1	125–499
2	500–874
3	875–999

With this scheme, the random numbers 213, 109, 915, 657, and 359, for example, represent 1, 0, 3, 2, and 1 heads in repeated flips of three coins.

Proceeding as in this last example, we can simulate any kind of probability distribution, and this is usually much more satisfactory than tossing coins, drawing numbered slips out of a hat, rolling dice, or gambling with other kinds of physical models. In fact, this is what we did in the sampling experiment discussed in the text, where we took 40 random samples of size 5 from a simulated Poisson distribution with $\mu = 9$ and $\sigma = 3$ (see page 188). Getting the required probabilities from a handbook of statistical tables, we used the following coding:

Number of Incoming Calls	Probability	Random Digits
0	0.000	
1	0.001	000
2	0.005	001–005
3	0.015	006–020
4	0.034	021–054
5	0.061	055–115
6	0.091	116–206
7	0.117	207–323
8	0.132	324–455
9	0.132	456–587
10	0.119	588–706
11	0.097	707–803
12	0.073	804–876
13	0.050	877–926
14	0.032	927–958
15	0.019	959–977
16	0.011	978–988
17	0.006	989–994
18	0.003	995–997
19	0.001	998
20	0.001	999

It will be left to the reader to verify that this assignment of random numbers provides the correct probabilities for the various outcomes. To illustrate how a sample of size 5 is obtained with this scheme, let us use the 13th, 14th, and 15th columns on page 446, starting from the top. Getting 889, 281, 202, 494, and 561, we note that the first number falls into the interval 877–926, the second falls into the interval 207–323, . . . and we thus translate these random numbers into a sample containing the values 13, 7, 6, 9, and 9. The main thing we watch in a problem like this is that the sets of random numbers assigned to the individual outcomes are proportional in size to the corresponding probabilities.

Some applied problems in which random numbers are used to simulate actual operations of a business (or parts of a business) will be taken up later in Chapter 13 under the heading of "Monte Carlo Methods"; this is merely another name for the simulation of situations involving uncertainties by means of random numbers or other gambling devices.

Technical Note 7   (The Binomial Distribution and the Normal Curve)

In Chapter 5 we obtained a formula for the probability of getting x successes in n trials when the probability of a success is p for each trial and the trials are independent. This formula for the so-called *binomial distribution* is easy to use when n is small, but it becomes troublesome when n is large. Fortunately, it can be shown that in that case the binomial distribution can be approximated closely with a normal distribution having the mean $\mu = np$ and the standard deviation $\sigma = \sqrt{np(1 - p)}$. (These are the expressions we gave on pages 150 and 152 for the mean and the standard deviation of the binomial distribution.) A good rule-of-thumb is to use this approximation only when np as well as $n(1 - p)$ exceed 5.

To illustrate this normal curve approximation of the binomial distribution, let us first consider the probability of getting 4 heads in 12 tosses of a balanced coin. Substituting $n = 12$, $x = 4$, and $p = 1/2$ into the formula on page 137, we get

$$\binom{12}{4}\left(\frac{1}{2}\right)^4\left(1 - \frac{1}{2}\right)^8 = \frac{495}{4,096}$$

or approximately 0.12. To determine the normal curve approximation to this probability, we shall have to employ the *continuity correction* mentioned on page 198, namely, represent 4 (heads) by the interval from 3.5 to 4.5. Since $\mu = 12(\frac{1}{2}) = 6$ and $\sigma = \sqrt{12(\frac{1}{2})(\frac{1}{2})} = 1.732$, we find that the values between which we want to determine the area under the standard normal curve are

$$\frac{3.5 - 6}{1.732} = -1.44 \quad \text{and} \quad \frac{4.5 - 6}{1.732} = -0.87$$

(see Figure 7.22). The corresponding entries in Table I are 0.4251 and

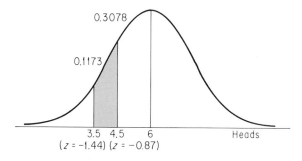

FIGURE 7.22

0.3078, and the required probability is $0.4251 - 0.3078 = 0.1173$. Clearly, the difference between this value and the exact value obtained above is negligible for most practical purposes.

The normal curve approximation of the binomial distribution is particularly useful in problems where we would otherwise have to use the formula for the binomial distribution repeatedly to obtain the values of many different terms. Suppose, for example, that the probability that a person responds to a mail questionnaire is 0.18, and that we want to know the probability of getting at least 12 replies to 100 questionnaires. (In other words, we want to find the probability of getting "at least 12 successes in 100 trials" when the probability of a success is 0.18.) If we tried to solve this problem by using the formula for the binomial distribution, we would have to find the sum of the probabilities corresponding to 12, 13, 14, . . ., and 100 successes (or those corresponding

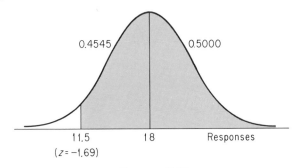

FIGURE 7.23

to 0, 1, 2, . . ., and 11). Evidently, this would involve a tremendous amount of work. On the other hand, using the normal curve approximation we have only to find the shaded area of Figure 7.23, namely, the area to the right of 11.5. Note that we are again using the continuity correction according to which 12 is represented by the interval from 11.5 to 12.5 and, in general, each integer k is represented by the interval from $k - \frac{1}{2}$ to $k + \frac{1}{2}$.

Since $\mu = 100(0.18) = 18$ and $\sigma = \sqrt{100(0.18)(0.82)} = 3.84$, we find that in standard units 11.5 becomes

$$\frac{11.5 - 18}{3.84} = -1.69$$

and that the desired probability is $0.4545 + 0.5000 = 0.9545$. This means that we can expect to get at least 12 replies to 100 questionnaires about 95 per cent of the time, provided that 0.18 is the correct figure for the probability of getting an individual reply. It is interesting to note that, rounded to two decimals, the *actual* value of this probability (obtained from an appropriate table) is 0.96.

Technical Note 8 (The Use of Probability Graph Paper)

There are various ways in which we can test whether an observed distribution fits the over-all pattern of a normal curve. The one which we shall discuss here is not the best; it is largely subjective, but it has the decided advantage that it is extremely easy to perform. To illustrate this technique, let us refer to the distribution of the 40 means of Figure 7.3 which, according to the Central Limit Theorem, should have roughly the shape of a normal curve. Converting this distribution into a "less than" percentage distribution (see page 16), we obtain

	Percentage of the Means
less than 6.5	0.0
less than 7.5	7.5
less than 8.5	25.0
less than 9.5	52.5
less than 10.5	77.5
less than 11.5	95.0
less than 12.5	100.0

Before we actually plot this cumulative distribution on the special paper illustrated in Figure 7.24, let us first investigate the scales of this kind of graph paper. As can be seen from Figure 7.24, the cumulative percentage scale is already marked off in the rather unusual pattern which makes the paper suitable for our special purpose. The other scale consists of equal subdivisions that are not labeled; in our problem they will be used to indicate the class boundaries 7.5, 8.5, 9.5, 10.5, and 11.5. This kind of graph paper (which is commercially available) is called *arithmetic probability paper*.

If we now plot the cumulative "less than" percentages corresponding to 7.5, 8.5, 9.5, 10.5, and 11.5, we obtain the points shown in Figure 7.24. *If such points lie very close to a straight line, we consider this as evidence that the distribution follows the pattern of a normal distribution.* In our example, the five points lie very close to the dotted line and we conclude that the over-all shape of the distribution of the 40 means

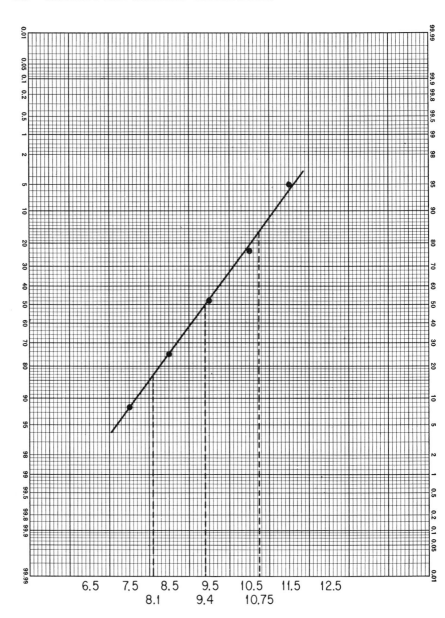

FIGURE 7.24 Arithmetic probability paper.

follows closely the pattern of a normal distribution. Note that in Figure 7.24 we did not plot points corresponding to 0 or 100 per cent of the data; as we pointed out earlier, the normal curve never quite reaches the horizontal axis no matter how far we go in either direction away from the mean.

The special graph paper which we have used in this example also provides us with a quick estimate of the mean and the standard deviation of a distribution, provided it has the shape of a normal distribution. To get the mean, we read off the value which corresponds to 50 per cent on the special percentage scale, and in our example we get 9.4. This agrees with the result indicated on page 191. Since roughly 68 per cent of the area under the normal curve corresponds to the interval from one standard deviation below the mean to one standard deviation above the mean, we can get an estimate of the standard deviation by reading off the values corresponding to 16 per cent and 84 per cent, and dividing the difference between these two values by two. In our example, we read off the values 8.1 and 10.75 corresponding to 16 per cent and 84 per cent, and we estimate the standard deviation as $\dfrac{10.75 - 8.1}{2} = 1.325$. This is very close to the result indicated on page 191.

EIGHT
DECISION MAKING: ESTIMATION

Problems of Estimation

According to some dictionaries, an estimate is a valuation based on opinion or roughly made from imperfect or incomplete data. Although this definition may be appropriate for a father's highly opinionated estimate of the ability of his son, a spy's imperfect estimate of a nation's military strength, or a politician's wishful thinking based only on returns from his own precinct, this is *not* how the term "estimate" is used in statistics. At least, this is not how it is used unless we are very careful in explaining what we mean by "opinion" and "incomplete," and if we ignore the terms "roughly" and "imperfect." In statistics we allow estimates based on opinions only if such opinions are based on sound judgment and experience, and we consider estimates based on "incomplete" data only if this means that we are using scientifically selected samples (rather than knowledge about entire populations).

Statistical methods of estimation find applications almost anywhere, in business, in science, as well as in everyday life. *In business*, a finance company may wish to estimate what proportion of its customers plan to buy a new car within the next calendar year, a contractor may wish to estimate the average monthly rent paid for two-room apartments in the city where he is planning to erect some new units, and a manufacturer of television tubes may wish to estimate how much variation there is in the lifetimes of his product. *In science*, a biologist may wish to estimate what proportion of a certain kind of insect is born physically defective, a psychologist may wish to estimate the average (mean) time it takes an adult to react to a given stimulus, and an engineer may wish to estimate how much variability there is in the strength of a new alloy. Finally, *in everyday life*, we may want to estimate what proportion of car accidents are due to faulty brakes, we may be interested in estimating the average time it takes to iron a shirt, and we may wish to know how much variation one can expect in a child's performance in school. Note that in each case we gave three examples: One dealing with the estimation of a *percentage or proportion*, one dealing with the estimation of a *mean*, and one dealing with an appropriate measure of *variation*. These (and in particular the first two) are the parameters with which we are concerned in most problems of estimation.

Referring again to the business examples, the finance company may estimate the proportion of potential new car buyers as 0.24, the contractor may estimate the required mean rent as $112.50, and the manufacturer may estimate the standard deviation of the lifetimes of all his tubes as 85 hours. Estimates like these are called *point estimates*, since each one consists of a single number, that is, a single point on the real number scale. Although this may be the most common way of expressing an estimate, point estimates have the serious shortcoming that they do not tell us anything about their relative merits; that is, they do not tell us how close we can expect such an estimate to be to the quantity it is supposed to estimate. In other words, *point estimates do not tell us anything about the intrinsic accuracy or precision of the method of estimation which is being used*. For instance, if an advertisement claims on the basis of "scientific" evidence that 75 per cent of all doctors prefer Brand Z cigarets, this would *not* be very meaningful if the claim were based on interviews with only 4 doctors among whom 3 happen to prefer Brand Z. However, the claim would become increasingly meaningful if it were based on interviews with 100 doctors, 400 doctors, or perhaps even 1,000 doctors. This illustrates why point estimates should always be accompanied by some information, some statement, which makes it possible to judge their merits. How this is done will be explained in the next section and in later parts of this chapter.

In most of the material covered in this chapter we shall assume that our estimates are to be based only on direct observations or measurements. If this kind of information is to be supplemented with collateral information, say, a person's experience and subjective judgment, we may have to use some form of *Bayesian inference*, like the one which we employed in Exercise 7 on page 153. Another example of a Bayesian inference (as it pertains to the estimation of means) is given in Exercise 12 on page 228.

The Estimation of Means

To illustrate the various problems we face in the estimation of a mean, let us consider the following example. For purposes of planning, scheduling, budgeting, and targeting a very large defense project, a major airframe manufacturer wishes to estimate the average time required to perform a certain mechanical assembly job, called "Job R." The performance times for thousands of times that the job has been performed in the past are available from company records, and the following figures constitute a random sample of size 40 taken from these job times (in hours):

$$
\begin{array}{cccccccc}
36.5 & 40.0 & 30.9 & 41.2 & 44.1 & 40.5 & 43.3 & 23.0 \\
40.5 & 35.8 & 21.9 & 34.6 & 34.2 & 39.6 & 46.1 & 28.7 \\
39.8 & 59.1 & 34.4 & 46.3 & 26.0 & 50.3 & 41.8 & 38.4 \\
49.9 & 31.0 & 54.5 & 40.4 & 53.4 & 31.9 & 36.5 & 37.5 \\
45.3 & 48.5 & 30.7 & 43.6 & 41.7 & 44.6 & 49.2 & 51.8
\end{array}
$$

The mean of this sample is $\bar{x} = 40.2$ hours, and in the absence of other information we shall use it as an estimate of μ, the *true* average time it takes for Job R.

To comply with the suggestion that point estimates should always be accompanied by information which makes it possible to judge their merits, we might add that the size of the sample on which this estimate is based is $n = 40$ and that the sample standard deviation is $s = 8.52$ hours. Unfortunately, this kind of information is meaningful only to those who have some knowledge of statistics. To make it meaningful also to the layman, let us go back briefly to the discussion of the preceding chapter, in particular to that dealing with the sampling distribution of the mean. Of course, we know that sample means will fluctuate from sample to sample, but we also know that the mean and the standard deviation of the distribution which describes these fluctuations (the sampling distribution of $\bar{x}$) are μ and $\sigma/\sqrt{n}$, where μ and σ are the mean and the standard deviation of the (supposedly infinite) population from which the sample was obtained. Making use of the fact that this sampling distribution can be approximated closely with a normal curve, we can now assert with a probability of 0.95 that $\bar{x}$ will differ from μ by less than 1.96 standard deviations (see Exercise 3 on page 208), or in other words

that $\bar{x}$ *will differ from* μ *by less than* $1.96 \dfrac{\sigma}{\sqrt{n}}$. *Since* $\bar{x} - \mu$ *is the error*

we make when we use $\bar{x}$ *as an estimate of* μ, *we can thus say that we are*

"95 per cent sure" that the magnitude of this error will be less than $1.96 \dfrac{\sigma}{\sqrt{n}}$.

Using the further results obtained in Exercise 3 on page 208, namely, that 98 per cent of the area under the standard normal distribution falls between -2.33 and 2.33 and that 99 per cent of the area falls between -2.58 and 2.58, *we can similarly assert with a probability of 0.98 that the*

error will be less than $2.33 \dfrac{\sigma}{\sqrt{n}}$ *or with a probability of 0.99 that the error*

will be less than $2.58 \dfrac{\sigma}{\sqrt{n}}$.

The result we have obtained here involves one complication: To be able to say something about the possible size of the error we might make when using $\bar{x}$ as an estimate of μ, we must know σ, the standard deviation of the population. Since this is not the case in most practical situations, we have no choice but to replace σ with an estimate, usually the sample standard deviation s. In general, this is considered to be reasonable provided the sample size is sufficiently large, and by "sufficiently large" we mean 30 or more.

Returning now to our numerical example, we can assert with a probability of 0.95 that if we estimate the *true* average time it takes to perform Job R as 40.2 hours, the error of this estimate is less than

$$1.96 \frac{s}{\sqrt{n}} = 1.96 \frac{8.52}{\sqrt{40}} = 2.64 \text{ hours}$$

Note that either the error of our estimate is less than 2.64 hours or it is not, *and we really don't know which.* However, if we had to bet, 19 to 1 (95 to 5) would be fair odds that the error is less than 2.64 hours. In other words, *the method we used to calculate the maximum error of 2.64 hours* *"works" 95 per cent of the time.*

When σ is unknown and n is less than 30, the method explained above cannot be used. However, there exists a modification of the formula for the maximum error to which we are exposed that applies also to small samples (n less than 30), provided it is reasonable to assume that the population from which the sample is obtained, or better its distribution, has roughly the shape of a normal curve. This modification is discussed in Technical Note 9 on page 243.

An interesting feature of the formula for the maximum error is that it can also be used to determine the sample size that is required to attain a desired degree of precision. Suppose we want to use the mean of a random sample to estimate the mean of a population and we want to be able to assert with a probability of 0.95 that the error of this estimate will be less than some quantity E. We can thus write

$$E = 1.96 \frac{\sigma}{\sqrt{n}} \qquad \star$$

and upon solving this equation for n we get

$$n = \left[\frac{(1.96)\sigma}{E} \right]^2 \qquad \star$$

Note that this formula cannot be used unless we know (or can approximate) the standard deviation of the population whose mean we want to estimate. Also, if the probability is to be changed from 0.95 to 0.98 or 0.99, we simply substitute 2.33 or 2.58 for 1.96 into the formula for n.

To illustrate this technique, suppose we want to estimate the average age of the presidents of major industrial concerns in the United States and that we want this estimate to be off by at most 1 year with a probability of 0.98. Suppose also that (on the basis of experience with similar data) it is reasonable to let σ be 5 years. Substituting these values into the formula for n with 2.33 instead of 1.96, we obtain

$$n = \left[\frac{(2.33)5}{1} \right]^2 = 135.7$$

and it follows that a sample of size $n = 136$ will suffice for the stated purpose. In other words, if we base our estimate on a random sample of size 136, we can assert with a probability of 0.98 that our estimate is within 1 year of the true mean.

The error we make when using a sample mean to estimate the mean of a population is given by the difference $\bar{x} - \mu$, and the fact that the *magnitude* of this error is less than $1.96 \dfrac{\sigma}{\sqrt{n}}$ can be expressed by means of the inequality*

$$-1.96 \frac{\sigma}{\sqrt{n}} < \bar{x} - \mu < 1.96 \frac{\sigma}{\sqrt{n}}$$

Applying some simple algebra, we can rewrite this as

$$\bar{x} - 1.96 \frac{\sigma}{\sqrt{n}} < \mu < \bar{x} + 1.96 \frac{\sigma}{\sqrt{n}} \qquad \star$$

and we can now assert with a probability of 0.95 that this inequality is satisfied for any given sample, namely, that the interval from $\bar{x} - 1.96 \dfrac{\sigma}{\sqrt{n}}$ to $\bar{x} + 1.96 \dfrac{\sigma}{\sqrt{n}}$ actually contains the mean we are trying to estimate. An interval like this is called a *confidence interval*, its endpoints are called *confidence limits*, and the probability with which we can assert that such an interval will "do its job," namely, that it will contain the quantity we are trying to estimate, is called the *degree of confidence*. Incidentally, if we want to use a degree of confidence of 0.98 or 0.99 instead of 0.95, we have only to substitute 2.33 or 2.58 for 1.96.

When σ is unknown and n is 30 or more, we proceed as before and estimate σ with the sample standard deviation s. The resulting 0.95 *large-sample confidence interval* for μ becomes

$$\bar{x} - 1.96 \frac{s}{\sqrt{n}} < \mu < \bar{x} + 1.96 \frac{s}{\sqrt{n}} \qquad \star$$

and if we substitute 2.33 or 2.58 for 1.96, we obtain the corresponding 0.98 or 0.99 large-sample confidence interval for μ. A corresponding *small-sample confidence interval* for μ, used when σ is unknown, n is less than 30, and the population distribution can be approximated closely with a normal curve, is given in Technical Note 9 on page 243.

---

* In case the reader has had no experience working with inequalities, let us briefly explain that $a < b$ means "a is less than b."

Applying this technique to our numerical example where we had $n = 40$, $\bar{x} = 40.2$, and $s = 8.52$ (see page 222), we obtain the following 0.95 confidence interval for the "true" average number of hours it takes to perform Job R:

$$40.2 - 1.96 \frac{8.52}{\sqrt{40}} < \mu < 40.2 + 1.96 \frac{8.52}{\sqrt{40}}$$

$$37.56 < \mu < 42.84$$

Had we wanted to calculate a 0.98 confidence interval for this example, we would have obtained

$$37.06 < \mu < 43.34$$

and this illustrates the interesting fact that *the surer we want to be, the less we have to be sure of.* In other words, if we increase the degree of certainty (the degree of confidence), the confidence interval becomes wider and thus tells us less about the quantity we want to estimate.

When we estimate the mean of a population with the use of a confidence interval, we refer to this kind of estimate as an *interval estimate.* In contrast to a point estimate, an interval estimate requires no further elaboration about its relative merits; this is taken care of indirectly by the degree of confidence and its actual width. To summarize, we can estimate the mean of a population either with an interval estimate or with a point estimate accompanied by some statement about the possible size of the error. Which method of estimation we use in any given situation will have to depend on the purpose for which the estimate is made, the audience for which it is intended, and similar nonstatistical considerations.

EXERCISES

1. A manufacturing company wants to estimate for a product that is custom made the mean time that elapses between the date of contract and the date of delivery. From a large file the company takes a random sample of 100 records and finds the mean time to be 85 days with a standard deviation of 15 days. If this mean of 85 days is used to estimate the desired mean time lapse between date of contract and date of delivery, what can be said with a probability of 0.95 about the possible size of the error?

2. A random sample of size 72 is taken from very extensive records or cash awards made to the employees of a company for helpful sugges-

tions. If the mean of this sample is $140 and its standard deviation is $25, construct a 0.95 confidence interval for the true mean of all the cash awards.

3. A sample of 36 fuses is randomly selected from a very large shipment and subjected to tests under prescribed conditions. The mean blowing time of the 36 fuses was found to be 12.15 seconds with a standard deviation of 0.12 seconds.

   (a) What can be said with a probability of 0.98 about the possible size of the error, if this mean of 12.15 seconds is used to estimate the mean blowing time of all the fuses in the very large shipment?

   (b) Use the data to construct a 0.99 confidence interval for the mean blowing time of all the fuses in the very large shipment.

4. In a cooking class 50 students prepare cookies with a given recipe requiring 8 ounces of peanut butter. On the average they obtain 31.3 cookies with a standard deviation of 1.4 cookies.

   (a) What can one assert with a probability of 0.99 about the possible size of the error, if this mean of 31.3 is used to estimate the average number of cookies obtained in all past, present, and future batches made with the given recipe?

   (b) Use the sample data to construct a 0.95 confidence interval for the true average number of cookies obtained with the given recipe.

5. A random sample of 40 No. 10 cans of sliced pineapple has a mean weight of 67 ounces and a standard deviation of 2 ounces. With what probability can we assert that the estimate of 67 ounces differs from the true average weight of all the cans from which the sample was obtained by less than 0.5 ounces? (*Hint:* Substitute z for 1.96 in the formula for E on page 224, solve for z, and find the normal curve area between $-z$ and z.)

6. A sample of 64 scores on an achievement test given to thousands of college freshmen has a mean of 245 and a standard deviation of 39. If this mean of 245 is used to estimate the average score obtained by all the college freshmen who took the test, with what probability can we assert that this estimate is "off" by not more than 10? (*Hint:* Substitute z for 1.96 in the formula for E on page 224, solve for z, and find the normal curve area between $-z$ and z.)

7. Before bidding on a contract, a manufacturer wants to be "98 per cent certain" that the company is in error by less than 5 minutes in its estimate of the average time required to perform a certain task. If the standard deviation of the performance times is assumed to be 15 minutes (on the basis of collateral information), how many times should the task be performed experimentally in order to estimate the true mean performance time?

8. A company wants to estimate with a degree of confidence of 0.95 and with an error not greater than $4.00 the true mean dollar size of orders for a particular item. How large a sample must the company take from its very extensive records to meet this requirement, if σ is assumed to equal $20.00?

9. If a sample constitutes an appreciable portion of a finite population (say, 5 per cent or more), the various formulas of the last section must be modified by basing them on the standard error formula of Theorem Q rather than that of Theorem R. For instance, the formula for E on page 224 becomes

$$E = 1.96 \frac{\sigma}{\sqrt{n}} \sqrt{\frac{N-n}{N-1}}$$

If a sample of 40 charges for service on a certain product randomly selected from a population of 160 such charges has a mean of $60.00 and a standard deviation of $20.00, what can be asserted with a probability of 0.95 about the possible size of the error if this mean is used to estimate the average of the 160 charges? Compare the result with that which would have been obtained if the "finite population correction factor" $\sqrt{\frac{N-n}{N-1}}$ had erroneously been omitted.

10. If the population from which the sample is obtained has roughly the shape of a normal distribution, the first confidence interval formula on page 225 applies also when n is small. Using it in connection with the samples obtained in Exercise 11 on page 194, the confidence limits can be written as $\bar{x} \pm 1.96 \frac{2}{\sqrt{5}}$ or as $\bar{x} \pm 1.75$, since $\sigma = 2$ and $n = 5$. Calculate a corresponding 0.95 confidence interval for each of the 100 samples obtained in that exercise and check what proportion contain the population mean which is $\mu = 6$. How does this proportion compare with expectations?

11. The 40 samples on page 188 were obtained from a bell-shaped distribution having the mean $\mu = 9$ and the standard deviation $\sigma = 3$. Assuming that the shape of this distribution is sufficiently close to that of normal distribution to use the 0.95 confidence limits $\bar{x} \pm 1.96 \frac{\sigma}{\sqrt{n}}$ calculate a corresponding 0.95 confidence interval for each of the 40 samples. Check what percentage of these confidence intervals actually contain μ and compare this figure with the 95 per cent we might expect.

12. (*A Bayesian inference*) Having had some experience with similar situations, three statisticians guess (or estimate subjectively) that the average daily demand for a new product will be, respectively, $\mu = 110$

$\mu = 120$, and $\mu = 124$ units. It is assumed that one of these figures must be correct and that the standard deviation of the daily demand for the new product is $\sigma = 25$.

(a) If figures are obtained on the daily demand for the new product on 100 days, find the probability that the mean of this sample will exceed 122.5 when $\mu = 116$.

(b) Find the probabilities [corresponding to the one asked for in part (a)] when $\mu = 120$ and $\mu = 124$.

(c) If the sample mean actually exceeds 122.5 and *a priori* the three statisticians are assumed to be about equally reliable (without direct information we assign each of their respective estimates a probability of $1/3$), what is the probability that $\mu = 124$? (*Hint:* Use Theorem N on page 132, letting A be the event that the sample mean exceeds 122.5, and letting B_1, B_2, and B_3 be the respective events that $\mu = 116$, $\mu = 120$, and $\mu = 124$.)

(d) Also find the probabilities that $\mu = 116$ and $\mu = 120$ given that the sample mean exceeds 122.5 and that the three statisticians are about equally reliable.

(e) Looking upon the probabilities obtained for the three values of μ in parts (c) and (d) as the values of a probability distribution for μ, calculate the mean of this probability distribution as a *Bayesian estimate* of the true average daily demand for the new product.

(*The exercises which follow are based on the material in Technical Note 9.*)

13. In a materials control study a large company selects a random sample of 4 item material costs from a large file of such costs which are assumed to be approximately normally distributed. If the sample mean is $\bar{x} = \$24.36$ and the sample standard deviation is $s = \$2.05$, construct a 0.95 confidence interval for the true average material costs of these items.

14. Test runs performed under standard conditions with 5 models of an experimental engine showed that on the average 2.6 gallons of gasoline were consumed in an hour with a standard deviation of 0.2 gallons of gasoline. If 2.6 is used as an estimate of the true average number of gallons this kind of engine will consume in an hour, what can we say with a probability of 0.95 about the possible size of the error of this estimate?

15. On page 34 we referred to a problem in which a manufacturing company was interested in determining the mean impact strength of thousands of wooden panels on the basis of a random sample of size 5. Using the figures given on that page, namely, 3,000, 3,210, 3,150, 3,400,

and 3,290 psi, construct a 0.98 confidence interval for the true averag
impact strength of the panels.

16. On page 52 we used a sample mean of $10.00 to estimate the tru
mean of all gifts to the United Fund in a certain area, and we suggeste
at the time that knowledge of the sample standard deviation s
important in judging the "closeness" of this estimate. Using the fac
that s equalled 4 and n equalled 6, what can we say with a probabilit
of 0.95 about the possible size of the error of this estimate?

17. A random sample of 9 breech blocks for an antiaircraft gun has a mea
of 0.6495 inches and a standard deviation of 0.0006 inches for a certai
dimension. Construct a 0.99 confidence interval for the true averag
value of this dimension.

18. A random sample of 6 daily scrap records (where scrap is expressed as
percentage of material requisitioned) shows 3.4, 4.0, 3.8, 6.0, 5.
and 4.4 per cent scrap. Construct a 0.98 confidence interval for th
true average percentage of scrap.

The Estimation of Proportions

The information that is commonly available for the estimation of
proportion (percentage, or probability) is the relative frequency wit
which a given event has occurred. If an event occurs x times out of n, th
relative frequency of its occurrence is x/n, and we generally use th
sample proportion to estimate the true proportion p with which we a
concerned. For example, if 316 of 400 housewives interviewed in a stud
preferred a new sweetened fruit soup to an unsweetened one, then $\dfrac{x}{n}$

$\dfrac{316}{400} = 0.79$, and we can use this figure as a point estimate of the tru
proportion of housewives preferring the new sweetened fruit soup to th
unsweetened one. Similarly, a large brokerage house might estimate
0.64 the proportion of its customers who recently sold stock to establis
losses for income tax purposes, if a sample check of 250 accounts show(
160 with sales for the given purpose.

In the remainder of this section we shall assume that the situations wit
which we are dealing satisfy (at least approximately) the conditions of tl
binomial distribution (see page 138). Our information will consist of ho
many successes there are in a given number of trials, and it will t
assumed that the trials are independent and that the probability of

success is p for each trial. In fact, p is the unknown proportion we are trying to estimate. Thus, the sampling distribution which describes the chance fluctuations of our estimates is essentially the binomial distribution, for which we indicated on pages 150 and 152 that its mean and its standard deviation are $\mu = np$ and $\sigma = \sqrt{np(1 - p)}$. An important aspect of these formulas is that they involve the "true" proportion p and, so far as σ is concerned, this causes some difficulties. In order to avoid these complications, at least for the moment, we shall begin by constructing confidence intervals for p with the use of tables designed specially for this purpose.

Tables V(a) and V(b) on pages 442 and 443 provide 0.95 and 0.99 confidence intervals for proportions; they apply to situations where the conditions underlying the binomial distribution are met at least approximately, they are easy to use, and they require practically no calculations. If a sample proportion is less than or equal to 0.50, we begin by marking the value obtained for x/n on the *bottom scale;* we then go up vertically until we reach the two contour lines (curves) which correspond to the size of the sample, and read the confidence limits for p off the *left-hand scale,* as indicated in Figure 8.1. If the sample proportion is greater than 0.50, we mark the value obtained for x/n on the *top scale,* go down vertically until we reach the two contour lines (curves) which correspond

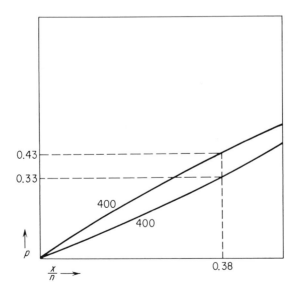

FIGURE 8.1

to the size of the sample, and read the confidence limits for p off the *right-hand scale*, as indicated in Figure 8.2.

To illustrate the use of Tables V(a) and V(b) when the sample proportion is less than or equal to 0.50, suppose that in a random sample of

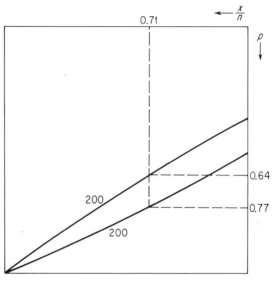

FIGURE 8.2

400 voters 152 are for a certain piece of legislation while 248 are against it. Marking $\dfrac{x}{n} = \dfrac{152}{400} = 0.38$ on the bottom scale of Table V(a) and proceeding as in Figure 8.1, we find that a 0.95 confidence interval for the true proportion of voters favoring the given piece of legislation is given by

$$0.33 < p < 0.43$$

In words, we can assert with a probability of 0.95 that the actual proportion of voters favoring the given piece of legislation is contained in the interval from 0.33 to 0.43. Had we wanted a 0.99 confidence interval for this proportion, Table V(b) would, similarly, have yielded

$$0.32 < p < 0.44$$

Note that the interval gets wider when the degree of confidence is increased.

To illustrate the use of Tables V(a) and V(b) when the sample proportion is greater than 0.50, suppose that a large bank wants to estimate what proportion of families without liquid assets have installment debts for automobiles, consumer purchases, etc.). Suppose, also, that a sample survey of 200 families without liquid assets included 142 with installment debts of some sort. Marking $\dfrac{x}{n} = \dfrac{142}{200} = 0.71$ on the *top scale* of Table V(a) (halfway between 0.70 and 0.72), and proceeding as in Figure 8.2, we find that the desired 0.95 confidence interval for the true proportion is

$$0.64 < p < 0.77$$

Using Table V(b) we similarly find that

$$0.62 < p < 0.79$$

is a 0.99 confidence interval for the true proportion of families without liquid assets which have installment debts of some sort. In words, we can assert with a probability of 0.95 that the actual proportion of families without liquid assets which have installment debts is contained in the interval from 0.64 to 0.77, and we can assert with a probability of 0.99 that the true proportion is contained in the interval from 0.62 to 0.79.

Note that in both of our examples Tables V(a) and V(b) had contour lines (curves) corresponding to the size of the samples; for values of n other than 8, 10, 12, 16, 20, 24, 30, 40, 60, 100, 200, 400, and 1,000, we literally have to read between the lines. For instance, the reader may wish to verify that for $x = 20$ and $n = 50$, Table V(a) gives the 0.95 confidence interval

$$0.26 < p < 0.55$$

When n is large and p is not too close to either 0 or 1, the binomial distribution can be approximated fairly well with a normal distribution having the mean $\mu = np$ and the standard deviation $\sigma = \sqrt{np(1 - p)}$ (see Technical Note 7 on page 214). Duplicating the argument on page 223, we can thus assert with a probability of 0.95 that the value which we obtain for x will differ from $\mu = np$ by less than $1.96\sqrt{np(1 - p)}$; *dividing everything by* n, this is equivalent to the assertion that the sample proportion x/n will differ from p by less than $1.96\sqrt{\dfrac{p(1 - p)}{n}}$. *Since the difference between x/n and p is the error which we make when using x/n as an estimate of p, we can thus assert with a probability of 0.95 that this error will be less than*

$$1.96\sqrt{\dfrac{p(1 - p)}{n}}$$

An unfortunate feature of this result is that we cannot calculate the size of the maximum error unless we know p, and of course p is the quantity we are trying to estimate. However, substituting x/n for p as an approximation, *we can assert with a probability of (roughly) 0.95 that the error will be less than*

$$1.96 \sqrt{\frac{\dfrac{x}{n}\left(1 - \dfrac{x}{n}\right)}{n}} \qquad \bigstar$$

In view of these various approximations (first we approximated the binomial distribution with a normal distribution, and then we approximated p with x/n), it is preferable to use this method of assaying the possible size of the error only if n is greater than or equal to 100.

To illustrate this technique, let us refer again to the example on page 232, where we had $x = 152$ and $n = 400$ in an experiment designed to estimate the true proportion of voters favoring a certain piece of legislation. Using the *point estimate* of $152/400 = 0.38$, we can now add that we are "95 per cent sure" that the error of this estimate is less than

$$1.96 \sqrt{\frac{(0.38)(0.62)}{400}} = 0.048$$

Note that $0.38 - 0.048 = 0.332$ and $0.38 + 0.048 = 0.428$ are very close to the 0.95 confidence limits we obtained on page 232 with the use of Table V(a). In fact, these values constitute the *large-sample confidence limits* suggested in Exercise 4 on page 236.

If we wanted to be able to assert with a probability of 0.98 or 0.99 that the error of our estimate is less than some appropriate amount, we could obtain this amount from the above expression after substituting 2.33 or 2.58 for 1.96. Thus, referring again to the installment debt example where we had $x = 142$ and $n = 200$, we can assert with a probability of 0.99 that if we estimate the true proportion as $142/200 = 0.71$, the error of this estimate is less than

$$2.58 \sqrt{\frac{(0.71)(0.29)}{200}} = 0.083$$

Note that 0.71 ± 0.083 gives values which are very close to the corresponding 0.99 confidence limits obtained on page 233 with the use of Table V(b).

As in the estimation of means, we can use the expression for the maximum error to determine how large a sample is needed to attain a desired degree of precision. If we want to be able to assert with a probability of 0.95 that our sample proportion will differ from the "true" proportion p by less than some quantity E, we can write

$$E = 1.96 \sqrt{\frac{p(1 - p)}{n}} \qquad \star$$

and upon solving for n, we get

$$n = p(1 - p) \left[\frac{1.96}{E}\right]^2 \qquad \star$$

Since this formula requires knowledge of p, the quantity we are trying to estimate, it cannot be used exactly as it stands. However, it can be shown that $p(1 - p)$ is at most equal to 1/4, and that it assumes this maximum value only when $p = 1/2$. *It follows that it is always "safe" to use the above formula with $p = 1/2$, although the resulting sample size may be unnecessarily large.* In case we do have some information about the possible range of values p might assume in a given example, we can take this into account in determining n. For instance, if it is reasonable to suppose that the proportion we are trying to estimate lies on the interval from 0.60 to 0.80, we substitute into the above formula whichever value is closest to 0.50; in this particular case we would substitute $p = 0.60$.

To illustrate this technique, suppose we want to estimate what proportion of household goods advertised in the classified ads of a local newspaper actually gets sold through this form of advertising. Suppose, also, that we want to be "95 per cent sure" that the error of our estimate is less than 0.05. *Having no idea what the true proportion might be,* we substitute $E = 0.05$, $p = 1/2$, and we get

$$n = \left(\frac{1}{2}\right)\left(\frac{1}{2}\right)\left[\frac{1.96}{0.05}\right]^2 = 384.16$$

Hence, if we base our estimate on a sample of size $n = 385$, we can assert with a probability of (at least) 0.95 that the sample proportion will not be "off" by more than 0.05. (We added the words "at least" because the sample size of 385 may actually be larger than required since we substituted $p = 1/2$.)

Had we known in this example that the quantity we are trying to estimate is in the neighborhood of, say, 0.30, the formula for n would have yielded

$$n = (0.30)(0.70)\left[\frac{1.96}{0.05}\right]^2 = 323$$

This illustrates the fact that if we do have some information about the possible size of the proportion we hope to estimate, this can appreciably reduce the size of the required sample. (Of course, if we wanted to use a probability of 0.98 or 0.99 in this kind of example, we would have only to substitute 2.33 or 2.58 for 1.96 in the formula for n.)

EXERCISES

1. The records of a large shoe store show that over a given period 720 of the 1,000 persons who entered the store bought at least one pair of shoes. Treating this as a random sample of *all* potential customers, construct a 0.95 confidence interval for the actual proportion of persons entering the store who will buy at least one pair of shoes.

2. In connection with the shoe store referred to in Exercise 1, the store's records also show that of the 400 men who bought shoes during a given period of time, 240 also bought socks. Treating this as a random sample of *all* potential male customers, find a 0.99 confidence interval for the actual proportion of male customers who buy socks as well as shoes.

3. A new candy vending machine installed in a bus terminal failed (did not either return the coin or release the candy) 16 times in the first 400 times it was used. Construct a 0.95 confidence interval for the true proportion of the time the machine will fail.

4. In a study of package design, a national manufacturer wants to determine what proportion of purchases of razor blades for use by men are actually made by women. If a random sample of 1,000 such purchases includes 220 made by women, construct a 0.95 per cent confidence interval for the actual proportion of such purchases made by women (a) using Table V(a), and (b) using the 0.95 *large-sample* confidence limits

$$\frac{x}{n} \pm 1.96 \sqrt{\frac{\frac{x}{n}\left(1 - \frac{x}{n}\right)}{n}}$$

suggested on page 234.

5. The largest bank in the country (with 26,000 employees) is considering a plan under which, at the employee's option, his pay will be deposited

directly in his checking account with the bank. In order to determine computer work loads, the bank wants to estimate the number of employees who will elect the plan, and it finds that in a random sample of size 200 there were 160 employees preferring the new option.

(a) Use Table V(b) to construct a 0.99 confidence interval for the true proportion of the employees who prefer the new option.

(b) Use the confidence limits of Exercise 4 with 2.58 substituted for 1.96 to construct a 0.99 confidence interval for the true proportion of the employees who prefer the new option. Compare with the result obtained in part (a).

(c) Use the result obtained in part (a) to construct a 0.99 confidence interval for the *number* of employees who prefer the new option.

6. In a survey to determine attitude towards various design and styling factors, a major automobile manufacturer takes a random sample of 500 owners of its station wagons. If 450 of these owners would prefer to have the third seat in a three-seat wagon facing the front, what can the company assert with a probability of 0.95 about the possible size of the error in the estimate of 0.90?

7. A large laundry records for one of its plants the number of shirts processed and the number rejected at final inspection because of faulty work. What can the management of the company assert with a probability of 0.98 about the possible size of the error, if it estimates the true proportion of shirts rejected at final inspection as 0.05 on the basis of a random sample of 300 shirts of which 15 were rejected?

8. An auditor wants to estimate the proportion of freight bills in a very large file that are in error (wrong rate, wrong extension, etc.).

(a) How large a random sample must he take to be 95 per cent sure that the sample estimate will not be off by more than 1 per cent? Assume that the auditor has no idea about the possible size of the true value of the proportion.

(b) How large a random sample must he take to be 95 per cent sure that the sample estimate will not be off by more than 1 per cent, if he can assume from experience that the true value is near 0.04?

9. A manufacturing company wants to determine what proportion of the thousands of items it buys are actually discounted from the list prices. If it wishes to estimate this proportion so that it can be asserted with a probability of 0.99 that the estimate is off by less than 5 per cent, how large a sample will the company have to take?

10. An insurance company, considering a "safe-driver plan" (with reduced rates on liability insurance for drivers who have neither had an accident

nor been cited for a traffic violation in the three previous years), want
to estimate what proportion of its many policy holders would qualify
for the plan. How large a random sample will have to be taken from
the company's files so that one can assert with a probability of 0.95
that the difference between the sample proportion and the true proportion will not exceed 0.02?

11. A large university is considering switching from the quarter plan to
the trimester plan and it wants to determine student attitude towards
such a change.

   (a) In the absence of any knowledge about the possible value of p
   what is the smallest random sample of student opinion needed so
   that the college can assert with a probability of 0.95 that the
   sample proportion will not be "off" by more than 4 per cent?

   (b) How would the sample size required in part (a) be affected, if it
   were known that in similar studies performed at other universities
   the proportion of students favoring the change was about 0.70?

12. If a sample constitutes a substantial portion (say, 5 per cent or more)
of a population, the methods of this section cannot be used without
appropriate modifications. If the sample itself is large, we can use
the same *correction factor* as in the estimation of means, and we can
write approximate 0.95 confidence limits for p as

$$\frac{x}{n} \pm 1.96 \sqrt{\frac{\frac{x}{n}\left(1 - \frac{x}{n}\right)}{n}} \cdot \sqrt{\frac{N - n}{N - 1}}$$

where N is, as before, the size of the population.

   (a) Referring to Exercise 11, suppose that in order to determine faculty
   sentiment toward the change, 250 of the 1,000 full-time members
   of the university are interviewed. Construct a 0.95 confidence
   interval for the true proportion of faculty members preferring
   the change, if the sample contained 195 who prefer the change.

   (b) A trade association took a random sample of 100 of its 300 member
   companies of whom 60 reported that new orders and production
   were up in a given month. Construct a 0.95 confidence interval
   for the true proportion of the trade association's member companies which had increased orders and production in the given
   month.

Further Problems of Estimation

So far we have learned how to construct confidence intervals for means
and proportions, and we have learned how to evaluate the precision of the

corresponding point estimates of μ and p. Although this will take care of a great variety of situations—in fact, the vast majority of problems of estimation—similar methods can be used to estimate other parameters of populations. By studying the sampling distributions of appropriate statistics, statisticians have developed confidence intervals for population standard deviations, medians, quartiles, and the like. In principle, the ideas are always the same and the main difficulty lies in the fact that some of these sampling distributions are mathematically quite involved. Fortunately, this difficulty is resolved by the important result that for *large samples* many of these sampling distributions can be approximated with normal curves. This means that if S is some statistic calculated from a large random sample, we can often write a 0.95 confidence interval for the population parameter which is estimated by S as

$$S - 1.96 \cdot \sigma_S < \text{population parameter} < S + 1.96 \cdot \sigma_S \qquad \bigstar$$

Here σ_S is the standard deviation of the sampling distribution of S, or in other words, σ_S is the *standard error of S*. If S happened to be a sample mean, we already know that for samples from infinite populations σ_S would equal $\dfrac{\sigma}{\sqrt{n}}$; in fact, the above confidence interval will reduce to the one on page 225. If S happened to be a sample proportion, σ_S would equal $\sqrt{\dfrac{p(1 - p)}{n}}$ and, after substituting x/n for p, the above confidence interval will reduce to the one of Exercise 4 on page 236. Note that, as before, we can change the degree of confidence from 0.95 to 0.98 or 0.99 by substituting 2.33 or 2.58 for 1.96.

When we first discussed the standard deviation in Chapter 3, we demonstrated how important it can be to have some knowledge (that is, some estimate) of the standard deviation of a population. As we have already done on several occasions, population standard deviations are usually estimated by means of sample standard deviations, and if s is the standard deviation of a *large* random sample, it can be shown that its standard error is given by

$$\sigma_s = \frac{\sigma}{\sqrt{2n}}$$

Here σ is the population standard deviation we are trying to estimate. If we now substitute this expression into the above confidence interval formula, we get

$$s - 1.96 \frac{\sigma}{\sqrt{2n}} < \sigma < s + 1.96 \frac{\sigma}{\sqrt{2n}}$$

and some simple algebra leads to the following *0.95 confidence interval for σ*:

$$\frac{s}{1 + \dfrac{1.96}{\sqrt{2n}}} < \sigma < \frac{s}{1 - \dfrac{1.96}{\sqrt{2n}}} \qquad \bigstar$$

Note that this confidence interval should be used only for large samples, namely, for $n \geq 30$.

Referring again to the numerical example on page 222 and substituting $n = 40$ and $s = 8.52$, we obtain

$$\frac{8.52}{1 + \dfrac{1.96}{\sqrt{80}}} < \sigma < \frac{8.52}{1 - \dfrac{1.96}{\sqrt{80}}}$$

$$6.98 < \sigma < 10.92$$

and we can thus assert with a probability of 0.95 that the interval from 6.98 to 10.92 hours contains σ, the true standard deviation of the number of hours it takes to perform Job R.

In the preceding discussion we arbitrarily chose 0.95, 0.98, and 0.99 as the probabilities in terms of which we appraised the possible size of the errors of our estimates. Nowadays these are the values which are most commonly used, but it has been the practice in the past to use also a probability of 0.50; we can then say that there is a fifty-fifty chance that the error of our estimate is less than a corresponding quantity called the *probable error*. Since 50 per cent of the area under the standard normal distribution lies between -0.6745 and 0.6745 (Table I is not sufficiently detailed for this purpose as it only shows that this value must lie between 0.67 and 0.68), we can write the formula for the *probable error of the mean* as

$$0.6745 \frac{\sigma}{\sqrt{n}}$$

This means that if a sample is used to estimate the mean of a population there is a fifty-fifty chance that the error will be less than $0.6745 \dfrac{\sigma}{\sqrt{n}}$.

Corresponding formulas for the *probable error of a proportion* and the *probable error of a sample standard deviation* are given by

$$0.6745 \sqrt{\frac{p(1-p)}{n}} \quad \text{and} \quad 0.6745 \frac{\sigma}{\sqrt{2n}}$$

Nowadays, probable errors are used mainly in military applications, where they serve as a measure of reliability or precision in gunnery, bombardment, and so forth.

The methods discussed in this chapter have been based on several assumptions. Foremost, we have always assumed that we were dealing with random samples and that these samples came from very large (or infinite) populations. The first of these assumptions is essential, and its violation makes everything we have discussed in this chapter invalid. The assumption that we are sampling from very large or infinite populations is necessary because, otherwise, we cannot use $\dfrac{\sigma}{\sqrt{n}}$ for the standard error of the mean and we would not satisfy (even approximately) the conditions underlying the binomial distribution. However, if we violate this second assumption, we are not in serious trouble. In fact, it is "safe" to use the methods of this chapter even when a sample constitutes a sizeable portion of the population *in the sense that we would be making our confidence intervals unnecessarily wide and the appraisal of our errors unnecessarily large*. As we saw in Exercise 9 on page 228 and in Exercise 12 on page 238, this can be avoided by making appropriate modifications.

EXERCISES

1. Referring to Exercise 1 on page 226, construct a 0.95 confidence interval for the true standard deviation of the time that elapses between the date of contract and the date of delivery of the given custom made product.

2. Referring to Exercise 5 on page 227, construct a 0.95 confidence interval for the true standard deviation of the weights of all the cans of sliced pineapple from which the sample was obtained.

3. Take the square root of each of the 40 sample variances given in Exercise 7 on page 194 and then calculate the standard deviation of these 40 sample standard deviations. Compare the result with the value one

might expect in accordance with the standard error formula $\sigma_s = \dfrac{\sigma}{\sqrt{2n}}$, where $\sigma = 3$ and $n = 5$.

4. For large samples from populations having roughly the shape of a normal distribution, it can be shown that the *standard error of the median* (the standard deviation of the sampling distribution of the median) is given by $1.2533 \dfrac{\sigma}{\sqrt{n}}$, where σ is the population standard deviation and n is the size of the sample. Verify that a median based on a random sample of size 100 and a mean based on a random sample of size 64 are thus about *equally reliable* estimates of the mean of a population having approximately the shape of a normal distribution.

5. In Exercise 6 on page 193, the reader was asked to find the standard deviation of the medians of the 40 samples given on page 188. Compare this value with what we might expect using the standard error formula of Exercise 4.

A Word of Caution

The methods we have studied in this chapter are *standard methods* which apply to a wide variety of *standard situations*. However, we often run into situations which are far from being "standard," and the methods of this chapter must, therefore, be used with a good deal of discretion. As a word of caution, let us relate the following story, a favorite of the late A. L. Bailey, who for many years served as Chief Actuary (Casualty) of the Insurance Department of the State of New York:

"Let us assume that you are a naturalist of some note and have made trips through all of North and South America, Europe, Asia, and Africa, and have made a special study of deer. In all of these travels you have noticed the one general fact that all of the deer of the various areas were tan-colored brown. There was, however, one outstanding exception. On a visit to the Bronx Zoo, you saw one albino deer and, in discussing that animal with fellow naturalists, you heard of several other such rare cases. You and I are now taking a trip to Australia for the first time and shortly after landing we go into the bush and we see our first Australian deer. It is tan-colored brown and I ask you just as a sporting proposition, what odds you would give me that most of the deer in Australia are tan-colored brown. I am sure that you would give me at least in the neighborhood of ten to one. Having later found that practically all of the deer in Australia are tan-colored brown, we continue our travels and go to New Zealand. When we go into the wooded area, we finally meet our first New Zealand deer and, lo!—it is a white one. Again, I ask you to name your odds; but now I propose that most of the deer in New Zealand are white. I doubt very much whether you would even consider giving me even money on that."

The moral of this story is that we must often use past experience, relevant collateral facts, as well as direct observations in estimating probabilities (or other parameters) that are needed for making wise decisions. We might, thus, use *Bayesian inferences* like the one given in the text on page 139 or like those of Exercises 14 and 15 on page 135 and Exercise 12 on page 228. Unfortunately, this has the decided disadvantage that it would then be virtually impossible to construct confidence intervals or reasonably appraise the size of our errors.

Technical Note 9 (Small-sample Confidence Intervals for Means)

When we learned how to construct confidence intervals for μ earlier in this chapter, we assumed that the sample size was sufficiently large to treat the sampling distribution of $\bar{x}$ as if it were a normal distribution, and to replace σ in the standard error formula with the sample standard deviation s. Using the Central Limit Theorem, we justified the first of these assumptions without saying anything about the nature of the population, the shape of its distribution, and so forth. In order to develop corresponding theory that applies also to small samples, we shall now have to assume that the population from which we are sampling (or, better, its distribution) has roughly the shape of a normal distribution. We can then base our methods on the statistic

$$t = \frac{\bar{x} - \mu}{s/\sqrt{n}} \qquad \bigstar$$

whose sampling distribution is called the *t distribution*. (More specifically, it is called the *Student-t distribution*, as it was first investigated by W. S. Gosset, who published his writings under the pen name of "Student.") The shape of this distribution is very much like that of the normal curve; it is symmetrical with zero mean, but there is a slightly higher probability for getting values falling into the two tails (see Figure 8.3). Actually, the shape of the t distribution depends on the size of the sample or, better, on the quantity $n - 1$, which is called the *number of degrees of freedom.**

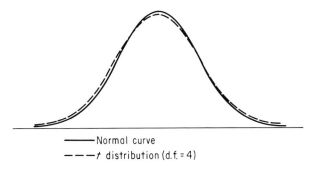

——— Normal curve

— — — t distribution (d.f. = 4)

FIGURE 8.3

Dealing with the standard normal distribution, we found that 95 per cent of the area under the curve falls between -1.96 and 1.96. As is illustrated in Figure 8.4, the corresponding values for the t distribution are $-t_{.025}$ and $t_{.025}$, and since these quantities depend on $n - 1$ (the number of degrees of freedom), their values must be looked up in a special table. Table II on page 438 contains (among others) the values of $t_{.025}$ with the number of degrees of freedom going from 1 to 29. Note that as the number of degrees of freedom increases, $t_{.025}$ approaches 1.96, the corresponding value for the normal distribution.

Duplicating the argument used on page 225, we now find that a *0.95 small-sample confidence interval for μ* is given by

$$\bar{x} - t_{.025} \frac{s}{\sqrt{n}} < \mu < \bar{x} + t_{.025} \frac{s}{\sqrt{n}} \qquad \star$$

---

* It is difficult to explain at this time why one should want to assign a special name to $n - 1$ which, after all, is only the sample size minus 1. However, we shall see in the next chapter that there are other applications of the t distribution, where the number of degrees of freedom is defined in a different way. The reason for the term "degrees of freedom" lies in the fact that if we know $n - 1$ of the deviations from the mean, then the nth is automatically determined (see argument on page 51). Since the sample standard deviation measures variation in terms of the squared deviations from the mean, we can thus say that this estimate of σ is based on $n - 1$ *independent quantities* or that we have $n - 1$ degrees of freedom.

The only difference between this confidence interval formula and the one on page 225 is that $t_{.025}$ takes the place of 1.96. Similarly, 0.98 and 0.99 confidence intervals can be obtained by replacing $t_{.025}$ with $t_{.010}$ or $t_{.005}$; these values are also given in Table II.

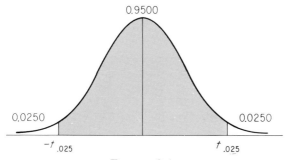

FIGURE 8.4

To illustrate the calculation of a small-sample confidence interval for μ, let us return to the example on page 49, where we wanted to estimate the true average drained weight of all cans of fruit salad of a certain size put up by a large canner. Using the random sample referred to on that page, for which the drained weights of 3 cans were 14.0, 13.8, and 14.2 ounces, we have $\bar{x} = 14.0$, $s = 0.20$, and, hence,

$$14.0 - 4.303 \; \frac{0.20}{\sqrt{3}} < \mu < 14.0 + 4.303 \; \frac{0.20}{\sqrt{3}}$$

$$13.5 < \mu < 14.5$$

where 4.303 is the value of $t_{.025}$ given by Table II for $3 - 1 = 2$ degrees of freedom. Note that in order to use this method we had to assume that the shape of the population distribution, the drained weights of all the cans of the given kind put up by the canner, can be approximated closely with a normal curve.

If the mean of a small random sample is used as a *point estimate* of μ, we can also appraise the possible size of the error using the t distribution instead of the normal curve. The only change needed in the expression for the maximum error is that $t_{.025}$ replaces 1.96 ($t_{.010}$ replaces 2.33 or $t_{.005}$ replaces 2.58). To illustrate this technique, let us refer again to the sample on page 48, which consisted of the following measurements of the compressive strength of a certain kind of steel:

71,000   45,250   70,400   81,350   42,000 psi

The mean and the standard deviation of this sample are $\bar{x} = 62{,}000$ and $s = 17{,}350$, and since $t_{.025}$ for $5 - 1 = 4$ degrees of freedom equals 2.776, we find that

$$E = t_{.025} \frac{s}{\sqrt{n}} = 2.776 \; \frac{17350}{\sqrt{5}} = 21{,}540 \text{ psi}$$

Thus, if we estimate the true average strength of all the steel from which this sample was obtained as 62,000 psi, we can assert with a probability of 0.95 that our error is less than 21,540 psi. This illustrates the fact that *although we can make logically correct inferences on the basis of very small samples, our results are apt to involve considerable errors and our confidence intervals are apt to be rather wide.*

NINE
DECISION MAKING: TESTS OF HYPOTHESES

Two Kinds of Errors

In Chapter 8 we studied decision problems in which we had to decide upon a value for such things as the "true" average time it takes to assemble a piece of machinery, the "true" proportion of housewives in a Chicago suburb who prefer one detergent to another, a "true" measure of the variability of the content of jars of instant coffee, and so on. We referred to these problems as *problems of estimation;* in each case we had to estimate the actual value of a parameter of a population. In this chapter we shall investigate decision problems that are of a somewhat different nature; we will be asked to decide, for instance, whether it is reasonable to maintain that a "twist" of 30.0 in-lb is required, on the average, to open a certain kind of jar, whether a manufacturer is justified in claiming that a new drycleaning fluid will remove at least 90 per cent of all spots, whether the variability of a shipment of steel is within specifications, and so on. These are all problems of *testing hypotheses;* in each case we must decide whether to accept or reject a hypothesis (an assumption, or a claim) concerning a parameter of a population.

To give an example that is typical of the kind of situation we face when testing a statistical hypothesis, suppose that a food processing plant uses a machine to put metal lids on pint jars of mayonnaise and that this machine is set so that, on the average, a "twist" of 30.0 in-lb (inch-pounds) will be required to remove the lids. Suppose, also, that it is known from long experience that the variability of the "sets" is stable and given by a standard deviation of $\sigma = 2.0$ in-lb. As it is desirable that the lids be neither too loose, which might cause spoilage, nor too tight, which might infuriate housewives, it is necessary to check each lot to see whether the machine is properly adjusted. To test a given lot, 16 jars are randomly selected and a torquemeter is used to determine the twist required to open each jar. The mean of these 16 measurements is then used to decide whether to accept or reject the hypothesis that the adjustment of the machine is under control. Specifically, *the management of the company accepts the hypothesis that $\mu = 30.0$ in-lb if the mean of the sample values falls between 28.8 and 31.2 in-lb; otherwise the hypothesis is rejected and an engineer is called in to adjust the machine.*

This provides a clear-cut criterion for deciding whether the machine is setting the lids as it should, but unfortunately it is not infallible. Since there is some variation among the settings, it could happen purely by chance that the mean of the 16 measurements exceeds 31.2 in-lb or is less than 28.8 in-lb even though the machine is actually adjusted so that $\mu = 30.0$ in-lb. If this happened, the company would waste time and money in having the machine gone over by an engineer. The chance of this happening could be reduced by choosing wider limits, say, by accepting the hypothesis that $\mu = 30.0$ in-lb if the sample mean falls between 27.5 and 32.5 in-lb, but this would increase another risk to which the company is exposed. This is the risk of obtaining a sample mean between 27.5 and 32.5 in-lb (or whatever other wider limits are being used) even though the machine is *not* properly adjusted. In other words, it is the risk of deciding that the machine is properly adjusted, while actually an average twist of, say, 27.0 in-lb or 32.0 in-lb is required to open the jars. If $\mu = 27.0$ in-lb, the company will ship jars which may well spoil in transit or storage; if $\mu = 32.0$ in-lb, the company will ship jars which may well create ill will, being too hard to open by hand.

Before adopting the above criterion (or, for that matter, any criterion), it would be wise for the management of the company to investigate what the chances are that the criterion might lead to a wrong decision. To this end, let us first investigate the possibility of getting a sample mean less than 28.8 in-lb or greater than 31.2 in-lb even though the adjustment of the machine is correct. In the language of statistics (especially that of Chapter 7), this means that we are interested in the probability of obtaining a sample mean less than 28.8 in-lb or greater than 31.2 in-lb when taking a random sample of size 16 from a population whose mean and standard deviation are $\mu = 30.0$ in-lb and $\sigma = 2.0$ in-lb. This probability is represented by the shaded area of Figure 9.1, and using the

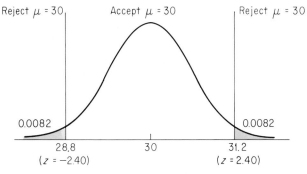

FIGURE 9.1

normal curve approximation to the sampling distribution of the mean, it is easily found. According to Theorem R, the standard deviation of this sampling distribution (namely, the standard error of the mean) is given by $\dfrac{\sigma}{\sqrt{n}}$, and for our example we, thus, obtain $\dfrac{2.0}{\sqrt{16}} = 0.50$. Hence, the dividing lines of the criterion are (in standard units)

$$\frac{31.2 - 30.0}{0.50} = 2.40 \quad \text{and} \quad \frac{28.8 - 30.0}{0.50} = -2.40$$

and it follows from Table I that the area in each tail of the sampling distribution of Figure 9.1 is $0.5000 - 0.4918 = 0.0082$. It follows that the probability of getting a value in either tail of this distribution, namely, *the probability of erroneously rejecting the hypothesis that the machine is properly adjusted*, is $0.0082 + 0.0082 = 0.0164$. Whether this is an acceptable risk is a matter of executive decision (and not of statistics); if necessary, it could be modified by changing the dividing lines of the criterion and (or) the size of the sample.

    Let us now look at the other kind of situation, where the machine has gone out of control, but the sample mean does not indicate that anything is amiss. Suppose, for instance, that the average twist required to open the jars has shifted to 32.0 in-lb. The probability of *not* detecting this shift with the given criterion is represented by the shaded area of Figure 9.2, namely, the area under the curve between 28.8 and 31.2 in-lb. The

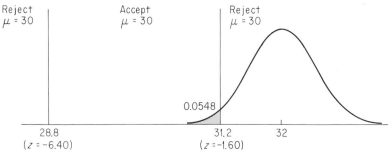

FIGURE 9.2

mean of this sampling distribution of $\bar{x}$ is $\mu = 32.0$, the standard deviation is as before $\dfrac{\sigma}{\sqrt{n}} = \dfrac{2.0}{\sqrt{16}} = 0.50$, and the dividing lines of the criterion shown in Figure 9.2 are (in standard units)

$$\frac{28.8 - 32.0}{0.50} = -6.4 \quad \text{and} \quad \frac{31.2 - 32.0}{0.50} = -1.60$$

It follows from Table I that the shaded area is $0.5000 - 0.4452 = 0.0548$, since the area to the left of $z = -6.4$ is negligible. We have thus shown that under the given conditions *the probability of erroneously accepting the hypothesis that the machine is performing as it should* is approximately 0.055. It is again a matter of executive decision (and not of statistics) whether this represents an acceptable risk.

To summarize what we have done, let us refer to the hypothesis that the machine is properly adjusted (that $\mu = 30.0$ in-lb) as Hypothesis *H*. Clearly, this hypothesis is either true or false, it is either accepted or rejected, and we are faced with the situation described in the following table

	H is True	*H is False*
Accept H	Correct decision	Type II error
Reject H	Type I error	Correct decision

If the hypothesis is *true and accepted* or *false and rejected*, we are in either case making a correct decision; if the hypothesis is *true but rejected*, we are committing an error called a *Type I error* (the error of rejecting a true hypothesis); if the hypothesis is *false but accepted*, we are committing an error called a *Type II error* (the error of accepting a false hypothesis). Whether an error is a Type I error or a Type II error will, thus, depend on how we formulate whatever hypothesis we want to test. For example, if H is the hypothesis that the Republican candidate will win a certain gubernatorial election, we will be committing a Type I error if we erroneously predict that his opponent will win the election. However, this same error would be a Type II error if we formulate H as the hypothesis that the Republican candidate will lose. (In the first case we erroneously reject H and in the second case we erroneously accept it.)

The scheme outlined above is reminiscent of what we did in Chapter 6, when we looked upon decision problems as games between two or more opponents, with each having the choice of several moves (or strategies). Analogous to the decision Mr. Jones had to make concerning the soft drink concession and the hot coffee and donut stand, we now have to decide whether to accept or reject Hypothesis H; analogous to Nature's decision between a very hot summer and a relatively cool summer, Nature now has control over Hypothesis H's being true or false. We can, thus, look upon a statistical decision problem as a game, where one player is the individual (or group of individuals) who has to make the decision, while the other player, Nature, has control over the statistical parameters with which the decision is concerned. The main difficulty in carrying this analogy much further is that in actual practice we can seldom put "cash values" on the various outcomes, as we did in Chapter 6. In our numerical example, we commit a Type I error when we erroneously reject the hypothesis that the machine is properly adjusted, and the only consequences might be the time and money involved in having somebody check the machine. However, when we erroneously accept the hypothesis and commit a Type II error, we expose ourselves to consequences that are difficult to evaluate: How big is the loss due to spoilage if the lids are too loose? How big is the loss in sales or good will if customers are aggravated by lids that are too tight? The whole question of assigning cash values to the consequences of all possible outcomes poses, in general, serious difficulties, and it limits the application of game theory to statistical problems of decision making. After all, how can one put a cash value on the error of accepting inferior steel for the construction of a bridge; what are the "cash" consequences of someone's deciding against the promotion of a certain executive, who might conceivably pull his firm out of the red; and how can one possibly evaluate in terms of money the consequences of a manufacturer's decision not to market a new drug, which might possibly save hundreds of lives? Of course, the seriousness of such consequences will determine, to some extent, whether a decision criterion presents acceptable risks. For instance, cost factors will determine in our numerical example whether 0.0164 (the probability of committing a Type I error) is acceptable, too high, or maybe too low. Also, the seriousness of the consequences of having mayonnaise jars requiring an average twist of 32.0 in-lb rather than 30.0 in-lb will determine whether 0.0548 (the probability of committing a Type II error) is acceptable, too high, or too low. In case the reader is curious to know under what conditions we might describe a risk as being *too low*, we have only to point out that it might be possible to reduce the cost of the testing procedure, say, by taking 12 observations instead of 16, and still keep the two risks within reasonable bounds.

In our example, we arbitrarily chose $\mu = 32.0$ in-lb as the alternative value for which we calculated the probability of committing a Type II error, namely, the probability of *not* detecting a shift in the adjustment of the machine. If the shift were *very small* (say, to 30.01 in-lb or to 29.99 in-lb) the consequences could probably be ignored. On the other hand, it might be of interest to know the probabilities of *not* detecting shifts to such values as 27.0 in-lb, 28.5 in-lb, 31.0 in-lb, or 32.5 in-lb in the average performance of the machine. Duplicating the method used earlier in this section, namely, approximating the sampling distribution of $\bar{x}$ with a normal distribution, the reader will be asked to verify in Exercise 5 on page 255 the values shown in the following table:

Value of μ	Probability of Type II Error	Probability of Accepting H
27.5	0.005	0.005
28.0	0.055	0.055
28.5	0.27	0.27
29.0	0.66	0.66
29.5	0.92	0.92
30.0	–	0.98
30.5	0.92	0.92
31.0	0.66	0.66
31.5	0.27	0.27
32.0	0.055	0.055
32.5	0.005	0.005

Using a normal curve table more extensive than Table I, it can also be shown that for $\mu = 27.0$ as well as for $\mu = 33.0$ the corresponding probabilities are 0.0002.

Since a Type II error is committed in our example when Hypothesis H is accepted when actually μ is not equal to 30.0 in-lb, the entries of the third column of the table are identical with those of the second column, except for the value which corresponds to $\mu = 30.0$ in-lb. If $\mu = 30.0$ in-lb and, hence, H *is true*, the probability of accepting H is the probability of *not committing a Type I error*, namely, $1 - 0.0164 = 0.9836$ or approximately 0.98.

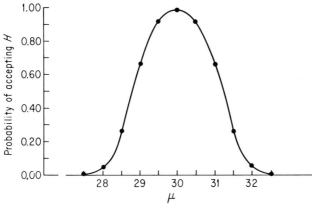

FIGURE 9.3. Operating characteristic curve.

Plotting the probabilities of accepting H as we did in Figure 9.3, we obtain a curve called the *operating characteristic curve* of the test criterion, or simply its *OC-curve*. An operating characteristic curve provides a good over-all picture of the advantages and disadvantages of a test criterion. For all values of the parameter except the one assumed under Hypothesis H it gives the probability of committing a Type II error; for the value assumed under H (in our case $\mu = 30.0$), it gives the probability of *not* committing a Type I error. Inspection of an operating characteristic curve, thus, enables us to decide whether the risks connected with a particular decision criterion are acceptable, too high, or too low. It is important to remember that the OC-curve of Figure 9.3 applies *only* to the special test where the hypothesis that $\mu = 30.0$ in-lb is accepted if the mean of a random sample of size 16 falls between 28.8 and 31.2, and where σ is known to equal 2.0 in-lb. Changing the test criterion or the sample size will correspondingly change the shape of the operating characteristic curve (see Exercises 6 and 7 on page 255); in fact, an

OC-curve can often be made to assume a particular desired shape by appropriate choice of the sample size and (or) the dividing lines of the test criterion.

A detailed study of operating characteristic curves would go considerably beyond the scope of this text, and the purpose of our illustration was mainly to demonstrate how statistical methods can be used to analyze and describe various risks connected with a decision criterion. Of course, these methods are not limited to the special hypothesis we formulated for the mayonnaise-jar example; Hypothesis *H* could have been the hypothesis that a shipment will arrive on time, the hypothesis that the demand for a product will remain unchanged, the hypothesis that the price of coffee will go up as much as the price of tea, the hypothesis that a new business venture will succeed—to name but a few of countless possibilities.

EXERCISES

1. Suppose that on the basis of a sample we want to test the hypothesis that the average price charged for 3-bedroom homes in the Phoenix area is $14,500. Explain under what conditions we would be committing a Type I error and under what conditions we would be committing a Type II error.

2. Suppose that a psychological testing service is asked to check whether Mr. Blue is emotionally fit to assume the presidency of a large corporation. What type of error is committed if the hypothesis that he is fit for the job is erroneously accepted? What type of error is committed if this hypothesis is erroneously rejected?

3. The management of a company wants to test the claim (hypothesis) that a new automatic mail sorter is more efficient than sorting by hand. Explain under what conditions they would be making Type I and Type II errors.

4. Whether an error is a Type I error or a Type II error depends on how we formulate the hypothesis we want to test. To illustrate this, suppose that the advertising director of a firm is concerned with the effectiveness of direct-mail solicitations.

   (a) If he formulates the hypothesis "direct-mail solicitations are at least 20 per cent effective," explain under what conditions he would be committing Type I and Type II errors.

   (b) If he formulates the hypothesis "direct-mail solicitations are less than 20 per cent effective," explain under what conditions he would be committing Type I and Type II errors.

5. Duplicating the method used in the text to calculate the probability of a Type II error for $\mu = 32.0$, verify the values shown in the table on page 252.

6. Suppose that in the example discussed in the text the criterion is changed so that the hypothesis that the machine is properly adjusted (the hypothesis that $\mu = 30.0$ in-lb) is accepted if the sample mean falls between 29.0 and 31.0; otherwise the hypothesis is rejected.

   (a) Calculate the probability of committing a Type I error with this criterion.
   (b) Calculate the probabilities of committing Type II errors with this criterion when μ equals, respectively, 27.5, 28.0, 28.5, 29.0, 29.5, 30.5, 31.0, 31.5, 32.0, and 32.5. (Note that due to the symmetry of the criterion only 5 of these values have actually to be calculated.)
   (c) Draw the OC-curve of this criterion and compare it with the one shown in Figure 9.3.

7. Suppose that in the example discussed in the text the criterion is changed so that the hypothesis that the machine is properly adjusted (the hypothesis that $\mu = 30.0$ in-lb) is accepted if the sample mean falls between 28.5 and 31.5; otherwise the hypothesis is rejected.

   (a) Calculate the probability of committing a Type I error with this criterion.
   (b) Calculate the probabilities of committing Type II errors with this criterion when μ equals, respectively, 27.5, 28.0, 28.5, 29.0, 29.5, 30.5, 31.0, 31.5, 32.0, and 32.5. (Note that due to the symmetry of the criterion only 5 of these values have actually to be calculated.)
   (c) Draw the OC-curve of this criterion and compare it with the ones of Figure 9.3 and part (c) of Exercise 6.

Null Hypotheses and Significance Tests

In the example of the preceding section we had more difficulties with Type II errors than with Type I errors, and this was due to the fact that we formulated our hypothesis in such a way that the probability of a Type I error could actually be obtained. Had we formulated instead the hypothesis that $\mu \neq 30.0$ in-lb, namely, the hypothesis that the machine is *not* properly adjusted, we would not have been able to calculate the probability of committing a Type I error; at least, we would not have been able to do so without specifying to what extent the machine might be out of adjustment.

In choosing the hypothesis which we referred to as Hypothesis H in our example, we followed the general rule of *always formulating hypotheses in such a way that we know what to expect if they are true.* As it was known that $\sigma = 2.0$ in-lb, the hypothesis $\mu = 30.0$ in-lb (and the theory of Chapter 7) enabled us to calculate probabilities concerning the sampling distribution of $\bar{x}$; in particular, we were able to calculate the probability that the mean of a random sample of size 16 is less than 28.8 or greater than 31.2 in-lb, namely, the probability of committing a Type I error.

To follow the rule given in italics in the last paragraph, we often have to assume (hypothesize) the exact opposite of what we may want to prove. If we want to show that one secretary works faster than another, we formulate the hypothesis that there is *no difference* in their performance. Similarly, if we want to show that a new advertising campaign helps to increase sales, we formulate the hypothesis that it does not, and if we want to show that one psychological test provides a better criterion for selecting executives than another test, we formulate the hypothesis that there is *no difference* in the effectiveness of the two tests. Since we assume that there is *no difference* in the performance of the secretaries, *no difference* in sales regardless of whether the new advertising campaign is employed, and *no difference* in the effectiveness of the psychological tests, we refer to hypotheses like these as *null hypotheses.*

Although we avoid one kind of difficulty by always formulating hypotheses so that the probability of a Type I error can be calculated, this will not help insofar as Type II errors are concerned. The only time there is no difficulty in finding the probabilities of either kind of error is when we test a *specific* hypothesis against a *specific* alternative, as we did when we tested the specific hypothesis $\mu = 30.0$ in-lb against the specific alternative $\mu = 32.0$ in-lb.

A possible escape from the difficulties connected with Type II errors is to avoid this kind of error altogether. To illustrate how this might be done, suppose we want to test our suspicion that one check-out clerk in a large supermarket makes on the average more mistakes than the others, where the others are known to make on the average 18 mistakes per day with a standard deviation of 4. Suppose, furthermore, that we watch this clerk for 10 days and then test the null hypothesis that there is no difference between his performance and that of the other check-out clerks, namely, the null hypothesis that $\mu = 18$ applies also to this clerk, on the basis of the following criterion:

reject the null hypothesis if the clerk averages more than 20 errors per day; otherwise reserve judgment.

Note that with this criterion there is no need to calculate the probability of committing a Type II error; we never really accept the null hypothesis and, hence, we cannot possibly make the mistake of accepting a false hypothesis.

The procedure we have just outlined is referred to as a *test of significance*. If the difference between what we expect and what we get is so large that it cannot reasonably be attributed to chance, we reject the null hypothesis on which our expectation is based. If the difference between what we expect and what we get is so small that it can well be attributed to chance, we say that the result is *not (statistically) significant*. We then reserve judgment or accept the null hypothesis depending on whether a definite decision, a definite action one way or the other, is required. In the above example, our suspicion that the clerk is worse than the others is confirmed if he averages more than 20 mistakes; in that case it is felt that the difference between the sample mean and $\mu = 18$ is too large to be attributed to chance. (The reader will be asked to verify in Exercise 4 on page 261 that the probability of getting a mean greater than 20 when μ equals 18 is, in fact, 0.06.) If the clerk averages 20 mistakes or fewer, we simply state that *the test did not definitely confirm our suspicion* (but we might nevertheless remain suspicious). Note that as in most criminal proceedings the burden of proof is put on the prosecution, and that the "defendant" is found not guilty unless his guilt is proven beyond a reasonable doubt.

Referring again to the mayonnaise-jar example, we could convert the criterion on page 248 into that of a significance test by rewriting it in the following form:

reject the Hypothesis H (that $\mu = 30.0$ in-lb) if the mean of the 16 sample values is less than 28.8 or greater than 31.2 in-lb; reserve judgment if it falls on the interval from 28.8 to 31.2 in-lb.

So far as the rejection of Hypothesis H is concerned, the rule has remained unchanged and the probability of a Type I error is still the same. However, so far as the acceptance of H is concerned, we are now playing it safe by reserving judgment. (Of course, this raises the question whether we can really afford to reserve judgment in ⁺his example. If production is to continue, the machine either must be left alone or it must be adjusted; hence, a decision must be reached one way or the other, we cannot reserve judgment, and we cannot escape the possibility of committing a Type II error. We have no choice here but to calculate the probabilities of committing Type II errors for pertinent values of μ and, if necessary, investigate the entire OC-curve. Whether or not we can afford to reserve judgment in any given situation will have to depend on the nature of the problem, the consequences, and so forth.)

Since the general problem of testing hypotheses and constructing statistical decision criteria is fairly complicated (and generally presents some difficulties to the beginner), it will help to proceed systematically as outlined in the following steps:

1. *We formulate a (null) hypothesis in such a way that the probability of a Type I error can be calculated; we also formulate an alternative hypothesis so that the rejection of the null hypothesis is equivalent to the acceptance of the alternative hypothesis.*

In the mayonnaise-jar example the null hypothesis was $\mu = 30.0$ in-lb and, even though we did not say so specifically, the alternative hypothesis was $\mu \neq 30.0$ in-lb. (After all, we were interested in determining whether the machine had gone out of adjustment in either direction.) We refer to this kind of alternative as a *two-sided alternative*, since we want to reject the null hypothesis if the average setting of the machine has become less than 30.0 in-lb and also if it has become greater than 30.0 in-lb. An instance where we use a *one-sided alternative* is provided by the supermarket-clerk example. Here the null hypothesis is $\mu = 18$ and the alternative hypothesis is $\mu > 18$, since we are interested in confirming our suspicion that the particular clerk makes on the average more mistakes than the others. (Had we been interested in the question whether this clerk is different, *better or worse*, than the other clerks, we would have used the two-sided alternative $\mu \neq 18$; and if we disliked the clerk for personal reasons and did not want to retain him unless he could prove himself superior to the other clerks, we would use the one-sided alternative $\mu < 18$ and fire him unless the hypothesis $\mu = 18$ can be rejected.) Beginners often find it difficult to decide upon an appropriate one-sided or two-sided alternative, and we want to stress the fact that which way to proceed depends entirely on the nature of the problem.

2. *We specify the probability of committing a Type I error, usually at 0.05 or 0.01; if possible, desired, or necessary, we may also make some specifications about the probabilities of Type II errors for specific alternatives.*

The probability of committing a Type I error is usually referred to as the *level of significance* at which the test is being conducted, and it is denoted by the Greek letter α (*alpha*). Thus, if we write $\alpha = 0.05$ in connection with a decision criterion, this means that we risk a Type I error with a probability of 0.05. As we have pointed out before, the decision whether to use 0.05, 0.01, or some other value, will have to depend on whatever consequences there may be to committing a Type I error. Generally speaking, the more serious the consequences of an error of this sort, the smaller the risk of committing it one is willing to take. The Greek letter β (*beta*) is often used to denote the probability of committing a Type II error; we can, thus, write $\alpha = 0.0164$ and $\beta = 0.0548$ for the criterion on page 248, provided we use the specific alternative $\mu = 32.0$ in-lb.

3. *We use suitable statistical theory to construct a criterion for testing the (null) hypothesis formulated in step 1 against the alternative given in step 1 at the level of significance specified in step 2.*

In the mayonnaise-jar example, we based the criterion on the normal curve approximation to the sampling distribution of $\bar{x}$; in general, it will have to depend on the *statistic* upon which we may want to base the decision and on the corresponding sampling distribution. A considerable portion of the remainder of this book will be devoted to the construction of such criteria. This usually involves choosing an appropriate statistic, specifying the sample size, and then determining the dividing lines (*critical values*) of the criterion. As we shall see later, it is essential for this purpose to know whether we are dealing with a one-sided or a two-sided alternative. As can be seen from our illustrations, we used a *two-sided test* (or *two-tail test*) with the two-sided alternative in the mayonnaise-jar example, rejecting the null hypothesis for small as well as large values of $\bar{x}$; in the supermarket-clerk example we used a *one-sided test* (or *one-tail test*) with the one-sided alternative $\mu > 18$, rejecting the null hypothesis only for large values of $\bar{x}$. In general, a test is said to be *one-sided* or *two-sided* (*one-tailed* or *two-tailed*), depending on whether the null hypothesis is rejected for values of the statistic falling into *either* or *both* tails of its sampling distribution.

4. *We specify whether the alternative to rejecting the hypothesis formulated in step 1 is to accept it or to reserve judgment.*

As we saw in our examples, this will have to depend on the nature of the problem, possible consequences and risks, and whether a decision one way or the other must be reached. Quite often we accept a null hypothesis with the tacit hope that we are not exposing ourselves to excessively high risks of committing *serious* Type II errors. Of course, if it is necessary and we have enough information, we can always calculate the probabilities required to get an over-all picture from the OC-curve of the test criterion.

Before we go into the various special tests treated in the next few sections, let us point out that the discussion of this section and the preceding section is not limited to tests concerning means. The concepts we have introduced apply equally well to hypotheses concerning proportions, population standard deviations, the randomness of samples, relationships among several variables, trends of time series, and so forth.

EXERCISES

1. The management of a food processing plant is considering the installation of new equipment for sorting olives. If μ_1 is the average number of olives sorted per hour by their old machine and μ_2 is the corresponding average for the new machine, the null hypothesis they shall want to test is $\mu_1 = \mu_2$.

    (a) What alternative hypothesis should they use if they do not want to buy the new equipment unless it is definitely proven superior? In other words, the burden of proof is put on the new equipment and the old equipment will be kept unless the null hypothesis can be rejected.

    (b) What alternative hypothesis should they use if they want to buy the new equipment (which has some other nice features) unless the old equipment is actually superior? Note that now the burden of proof is on the old equipment and the new machine will be bought unless the null hypothesis can be rejected.

(c) What alternative hypothesis should they use so that the rejection of the null hypothesis could lead either to buying the new machine or to keeping the old one?

2. A company gives its typists an A rating if they can average more than 80 words a minute, and a B rating if they average less than 80 words a minute. To classify (or reclassify) a typist, they give her a test designed to test the null hypothesis that $\mu = 80$, where μ is the average number of words she can type per minute.

(a) What alternative hypothesis should the personnel manager use if he does not want to give a typist the higher rating unless she can definitely prove herself superior? In other words, the burden of proof is on the typist, and she will be given the lower rating unless the null hypothesis can be rejected.

(b) What alternative hypothesis should the personnel manager use if he does not want to put the burden of proof on the typist? That is, she will be given the higher rating unless the null hypothesis can be rejected.

3. Using standard treatment, the mortality rate of a certain disease is known to be 0.04. Investigating the effectiveness of a new drug in the treatment of this disease, the manufacturer of the drug wants to test the null hypothesis $r = 0.04$ against a suitable alternative, where r is the mortality rate of the disease treated with the new drug.

(a) What alternative hypothesis should the manufacturer use if he is very careful and does not want to introduce the new drug unless it is definitely proven superior?

(b) What alternative hypothesis should the manufacturer use if he is very anxious to put the drug on the market? That is, he does not want to put the burden of proof on the new drug; he wants to market it unless it is definitely proven inferior to the standard treatment of the disease.

4. Verify for the supermarket-clerk example on page 257 that the probability of committing a Type I error is approximately 0.06.

Tests Concerning Means

To illustrate the steps outlined in the preceding section, let us begin with two tests which, for all practical purposes, are equivalent to the ones used in the mayonnaise-jar and supermarket-clerk examples. The first test, as it will be applied here, is designed to answer an insurance company's request for information whether or not private passenger cars are driven, on the average, 12,000 miles a year. It is assumed to be known that the variability of such figures (mileages) is given by a standard deviation of $\sigma = 1,800$ miles. As in the mayonnaise-jar example, it is decided to base the test on the mean of a random sample; specifically, the mean of the mileages of 100 private passenger cars.

Beginning with step 1 we first formulate the null hypothesis to be tested and the two-sided alternative hypothesis as

$$Hypothesis:\quad \mu = 12,000 \text{ miles}$$

$$Alternative:\quad \mu \neq 12,000 \text{ miles}$$

Next, we specify the level of significance as $\alpha = 0.05$, and this is where we depart from the procedure of the mayonnaise-jar example. On page 248 we specified the test criterion and then calculated the probability of a Type I error; now we reverse the procedure, specifying α and then

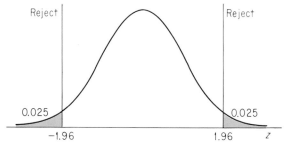

FIGURE 9.4

choosing an appropriate criterion. Another departure from the mayonnaise-jar example is that we shall formulate the criterion in *standard units* (see page 57), which has the advantage that it will make the criterion applicable to a great variety of problems. Approximating the sampling distribution of $\bar{x}$, as before, with a normal distribution, the criterion we shall use is shown in Figure 9.4. The dividing lines of the criterion are $z = -1.96$ and $z = 1.96$, which makes the areas in the two tails of the distribution (the shaded regions of Figure 9.4) both equal to 0.025. Since the standard deviation of this sampling distribution is given by $\dfrac{\sigma}{\sqrt{n}}$ the test criterion of Figure 9.4 may be expressed as follows:

reject the hypothesis (and accept the alternative) if $z < -1.96$ or $z > 1.96$; accept the hypothesis (or reserve judgment) if $-1.96 \leq z \leq 1.96$, *where*

$$z = \frac{\bar{x} - \mu_0}{\sigma/\sqrt{n}}$$ ★

and where μ_0 is the value of μ assumed under the given hypothesis.

To apply this test, let us suppose that the mean obtained for the mileages of the 100 private passenger cars is $\bar{x} = 12{,}410$ miles. Substituting this value together with $\mu_0 = 12{,}000$, $\sigma = 1{,}800$, and $n = 100$ into the formula for z, we obtain

$$z = \frac{12{,}410 - 12{,}000}{1{,}800/\sqrt{100}} = 2.28$$

Since this value exceeds 1.96, the hypothesis must be rejected and we conclude that the average annual mileage for private passenger cars is *not* 12,000 miles. In fact, the figures indicate that this average must actually be higher.

We used a two-tail test in this last example, because we originally formulated the two-sided alternative $\mu \neq 12{,}000$. Clearly, this alternative is supported by evidence falling into either tail of the sampling distribution of Figure 9.4. To give an example where it is appropriate to use a one-sided alternative and, correspondingly, a one-tail test, suppose that a consumer testing service wants to investigate the claim that the average net weight of jars of a certain kind of jam is 12.0 ounces, as stated on their labels. It is assumed to be known that the variability of the weights of such jars of jam is given by a standard deviation of $\sigma = 0.24$ ounces. Looking at this problem from the consumer's point of view only, the hypothesis to be tested and its one-sided alternative must be

Hypothesis: $\mu = 12.0$ ounces

Alternative: $\mu < 12.0$ ounces

Evidently, there would be no reason to complain from the consumer's point of view if μ were actually greater than 12.0 ounces. Formulating the alternative in this way, is the burden of proof on the consumer or the producer of the jam?

Choosing again a level of significance of 0.05, the normal curve approximation to the sampling distribution of $\bar{x}$ leads to the test criterion shown in Figure 9.5, where the dividing line, $z = -1.64$, is such that the shaded area in the left-hand tail equals 0.05. Formally, this criterion can be stated as follows:

reject the hypothesis (and accept the alternative) if $z < -1.64$; accept the hypothesis (or reserve judgment) if $z \geq -1.64$, where

$$z = \frac{\bar{x} - \mu_0}{\sigma/\sqrt{n}} \qquad \star$$

and where μ_0 is the value of μ assumed under the given hypothesis.

To show how this test is applied, let us suppose that a random sample of 36 jars of the given kind of jam had a mean weight of $\bar{x} = 11.97$ ounces.

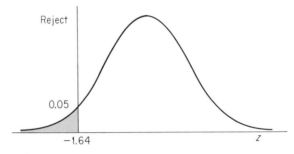

FIGURE 9.5

Substituting this value together with $\mu_0 = 12.0$, $\sigma = 0.24$, and $n = 36$ into the above formula for z, we obtain

$$z = \frac{11.97 - 12.0}{0.24/\sqrt{36}} = -0.75$$

Since this value is *not* less than -1.64, the hypothesis cannot be rejected and we either accept the claim that the average net weight of a jar of this kind of jam is 12.0 ounces, or we reserve judgment by simply stating that *the sample mean of 11.97 did not differ sufficiently from 12.0 to disprove the claim.* (We might add that this test gives poor protection against accepting the hypothesis $\mu = 12.0$ ounces when μ is greater than 12.0, but this does not matter from the consumer's point of view; he does not need any protection against getting more than he pays for.)

Had the above experiment been performed by the producer of the jam who (in contrast to the consumer) does not want to have too much jam in the average jar (and who is concerned only with this), he would have used the alternative hypothesis $\mu > 12.0$ ounces. The resulting test is shown in Figure 9.6, and the hypothesis is rejected if $z > 1.64$, with z calculated in the same way as before. One might say that this test is the *mirror image* of the one of Figure 9.5. Using the same data as before, the producer of the jam would also have been unable to reject the hypothesis that the true average net weight of a jar of his jam is 12.0 ounces; clearly, $z = -0.75$ is less than 1.64.

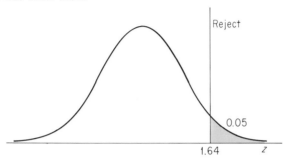

FIGURE 9.6

In all of these illustrations we arbitrarily used a level of significance of 0.05. Had we wanted to use $\alpha = 0.01$ in the first example, the dividing lines for the two-tail test would have been $z = -2.58$ and $z = 2.58$. Similarly, we would have used the critical value $z = -2.33$ for the one-tail test of Figure 9.5, and the critical value of $z = 2.33$ for the one-tail test of Figure 9.6. Note that if we had used $\alpha = 0.01$ in the first example, we would not have been able to reject the hypothesis that private passenger cars travel on the average 12,000 miles per year. *This illustrates the very important point that the level of significance should always be specified before any tests are actually performed. This will spare us the temptation of later choosing a level of significance which may happen to suit our particular objectives.*

A serious shortcoming of the methods described in this section is that they require knowledge of σ, the standard deviation of the population from which the sample is obtained. Since σ is unknown in many (in fact, most) practical applications, we have no choice but to replace it with an estimate. If n is large (30 or more), it is customary to use the methods of this section with σ replaced by the sample standard deviation s, namely, with z calculated according to the formula

$$ z = \frac{\bar{x} - \mu_0}{s/\sqrt{n}} \qquad \bigstar $$

It is for this reason that these methods are sometimes referred to as *large-sample tests*. If *n* is small, we have to use the alternate tests described in Technical Note 10 on page 292. The main difference between these *small-sample tests* and the ones described above is that they are based on the Student-*t* distribution instead of the normal curve. This is the sampling distribution we introduced first in Technical Note 9 in connection with the problem of estimating μ on the basis of small samples.

Differences Between Means

There are many statistical problems in which we must decide whether an observed difference between two sample means may be attributed to chance. We may want to decide, for instance, whether there is really a difference between two kinds of steel, if a sample of one kind had an average strength of 56,800 psi while a sample of another kind had an average strength of 55,600 psi. Similarly, we may want to decide on the basis of samples whether there actually is a difference in the size of delinquent charge accounts in two branches of a department store, whether men can perform a given task faster than women, whether one kind of television tube is apt to last longer than another, and so on.

The method which we shall employ to test whether an observed difference between two sample means may be attributed to chance is based on the following theory: *If $\bar{x}_1$ and $\bar{x}_2$ are the means of two large independent random samples of size n_1 and n_2, the sampling distribution of the statistic $\bar{x}_1 - \bar{x}_2$ can be approximated closely with a normal curve having the mean $\mu_1 - \mu_2$ and the standard deviation*

$$\sqrt{\frac{\sigma_1^2}{n_1} + \frac{\sigma_2^2}{n_2}}$$

where μ_1, μ_2, σ_1, and σ_2 are, respectively, the means and the standard deviations of the two populations from which the two samples were obtained.

By "independent" samples we mean that the selection of one sample is in no way affected by the selection of the other. Thus, the theory does *not* apply to "before and after" kinds of comparisons, nor does it apply, say, to the comparison of the I.Q.'s of husbands and wives. A special method for handling this kind of problem is referred to in Exercise 19 on page 272.

One difficulty in applying the above theory is that in most practical applications σ_1 and σ_2 are unknown. However, since we are limiting ourselves to large samples (neither n_1 nor n_2 should be less than 30), it is quite reasonable to substitute the sample standard deviations s_1 and s_2 for σ_1 and σ_2, and write the formula for the *standard error of the difference between two means* as

$$\sqrt{\frac{s_1^2}{n_1} + \frac{s_2^2}{n_2}}$$

To illustrate how this theory is applied, suppose we want to compare the weekly food expenditures of married couples without children in two cities. Taking random samples of size 100 and 120, respectively, the results of this investigation may be summarized as follows:

$$n_1 = 100, \quad \bar{x}_1 = \$32.46, \quad s_1 = \$8.12$$

$$n_2 = 120, \quad \bar{x}_2 = \$29.15, \quad s_2 = \$7.87$$

Letting μ_1 and μ_2 represent the true average weekly food expenditures of married couples without children in the two cities, the null hypothesis we shall want to test and the two-sided alternative are

Hypothesis: $\mu_1 - \mu_2 = 0$

Alternative: $\mu_1 - \mu_2 \neq 0$

Specifying that the level of significance is to be $\alpha = 0.05$, we shall again use the criterion of Figure 9.4, although z must, of course, be calculated in a different way. Formally, this criterion may be stated as follows:

reject the null hypothesis (and accept the alternative) if $z < -1.96$ or $z > 1.96$; accept the null hypothesis (or reserve judgment) if $-1.96 \leq z \leq 1.96$, where

$$z = \frac{\bar{x}_1 - \bar{x}_2}{\sqrt{\frac{s_1^2}{n_1} + \frac{s_2^2}{n_2}}} \qquad \star$$

Note that this formula for z is obtained by subtracting from $\bar{x}_1 - \bar{x}_2$ the mean of its sampling distribution (which under the null hypothesis is $\mu_1 - \mu_2 = 0$), and then dividing by the standard deviation of its sampling distribution with s_1 and s_2 substituted for σ_1 and σ_2.

Substituting the numerical values given for our example, we obtain

$$z = \frac{32.46 - 29.15}{\sqrt{\dfrac{(8.12)^2}{100} + \dfrac{(7.87)^2}{120}}} = 3.06$$

and since this value exceeds 1.96, we conclude that the observed difference between the average weekly food expenditures of $32.46 and $29.15 is *significant*. In other words, we conclude that there actually is a difference in the true average weekly food expenditures of married couples without children in the two cities. (Incidentally, if we had wanted to use a level of significance of 0.01 in this example, the dividing lines of the criterion would have been -2.58 and 2.58, and the null hypothesis would also have been rejected.)

As we have pointed out earlier, the above significance test for the difference between two means applies only to large samples. A method which can be used also for small samples (although it has some other restrictions) is given in Technical Note 10 on page 292. This small-sample test is again based on the Student-t distribution instead of the normal curve. Furthermore, a significance test for differences among more than two sample means will be taken up in Chapter 12 under the heading of "Analysis of Variance."

EXERCISES

1. Following the introduction of plastic pins, a number of bowlers reported that their scores had dropped. In a test arranged by a pin manufacturer, a good bowler whose average score (using wooden pins) is 182 pins with a standard deviation of 28 pins was asked to roll 100 lines using the new pins. Using a level of significance of 0.05, is there reason to believe that the new pins have adversely affected his score, if he averaged 171 pins?

2. A manufacturer wants to test whether the average performance level for an operation involving the sorting of certain items is 150 correct classifications per hour. If a random sample of 80 individuals tested showed an average of 148.2 correct classifications with a standard deviation of 15.4, check at a level of significance of 0.05 whether this is sufficient evidence to reject the hypothesis that the true mean of the population sampled is 150.

3. A standardized test of the ability to think scientifically has been administered thousands of times with a mean score of 84 and a standard deviation of 10.4 points. A group of 50 students is randomly selected for instruction in a course in which special emphasis is placed on problem formulation, deductive and inductive logic, interpretation of data, and other aspects of scientific thinking. Following the instruction period, the students are given the standard test and their average score is 86.1. Show that this does *not* prove (at the 0.05 level of significance) that the special instruction raises the achievement level on the test. Can you give *three* possible reasons which might account for this result?

4. Investigating an alleged unfair trade practice, the Federal Trade Commission takes a random sample of 40 "9-ounce" candy bars from a large shipment, obtaining a mean of $\bar{x} = 8.94$ ounces and a standard deviation of $s = 0.12$ ounces. Test whether this constitutes evidence on which to base a finding of unfair practice, using an appropriate one-sided alternative and a level of significance of 0.01.

5. A random sample of boots worn by 60 combat soldiers in a desert region showed an average life of 1.16 years with a standard deviation of 0.62 years. Under standard conditions, these boots are known to have an average life of 1.33 years. Is there reason to assert at a level of significance of 0.05 that use in the desert causes the mean life of such boots to decrease?

6. A production process is designed to fill No. $1\frac{1}{4}$ cans with 14.5 ounces net weight of sliced pineapple. Although the mean weight varies from time to time, the standard deviation is considered to be stable and well established at 0.64 ounces. In order to test incoming lots for weight, a large buyer takes a random sample of 30 cans from each lot and determines the mean net weight.

   (a) For what values of $\bar{x}$ should the buyer reject the null hypothesis $\mu = 14.5$ ounces, if he wants to use a two-sided alternative and a level of significance of 0.05?

   (b) Using the criterion established in part (a), what is the probability that the buyer will fail to detect a lot whose actual mean is only 14.3 ounces?

7. Repeat Exercise 6 using the one-sided alternative $\mu < 14.5$ ounces, which would seem more appropriate for the buyer who does not care whether he gets too much.

8. Two randomly selected groups of 50 employees of a very large firm are taught an assembly operation by two different methods and then tested for performance. If the first group averaged 140 points with a standard deviation of 10 points while the second group averaged 135 points with

a standard deviation of 8 points, test at the 0.05 level whether the difference between their mean scores is significant.

9. In order to evaluate the clinical effects of a new steroid in treating chronically underweight persons, 40 such persons were given 25-mg dosages of the drug over a 12-week period, while another 40 such persons were given 50-mg dosages of the drug over the same period. After 6 months, it was observed that the persons in the first group had gained on the average 9 pounds with a standard deviation of 7 pounds, while those in the second group had gained on the average 11 pounds with a standard deviation of 6 pounds. Treating the two samples as random samples, test at the 0.05 level of significance whether there is a real difference in the average weight gains of persons receiving the two dosages.

10. To investigate the claim that women are better at a certain job than men, the personnel department of a large cotton textile mill gives an appropriate aptitude test to a random sample of 40 male employees and a random sample of 50 female employees. What will they conclude (at a level of significance of 0.01) if the men average 81.3 with a standard deviation of 10.2 while the women average 88.9 with a standard deviation of 11.4? (*Hint:* Modify the criterion on page 267 so that it applies to a test where we use a one-sided alternative and the desired level of significance.)

11. (*Control charts for means*) In industrial quality control it is often necessary to test the same hypothesis over and over again at regular intervals of time. Suppose, for example, that a process for making

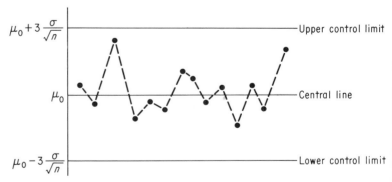

FIGURE 9.7

compression springs is under control if the free lengths of the springs have a mean of $\mu = 1.5$ inches; it is known from experience that the standard deviation of the free lengths of these springs is $\sigma = 0.02$ inches. In order to test whether the process is under control, random samples of size n are taken, say, every hour, and it is decided in each case on the basis of $\bar{x}$ whether to accept or reject the null hypothesis $\mu_0 = 1.5$. To simplify this task, quality control engineers use *control charts* like that of Figure 9.7, where the vertical scale is the scale of measurement of $\bar{x}$, the central line is at $\mu = \mu_0$ and the *upper and lower control limits* are at $\mu_0 + 3 \dfrac{\sigma}{\sqrt{n}}$ and $\mu_0 - 3 \dfrac{\sigma}{\sqrt{n}}$. Each sample mean is plotted on this chart and the process is considered to be in control so long as the $\bar{x}$'s fall between the control limits. Assuming that the data constitute random samples from a normal population, the probability of a Type I error is less than 0.003. Using $\mu_0 = 1.5$ and $\sigma = 0.02$, construct a control chart for the means of samples of size $n = 5$. Also plot on this chart the following data, constituting the means of such random samples taken at hourly intervals during the operation of the process: 1.510, 1.495, 1.521, 1.505, 1.524, 1.520, 1.488, 1.465, 1.529, 1.444, 1.531, 1.502, 1.490, 1.531, 1.475, 1.478, 1.522, 1.491, 1.491, 1.482. Was the process ever out of control?

12. In the production of certain shafts, a process is said to be in control if the outside diameters have a mean of $\mu = 2.500$ in. and a standard deviation of $\sigma = 0.002$ in.

    (a) Construct a control chart for the means of random samples of size 4.

    (b) Plot on the chart obtained in part (a) the following figures, representing the means of 25 such random samples taken at regular intervals of time: 2.5014, 2.5022, 2.4995, 2.5006, 2.4985, 2.5002, 2.5016, 2.4985, 2.4992, 2.5028, 2.5016, 2.5020, 2.5001, 2.4995, 2.5003, 2.5012, 2.4988, 2.4975, 2.5011, 2.4992, 2.5002, 2.5014, 2.4976, 2.5003, 2.5015. Was the process ever out of control?

(The exercises which follow are based on the material in Technical Note 10 on page 292.)

13. Test runs with 6 models of an experimental engine showed that they operated, respectively, for 17, 22, 18, 20, 19, and 18 minutes with 1 gallon of a certain kind of fuel. Is this evidence at the 0.01 level of significance that the models are not operating at a desired standard of 22 minutes under the given conditions?

14. A large institutional food buyer invites packers to submit samples from last season's fruit and vegetable pack for grading as a guide in requesting bids on the current season's pack. Using U.S.D.A. Standards for Grades and official draining sieves and scales, the buyer checks the submitted samples for (among other things) drained weight. If a submitted sample of 4 No. 10 cans of carrots has drained weights of 72.4, 71.6, 71.9, and 71.3 ounces, test at the 0.05 level of significance

whether this is in accordance with the prescribed average weight of 72 ounces.

15. A company wants to test whether (under specified operating conditions) the average tool life per sharpening of a multitoothed cutting tool (called a "broach") is 3,000 pieces against the alternative that it is less than 3,000 pieces. If 6 tests showed tool lives of 2,970, 3,020, 3,005, 2,900, 2,940, and 2,925 pieces, what conclusion will they reach using a level of significance of 0.05?

16. A company wants to compare the lifetimes of two stones used in an abrasive process (called "superfinishing"), which produces rapidly a fine microfinish on machined surfaces. In laboratory tests, hot rolled steel driveshafts of the same degree of surface roughness are processed for two minutes each under specified conditions using either of the two stones. If the average lifetime of 10 stones of the first kind was 60 pieces with a standard deviation of 5 pieces, while the average lifetime of 10 stones of the second kind was 64 pieces with a standard deviation of 3 pieces, is the difference between these two means significant at a level of significance of 0.05?

17. The company referred to in Exercise 16 wants to compare the efficiency of two different processes for surface grinding (removing metal by means of abrasive grinding wheels). The particular measure of efficiency used is the ratio of the volume of abrasive consumed on the job to the volume of stock removed from the work pieces. In 5 tests conducted on hardened steel under standard conditions, surface grinder Q showed efficiencies of 0.44, 0.38, 0.35, 0.40, and 0.43, while 5 similar tests with surface grinder R showed efficiencies of 0.41, 0.38, 0.47, 0.46, and 0.43. Test at the 0.05 level of significance whether the two surface grinders are equally efficient under the given conditions.

18. Tests are made on the lifetimes of samples of 5 wooden and 5 plastic bowling pins with the following results (in number of lines):

    Wood:　　1,500, 1,410, 1,625, 1,290, 1,785
    Plastic:　3,100, 2,765, 3,210, 2,942, 3,208

    Test at the 0.01 level of significance whether the difference between the means of the samples is significant.

19. If we want to study the effectiveness of a new diet on the basis of weights "before and after," or if we want to study whatever differences there may be between the I.Q.'s of husbands and wives, the methods introduced in this chapter cannot be used. The samples are not independent; in fact, in each case the data are *paired*. To handle data of this kind, we work with the (signed) differences of the paired data and test whether these differences may be looked upon as a sample from a population for which $\mu = 0$. If the sample is small, we use the t test

on page 293, and if it is large, we use the test on page 263. Apply this technique to the following data designed to test whether there is a systematic difference in the blood-pressure readings obtained with two different instruments:

	Reading Obtained with Instrument A	Reading Obtained with Instrument B
Patient 1	147	151
Patient 2	118	120
Patient 3	144	145
Patient 4	165	168
Patient 5	140	146
Patient 6	125	124
Patient 7	132	135
Patient 8	151	152

Use a level of significance of 0.05 to test whether there is a difference in the true average readings obtained with the two instruments.

20. In a study of the effectiveness of a reducing diet, the following "before and after" figures were obtained for a random sample of 10 adult married females in the age group from 30 to 40 (data in pounds):

	Before	After
. Mrs. A	134	131
Mrs. B	147	140
Mrs. C	165	164
Mrs. D	152	153
Mrs. E	139	133
Mrs. F	122	122
Mrs. G	138	135
Mrs. H	147	148
Mrs. I	153	147
Mrs. J	178	165

Use a level of significance of 0.01 to test the null hypothesis (that the diet is not effective) against a suitable one-sided alternative.

Tests Concerning Proportions

Once the reader has grasped the fundamental ideas underlying tests of hypotheses, the various tests we shall study in this and in later sections should not present any difficulties. The tests we shall discuss in this particular section apply to problems in which we must decide, on the basis of sample data, whether the true value of a proportion (percentage, or probability) equals a certain given value p. For instance, a management consulting firm studying cost control in a large laundry may want to know whether the true proportion of "cleaned" shirts rejected at final inspection because of faulty work is $p = 0.10$. Similarly, the personnel manager of a large textile mill may want to know whether 0.40 is the true proportion of employees recruited through newspaper ads who will pass a standard mechanical aptitude test without company training, and a manufacturer may want to know whether it is true that 60 per cent of all housewives (in a certain market area) prefer a new sweetened fruit soup to an unsweetened one.

Questions of this kind are usually decided on the basis of a sample proportion or the observed number of "successes" in n "trials." In the above examples, the management consulting firm would base its decision on the *number* (or proportion) of "cleaned" shirts rejected in a sample of, say, 400; the personnel manager would base his decision on the *number* of employees recruited by newspaper ads who pass the test, say, among 200 employees thus recruited; and the manufacturer would base his decision on the *number* of housewives preferring the sweetened soup, say, in a sample of 600 housewives selected at random.

The sampling distribution of the number of successes in n trials is the binomial distribution first studied in Chapter 5. In fact, when n is small, tests concerning a "true" proportion p (namely, tests concerning the parameter p of a binomial distribution) are usually based directly on tables of binomial probabilities, such as those referred to in the Bibliography at the end of this book. When n is large, however, we approximate the binomial distribution with a normal curve and (as was indicated on page 215) this approximation is usually satisfactory so long as np and $n(1 - p)$ both exceed 5. The mean and the standard deviation are taken as np and $\sqrt{np(1 - p)}$, respectively, in accordance with the formulas given on pages 150 and 152 in Chapter 6.

To illustrate this kind of test, let us return to the first of the examples given above, and let us suppose that the hypothesis and the two-sided alternative the management consulting firm wants to test at $\alpha = 0.05$ are

$$Hypothesis: \quad p = 0.10$$

$$Alternative: \quad p \neq 0.10$$

where p is the true proportion of "cleaned" shirts rejected at final inspection because of missing or broken buttons, dirt or grease spots, etc. The sample size is taken to be $n = 400$, and this makes it reasonable to use the normal curve approximation to the distribution of the number of successes in n trials. The appropriate test criterion is again the two-tail test of Figure 9.4, namely,

reject the hypothesis (and accept the alternative) if $z < -1.96$ or $z > 1.96$; accept the hypothesis (or reserve judgment) if

$$-1.96 \le z \le 1.96$$

where

$$z = \frac{x - np_0}{\sqrt{np_0(1 - p_0)}} \qquad \bigstar$$

and where p_0 is the value assumed for p under the given hypothesis.

To apply this criterion, suppose that the management consulting firm actually obtained a sample of size 400 which contained 45 shirts that did not pass final inspection. Substituting $x = 45$, $n = 400$, and $p_0 = 0.10$ into the above formula for z, we get

$$z = \frac{45 - 400(0.10)}{\sqrt{400(0.10)(0.90)}} = 0.83$$

and it follows that the hypothesis $p = 0.10$ *cannot be rejected.* Having to make a decision one way or the other, the management consulting firm will have to accept 0.10 as the true proportion of "cleaned" shirts that do not meet final inspection. (If, for some reason, the management consulting firm is reluctant to make this decision, they might continue the experiment by collecting further data.)

To give an example where it is appropriate to use a one-sided alternative let us return to the third of the examples mentioned on page 274. Let us suppose that the manufacturer is worried, in particular, about the alternative that the true proportion of housewives preferring the sweetened soup might be less than 0.60, in which case he would not consider it worthwhile to change his product, his advertising, and so forth. We thus have

Hypothesis: $p = 0.60$

Alternative: $p < 0.60$

where p is the true proportion of housewives who prefer the sweetened soup. Suppose, furthermore, that this hypothesis is to be tested on the basis of a random sample of size $n = 600$ at a level of significance of 0.05. Using again the normal curve approximation to the binomial distribution, the appropriate one-tail test is the one shown in Figure 9.5; the criterion is identical with the one given on page 264, the only distinction being that z is now calculated according to the formula

$$z = \frac{x - np_0}{\sqrt{np_0(1 - p_0)}}$$

where p_0 is the value assumed for p under the given hypothesis. If 321 of the 600 housewives actually expressed a preference for the new sweetened soup while 279 preferred the old kind, substitution into the above formula for z yields

$$z = \frac{321 - 600(0.60)}{\sqrt{600(0.60)(0.40)}} = -3.25$$

Since this value is less than -1.64, the manufacturer accepts the alternative $p < 0.60$ and decides *not* to change the soup.

As in the preceding section, the level of significance can be changed to $\alpha = 0.01$ by changing the dividing lines of the two-tail test to $z = -2.58$ and $z = 2.58$, and by changing the dividing line of the one-tail test to $z = -2.33$ or $z = 2.33$, depending on whether it is the test criterion of Figure 9.5 or the one of Figure 9.6.

Differences Among Proportions

There are many applications in which we must decide whether observed differences among two or more sample proportions (or percentages) are significant or whether they can be attributed to chance. For instance, if one mail-order solicitation yields a 10 per cent response while another more elaborate one yields a 12 per cent response, we may want to decide whether the observed 2 per cent difference is significant or whether it can be explained by chance. Similarly, if random samples of voters (100 with low incomes, 140 with average incomes, and 60 with high incomes) are asked how they would vote on a certain piece of legislation and the results are as shown in the following table,

	Voters with Low Incomes	*Voters with Average Incomes*	*Voters with High Incomes*
For the Legislation	58	77	27
Against the Legislation	42	63	33

it may be of interest to know whether the *actual proportions* of favorable votes are the same for all three groups. In other words, it is of interest to know whether the differences among 0.58, 0.55, and 0.45 (the sample proportions of favorable votes obtained for the three income groups) can be attributed to chance.

To illustrate how we handle this last kind of example, let us denote the true proportions of voters favoring the legislation in the three income groups p_1, p_2, and p_3. Thus, the null hypothesis we shall want to test and the alternative hypothesis are

$$Hypothesis: \quad p_1 = p_2 = p_3$$

$$Alternative: \quad p_1, p_2, \text{ and } p_3 \text{ are not all equal}$$

If the null hypothesis is true, we can combine the three samples and estimate the common proportion of voters favoring the legislation as

$$\frac{58 + 77 + 27}{100 + 140 + 60} = \frac{162}{300} = 0.54$$

With this estimate we would *expect* 100(0.54) = 54 votes for the legislation in the first sample, 140(0.54) = 75.6 in the second sample, and 60(0.54) = 32.4 in the third sample. Subtracting these figures from the totals for the respective samples, we would *expect* 100 − 54 = 46 votes against the legislation in the first sample, 140 − 75.6 = 64.4 in the second sample, and 60 − 32.4 = 27.6 in the third sample. These results are summarized in the following table, where the *expected frequencies* are shown in parentheses below those that were actually observed:

	Voters with Low Incomes	Voters with Average Incomes	Voters with High Incomes
For the Legislation	58 (54)	77 (75.6)	27 (32.4)
Against the Legislation	42 (46)	63 (64.4)	33 (27.6)

To test the null hypothesis $p_1 = p_2 = p_3$, we now compare the frequencies that were actually observed with those we could expect if the null hypothesis were true. It stands to reason that the null hypothesis should be accepted if the two sets of frequencies are very much alike; after all, we would then have obtained almost exactly what we could have expected if the null hypothesis were true. On the other hand, if the discrepancies between the two sets of frequencies are large, the observed frequencies do not agree with what we could expect, and this is an indication that the null hypothesis must be false.

Writing the observed frequencies as f's and the expected frequencies as e's, we shall base their comparison on a statistic called x^2 (*chi-square*), namely,

$$\chi^2 = \Sigma \frac{(f - e)^2}{e} \qquad \star$$

Since this notation is rather abbreviated, let us restate in words that x^2 is the sum of the quantities obtained by dividing $(f - e)^2$ by e separately for each "cell" of the table. For our example we thus obtain

$$\chi^2 = \frac{(58 - 54)^2}{54} + \frac{(77 - 75.6)^2}{75.6} + \frac{(27 - 32.4)^2}{32.4}$$

$$+ \frac{(42 - 46)^2}{46} + \frac{(63 - 64.4)^2}{64.4} + \frac{(33 - 27.6)^2}{27.6}$$

$$= 2.656$$

If there is a close agreement between the f's and e's, the differences $f - e$ and hence χ^2 will be small; if the agreement is poor, some of the differences $f - e$ and hence χ^2 will be large. *Consequently, we reject the null hypothesis if χ^2 is large, and we accept it or reserve judgment if χ^2 is small.* The exact criterion for this decision is based on the sampling distribution of the χ^2 statistic, which can be approximated very closely by a theoretical distribution called the *chi-square distribution*. The criterion which is based on this sampling distribution is shown in Figure 9.8; using a level of significance of 0.05, the dividing line of the criterion, $\chi^2_{.05}$, is such that the shaded area in Figure 9.8 is 0.05. Its value may be obtained from Table III. The chi-square distribution, like the Student-t distribution introduced on page 243, depends on a parameter called the *number of degrees of freedom*. In our example the number of degrees of freedom is 2 and, in general, in the comparison of k sample proportions it is $k - 1$. (Intuitively, we can justify this formula for the number of degrees of freedom with the argument that if we calculate $k - 1$ of the *expected* frequencies in either row of the table, all the other expected frequencies may be obtained by subtraction from the totals of appropriate rows or columns.)

Referring back to our numerical example, we find from Table III that $\chi^2_{.05}$ for $3 - 1 = 2$ degrees of freedom equals 5.991. Since 2.656, the value which we actually obtained for χ^2, is less than 5.991, the null hypothesis cannot be rejected. We conclude that income is *not* a factor in voters' opinion concerning the legislation (or we reserve judgment by stating simply that the observed differences among the sample proportions are not significant).

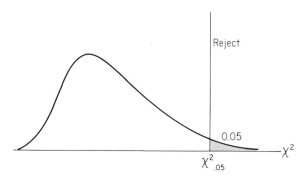

FIGURE 9.8

In general, if we want to compare k sample proportions, we first calculate the expected frequencies as we did on page 277. Combining the data, we estimate p as

$$\frac{x_1 + x_2 + \ldots + x_k}{n_1 + n_2 + \ldots + n_k} \qquad \star$$

where the n's are the sizes of the respective samples and the x's are the corresponding numbers of successes. Multiplying the n's by this estimate of p, we obtain the expected frequencies for the first row of the table, and subtracting these values from the totals of the corresponding samples, we obtain the expected frequencies for the second row of the table. (Note that the expected frequency for any one of the cells may also be obtained by multiplying the total of the row to which it belongs by the total of the column to which it belongs, and dividing by the grand-total, $n_1 + n_2 + \ldots + n_k$, for the entire table.)

Next, χ^2 is calculated according to the formula

$$\chi^2 = \Sigma \frac{(f - e)^2}{e} \qquad \star$$

with $(f - e)^2/e$ determined separately for each of the $2k$ cells of the table. The criterion for testing the null hypothesis $p_1 = p_2 = \ldots = p_k$ against the alternative that these p's are not all equal then reads as follows:

reject the null hypothesis (and accept the alternative) if $\chi^2 > \chi^2_{.05}$; accept the null hypothesis (or reserve judgment) if $\chi^2 \leq \chi^2_{.05}$, where the value of $\chi^2_{.05}$ is based on $k - 1$ degrees of freedom.

This test is designed for a level of significance of 0.05, but if we want to use $\alpha = 0.01$, we have only to substitute $\chi^2_{.01}$ for $\chi^2_{.05}$. Incidentally, when calculating the expected frequencies it is customary to round to the nearest integer or to one decimal, as we did in our example. The entries in Table III are given to three decimals, but there is seldom any need to carry more than two decimals in calculating the value of the χ^2 statistic itself. It should also be noted that since the above test is only approximate, it is best not to use it when one (or more) of the expected frequencies is less than 5.

The method which we have discussed can be used only to test against the null hypothesis that the p's are not all equal. However, in the special case where $k = 2$ and we are interested in the significance of the difference between two sample proportions, we can test against either of the alternatives $p_1 < p_2$ or $p_1 > p_2$ by using an *equivalent test* based on the normal curve rather than the chi-square distribution. This alternative procedure is discussed in Exercise 10 below.

EXERCISES

1. A political party organization claims that, based on its own poll, Candidate M is favored by 70 per cent of the eligible voters. Test at a level of significance of 0.05 whether this claim is exaggerated in the light of results published by a (usually highly reliable) independent survey showing that in a random sample of 600 voters only 377 favored Candidate M.

2. A doctor wishes to determine whether a new skeletal muscle relaxant will produce beneficial results in a significantly higher proportion of patients suffering from various severe neurological disorders than the 0.80 proportion receiving beneficial results from standard treatment. If in a random sample of 100 patients 85 obtained beneficial results

from the new muscle relaxant, how should the doctor interpret this at a level of significance of 0.10?

3. To test the Student Daily's claim that only 30 per cent of the students attending a certain large university favor an administration plan to increase student activity fees to help build a new student union, the administration interviews a random sample of 400 students. If 158 students in the sample favor the plan, is this evidence at the 0.05 level of significance that the newspaper claim is too low?

4. A large brokerage firm wants to test the claim that 80 per cent of its customers who sell stock to establish tax losses immediately reinvest the proceeds in other stocks. What conclusion should they arrive at (with $\alpha = 0.01$) if in a random sample of 150 sales made to establish tax losses there were 114 instances where the proceeds were immediately reinvested in other stocks?

5. The manager of the cafeteria of a large manufacturing company claims that at least 75 per cent of the employees who eat in the cafeteria would prefer to have smaller portions on the $1.00 "Special Plate" and a corresponding reduction in price to $0.90. What can the management of the company conclude at a level of significance of 0.05 if in a random sample of 300 employees who eat at the cafeteria 238 are in favor of the change?

6. In auditing a company's records, an accounting firm wants to check whether $p = 0.015$ is a reasonable estimate of the proportion of freight bills that were in error (wrong rate, incorrect extension, etc.). What can they conclude at a level of significance of 0.05 if a random sample of 1,000 freight bills (taken from a file containing about 200,000 paid freight bills) contains 21 that were in error?

7. To determine the attitude of its field sales personnel toward whether the company should follow its present policy of maintaining profit levels on unit sales or adopt a proposed new high-volume, low-price policy, a national manufacturer took a sample of its salesmen in 4 broad geographic areas with the following results:

	North	South	East	West
Maintain Old Policy	42	22	54	52
Adopt New Policy	48	38	146	78

Find the expected frequencies under the null hypothesis that the true proportions of field men who favor the present policy are the same, calculate χ^2, and test the null hypothesis at a level of significance of 0.05.

8. A large city park and recreation department plants 1,000 tulip bulbs each of the highest-grade bulbs supplied by seed firms A, B, and C. Of the bulbs bought from these firms, 105, 70, and 95, respectively, failed to germinate. Use a level of significance of 0.05 to test the hypothesis that the true proportion of bulbs (of the given grade) that fail to germinate is the same for all three firms.

9. Tests are made on the proportion of defective castings produced by two molds. If among 100 castings from mold I there were 14 defectives while among 200 castings from mold II there were 36 defectives, test the null hypothesis that there is no difference between the true proportions of defective castings produced by the two molds. Use a level of significance of 0.01.

10. Repeat Exercise 9, basing your decision on the statistic

$$z = \frac{\dfrac{x_1}{n_1} - \dfrac{x_2}{n_2}}{\sqrt{p(1-p)\left(\dfrac{1}{n_1} + \dfrac{1}{n_2}\right)}} \quad \text{with} \quad p = \frac{x_1 + x_2}{n_1 + n_2}$$

whose sampling distribution is approximately the standard normal distribution provided that both samples are large. The criterion for this two-tail test is again the one shown in Figure 9.4, with 2.58 substituted for 1.96 to change the level of significance to 0.01. Also verify that the *square* of the value obtained for z in this exercise equals the value obtained for χ^2 in Exercise 9.

11. In order to test the claim that more women than men prefer a fully reclining front seat with a headrest, an automobile manufacturer selects random samples of 100 men and 100 women and asks each the following question: "In your next car will you probably buy for about $25 extra a fully reclining front seat with a headrest?" If in the samples 42 men and 73 women say that they will probably buy this feature, what can the manufacturer conclude about the above claim (using a level of significance of 0.05)? (*Hint:* Use an appropriate one-sided alternative and base your decision on the statistic of Exercise 10.)

12. A marketing study conducted in Detroit showed that in a random sample of 100 married women who work full time 72 prefer to buy lima beans frozen rather than canned, while in a random sample of 100 married women who do not work full time only 67 prefer to buy lima beans frozen rather than canned.

(a) Test for the significance of the difference between the two sample proportions (with $\alpha = 0.05$) using the χ^2 statistic discussed in the text.

(b) Test for the significance of the difference between the two sample proportions (with $\alpha = 0.05$) using the z statistic of Exercise 10. Verify that the *square* of the value obtained for the z statistic equals the value obtained for the χ^2 statistic in part (a).

13. (*Control charts for attributes*) In order to control the proportion of defectives or other characteristics (attributes) of mass-produced items, quality control engineers take random samples of size n at regular intervals of time and plot their results (the sample proportions) on a *control chart* like that of Figure 9.9. If the production process is considered to be under control when the true proportion of defectives is

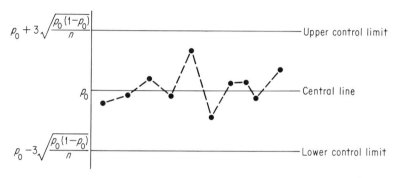

FIGURE 9.9

p_0, the *central line* of the control chart for the proportion of defectives is at p_0, and the *3-sigma upper and lower control limits* are at

$$p_0 + 3\sqrt{\frac{p_0(1 - p_0)}{n}} \quad \text{and} \quad p_0 - 3\sqrt{\frac{p_0(1 - p_0)}{n}}$$

As was explained in connection with Figure 9.7, a process is assumed to be under control so long as the sample proportions, plotted on the control chart, remain between the two control limits.

Construct a control chart for the proportion of defectives obtained in repeated random samples of size 100 from a process which is considered to be under control when $p_0 = 0.20$. Given that 24 consecutive samples of size 100 contained, respectively, 23, 14, 19, 25, 20, 18, 13, 27, 24, 25, 21, 20, 30, 24, 17, 23, 19, 16, 13, 19, 21, 20, 25, and 34 defectives, plot the corresponding proportions on the control chart and comment on the performance of the process.

14. Construct a control chart (see Exercise 13) for the proportion of defectives obtained in repeated random samples of size 400 from a process which is considered to be under control when $p_0 = 0.10$. Given that 25 consecutive samples of size 400 contained, respectively, 41, 32, 55,

49, 37, 45, 40, 23, 35, 27, 47, 45, 38, 40, 42, 36, 48, 50, 36, 25, 20, 34, 28, 25, and 24 defectives, plot the corresponding proportions on the control chart and comment on the performance of the process.

Contingency Tables

The χ^2 statistic plays an important role in many other tests dealing with *count data*, that is, in problems where our information is obtained by counting rather than measuring. The method we shall discuss in this section is an extension of that of the preceding section and to illustrate it, suppose we want to determine whether there exists a relationship between the incomes of salesmen of hotel supplies and their educational background. Suppose, furthermore, that in a random sample of size $n = 400$ we obtained the results which are summarized in the following *contingency table* (this term is generally used in connection with two-way tables in which items, objects, persons, etc., are classified according to two characteristics):

	No College Education	Some College but No Degree	College Graduate	
Income under $8,000	63	78	29	170
Income between $8,000 and $12,000	48	82	45	175
Income over $12,000	9	20	26	55
	120	180	100	400

The null hypothesis we shall want to test is that for this kind of salesman income and educational background are *independent* (or in other words that there is no relationship between the income of salesmen of hotel supplies and their formal education). If this null hypothesis is true, the probability of randomly selecting a salesman of hotel supplies for our sample who has an income under $8,000 and no college education equals the *product* of the probability that he has an income under $8,000 and the probability that he has no college education (see Theorem L on page 129). Using the row and column totals of the above table to *estimate* these two probabilities, we obtain $\frac{170}{400}$ for the probability that a salesman of hotel supplies has an income under $8,000, and $\frac{120}{400}$ for the probability that he has no college education. Hence, we estimate the "true proportion" of salesmen of hotel supplies with incomes under $8,000 and no college education as $\frac{170}{400} \cdot \frac{120}{400}$, and in a sample of size 400 we would *expect* to find $\frac{170}{400} \cdot \frac{120}{400} \cdot 400 = \frac{170 \cdot 120}{400} = 51$ salesmen to fit this description.

Having thus obtained the *expected frequency* for the first cell of the first row of our table, it should be noted that after cancelling 400's, we obtained this value by multiplying the total of the first row by the total of the first column and then dividing by the grand-total of 400. In general we can (as on page 279) find the expected frequency for any one cell of a contingency table by *multiplying the total of the row to which it belongs by the total of the column to which it belongs and then dividing by the grand-total for the whole table.* Using this procedure, we obtain an expected frequency of $\frac{170 \cdot 180}{400} = 76.5$ for the second cell of the first row, and $\frac{175 \cdot 120}{400} = 52.5$ and $\frac{175 \cdot 180}{400} = 78.75$ for the first two cells of the second row. As it can be shown that the sum of the expected frequencies for each row or column must equal the sum of the corresponding observed frequencies, we obtain an expected frequency of

$$170 - (51 + 76.5) = 42.5$$

for the third cell of the first row,

$$175 - (52.5 + 78.75) = 43.75$$

for the third cell of the second row, and

$$120 - (51 + 52.5) = 16.5$$
$$180 - (76.5 + 78.75) = 24.75$$

and

$$100 - (42.5 + 43.75) = 13.75$$

for the three cells of the third row. Rounding the expected frequencies to one decimal, these results are summarized in the following table, where the expected frequencies are shown in parentheses below the frequencies that were actually observed:

	No College Education	Some College but No Degree	College Graduate
Income under $8,000	63 (51)	78 (76.5)	29 (42.5)
Income between $8,000 and $12,000	48 (52.5)	82 (78.8)	45 (43.8)
Income over $12,000	9 (16.5)	20 (24.8)	26 (13.8)

From here on, the work is like that of the preceding section; we calcu-late the χ^2 statistic according to the formula

$$\chi^2 = \Sigma \frac{(f - e)^2}{e} \qquad \bigstar$$

with $(f - e)^2/e$ calculated separately for each cell of the table. Then we use the criterion of Figure 9.8 as it is formulated on page 280, with the one exception that the number of degrees of freedom is given by a different formula. If a contingency table has r rows and k columns, the number of degrees of freedom for χ^2 is $(r - 1)(k - 1)$. In our numerical example it is $(3 - 1)(3 - 1) = 4$ and it should be noted that after we had calcu-lated four of the expected frequencies, all the others were obtained by subtraction from the totals of appropriate rows or columns.

Returning now to the observed and expected frequencies ˮof the above table, we get

$$\chi^2 = \frac{(63 - 51)^2}{51} + \frac{(78 - 76.5)^2}{76.5} + \frac{(29 - 42.5)^2}{42.5} + \frac{(48 - 52.5)^2}{52.5}$$

$$+ \frac{(82 - 78.8)^2}{78.8} + \frac{(45 - 43.8)^2}{43.8} + \frac{(9 - 16.5)^2}{16.5} + \frac{(20 - 24.8)^2}{24.8}$$

$$+ \frac{(26 - 13.8)^2}{13.8}$$

$$= 22.81$$

and since this value exceeds 9.488, the value of $\chi^2_{.05}$ for 4 degrees of freedom, the null hypothesis must be rejected. In other words, we have shown that there exists a significant dependence (or relationship) between the income and educational background of salesmen of hotel supplies.

Goodness of Fit

In this section we shall treat a further application of the χ^2 criterion, in which we compare an observed frequency distribution with a distribution we might expect according to theory or assumptions. To illustrate this method, let us return to the binomial distribution studied in Chapter 5, in particular to the one pertaining to the number of heads obtained in 3 flips of a balanced coin (or when flipping three balanced coins). As we saw on page 136, the probabilities of getting 0, 1, 2, or 3 heads are, respectively, $\frac{1}{8}$, $\frac{3}{8}$, $\frac{3}{8}$, and $\frac{1}{8}$. Suppose now that we actually toss 3 coins 240 times and that we obtain the results shown in the "observed frequency" column of the following table:

Number of Heads	Observed Frequency	Expected Frequency
0	21	30
1	101	90
2	83	90
3	35	30

The expected frequencies in the right-hand column were obtained by multiplying each of the corresponding probabilities by 240. [In other words, the number of times we expect 0 heads is $240(\frac{1}{8}) = 30$, the number of times we expect 1 head is $240(\frac{3}{8}) = 90$, and so on.]

As can be seen by inspection, there are some discrepancies between the observed frequencies and those provided by the binomial distribution; to check whether they may be attributed to chance, we calculate χ^2 by means of the formula

$$\chi^2 = \Sigma \, \frac{(f - e)^2}{e} \qquad \qquad \bigstar$$

If it turns out that the value we obtain for χ^2 is *too large* we reject the null hypothesis, namely, the hypothesis that the binomial distribution provides the appropriate theory for describing the given experiment.

(Actually, rejection of the null hypothesis would imply that either the coins are not all properly balanced or that they are not randomly flipped.) Substituting the above frequencies into the formula for χ^2, we get

$$\chi^2 = \frac{(21 - 30)^2}{30} + \frac{(101 - 90)^2}{90} + \frac{(83 - 90)^2}{90} + \frac{(35 - 30)^2}{30}$$

$$= 5.42$$

To decide whether this value is large enough to reject the null hypothesis, we again use the criterion on page 280, the one shown in Figure 9.8, with the only difference that in a problem of *goodness of fit* we use a different rule for the number of degrees of freedom. In general, *the number of degrees of freedom for this kind of test is given by the number of terms $(f - e)^2/e$ added in obtaining χ^2 minus the number of quantities, obtained from the observed data, that are used in calculating the expected frequencies.*

In our numerical example we had 4 terms in the formula for χ^2, and the only quantity needed from the observed data to calculate the expected frequencies was the total frequency of 240. Hence, the number of degrees of freedom is $4 - 1 = 3$, and for a level of significance of 0.05 Table III yields $\chi^2_{.05} = 7.815$. Since $\chi^2 = 5.42$ is less than this critical value, the null hypothesis cannot be rejected and we say that the binomial distribution provides a good fit to the data.

The method we have illustrated in this section is used quite generally to test how well theoretical distributions fit (or describe) observed data. In the exercises which follow, we shall thus test whether it is reasonable to treat an observed distribution as if it had (at least approximately) the shape of a normal distribution, and we shall also test whether a given set of data supports the assumption of the Poisson distribution introduced in Exercise 11 on page 141.

EXERCISES

1. A large department store operating several branches in a metropolitan area wants to determine whether there is a relationship between employees' length of service and their opinion concerning the merits of the store's annual "Back to School" sale. The table below shows the judgments of a random sample of 440 employees of the store:

	2 Years of Service or Less	3–5 Years of Service	6–10 Years of Service	More than 10 Years of Service
Sale is Very Good	48	51	43	35
Sale is Satisfactory	22	42	59	57
Sale is Poor	15	22	33	13

Find the expected frequencies under the null hypothesis that there is no relationship between length of service and opinion concerning the sale, calculate χ^2, and test the null hypothesis at a level of significance of 0.05.

2. An opinion research organization wants to determine whether there is any relationship between the quality of interviewers' work and their scores on an introvert-extrovert test of personality. Each interviewer is rated by his supervisor as being above average, average, or below average on the basis of such factors as persistence, need for supervision, complaints from alleged respondents, neatness in completing schedules, and so on. The results are as shown in the following table:

	Work above Average	Work is Average	Work below Average
Introvert	18	28	14
Average	37	63	30
Extrovert	15	29	16

Find the expected frequencies under the null hypothesis that there is no relationship, calculate χ^2, and test the null hypothesis at a level of significance of 0.05. What can one conclude about the effectiveness of this personality test in predicting whether a person applying for a position with the opinion research organization will turn out to be a good interviewer?

3. A trade publication wants to determine the attitudes of managers in various fields toward the value to business of such "prestige" type of activities as special expenditures for research, sponsorship of such events as science fairs, awarding college and university fellowships, and so on. The results of a poll of 500 managers in four fields showed the following results:

	Chemical	Oil	Electrical	Automobile
Of Little Value	50	25	30	20
Of Some Value	40	30	40	15
Of Great Value	75	55	80	40

Test at a level of significance of 0.01 whether there is any relationship between a manager's attitude towards such activities and the area of his employment.

4. The following table contains a distribution obtained for 320 tosses of 5 coins and the corresponding expected frequencies obtained by multiplying by 320 the binomial probabilities of 1/32, 5/32, 10/32, 10/32, 5/32, and 1/32:

Number of Heads	Observed Frequency	Expected Frequency
0	13	10
1	49	50
2	87	100
3	109	100
4	56	50
5	6	10

Test for goodness of fit at a level of significance of 0.05.

5. Test at the 0.05 level of significance whether a die is properly balanced if 120 rolls yielded the following results: 1 occurred 23 times, 2 occurred 21 times, 3 occurred 15 times, 4 occurred 17 times, 5 occurred 26 times, and 6 occurred 18 times.

6. The following is a distribution of the speeds with which 400 westbound cars passed a checkpoint on U.S. 80 in Arizona:

Speed (in miles per hour)	Number of Cars
39 or less	12
40–44	26
45–49	80
50–54	130
55–59	104
60 and over	48

The mean of these speeds, calculated before they were grouped, is $\bar{x} = 52.5$ mph and their standard deviation is $s = 6.6$ mph.

(a) Given a normal curve with $\mu = 52.5$ and $\sigma = 6.6$, find the area under the curve to the left of 39.5, between 39.5 and 44.5, between 44.5 and 49.5, between 49.5 and 54.5, between 54.5 and 59.5, and to the right of 59.5.

(b) Multiply by 400 the normal curve areas obtained in part (a), getting thus the *expected normal curve frequencies* corresponding to the six classes of the given distribution.

(c) Calculate χ^2 and test the null hypothesis that the given data may be looked upon as a random sample from a population having roughly the shape of a normal distribution. Use a level of significance of 0.05. (*Hint:* The number of degrees of freedom for testing the fit of a normal distribution by this method is $k - 3$, where k is the number of classes in the distribution.)

7. Use the method of Exercise 6 to test whether it is reasonable to look at the distribution of the 40 means of Figure 7.3 on page 189 as having roughly the shape of a normal distribution. Use a level of significance of 0.01. (As was indicated on page 191, the mean and the standard deviation of this distribution are 9.4 and 1.32, respectively.)

8. A company observed that in a 100-day period there were 12, 25, 28, 16, 10, 5, 3, and 1 days on which 0, 1, 2, 3, 4, 5, 6, and 7 or more record changes, respectively, were necessary for a certain record file. Is it reasonable to suppose at the 0.05 level of significance that the distribution of the daily number of required changes may be satisfactorily described by a Poisson distribution with $\lambda = 2$? Calculate the probabilities for 0, 1, 2, 3, 4, 5, and 6 record changes with the formula given in Exercise 12 on page 142, and then obtain the probability for "7 or more" by subtraction. Since none of the expected frequencies should be less than 5 (see page 280), it may be necessary to combine some of the classes of the distribution.

A Word of Caution

There is an interesting analogy between significance testing and the principle of criminal law that a person is presumed innocent until he is proven guilty. In significance tests the burden of proof is on us to show that observed differences (discrepancies between several sets of data or discrepancies between theory and practice) are too large to be reasonably attributed to chance; in criminal proceedings, the burden of proof is on the prosecution, which must show beyond any reasonable doubt that the defendant is guilty. Thus, it can happen that a guilty party is found "not guilty" simply because the prosecution did not have quite enough evidence to get a conviction. Similarly, we may fail to reject a null hypothesis due to the vagaries of Lady Luck or simply because we do not have enough data to "get a conviction." The fact that a party is found "not guilty" in a court of law does not necessarily imply that he is considered innocent, say, in the eye of the public. Similarly, if we are unable to reject a null hypothesis, this does not mean that we must necessarily accept it; it was for this reason that we introduced the prerogative of reserving judgment whenever such an action is feasible and appropriate.

Also, it must be remembered that in statistics the term "significant" is used in a special technical sense. If we say that something is "statistically significant," it does not follow that it is necessarily significant in the sense of being particularly meaningful or of any practical importance. It can well happen that we get a significant difference in public response to two products (say, the unsweetened and sweetened fruit soups referred to on page 274), while the actual difference is so small that it is "commercially insignificant"—it does not warrant the expense of switching from one product to the other. This kind of difficulty would not arise if we viewed problems of hypothesis testing within the more general and wider framework of *decision theory*, where we would consider also the consequences that are involved. However, this would present other problems (see page 251) that are difficult to surmount. In any case, the methods presented in this chapter are widely used and they have proved themselves extremely valuable in industry, in management, and in virtually all of the natural and social sciences.

Technical Note 10 (Small-sample Tests Concerning Means)

If n is small (less than 30) we proceed as in Technical Note 9, assuming that the population from which we are sampling has roughly the shape of a normal distribution, and we base our methods on the statistic

$$t = \frac{\bar{x} - \mu}{s/\sqrt{n}} \qquad \bigstar$$

whose sampling distribution is the Student-t distribution with $n - 1$ degrees of freedom (see Figure 8.3 on page 244). Since the above formula

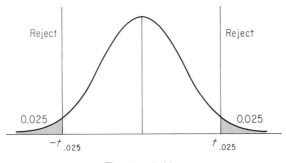

FIGURE 9.10

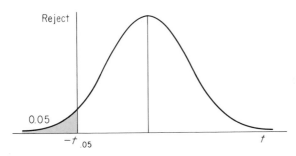

FIGURE 9.11

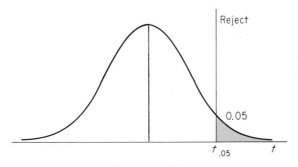

FIGURE 9.12

for t is identical with the one for z given on page 265, where we replaced σ by s, the only difference between the small-sample tests and the large-sample tests concerning means is in the dividing lines of the criteria. Using $\alpha = 0.05$, the dividing lines for the two-tail test are $-t_{.025}$ and $t_{.025}$ instead of -1.96 and 1.96, and the dividing line for the one-tail test is either $-t_{.05}$ or $t_{.05}$ instead of -1.64 or 1.64, depending on whether the alternative hypothesis is $\mu < \mu_0$ or $\mu > \mu_0$ (see Figures 9.10, 9.11, and

9.12). For $\alpha = 0.01$, the corresponding dividing lines for the two-tail test are $-t_{.005}$ and $t_{.005}$, and the one for the one-tail test is either $-t_{.01}$ or $t_{.01}$. All of these critical values of t may be obtained from Table II, with the number of degrees of freedom equal to $n - 1$.

To illustrate this kind of test, suppose we want to investigate whether certain mechanical equipment can (on the average) sort a firm's completely randomized lists of inventory item numbers in 20 minutes. In order to test the hypothesis $\mu = 20$ minutes against the one-sided alternative $\mu > 20$ minutes, so that the rejection of the null hypothesis implies that the equipment is *too slow* for the job, 8 such lists are run through the equipment. The results are that they required on the average 23.4 minutes with a standard deviation of 2.7 minutes. Substituting $n = 8$, $\bar{x} = 23.4$, $\mu = 20.0$, and $s = 2.7$ into the formula for t, we get

$$t = \frac{23.4 - 20.0}{(2.7)/\sqrt{8}} = 3.56$$

Since this exceeds 1.895, the value of $t_{.05}$ for $8 - 1 = 7$ degrees of freedom, the null hypothesis must be rejected, and we conclude that the equipment is too slow for the job.

The Student-t distribution also provides a small-sample criterion for tests concerning the *difference between two means*. To use this criterion, we have to assume that the two samples come from populations which can be approximated closely with normal distributions and which, furthermore, have *equal variances*. Specifically, we test the null hypothesis $\mu_1 = \mu_2$ against the two-sided alternative $\mu_1 \neq \mu_2$ with the statistic

$$t = \frac{\bar{x}_1 - \bar{x}_2}{\sqrt{\dfrac{\Sigma (x_1 - \bar{x}_1)^2 + \Sigma (x_2 - \bar{x}_2)^2}{n_1 + n_2 - 2} \cdot \left(\dfrac{1}{n_1} + \dfrac{1}{n_2}\right)}} \qquad \bigstar$$

where $\Sigma (x_1 - \bar{x}_1)^2$ is the sum of the squared deviations from the mean of the first sample while $\Sigma (x_2 - \bar{x}_2)^2$ is the sum of the squared deviations from the mean of the second sample. Note that since, by definition, $\Sigma (x_1 - \bar{x}_1)^2 = (n_1 - 1) \cdot s_1^2$ and $\Sigma (x_2 - \bar{x}_2)^2 = (n_2 - 1) \cdot s_2^2$, the above formula can be simplified somewhat when the two sample variances have already been calculated from the data.

Under these assumptions, it can be shown that the sampling distribution of this t-statistic is the Student-t distribution with $n_1 + n_2 - 2$

degrees of freedom. Using a 0.05 level of significance (and the two-sided alternative) the criterion for this test is again the one shown in Figure 9.10.

To illustrate this small-sample test for the difference between two means, let us refer to the example on page 63, where we compared the average square footage covered by one-gallon cans of certain kinds of paint. Limiting our comparison here to Brands A and C, we have the following data concerning the number of square feet covered, respectively, by 5 one-gallon cans of each kind of paint:

$$\textit{Brand A:} \quad 505, \quad 516, \quad 478, \quad 513, \quad 503$$
$$\textit{Brand C:} \quad 496, \quad 485, \quad 490, \quad 520, \quad 484$$

The means of these two samples are 503 and 495, and we shall now want to test whether the difference of 8 is significant. In order to calculate t according to the above formula, we first determine

$$\Sigma \ (x_1 - \bar{x}_1)^2 = 2^2 + 13^2 + 25^2 + 10^2 + 0^2 = 898$$

$$\Sigma \ (x_2 - \bar{x}_2)^2 = 1^2 + 10^2 + 5^2 + 25^2 + 11^2 = 872$$

Substituting these values together with $n_1 = n_2 = 5$, $\bar{x}_1 = 503$, and $\bar{x}_2 = 495$ into the formula for t, we obtain

$$t = \frac{503 - 495}{\sqrt{\dfrac{898 + 872}{5 + 5 - 2} \cdot \left(\dfrac{1}{5} + \dfrac{1}{5}\right)}} = 0.85$$

Since 0.85 falls between -2.306 and 2.306, where 2.306 is the value of $t_{.025}$ for $5 + 5 - 2 = 8$ degrees of freedom, it follows that the difference between the two sample means is *not significant*. (A method for comparing the means obtained for all three of the paints will be taken up later in Chapter 12 under the heading of "Analysis of Variance.")

TEN
DECISION MAKING: PROBLEMS OF PREDICTION

association (Correlation)

Curve Fitting

The foremost objective of many statistical investigations in busines and economics is to make predictions—that is, to forecast such things a the demand for a new product, the growth of an industry, the futur value of a piece of property, the performance of a new salesman, traffi on a new freeway, and so forth. Although predictions based on statistica information may sometimes (providentially) agree with the exact value they are intended to predict, this is the exception rather than the rule It must constantly be kept in mind that, by their very nature, prediction based on statistical information cannot always be right; at best, they ca be formulated only in terms of probabilities and one must be satisfied if one is right a high percentage of the time or if one's predictions ar *on the average* reasonably close.

Whenever possible, scientists strive to express, or approximate, rela tionships between quantities that are known and quantities they want t predict in terms of mathematical equations. This approach has bee very successful in the natural sciences; it is known, for instance, that at constant temperature the relationship between the volume (y) of a gas and its pressure (x) is given by the formula

$$x \cdot y = k$$

where k is a numerical constant. Similarly, in biology it has been discovered that the size of a culture of bacteria (y) can be expressed in terms of the time (x) it has been exposed to certain favorable conditions by means of the formula

$$y = a \cdot b^x$$

where a and b are numerical constants.

Businessmen and economists have borrowed and continue to borrow liberally from the tools of the natural sciences. Among others, the two aforementioned equations are often used to describe relationships between such things as the total consumption and the price of a commodity, a company's sales and the number of years it has been in operation, the size of an order and unit cost, and so on. To give a concrete example, it can be shown, for instance, that the annual sales of life insurance in a certain southern state may be forecast quite accurately by means of the formula

$$y = 160(1.20)^x$$

where y represents sales in millions of dollars, while x is the number of years that have elapsed between 1946 and the year whose sales we want to predict. Substituting $x = 24$, we might thus predict 1970 life insurance sales of

$$160(1.20)^{24} = 1,480 \text{ million dollars}$$

for the given state. (As a word of warning, we might add that this constitutes quite an *extrapolation*; that is, we are going considerably beyond the time period on the basis of which the equation was originally obtained, and we are proportionally sticking out our necks.)

Of the many equations that can be used for purposes of prediction, the simplest and the most widely used is the linear equation (in two unknowns), which is the form

$$y = a + bx$$

where a and b are numerical constants. Once these constants are known (usually, they are estimated on the basis of sample data), we can calculate a predicted value of y for any given value of x simply by substitution. *Linear equations are useful and important not only because there exist many relationships that are actually of this form, but also because they often provide close approximations to relationships which would otherwise be difficult to describe in mathematical terms.*

The term "linear equation" arises from the fact that, when plotted on ordinary graph paper, all pairs of values of x and y which satisfy an equation of the form $y = a + bx$ will fall on a straight line. To illustrate, let us consider the equation

$$y = 1.22 - 0.03x$$

whose graph is shown in Figure 10.1. In this equation, x stands for road width (in yards) and y stands for the corresponding number of accidents

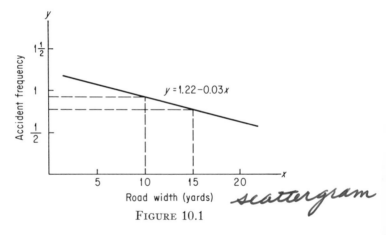

Road width (yards) *scattergram*

FIGURE 10.1

occurring per million vehicle miles; the constants 1.22 and -0.03 were obtained from a study of a state highway department. If the width of a road is 10 yards, the predicted number of accidents per million vehicle miles is $1.22 - 0.03(10) = 0.92$, and by similar substitution, if the width of a road is 15 yards, the predicted number of accidents per million vehicle miles is 0.77. Any pair of values of x and y satisfying the above equation constitutes a point (x, y) which falls on the line of Figure 10.1.

In any problem of prediction in which we want to use some kind of mathematical equation, we face essentially *three* kinds of problems. First, we must decide what kind of curve is to be used; namely, we must decide whether it is to be a straight line, a parabola of the form

$$y = a + bx + cx^2$$

an exponential curve like the one used earlier in the insurance example on page 297, or one of many other kinds of curves. This question is usually decided by inspecting the data from which the predicting equation is to be obtained; we plot the data on ordinary graph paper, sometimes on special logarithmic or log-log graph paper, and we thus decide upon the kind of curve that will give a reasonably good fit. (There exist methods for putting this decision on a less subjective basis, but we shall not go into them in this introductory text.)

To illustrate this procedure (as well as subsequent problems of curve fitting), suppose that a metals company, manufacturers of ball bearings, bushings, compression springs, shafts, and many other parts used in precision instruments and machinery, wishes to study the relationship between the "quality" of parts of a certain kind and the processing time for the part. The quality characteristic under consideration is hardness; a hardness number (referred to simply as "quality") is calculated for each part by a special formula using data gathered in tests in which a spherical ball subjected to a given compressive load is used to penetrate or indent the surface of the part. The following data show the results of tests conducted on a random sample of 10 parts of a given kind. The two numbers given for each part are the number of minutes spent in processing the part, x, and the quality (hardness) of the part, y:

Processing Time x	Quality y
15	180
12	140
20	230
17	190
12	160
25	300
22	270
9	110
18	240
30	320

Plotting the points corresponding to these 10 pairs of values as we have done in Figure 10.2, it is apparent that although the points do not actually fall on a straight line, the over-all pattern of the relationship is pretty well described by the dotted line. Consequently, we feel justified in deciding that a straight line will describe the relationship between processing time and the given quality characteristic reasonably well.

We now face the second problem of curve fitting, namely, that of finding the equation of the line (or whatever other kind of curve we may have decided upon) which in some sense provides the best possible fit to our data and which, we hope, will later yield the best possible predictions. Logically speaking, there is no limit to the number of straight lines we can draw on a piece of paper; some of these are such obviously poor fits that they can be ruled out immediately, but there are many left which seem to provide a fairly good fit. In order to single out one line as the one which "best" fits our data, we will have to state specifically

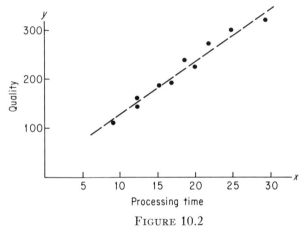

FIGURE 10.2

what we mean here by "best"; in other words, we will have to state precisely *in what sense* the line is to provide the "best" fit to the data. If all the points actually fell on a straight line, the criterion would be self-evident, but that is an extreme case we cannot expect to encounter very often in practical applications. In general, we shall have to be satisfied with a line having certain desirable (though not perfect) characteristics. The criterion that is most widely used for this purpose (that is, for defining a "best" fit), is the criterion of *least squares*, which we shall explain in the next section. It dates back to the early part of the nineteenth century and the French mathematician Adrien Legendre. Nowadays, least squares methods are widely used in various branches of statistics.

Leaving the mechanics of the method of least squares to the next section, let us suppose, for the moment, that by using this method we

)btained the equation

$$y' = 24.43 + 10.53x$$

'or our numerical example. Note that we have put a prime on the y in
order to differentiate between the value of y which was actually observed
or a certain value of x and the corresponding value obtained with the
ise of the equation of the line (see Figure 10.3).

The equation which we have obtained is the desired "predicting"
equation, namely, the equation which now enables us to predict the
quality of a part in terms of the length of time that it was processed.

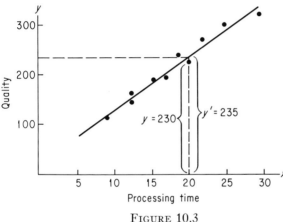

FIGURE 10.3

'or instance, for a part processed 20 minutes we can predict a quality
hardness) of

$$y' = 24.43 + 10.53(20) = 235.03$$

or, roughly, 235.

Having obtained the equation of a line by the method of least squares
and having used it to make a prediction, we must now face the third
basic problem of curve fitting; we must ask ourselves such questions as

"How good are the values we obtained for the constants a and b in
the equation $y = a + bx$? After all, the numbers 24.43 and 10.53
are only estimates based on sample data."

"How are we to interpret the predicted quality of a part processed
for 20 minutes? It would hardly seem reasonable to suppose that
all parts processed for 20 minutes have the identical hardness."

"How can we obtain limits, two numbers, which are indicative of the goodness of a prediction in the same way in which a confidence interval is indicative of the goodness of an estimate, say, of the mean of a population?"

Before we try to answer any of these questions, let us point out a fundamental difference between the problem in which we predicted the 1970 life insurance sales in a certain southern state and the two problems in which we predicted accident frequency in terms of road width and the quality of certain parts in terms of their processing time. Whereas the life insurance prediction is, so to speak, a "one shot" affair—there is only one correct figure for these 1970 life insurance sales—the situation is quite different in the other two examples. The prediction that there will be 0.92 accidents per million vehicle miles on a stretch of road whose width is 10 yards can be applied to many different roads having this particular width; as a matter of fact, it can even be applied to the same stretch of road for different periods of time. Similarly, the prediction that a part processed 20 minutes will have a quality rating of 235 can be applied to as many parts as the manufacturer may wish to process for 20 minutes. Clearly, we cannot reasonably expect 0.92 accidents per million vehicle miles for *every* road whose width is 10 yards, and we cannot reasonably expect *every* part processed by the manufacturer for 20 minutes to have a hardness rating of 235. These two phenomena are random phenomena: they are subject to chance fluctuations, and we can at best say that *on the average* there are 0.92 accidents per million vehicle miles on a road whose width is 10 yards, or that a part processed for 20 minutes by the given manufacturer will *on the average* have a hardness rating of 235. We thus look at each of these predicting equations as representing a *curve of means*, or as a *regression equation*, which gives for each x an estimate of the *mean* of the corresponding distribution of the y's.*

To give another example, suppose that a study of the ages and second-hand prices charged for a certain make of two-door sedan yielded the following predicting equation, where x is the age in years and y is the price in dollars:

$$y' = 1{,}708 - 136x$$

---

* The term *regression*, as it is used here, is due to Francis Galton; he employed it first in connection with a study of the heights of fathers and sons, observing a regression (or turning back) from the heights of sons to the heights of their fathers.

Substituting $x = 4$ into this equation, we obtain $y' = \$1,164$, and according to what we have just said this means that the *average price* of 4-year-old models of this kind of car is estimated as $\$1,164$. Some will cost less, some will cost more, but we estimate that *on the average* their price is $\$1,164$.

In each of these last three examples we used an expression of the form $a + bx$ (with a and b determined on the basis of appropriate data) to estimate the true mean of y for a given value of x. Now, if the true mean of y for a given value of x is denoted $\alpha + \beta x$, we can look upon a as an estimate of α (*alpha*) and b as an estimate of β (*beta*). Thus, if the true average quality of a part processed x minutes is $\alpha + \beta x$, we look upon $a = 24.43$ as an estimate of α and $b = 10.53$ as an estimate of β. Similarly, for the accident-frequency and road-width example we estimate the *regression coefficients* α and β as 1.22 and -0.03, and for the example dealing with the ages and prices of certain cars we estimate the corresponding quantities as 1,708 and -136.

Let us now return to the three questions posed on page 301, of which the second has actually been answered already in the preceding discussion. Rephrasing the first question, we can now ask, "how good are the estimates a and b which we obtained for the regression coefficients α and β?" Although the technical detail is fairly involved, there exist methods which enable us to construct confidence limits for α and β, and we can thus evaluate the "goodness" of our estimates by the methods of Chapter 8. How this is done for β is illustrated in Exercise 10 on page 319; we shall not go into it here, since the most convenient form of the computing formula involves the *correlation coefficient*, which we have not yet discussed. Let us point out, though, that in most problems we are more interested in β, the *slope* of the regression line, than in α. In the road-width and accident-frequency example, β measures the change in accident frequency which corresponds to a unit (one yard) increase in road width, while in the processing-time and hardness example, β measures the increase in quality per unit (one minute) increase in processing time. Determining the change in y which is associated with a unit change in x is often the most important objective of a study. On the other hand, α merely measures the value on the line which corresponds to $x = 0$, and in many cases this has no practical significance at all. It should also be pointed out that there exist methods for putting confidence limits on $\alpha + \beta x$ for a given value of x, that is, confidence limits for the true mean of the y's for a given value of x (see Exercise 12 on page 312).

The answer to the third question on page 302 will be given in Technical Note 11 on page 348, where we shall give a method for calculating so-called *limits of prediction*. Using this method, we will be able to assert, for instance, with a probability of 0.95 that the hardness rating of a part processed by the given manufacturer for 20 minutes will fall on the interval from 197 to 273.

The Method of Least Squares

If the reader has ever had the opportunity to analyze data which were plotted as points on a piece of graph paper, he has probably felt the urge

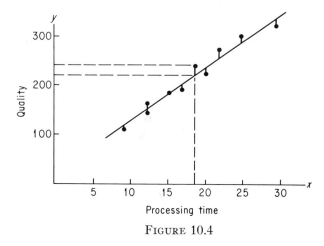

FIGURE 10.4

to take a ruler, juggle it around, and decide upon a line which, to the eye, presents a fairly good fit. There is no law which says that this cannot be done, but it certainly is not very "scientific." Another argument against freehand curve fitting is that it is largely subjective and, hence, there is no way of evaluating the "goodness" of subsequent predictions.

As it will be used in this chapter, the *least squares criterion* demands that the line which we fit to our data be such that *the sum of the squares of the vertical deviations (distances) from the points to the line is a minimum*. For our hardness and processing-time example, the method of least squares requires that the sum of the squares of the distances represented by the solid line segments of Figure 10.4 be as small as possible. The logic behind this approach may be explained as follows: considering, for example, the part which was processed for 18 minutes, we find that it had a hardness rating of 240. Reading the value which corresponds to

$x = 18$ directly off the line of Figure 10.4, we see that the corresponding "predicted" value is roughly $y' = 215$, so that the error of the prediction, represented by the vertical distance from the point to the line, is about $y - y' = 240 - 215 = 25$. There are 10 such errors corresponding to the 10 parts, and the least squares criterion demands that we minimize the sum of their squares. We do not minimize the sum of the deviations (distances), themselves, since some of the deviations are positive, some are negative, and their sum is always equal to zero.

To show how a least squares line is actually fitted to a set of data, let us consider n pairs of numbers $(x_1, y_1), (x_2, y_2), \ldots, (x_n, y_n)$, which might represent such things as automobile registrations and total gasoline sales in n different states, the incomes and medical expenditures of n families, the hardness and tensile strength of n parts made by a certain machine, the I.Q.'s of n fathers and sons, and so on. We shall always use the letter y for the variable which is to be predicted in terms of the other, that is, in terms of x, and we, therefore, write the predicting equation as

$$y' = a + bx$$

As was pointed out before, we use the symbol y' to distinguish between the *observed* values of y and the corresponding *calculated* values obtained with the equation of the line. For each of the n given values of x we thus have a *given* value of y and a *calculated* value y'.

The least squares criterion requires that we find the numerical values of the constants a and b appearing in the equation $y' = a + bx$ for which

$$\Sigma (y - y')^2$$

is as small as possible. In other words, we minimize the sum of the squares of the differences between the observed y's and the predicted y''s (see Figure 10.5). We shall not go through the actual derivation (which requires either calculus or a process called "completing the square"), but simply state the result that minimizing $\Sigma (y - y')^2$ yields the following two equations in the unknowns a and b:

$$\Sigma y = na + b(\Sigma x)$$
$$\Sigma xy = a(\Sigma x) + b(\Sigma x^2)$$

★

Here n is the number of pairs of observations, Σx and Σy are, respectively, the sums of the given x's and y's, Σx^2 is the sum of the squares of the x's, and $\Sigma\ xy$ is the sum of the products obtained by multiplying each of the given x's by the corresponding observed value of y. The above equations, whose solution gives the desired least squares values of a and b, are usually called the *normal equations*.

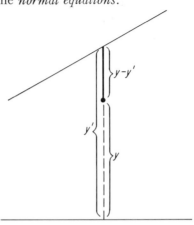

FIGURE 10.5

Returning now to our numerical example and copying the first two columns from page 299, we obtain the sums needed for substitution into the normal equations from the following table:

Processing Time x	Quality y	x^2	xy
15	180	225	2,700
12	140	144	1,680
20	230	400	4,600
17	190	289	3,230
12	160	144	1,920
25	300	625	7,500
22	270	484	5,940
9	110	81	990
18	240	324	4,320
30	320	900	9,600
180	2,140	3,616	42,480

Substituting $n = 10$ and the appropriate column totals into the two normal equations, we get

$$2{,}140 = 10a + 180b$$

$$42{,}480 = 180a + 3{,}616b$$

and we must now solve these two simultaneous linear equations; that is, we must find the values of a and b which *together* satisfy the two equations. There are several ways in which this can be done, and the reader may recall from elementary algebra that such equations can be solved by the *method of elimination* or by the use of determinants. In either case, we obtain $a = 24.43$ and $b = 10.53$.

To simplify this work, let us solve the two normal equations symbolically for a and b, so that the solution can then be obtained by direct substitution. Going through the necessary algebraic steps, we obtain

$$\bar{y} = a + b\bar{x}$$

$$a = \frac{(\Sigma\, y)(\Sigma\, x^2) - (\Sigma\, x)(\Sigma\, xy)}{n(\Sigma\, x^2) - (\Sigma\, x)^2} \qquad a = \bar{y} - b\bar{x}$$

$$b = \frac{n(\Sigma\, xy) - (\Sigma\, x)(\Sigma\, y)}{n(\Sigma\, x^2) - (\Sigma\, x)^2} \qquad \bigstar$$

and for our example we have

$$a = \frac{(2{,}140)(3{,}616) - (180)(42{,}480)}{10(3{,}616) - (180)^2} = \frac{91{,}840}{3{,}760} = 24.43$$

$$b = \frac{10(42{,}480) - (180)(2{,}140)}{10(3{,}616) - (180)^2} = \frac{39{,}600}{3{,}760} = 10.53$$

There is still another way of getting these values which is often used because of its convenience: first we calculate b using the above formula, and then we substitute this value into the first of the two normal equations to obtain a. We would thus get $2{,}140 = 10a + 180(10.53)$ or

$$a = \frac{2140 - 180(10.53)}{10} = 24.46, \text{ which (except for a slight rounding}$$

error) agrees with the value of a obtained before.

We can now write the equation of the least squares line for our numerical example as

$$y' = 24.43 + 10.53x$$

This is the "predicting" equation which we gave earlier on page 301, and as we illustrated at that time, the predicted value of y for any given value of x is obtained by multiplying x by 10.53 and adding 24.43. For $x = 20$, we thus obtained $y' = 24.43 + 10.53(20) = 235$; in other words, we predict that a part processed for 20 minutes will (on the average) have a quality rating of 235.

In the discussion of this section we have considered only the problem of fitting a straight line to paired data. More generally, the method of least squares can also be used to fit other kinds of curves and even "predicting equations" in more than two unknowns. Among the many equations that can be used to express relationships between more than two variables, the most widely used are *linear equations* of the form

$$y' = a + bx_1 + cx_2 + dx_3 + \dots$$

in which y is the variable to be predicted and the x's (of which there may be several depending upon the nature of the problem) are the known variables on which the predictions are to be based. For example, the equation

$$y' = 3.4892 - 0.0899x_1 + 0.0637x_2 + 0.0187x_3$$

arose in a study of the demand for beef and veal. Here y stands for the total consumption of federally inspected beef and veal in millions of pounds, x_1 stands for a composite retail price of beef in cents per pound, x_2 represents a composite retail price of pork in cents per pound, and x_3 stands for income as measured by a certain payroll index. The numerical constants of this equation were obtained by the method of least squares. In a situation like this, the method of least squares requires the solution of as many normal equations as there are variables, but this is no problem to a digital computer. Least squares equations involving 30 or more variables (whose solution by hand would require months of work) can be solved in a matter of minutes on a fast machine. Since problems like these are of great importance, suitable programs for various computers are readily available.

EXERCISES

1. Raw material used in the production of a synthetic fiber is stored in a place without humidity control. Measurements of the relative humidity in the storage place and the moisture content of a sample of the raw material (both in percentages) on 10 days (randomly selected over a given period of time) yielded the following results:

Humidity, x	46	30	34	52	38	44	40	45	34	60
Moisture content, y	10	7	9	13	8	12	11	11	7	14

(a) Construct suitable scales for x and y and plot the original data.

(b) Use the normal equations on page 305 to find a and b for the equation of the least squares line which will enable one to predict (estimate) the moisture content of the raw material going into production in terms of the humidity in the storage place. Plot the line on the chart obtained in part (a).

(c) Predict the moisture content of a batch of stored raw material when the humidity is 45 per cent (1) by substituting $x = 45$ into the equation of the line, and (2) by reading the estimate directly off the diagram completed in part (b).

2. In connection with planning servicing facilities for machines that require attention, a company wants to study the relationship between the number of machines waiting for attention at a given time and the average time required by operators to service the machines. More specifically, the company wants to know whether there is a tendency for operators to work faster (and reduce the service time) when the number of machines waiting for service is large. Accordingly, the company randomly selects 8 records showing the number of machines in line at the beginning of a given time period and the number of services completed by an operator during the period. The following are the data:

Machines in line, x	3	6	5	4	4	6	8	7
Number of completed services, y	3	2	3	5	3	6	6	4

(a) Use the formulas on page 307 to compute a and b and write the equation of the least squares line.

(b) Plot the original data and line obtained in part (a) on one diagram.

(c) Predict the average number of services an operator will complete during a period when there are 5 machines in line at the beginning of the period.

3. A study is made to determine the relationship between the area burned in forest fires in U.S. counties having a formal fire-control organization (with a county ranger, smoke-chaser assistants during the fire season, fire crew members, and so on, supported by annual fire-control appropriations) and the variable operating costs of the fire protection. (The ranger's salary is a fixed operating cost and unrelated to the area burned. Money over and above the ranger's salary which determines how much he can travel, the equipment and facilities he can buy, and how many men he can hire—the variable operating funds—directly affect the quality of fire protection.) A random sample of the annual figures for 12 counties shows the following variable operating expenses (in cents per acre) and the area burned (as a per cent of the protected area):

Variable Operating Funds x	Protected Area Burned y
2.8	0.09
1.7	0.24
1.9	0.36
2.5	0.12
2.7	0.20
0.8	0.40
1.5	0.34
2.8	0.14
2.2	0.22
1.2	0.42
2.1	0.30
0.7	0.48

(a) Use the normal equations to find a and b for the least squares line which will make it possible to predict area burned from knowledge of available variable operating funds.

(b) Plot the original data and the line obtained in part (a) on one diagram.

(c) Predict the percentage of protected area burned in a county having 2.0 cents per acre variable operating expenditures (1) by using the equation of the least squares line, and (2) by reading the prediction off the line plotted in part (b).

4. In learning computer programming, a large group of business administration students are given instructional materials and allowed to proceed at their own pace, handing in required assignments as they are completed. At the end of the "course," 10 students are randomly selected and given an achievement test. The following are the number of hours they required to complete the work and their grades on the test:

Hours spent, x	30	25	50	38	20	70	35	24	60	45
Test score, y	80	80	45	70	95	20	50	90	25	50

(a) Find the equation of the least squares line which will enable us to predict a student's achievement score in terms of the number of hours required to complete the course.

(b) Use the equation obtained in part (a) to determine the score we would expect a student to get on the test if he took 40 hours to complete the course.

5. An analytic chemist makes a study of the relationship between the nicotine and tar in cigarettes. Taking 9 different brands of king-size filter cigarettes, he obtains the following results:

Nicotine in smoke (mg), x	0.6	1.6	1.6	1.6	1.7	1.8	1.8	2.0	2.3
Tar in smoke (mg), y	11.8	16.5	17.2	24.1	25.2	20.6	22.8	22.4	19.3

(a) Find the equation of the least squares line by first computing b with the use of the formula on page 307 and then obtaining a by substituting this value of b into the first of the normal equations.

(b) Plot the original data and line on one diagram.

(c) Estimate the tar content of a cigarette which has 1.5 mg nicotine content in the smoke (1) by using the equation of the line obtained in (a), and (2) by reading the value directly off the line plotted in part (b). What does the scatter of the plot of the original data suggest about the possible merits of such predictions?

6. One phase of a large-scale sociological and economic study is devoted to the relationship between educational level and income. As part of this work an investigator takes a random sample of 8 cities in a 13-state geographical region and finds from 1960 decennial census data (published by the Bureau of the Census) what percentage of the city population are college graduates and the city's median income (in dollars). The following are the results:

Per Cent College Graduate x	Median Income y
7.2	4,244
6.7	4,915
17.0	7,020
12.5	6,215
6.3	3,816
23.9	7,566
6.0	4,438
10.2	5,387

(a) Find the equation of the least squares line with which one can predict a city's median income on the basis of the percentage of its population that are college graduates.

(b) Plot the original data as well as the least squares line on one diagram.

(c) Estimate the median income of a city having 12 per cent college graduates among its population.

7. Suppose that in Exercise 6 we had been interested in predicting a city's percentage of college graduates in terms of its median income. Interchanging x and y for the data of Exercise 6, find the corresponding least squares line and compare it with the one obtained in Exercise 6.

(The exercises which follow are based on the material in Technical Note 11 on page 348.)

8. Use the results of Exercise 1 to construct 0.95 limits of prediction for the moisture content of a batch of raw materials when the humidity is 45 per cent.

9. Use the values of a and b obtained in Exercise 2 to calculate first the standard error of estimate and then 0.95 limits of prediction for the number of services an operator will complete during a period when there are 5 machines in line at the beginning of the period.

10. Use the results of Exercise 3 to construct 0.99 limits of prediction for the percentage of protected area burned in a county having 2.0 cents per acre variable operating expenditures.

11. Using the values of a and b obtained in Exercise 5, calculate first the standard error of estimate and then 0.95 limits of prediction for the tar content of cigarettes having a nicotine content of 1.5 mg.

12. If it is desired to estimate the *mean* of y for a given value x_0, appropriate 0.95 confidence limits for $\alpha + \beta x_0$ can be written in the form $(a + bx_0) \pm B$, where B is almost identical with the quantity A (as given on page 349), except that inside the radical $\dfrac{n + 1}{n}$ is replaced by $\dfrac{1}{n}$. Apply this method to the example in the text and find 0.95 confidence limits for the *average quality* of a part processed for 20 minutes.

13. Apply the method suggested in Exercise 12 to the data of Exercise 2 (see also Exercise 9) and construct 0.95 confidence limits for the *average number of services* an operator will complete during a period when there are 5 machines in line at the beginning of the period.

Correlation

Having learned how to fit a least squares line to a set of paired data, let us now study a way of measuring how good the fit of such a line actually is in any given problem. To this end, let us first analyze the variability of the observed y's (in our example the variability in the quality of the 10 parts). As can be seen from the data on page 299, there is considerable variation among the y's, the smallest being 110 and the largest being 320. It is also apparent from these data as well as Figures 10.2 and 10.3 that this variation is not all due to chance. The fact that the 8th part tested had the low quality rating of 110 must be due, at least in part, to the fact that it was processed for only 9 minutes. Similarly, the fact that the 10th part tested had the high quality rating of 320 must be due, at least in part, to the fact that it was processed for the much longer period of

30 minutes. This raises the following question: *how much of the total variation of the y's can be attributed to chance and how much can be attributed to the relationship between the two variables x and y, namely, to the fact that the observed y's correspond to different values of x?*

As a measure of the total variation of the observed y's we can use their variance or, which is practically the same, the sum of squares

$$\Sigma \, (y - \bar{y})^2$$

namely, the variance multiplied by $n - 1$. As can be seen from the second column of the table on page 306, $\Sigma \, y = 2{,}140$, so that $\bar{y} = \dfrac{2{,}140}{10} = 214$ and, hence,

$$
\begin{aligned}
\Sigma \, (y - \bar{y})^2 &= (180 - 214)^2 + (140 - 214)^2 + (230 - 214)^2 \\
&\quad + (190 - 214)^2 + (160 - 214)^2 + (300 - 214)^2 \\
&\quad + (270 - 214)^2 + (110 - 214)^2 + (240 - 214)^2 \\
&\quad + (320 - 214)^2 \\
&= 43{,}640
\end{aligned}
$$

If *all* of this variation could be attributed to differences in processing time, the 10 points would all have to fall on a straight line (provided, of course, the relationship between processing time and quality is actually of this kind). The fact that they do not is an indication that there are other factors at play, and we shall assume that all of these other factors can be combined under the general heading of "chance."

Chance variation is thus measured by the amounts by which the points deviate from the line, namely, by the quantity

$$\Sigma \, (y - y')^2$$

which is the sum of the squares of the deviations represented by the solid line segments of Figure 10.4. (If all the points actually fell on a straight line, $\Sigma \, (y - y')^2$ would have to equal zero.) In order to compute this quantity for our example, we will first have to calculate the predicted values y' by substituting the given values of x into the least squares equation

$$y' = 24.43 + 10.53x$$

(An alternate, and easier, way of calculating $\Sigma \, (y - y')^2$ is given in the technical note on page 348.) We thus get $y' = 24.43 + 10.53(15)$

= 182.38 for the first part, $y' = 24.43 + 10.53(12) = 150.79$ for the second part, ..., and $y' = 24.43 + 10.53(30) = 340.33$ for the tenth part. Substituting these values together with the observed y's into $\Sigma (y - y')^2$, we obtain

$$\Sigma (y - y')^2 = (180 - 182.38)^2 + (140 - 150.79)^2 + \ldots$$
$$+ (320 - 340.33)^2$$
$$= 1,934$$

Hence, we can claim that

$$\frac{\Sigma (y - y')^2}{\Sigma (y - \bar{y})^2} \cdot 100 = \frac{1,934}{43,640} \cdot 100 = 4.43 \ per \ cent$$

of the variation in the quality of the parts can be attributed to chance; the remaining $100 - 4.43 = 95.57$ per cent of the variation in the quality of the parts is accounted for by differences in processing time.

Taking the square root of the proportion 0.9557 (namely, the proportion of the total variation in quality that is accounted for by differences in processing time), we obtain the so-called *coefficient of correlation*. Representing this statistic by the letter r, we have symbolically

$$r = \pm \sqrt{1 - \frac{\Sigma (y - y')^2}{\Sigma (y - \bar{y})^2}}$$

with the sign attached to r being the sign of b in the predicting equation. Thus, r is *positive* when the least squares line has an *upward slope*, that is, when the relationship between x and y is such that small values of y tend to go with small values of x and large values of y tend to go with large values of x. Correspondingly, r is *negative* when the least squares line has a *downward slope*, that is, when small values of y tend to go with large values of x and large values of y tend to go with small values of x. Corresponding to the sign of r, we say that there is a *positive* or a *negative correlation* (see Figure 10.6); when $r = 0$, we say that there is *no correlation*.

For our numerical example we obtain $r = + \sqrt{0.9557} = 0.978$, and we shall interpret this as follows: *the least squares line provides a very good fit and there is every indication that there is a strong relationship between the quality of the parts and their processing time.* Note that by virtue of its definition, a correlation coefficient must lie on the interval from -1 to $+1$, with $r = -1$ or $r = +1$ being indicative of a perfect fit, namely, of the fact that all the points actually fall on a straight line. When $r = 0$, none of the variation of the y's can be attributed to the relationship with x, and we say that there is no correlation; the fit is so poor that knowledge of x is of no help in the prediction of y.

The correlation coefficient is a very widely used measure of the correlation (relationship, association, dependence) between two variables. In

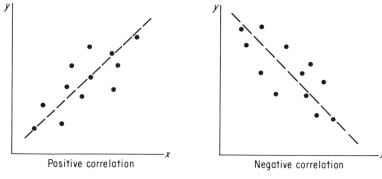

Positive correlation   Negative correlation

FIGURE 10.6

practice, its calculation is greatly simplified by using the computing formula

$$r = \frac{n(\Sigma\, xy) - (\Sigma\, x)(\Sigma\, y)}{\sqrt{n(\Sigma\, x^2) - (\Sigma\, x)^2}\ \sqrt{n(\Sigma\, y^2) - (\Sigma\, y)^2}} \qquad \bigstar$$

which is actually equivalent to the above formula used to define r. It has the added advantage that it automatically gives r the correct sign.

Although the computing formula for r may look rather formidable, it is quite easy to use. The quantities we have to substitute are $n, \Sigma\, x, \Sigma\, y,$ $\Sigma\, x^2, \Sigma\, xy, \Sigma\, y^2,$ and it should be noted that except for $\Sigma\, y^2$, they are the identical quantities which were required for the calculation of the coefficients a and b. Squaring the y's in the second column of the table on page 306 we obtain $\Sigma\, y^2 = 501,600$, and substituting this value together with $n = 10$ and the column totals on page 306 into the computing formula for r, we get

$$r = \frac{10(42,480) - (180)(2,140)}{\sqrt{10(3,616) - (180)^2}\ \sqrt{10(501,600) - (2,140)^2}}$$

$$= 0.978$$

This agrees, as it should, with the result which we obtained before.

As we have defined the coefficient of correlation, $100r^2$ gives the percentage of the total variation of the y's which is due to differences in x (due to the relationship with x). If in a given problem $r = 0.80$, then 64 per cent of the variation of the y's is accounted for by the relationship with x; similarly, if $r = 0.40$, only 16 per cent of the variation of the y's is accounted for by the relationship with x. In the sense of "percentage of variation accounted for" we can thus say that a correlation of $r = 0.80$ is *four times as strong* as a correlation of 0.40, and that a correlation of 0.60 is *nine times as strong* as a correlation of 0.20.

The coefficient of correlation is not only widely used, it is also widely *abused*. For one thing, it is often overlooked that a strong correlation is

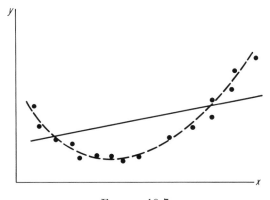

FIGURE 10.7

not necessarily indicative of a cause-effect relationship. For instance, a high positive correlation has been observed in a study of the relationship between teachers' salaries and liquor consumption, and a high negative r has been observed in a study of the annual per capita consumption of chewing tobacco in the United States and the number of automobile thefts reported in a sample of urban areas in the same years. We shall leave it to the reader's ingenuity to figure out why there might be strong correlations in these examples without there being any cause-effect relationships. Another example of this kind is discussed on page 347.

A point which is sometimes overlooked is that r measures only the strength of *linear* relationships. If we calculated r for the data of Figure 10.7, for example, we would get a value close to 0, even though there is evidently a very strong *curvilinear* relationship between the two variables; that is, the points representing the data are all very close to the dotted curve.

Finally, it is sometimes overlooked that when r is calculated on the basis of a sample, we may get a strong (positive or negative) correlation purely by chance, even though there is actually no relationship whatsoever between the two variables. To illustrate this point, suppose we take a pair of dice, one red and one green, we roll them five times, and we obtain the following results:

Red Die x	Green Die y
3	2
5	5
3	1
5	6
1	3

Calculating r for these data, we get the surprisingly high value $r = 0.66$, and this raises the obvious question whether there is anything wrong with the assumption that there is actually no relationship at all. *After all, one die does not know what the other one is doing.* In order to answer this question, we shall have to see whether this high value of r might be attributed to chance.

To test the null hypothesis of no correlation (the hypothesis that there is no relationship), we shall refer to a special table, which has been calculated on the basis of the sampling distribution of r when the x's and y's are sample values coming from populations having roughly the shape of normal distributions. Referring to Table VI,

we reject the null hypothesis of no correlation at the level of significance of 0.05 if the value of r calculated for a set of data exceeds $r_{.025}$ or if it is less than $-r_{.025}$.

If the value we obtain for r falls between $-r_{.025}$ and $r_{.025}$, we say that the correlation coefficient is *not significant*. Incidentally, if we want to use a level of significance of 0.01 in this test, we have only to substitute $r_{.005}$ for $r_{.025}$; the critical values $r_{.005}$ are also given in Table VI on page 444.

Applying this test to our numerical example (the processing time and quality of the 10 parts), we find that $r_{.025} = 0.632$ for $n = 10$. Since this is exceeded by 0.978, the value we obtained for r in this example, we reject the null hypothesis and conclude that there *is* a relationship between the processing time and the quality of the given kind of part. Applying the test to the example where we rolled a pair of dice, we find that $r_{.025} = 0.878$ for $n = 5$, which exceeds $r = 0.66$ (the value of r obtained in this example). Thus, the relationship observed in this small sample is not strong enough to persuade us that there is, in fact, a relationship between x and y; in other words, we attribute it entirely to chance.

EXERCISES

1. Calculate r for the humidity-moisture content data of Exercise 1 on page 308 and test for significance with $\alpha = 0.05$.

2. Calculate r for the data of Exercise 2 on page 309 and test at the 0.05 level of significance whether there is a relationship between the number of services an operator will perform in a period and the number of machines in line at the beginning of the period.

3. Calculate r for the data of Exercise 3 on page 310 and determine at the 0.01 level of significance whether there actually is a relationship between the percentage of protected area burned and variable operating expenditures.

4. Calculate r for the data of Exercise 4 on page 310 and test at the 0.05 level of significance whether there is a linear relationship between achievement and hours spent on the course.

5. Calculate r for the data of Exercise 6 on page 311 and test at the 0.01 level of significance whether there is a relationship between education and income.

6. Calculate r separately for each of the following sets of data:

	x	y			x	y
(a)	141	6	(b)		12	76
	110	4			45	25

Is there a way of avoiding all calculations in obtaining the required values of r?

7. In the study referred to in Exercise 6 on page 311, the following data were obtained for the median incomes (in thousands of dollars) in the 8 sample cities and the corresponding percentages of families in the cities owning a car:

Median Income x	Per Cent Owning Car y
7.0	68.2
4.4	49.4
5.4	52.9
4.9	50.9
7.6	70.4
4.2	52.6
3.8	48.5
6.2	60.0

Calculate r and test for significance at the 0.05 level of significance.

8. In a study concerned with predicting success in business, data were collected on a number of male M.B.A. graduates of a leading graduate school of business. Success for the men working in large organizations was expressed as a composite of organizational level of authority, degree of participation in deciding over-all company policy, and remuneration. Test at the 5 per cent level of significance whether there is a real relationship (for the population studied) between success in business and the following four variables:

   (a) Grade point average in 4-year college: $n = 72$ and $r = 0.14$.

   (b) Score on M-F scale of Strong Vocational Interest Blank: $n = 92$ and $r = 0.19$.

   (c) Leadership in undergraduate school: $n = 100$ and $r = 0.24$.

   (d) Score on College Admissions Test: $n = 80$ and $r = -0.01$.

9. State in each case whether you would expect to obtain a positive correlation, a negative correlation, or no correlation between:

   (a) The number of years of education of husbands and wives.

   (b) Income and size of family.

   (c) Hat size and intelligence.

   (d) Number of vice-presidents and net earnings of a corporation.

   (e) Dividends and earnings per share.

   (f) Temperature and inches of snow on the ground in Watertown, N.Y.

   (g) Hours of practice and golf scores.

10. Using r, it is possible to write 0.95 confidence limits for β (the *slope* of the least squares line) as

$$ b\left[1 \pm t_{.025} \cdot \frac{\sqrt{1 - r^2}}{r\sqrt{n - 2}}\right] $$

where b is calculated according to the formula on page 307 and the number of degrees of freedom for $t_{.025}$ is $n - 2$. Use this method to construct a 0.95 confidence interval for the slope of the least squares line obtained in Exercise 1 on page 308. (The value of r was obtained for these data in Exercise 1 above.)

11. Use the method of Exercise 10 to construct a 0.95 confidence interval for the slope of the least squares line obtained in Exercise 2 on page 309. (The value of r was obtained in Exercise 2 above.)

Time Series Analysis

As has been said in many different ways, the future belongs to those who plan for it best. This is true, in particular, in business and in economics. Of course, business planning is not an end in itself, but organized planning utilizing various statistical techniques (intended to assess past performance and estimate the success or failure of proposed strategies) seems to have everything in its favor. Aside from its intuitive appeal, there are the achievement records of many highly successful companies which treat planning as an organized activity and analyze exhaustively the many factors bearing on planning decisions. Marketing strategy is often planned in great detail for several years ahead, with enough flexibility built in to allow for whatever changes market conditions may require. Financial strategy is also widely planned, so that operating plans can be carried out and a proper balance maintained between distributed earnings and retained earnings necessary for future growth. Many manufacturing companies attempt to make their long-range planning (say, beyond a year) more effective by maintaining 10-year or longer projections on sales, profits, cash needs, and so forth, for all of their major product groups. No intelligent planning of needs for raw materials or production facilities can be done without some notion of projected future sales. This is far from all, of course; in determining an optimal production capacity, for instance, specific estimates, or predictions, of production cost, restrictions on capacity, etc., are required in addition to product and service demands.

Undoubtedly, the most important part of planning is predicting, or *forecasting*, the future values of various key variables on the basis of past data. Thus, one usually deals with statistical data which are collected, observed, or recorded at regular intervals of time and which are called *time series*. This term applies, for example, to the annual production of teel, monthly data on the number of employees in nonagricultural establishments in the United States, or the daily clearings in the Atlanta Clearing House. Although we shall limit ourselves to business and economic data, it must be recognized that neither the term "time series" nor the methods of analysis which we shall discuss in the next few sections are limited to these fields. Incidentally, we frequently abbreviate the term "time series" by referring to such data simply as "series"; we thus speak of a *series* of monthly farm prices, a *series* of weekly freight car loadings, and so forth.

Although our concern is with the future, time series analysis begins by looking backward. After all, it would be foolish not to put relevant experience from the past to use in planning for an uncertain future. We thus search for observable regularities and patterns, which are so persistent that they cannot be ignored. If we subsequently base our forecasts on such regularities and patterns, we are simply expressing the feeling that what has happened in the past will, to a greater or lesser extent, continue to happen or will again happen in the future.

Sometimes, when we look at the graph of a time series, we get the impression that it is the scrawling of a small child, and it is hard to believe that any kind of analysis will bring even some order into the irregular patterns. Nevertheless, if we make some simplifying assumptions, it becomes possible to identify, explain, and measure the fluctuations that appear in time series. Thus, we shall assume that there are four basic types of variation which, superimposed and acting in concert, account for the observed changes over a period of time and give the series its irregular appearance. These four *components* of a time series are:

1. *secular trend*
2. *seasonal variation*
3. *cyclical variation*
4. *irregular variation*

and we shall assume further that there is a multiplicative relationship between these four components, namely, that any particular value in a series can be looked upon as the product of factors which can be attributed to the four components.

Of course, this is only one of many possible models (schemes) we might use in studying time series. Although it ignores the hidden interactions and interrelationships in the data and the entire "complex of individually small shifts and nuances," it is the best place to begin one's study of the

analysis of time series and forecasting. Indeed, there is much of fundamental importance about the movements of data through time that can
be learned from this traditional approach, besides which the traditional
methods have been and continue to be widely used in practice. In many
instances, they provide very satisfactory results.

*By the secular (or long-term) trend of a time series we mean the smooth or
regular movement of a series over a fairly long period of time.* Intuitively
speaking, the trend of a time series displays the general sweep of its
development, or better, it characterizes the gradual and consistent pattern of its changes. In many series, the pattern is one of gradual growth

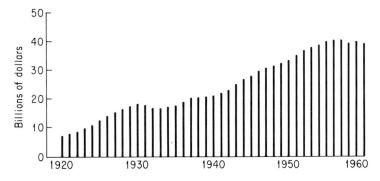

FIGURE 10.8. Industrial life insurance in force in
the United States. (*Source:* 1961 Life Insurance
Fact Book.)

or decline, which may be described reasonably well by means of a straight
line or some other sort of smooth curve. For example, Figure 10.8 shows
the over-all *upward trend* in the ownership of industrial life insurance
in the United States, while Figure 10.9 shows a persistent *downward trend*
in farm employment in the United States.

In time series work, as in regression analysis and curve fitting, straight
lines are widely used and easily fitted, but they are not always adequate.
The trends of many time series can be described reasonably well only by
more complicated kinds of curves. For example, the series on university
enrollment shown in Figure 10.10 has the general shape of an elongated
letter S, and no straight line can give even approximately a good fit.
The curve which has been fitted to it in Figure 10.10 is one of the so-called
growth curves, and it reflects a type of growth pattern that is frequently
observed in time series. In this book we shall study mainly linear

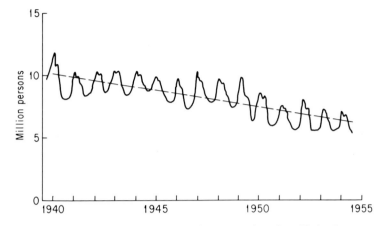

FIGURE 10.9. Farm employment in the United States. (*Source:* Statistical Abstracts of the United States.)

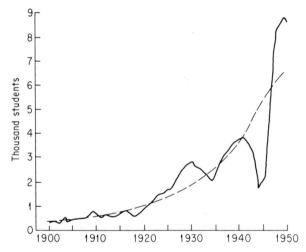

FIGURE 10.10. Enrollment at the University of Tennessee.

trends, although we shall give a method, the *method of moving averages*, which can be used in a wide variety of problems when a straight line would not give a good fit.

Seasonal variation, which consists of regularly repeating patterns like those shown in Figure 10.11, is quite easy to understand. The name implies a connection with the seasons of the year, like the variation found in the monthly production of automobiles or the quarterly consumption of electricity, but it is actually used to indicate any kind of periodic variation where the period is at most one year.

Few businesses are free from the effect of seasonal variations. The examination of almost any series of business data recorded on a quarterly, monthly, weekly, daily, or hourly basis, shows movements within the series which seem to occur again and again with some definite degree of regularity. Except for the holiday season, airline passenger traffic normally drops during the winter months; about two-thirds to three-fourths of the total annual business in the jewelry trade is done in the two months

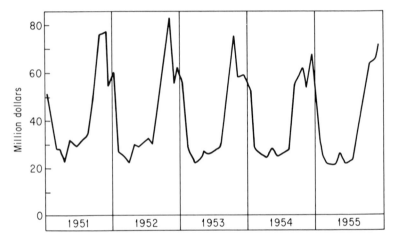

FIGURE 10.11. Monthly cash receipts from farm marketings in Tennessee. (*Source:* U.S. Department of Agriculture.)

before Christmas; automobile manufacturers' profits are usually lower in the third quarter of the year because of the model changeover; subway traffic on workdays is always heaviest in the early morning and late afternoon; and so on. An understanding of these patterns is of great importance to businessmen and economic planners. Even in cases where the seasonal variation is not itself of basic concern, it must often be measured statistically in order to facilitate the study of other types of variation.

After the trend and the seasonal variation have been eliminated statistically from a time series, we are left with *cyclical and irregular variations*. Cyclical variation is sometimes defined as the variation which remains in a time series after the trend, seasonal variations, and irregular fluctuations have been eliminated. Actually, there is more to it than that, but in classical time series analysis such a process of elimination is the usual way of measuring cyclical variation, that is, *business cycles*. Generally speaking, business cycles consist of recurring up and down movements of activity which differ from seasonal variations in that they extend over longer periods of time and, supposedly, result from entirely different sets of causes. Recurring periods of prosperity, recession, depression, and recovery, which constitute the phases of a complete business cycle, are considered to be due to other factors than the weather, social customs, and so on, which account for seasonal variations. Because of the great importance of cyclical swings of business to the social and economic life of this country, an enormous amount of effort has been spent in studying business cycles. Many theories have been proposed to account for particular cycles, but few explanations of these complicated phenomena have found any kind of general acceptance. Owing to its complexity, we shall not study this problem in this text.

Irregular variations of time series are those kinds of fluctuations that are either random (due to chance) or caused by such readily identifiable special events as elections, wars, floods, earthquakes, and so forth. So far as random variations are concerned, there is little to be said except that in the long run they will usually tend to average out. Of course, there is always the question whether, perhaps, all the fluctuations of a time series might be attributed to chance, and there exist appropriate tests of significance. One of these, a test based on so-called *"runs above and below the median"* is discussed in Technical Note 12 on page 350.

Irregular variations that are due to the occurrence of special events usually pose no serious problems. Most of the time they can easily be recognized and identified with the political changes, weather conditions, or sociological upheavals by which they are caused. They can then be eliminated from the data before we try to measure the trend, seasonal variation, or cyclical patterns.

Secular Trends

The most widely used method for fitting trends to time series is the method of least squares, with which we are already familiar. As we saw earlier, the problem of fitting a least squares line $y' = a + bx$ is essentially that of determining values of a and b which, for a given set of data, makes

$\Sigma \, (y - y')^2$ as small as possible. We found these two quantities either by solving the two normal equations on page 305 or by using the special formulas on page 307.

When dealing with time series where the x's practically always refer to successive years (days, weeks, or months), the problem of fitting a trend line by the method of least squares can be simplified considerably by performing the following change of scale (coding): letting x be the variable which measures time and taking the origin (the zero) of the new scale at the *middle* of the series, that is, at the middle of the x's, we number the years (or other time periods) so that in the new scale $\Sigma \, x = 0$. Thus, when dealing with an *odd* number of years, we assign $x = 0$ to the middle year and number the years $\dots, -5, -4, -3, -2, -1, 0, 1, 2, 3, 4, 5, \dots$. When dealing with an *even* number of years, there is no middle year, and we assign successive years the numbers $\dots, -7, -5, -3, -1, 1, 3, 5, 7,$ $\dots$, with -1 and 1 assigned to the two middle years. The advantage of having $\Sigma \, x = 0$ becomes apparent when we make this substitution in the two formulas on page 307. The formulas for a and b become

$$a = \frac{\Sigma \, y}{n} \quad \text{and} \quad b = \frac{\Sigma \, xy}{\Sigma \, x^2} \qquad \bigstar$$

and it is evident that they now involve much less work.

To illustrate how this simplification works, let us fit a least squares trend line to the total annual (net) sales of the Westinghouse Electric Corporation for the years 1952–1960:

Year	Net Sales (millions of dollars)
1952	1,454
1953	1,582
1954	1,636
1955	1,441
1956	1,525
1957	2,009
1958	1,896
1959	1,911
1960	1,956

Since we have an odd number of years (9 to be exact), we label them $-4, -3, -2, -1, 0, 1, 2, 3, 4$, and the sums needed for substitution into the formulas for a and b are obtained in the following table:

Year	x	y	xy	x^2
1952	-4	1,454	$-5,816$	16
1953	-3	1,582	$-4,746$	9
1954	-2	1,636	$-3,272$	4
1955	-1	1,441	$-1,441$	1
1956	0	1,525	0	0
1957	1	2,009	2,009	1
1958	2	1,896	3,792	4
1959	3	1,911	5,733	9
1960	4	1,956	7,824	16
	0	15,410	4,083	60

Substituting $n = 9$, $\Sigma y = 15,410$, $\Sigma xy = 4,083$, and $\Sigma x^2 = 60$ into the new formulas for a and b, we get

$$a = \frac{15,410}{9} = 1,712.2$$

$$b = \frac{4,083}{60} = 68.0$$

and the equation of the trend line may be written as

$$y' = 1,712.2 + 68.0x$$

Unless we state precisely what x and y mean in this equation, namely, the units and scales in which they are given, there is likely to be some confusion. It is advisable, therefore, to specify the origin of x and the units of both x and y in an explanatory legend added to the trend equation. For our example, we might write

$$y' = 1,712.2 + 68.0x$$

*(origin, 1956; x units, 1 year; y, annual
sales in millions of dollars)*

This makes it clear that 1,712.2 is the trend value for 1956 and that the *annual trend increment* (the year-to-year growth) in Westinghouse's annual sales is estimated at $68.0 million for the given period of time.

Using the equation we have obtained, we can now determine the *trend value* for any year by substituting the corresponding value of x. For instance, for 1952 we substitute $x = -4$ and get a trend value of $y' = 1,712.2 + 68.0(-4) = 1,440.2$, and for 1960 we substitute $x = 4$ and get a trend value of $y' = 1,712.2 + 68.0(4) = 1,984.2$. Plotting these two trend values and joining them by a straight line, we obtain the least squares trend line shown in Figure 10.12.

It is sometimes desirable, or necessary, to modify the trend equation by changing the origin of x, changing the units of x, or changing the units of y. To illustrate how this is done, let us first change the y units in the above equation from annual sales to *average monthly sales*. Since each y

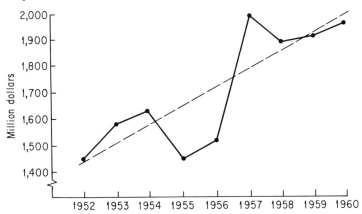

FIGURE 10.12. Sales of Westinghouse Electric Corporation, 1952–1960.

is thus divided by 12, the constants a and b in the trend equation must both be divided by 12, and we get

$$y' = 142.68 + 5.67x$$

(*origin, 1956; x units, 1 year; y, average*
monthly sales in millions of dollars)

Now let us modify the trend equation further by changing the x's so that they refer to successive months. Since b measures the *trend increment*, the increase or decrease of trend values corresponding to one unit of x, we shall have to divide b by 12, changing it thus from an *annual trend increment* to a *monthly trend increment*. Leaving the constant unchanged, we thus get

$$y' = 142.68 + 0.47x$$

(*origin, 1956; x units, 1 month; y, average*
monthly sales in millions of dollars)

Finally, let us change the origin of x from the middle of 1956, where it now, to, say, the middle of January 1956. (This kind of modification w be helpful later in connection with some problems of forecasting.) Since the middle of January 1956 is $5\frac{1}{2}$ months earlier than the middle of the year 1956, we shall have to subtract 5.5 monthly trend increments from the 1956 trend value of 142.68. The new value of a is thus

$$142.68 - 5.5(0.47) = 140.10$$

and we finally get

$$y' = 140.10 + 0.47x$$

(*origin, January 1956; x units, 1 month; y, average monthly sales in millions of dollars*)

Before we go any further, let us repeat the remark made on page 325, namely, that all the fluctuations of a time series might conceivably be due to chance. Before we fit a trend line or some other kind of trend equation, it is, therefore, recommended that we test whether it is actually worthwhile to go through all the work of fitting a trend to a given set of data. There are several tests we can use for this purpose, and one of them is given in Technical Note 12 on page 350. Several of the exercises on page 334 require the use of this technique.

On page 322 we described a secular trend as being indicative of the "general sweep" of the development of a time series. If it is uncertain whether the trend is linear or whether it might be better described by some other kind of curve, if we are not sure whether we are actually dealing with a trend or part of a cycle, and if we are not really interested in obtaining a mathematical equation, we can describe the over-all "behavior" of a time series quite well by means of an artificial series called a *moving average*. A moving average is obtained by replacing each value in a series by the mean of itself and some of the values directly preceding it and directly following it. For instance, in a *three-year moving average* calculated for annual data, each annual figure is replaced by the mean of itself and the annual figures corresponding to the two adjacent years; in a *five-year moving average* each annual figure is replaced by the mean of itself, those of the two preceding years, and those of the two years that follow. If the averaging is done over an *even* number of periods, say, 4 years or 12 months, the moving average will initially fall between successive years or months. In such cases, the values are customarily brought "back in line" by taking a subsequent two-year (or two-month) moving average. This procedure will be used later on page 339.

The basic problem in constructing a moving average is choosing an appropriate period over which the values are to be averaged. This will have to depend on what unwanted or distracting fluctuations are to be eliminated and, hence, it will have to depend on the nature of the data as well as the purpose for which the moving average is to be constructed. For instance, on page 339 we shall calculate a twelve-month moving average in order to eliminate annual seasonal patterns.

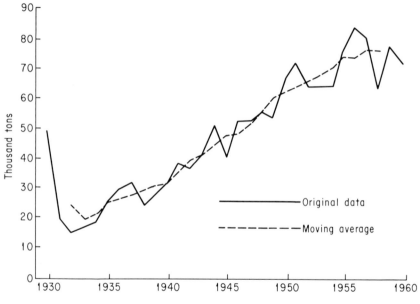

FIGURE 10.13. Average quarterly sales of gypsum products in the United States.

To illustrate the construction of moving averages, let us calculate a five-year moving average to *smooth* the time series of the average quarterly quantities of gypsum products (in thousands of short tons) sold or used in the United States for industrial purposes from 1930 through 1960. The third column of the table shows the *five-year moving totals*, which for any given year consist of the sum of that year's figure plus those of the two preceding and the two succeeding years. The last column, which contains the moving average, is obtained by dividing each of the corresponding moving totals by five. Both the original data and the five-year moving average are shown in Figure 10.13, and it should be observed that the moving average has substantially reduced the fluctuations of the series and given it a much smoother appearance. It should

	Gypsum Products Sold or Used	Five-year Moving Totals	Five-year Moving Averages
1930	49.4		
1931	19.7		
1932	15.3	119.8	24.0
1933	16.3	96.3	19.3
1934	19.1	106.3	21.3
1935	25.9	122.5	24.5
1936	29.7	129.8	26.0
1937	31.5	138.4	27.7
1938	23.6	143.4	28.7
1939	27.7	151.7	30.3
1940	30.9	156.3	31.3
1941	38.0	173.6	34.7
1942	36.1	196.0	39.2
1943	40.9	204.5	40.9
1944	50.1	218.1	43.6
1945	39.4	233.9	46.8
1946	51.6	248.1	49.6
1947	51.9	250.7	50.1
1948	55.1	277.1	55.4
1949	52.7	297.5	59.5
1950	65.8	308.7	61.7
1951	72.0	317.1	63.4
1952	63.1	327.6	65.5
1953	63.5	336.5	67.3
1954	63.2	348.0	69.6
1955	74.7	364.5	72.9
1956	83.5	363.6	72.7
1957	79.6	378.2	75.6
1958	62.6	374.7	74.9
1959	77.8		
1960	71.2		

so be noted that by using a moving average we lose a few years at ch end of the series; generally, this does not pose any problems unless a ries is very short or all values are needed for further calculations.

XERCISES

1. The number of manufacturing companies establishing new plants in a given city during the years 1956 through 1961 were, respectively, 9, 8, 4, 3, 4, and 2.

   (a) Plot the series.

(b) Use the formulas for a and b given in this section to fit a least squares line to the data, and give the equation of the line with an appropriate legend.

(c) Use the equation obtained in part (b) to calculate the 1956 and 1961 trend values and plot the least squares line on the chart showing the original data.

(*Hint:* Since there is an even number of years, use the coding -5, -3, -1, 1, 3, and 5; the origin for x will, thus, be between 1958 and 1959 and the x units will be 6 months.)

2. Modify the equation obtained in Exercise 1 by shifting the origin of x to (the middle of) 1960.

3. For the years 1952 through 1962, the total annual production of shoes and slippers (in millions of pairs) in the United States was 533.2, 532.0, 530.4, 585.4, 591.8, 597.6, 587.1, 637.4, 598.4, 593.3, and 619.4.

(a) Plot this series on ordinary graph paper.

(b) Use the formulas on page 326 to calculate the equation of the least squares line which best describes the trend of this series.

(c) Plot the least squares line on the chart made for the original data by drawing a straight line through the calculated 1952 and 1962 trend values.

4. Modify the trend equation obtained in Exercise 3 for use with monthly data, using January 1960 as the origin of the new equation.

5. The following figures show the shipments of Douglas Fir (in billions of board feet) for the years 1951 through 1962: 9.56, 10.15, 9.49, 9.41, 9.54, 8.74, 8.00, 8.44, 8.81, 8.29, 7.68, and 7.98.

(a) Fit a least squares trend line to this series and draw a graph showing the line together with the original data.

(b) Modify the trend equation obtained in part (a) so that the origin for x is June 1954, x units are 1 month, and y represents average monthly shipments.

6. Total annual sales of the Lockheed Aircraft Corporation for the years 1952–1962 were, respectively, 441, 820, 733, 676, 751, 879, 974, 1,304, 1,332, 1,445, and 1,753 millions of dollars.

(a) Fit a least squares trend line to this series and plot the line on a graph showing also the actual sales figures.

(b) Modify the trend equation of part (a) for use with monthly data showing January 1952 as the origin for x.

7. The following series shows the total cost (in millions of dollars) of magazine advertising placed for the years 1951 through 1962: 514, 554, 603, 597, 657, 692, 739, 693, 784, 854, 836, and 876.

(a) Use the formulas on page 326 to find the least squares line which best describes the growth of magazine advertising for the 1951–1962 period. Plot the line on a chart showing also the original data.

(b) Modify the trend equation of part (a) so that the origin for x is January 1962, the x units are 1 month, and y represents average monthly cost of magazine advertising in millions of dollars.

8. For the years 1952 through 1962, the total annual consumption of cotton in the United States (in millions of bales) was 9.2, 9.3, 8.5, 9.1, 9.0, 8.4, 8.1, 9.0, 8.7, 8.5, and 8.7.

   (a) Find the least squares line which best describes the downward trend of cotton consumption over this period, and plot the line on a chart showing also the original data.

   (b) Change the origin to June 1955, x units to 1 month, and y to average monthly consumption in millions of bales.

9. On pages 337–338 the monthly sales of women's apparel, accessory stores are given for the years 1956 through 1960. Verify that a least squares trend equation fit to this series can be written in the form $y' = 378.09 + 1.3354x$ (origin, January 1956; x units, 1 month; y, average monthly sales in millions of dollars). (*Hint:* Fit the least squares line to the five annual totals and then convert the equation to the form shown above.)

10. The following are the average monthly sales (in millions of dollars) of the rubber goods industries for the years 1930 through 1962: 70, 52, 40, 45, 57, 62, 76, 87, 71, 89, 96, 141, 158, 244, 280, 284, 262, 284, 279, 254, 335, 408, 410, 418, 384, 473, 469, 480, 449, 510, 510, 500, and 550. Calculate a three-year moving average and plot the original data as well as the moving average on ordinary graph paper.

11. Calculate a five-year moving average for the data of Exercise 10 and compare its graph with the one obtained in that exercise.

12. The following figures represent the average monthly production of kerosene (in thousands of barrels) for the years 1930–1961: 4,101, 3,537, 3,653, 4,081, 4,488, 4,651, 4,674, 5,442, 5,382, 5,710, 6,157, 6,049, 5,623, 6,023, 6,529, 6,752, 8,699, 9,201, 10,160, 8,513, 9,876, 11,132, 11,025, 10,276, 10,192, 9,761, 10,290, 9,077, 9,167, 9,222, 11,314, and 11,900.

   (a) Construct a three-year moving average and plot it on a diagram showing also the original data.

   (b) Construct a five-year moving average and plot it on the diagram obtained in part (a).

13. The following figures represent the average number of bales of cotton consumed per month during the years 1925 through 1962:

Year	Cotton Consumption	Year	Cotton Consumption
1925	536,044	1944	807,614
1926	556,971	1945	761,780
1927	671,085	1946	819,401
1928	547,673	1947	795,513
1929	587,491	1948	757,929
1930	448,149	1949	656,100
1931	453,655	1950	804,140
1932	418,084	1951	836,407
1933	517,550	1952	765,077
1934	451,595	1953	776,806
1935	470,889	1954	710,843
1936	591,980	1955	755,478
1937	618,166	1956	746,535
1938	491,856	1957	696,302
1939	614,155	1958	677,646
1940	671,020	1959	748,097
1941	882,190	1960	726,382
1942	952,787	1961	710,000
1943	888,829	1962	727,000

(a) Construct a 3-year moving average and plot it on a diagram showing also the original data.

(b) Construct a 7-year moving average and plot it on a diagram showing also the original data.

(*The exercises which follow are based on the material in Technical Note 12.*)

14. With 1957–59 = 100, the values of the Federal Reserve Board Index of Industrial Production for the years 1947–1962 are 65.7, 68.4, 64.7, 74.9, 81.3, 84.3, 91.3, 85.8, 96.6, 99.9, 100.7, 93.7, 105.6, 108.7, 109.8, and 118.2. Use the method of runs above and below the median to test at the 0.05 level whether there is a significant trend.

15. The total number of radio-phonograph sets (in thousands) produced by a certain company for the years 1942 through 1962 were 100, 120, 145, 151, 119, 108, 142, 150, 159, 143, 122, 138, 124, 112, 110, 122, 143, 152, 125, 117, and 168. Test at a level of significance of 0.01 whether there is a significant trend in the company's production of these units.

16. Test at a level of significance of 0.05 whether or not there is a significant trend in the Lockheed Aircraft sales given in Exercise 6.

17. Test at a level of significance of 0.05 whether there is a significant trend in the magazine advertising series of Exercise 7.

18. Test at a level of significance of 0.01 whether there is a significant trend in the kerosene production series of Exercise 12.

Seasonal Variation

Let us now turn to the problem of measuring *seasonal variation*, namely, those repeating patterns in a time series whose period is at most one year. An indicator of the way in which seasonal influences affect a time series is called a *seasonal index* or an *index of seasonal variation*. For monthly data, a seasonal index consists of 12 numbers, one for each month, with each number expressing that particular month's activity as a percentage of that of the average month. For instance, if the seasonal index for a store's January sales is 86, this means that typical January sales are 86 per cent of those of the average month. We used the word "typical" here because the percentage will vary somewhat from year to year; it is, itself, an average.

There are many ways in which seasonal variation can be measured, or a seasonal index can be constructed. These go all the way from rather crude measures based on very simple calculations to highly refined measures based on involved computer techniques. We shall illustrate the construction of a seasonal index by using the so-called *ratio-to-moving-average*, or *percentage-of-moving-average*, method. Until certain refinements were made possible by the use of high-speed computers, this method was probably the most widely used and the most generally satisfactory one available.

In constructing a seasonal index, our efforts are first aimed at eliminating trend, cyclical, and irregular variations from the series. The way this is done in the basic *ratio-to-moving-average method* is relatively simple. We begin by calculating a 12-month moving average in order to remove all seasonal movements from the series. Of course, in actual practice seasonal patterns vary somewhat from year to year, so that this will not necessarily eliminate all of the seasonal variation. It will eliminate most of it, however, and also most of the irregular variation. The 12-month moving average is, thus, an estimate of the trend and cyclical components of the series. Since we are assuming that any value in the original series is the *product* of factors attributed to the four basic components (secular trend, seasonal variation, cyclical variation, and irregular variation), dividing each value by the corresponding value of the 12-month moving average gives an estimate of the seasonal and irregular components in the series. In other words, dividing $T \cdot S \cdot C \cdot I$ by $T \cdot C$ leaves us with $S \cdot I$, the product of the factors attributed to seasonal and irregular variations. All that is left to do then is to eliminate, insofar as possible, the irregular fluctuations. This can be done by separately averaging the figures obtained for the different Januaries, Februaries, and so on. When one knows a good deal about the series being studied, it may also be possible to identify and eliminate irregular variations of the kind discussed on page 325. The effect of such erratic variations can also be reduced by using the *median* to average the values given for each month,

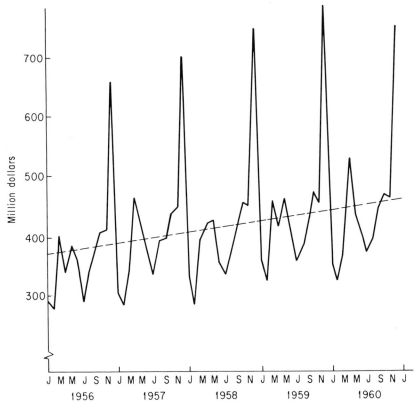

FIGURE 10.14. Sales of women's apparel, accessory stores, 1956–1960.

or perhaps the *modified arithmetic mean*, which is the mean of the values remaining after the smallest and largest values have been cast out. Moving averages may also be used for smoothing out irregular variations. In any event, by some sort of averaging we finally arrive at estimates of the seasonal factors alone.

The series we have chosen to illustrate this procedure is that of sales of women's apparel, accessory stores in the United States; the figures

SALES OF WOMEN'S APPAREL, ACCESSORY STORES
(MILLIONS OF DOLLARS)

		Sales (1)	12-Month Moving Total (2)	2-Month Moving Total (3)	Centered 12-Month Moving Average (4)	Percentages of 12-Month Moving Average (5)
1956	January	292				
	February	278				
	March	403				
	April	344				
	May	388				
	June	364				
			4,540			
	July	290		9,098	379.1	76.5
			4,558			
	August	338		9,121	380.0	88.9
			4,563			
	September	374		9,070	377.9	99.0
			4,507			
	October	405		9,133	380.5	106.4
			4,626			
	November	410		9,286	386.9	106.0
			4,660			
	December	654		9,337	389.0	168.1
			4,677			
1957	January	310		9,402	391.8	79.1
			4,725			
	February	283		9,502	395.9	71.5
			4,777			
	March	347		9,578	399.1	86.9
			4,801			
	April	463		9,631	401.3	115.4
			4,830			
	May	422		9,698	404.1	104.4
			4,868			
	June	381		9,783	407.6	93.5
			4,915			
	July	338		9,861	410.9	82.3
			4,946			
	August	390		9,887	412.0	94.7
			4,941			
	September	398		9,929	413.7	96.2
			4,988			
	October	434		9,933	413.9	104.9
			4,945			
	November	448		9,893	412.2	180.7
			4,948			
	December	701		9,873	411.4	170.4
			4,925			
1958	January	341		9,846	410.2	83.1
			4,921			
	February	278		9,825	409.4	67.9
			4,904			
	March	394		9,828	409.5	96.2
			4,924			
	April	420		9,871	411.3	102.1
			4,947			
	May	425		9,897	412.4	103.1
			4,950			
	June	358		9,943	414.3	86.4
			4,993			
	July	334		10,004	416.8	80.1
			5,011			
	August	373		10,066	419.4	88.9
			5,055			
	September	418		10,171	423.8	98.6
			5,116			
	October	457		10,229	426.2	107.2
			5,113			
	November	451		10,262	427.6	105.5
			5,149			
	December	744		10,350	431.2	172.5
			5,201			

SALES OF WOMEN'S APPAREL, ACCESSORY STORES (*Continued*)
(MILLIONS OF DOLLARS)

		Sales (1)	12-Month Moving Total (2)	2-Month Moving Total (3)	Centered 12-Month Moving Average (4)	Percentages of 12-Month Moving Average (5)
1959	January	359	5,223	10,424	434.3	82.7
	February	322	5,228	10,451	435.5	73.9
	March	455	5,238	10,466	436.1	104.3
	April	417	5,252	10,490	437.1	95.4
	May	461	5,252	10,504	437.7	105.3
	June	410	5,284	10,536	439.0	93.4
	July	356	5,288	10,572	440.5	80.8
	August	378	5,286	10,574	440.6	85.8
	September	428	5,211	10,497	437.4	97.9
	October	471	5,320	10,531	438.8	107.3
	November	451	5,294	10,614	442.2	102.0
	December	776	5,290	10,584	441.0	176.0
1960	January	363	5,304	10,594	441.4	82.2
	February	320	5,320	10,624	442.7	72.3
	March	380	5,335	10,655	444.0	85.6
	April	526	5,331	10,666	444.4	118.4
	May	435	5,344	10,675	444.8	97.8
	June	406	5,317	10,661	444.2	91.4
	July	370				
	August	394				
	September	443				
	October	467				
	November	464				
	December	749				

represent monthly sales in millions of dollars for the years 1956 through 1960. The original data are plotted in Figure 10.14 and they are given in column (1) of the preceding table. Note the pronounced seasonal pattern in the graph of Figure 10.14; together with an upward trend, these seem to be the dominating sources of variation in the data.

The first step in the calculations is to obtain the 12-month moving totals, which are shown in column (2). The first entry in this column, 4,540, is the *sum* of the 12 monthly sales figures for 1956, and it is recorded at the middle of the period, namely, between June and July 1956. The second entry in this column, 4,558, is obtained by subtracting the

January 1956 figure from 4,540 and adding the January 1957 figure; in other words, 4,558 is the *sum* of the 12 monthly sales from February 1956 through January 1957, and it is recorded at the middle of this period. The third and succeeding entries in the column are found by continuing this process of subtracting and adding monthly values.

In order to obtain a 12-month moving average which is *centered* on the original data, we next calculate two-month moving totals of the entries of column (2). These are shown in column (3), with the first entry being the sum of the first two values in column (2), the second entry being the sum of the second and third values in column (2), and so forth. Note that the entries in column (3) are recorded between those of column (2) and, hence, they are in line with (or centered on) the original data.

Since each entry of column (2) is the sum of 12 monthly figures and each entry of column (3) is the sum of two entries of column (2), or altogether the sum of 24 monthly figures, we finally obtain the centered 12-month moving average shown in column (4) by dividing each entry of column (3) by 24. The next step is to divide the original data month by month by the corresponding trend-cycle estimates (that is, the corresponding values of the moving average), and to multiply these ratios by 100. We thus arrive at the *percentages of moving average* shown in column (5). The reader will recall that this last step is designed to eliminate the trend and cyclical components from the data.

All that remains to be done is to eliminate the irregular variations as best we can, and to this end we rearrange the entries of column (5) as in the first five columns of the following table:

	1956	1957	1958	1959	1960	Median	Seasonal Index
January		79.1	83.1	82.7	82.2	82.4	82.2
February		71.5	67.9	73.9	72.3	71.9	71.8
March		86.9	96.2	104.3	85.6	91.6	91.4
April		115.4	102.1	95.4	118.4	108.8	108.6
May		104.4	103.1	105.3	97.8	103.8	103.6
June		93.5	86.4	93.4	91.4	92.4	92.2
July	76.5	82.3	80.1	80.8		80.4	80.2
August	88.9	94.7	88.9	85.8		88.9	88.7
September	99.0	96.2	98.6	97.9		98.2	98.0
October	106.4	104.9	107.2	107.3		106.8	106.6
November	106.0	108.7	105.5	102.0		105.8	105.6
December	168.1	170.4	172.5	176.0		171.4	171.1
						1,202.4	1,200.0

There are various ways in which we can average the figures given for each month; we chose the median for the reason indicated above. (Note that in this case where we have four values for each month, the median is, in fact, equivalent to the modified mean.) The 12 medians are shown in the second column from the right. Now, since the seasonal index for each month is supposed to be a percentage of the average month, the sum of the 12 values should equal 1,200. Actually, the medians total 1,202.4, and so we adjust for this by multiplying each of the medians by $\frac{1,200}{1,202.4} = 0.9980$. The final values of the seasonal index are shown in the column on the right.

The interpretation of this index is straightforward. For instance, January sales of women's apparel, accessory stores are typically 82.2 per cent of those of the average month; sales are usually relatively low in February, and December sales are typically 71.1 per cent *above* sales of the average month.

In using a seasonal index for any purpose, we must always be mindful of its limitations. An index is based on historical (past) data and we cannot reasonably expect seasonal patterns to remain completely constant over long periods of time. The method we have illustrated here applies to the description of *constant* seasonal patterns, or seasonal patterns which do not change very much. If there are pronounced changes in the seasonal pattern with the passage of time, the sort of index we have discussed will not be suitable. In a situation like that we would be faced with extremely difficult problems, which we shall not discuss.

Seasonal indexes are extremely important in various practical applications. We shall briefly explain two of these, the first in *deseasonalizing data* and the second in *forecasting*. Leaving the use of seasonal indexes in forecasting to the section which follows, let us discuss now the problem of deseasonalizing, namely, that of *removing* seasonal influences from a given set of data. Of course, nobody knows how things would have been if a series had been uninfluenced by seasonal factors, when seasonal fluctuations have actually occurred. So, when we speak of what things would have been like without seasonal fluctuations, it must be understood that we are speaking rather loosely. The notion of a series of data free from seasonal influences is imprecise, but it is a useful way of understanding the concept.

The process of removing seasonal variation, or deseasonalizing data, consists merely of dividing each value in a series by the corresponding value of the seasonal index and multiplying the result by 100 (or by dividing by the corresponding value of the seasonal index written as a *proportion*). The logic of this process is quite simple: if December toy sales are 180 per cent of those in the average month, taking 100/180 of the December sales would tell us what these sales would have been if there had been no seasonal variation.

We shall illustrate this process by deseasonalizing the 1960 sales of women's apparel, accessory stores, using the seasonal index obtained above. In the table which follows, the sales figures and the seasonal index are copied from pages 338 and 339, with the values of the seasonal index given as proportions and rounded to two decimals. The values in the right-hand column are the deseasonalized sales, and they are computed by dividing each month's actual sales by the corresponding value of the seasonal index.

1960	Sales	Seasonal Index	Deseasonalized Sales
January	363	0.82	443
February	320	0.72	444
March	380	0.91	418
April	526	1.09	483
May	435	1.04	418
June	406	0.92	441
July	370	0.80	462
August	394	0.89	443
September	443	0.98	452
October	467	1.07	436
November	464	1.06	438
December	749	1.71	438

Inspecting this table, we discover several interesting facts. For instance, there was an increase of $60 million from February to March, but it follows from the deseasonalized data that this increase is actually less than might have been expected in accordance with typical seasonal patterns. It would thus have been entirely unjustified to rejoice about this $60 million increase in sales. On the other hand, sales dropped by $29 million from May to June, but there is no need to worry; the drop is actually less than what might have been expected in accordance with typical seasonal patterns. All this is apparent from the deseasonalized data, and it illustrates very clearly why seasonal variations must be taken into account in the analysis of any kind of business data. Many important time series published regularly by the federal government are reported on a deseasonalized basis.

Forecasting

Now that we have attained some familiarity with time series and know how to measure some of their components, let us see how time series are used in forecasting. The rationale of basing forecasts on time series is that we are (hopefully) convinced that there is some regularity in the movement of data through time and that "what has happened in the past will, to a greater or lesser extent, continue to happen or will happen again in the future." Thus, the obvious way to forecast the trend of a time series is to extrapolate from the trend equation which describes the past. By "extrapolate" we mean extending it into the future, or otherwise estimating a value that lies beyond the range of values on the basis of which the trend equation was obtained.

To illustrate, suppose we are given the following trend equation which describes the long-term growth of a junior department store in a large shopping center in a metropolitan area:

$$y' = 1,440 + 72x$$

(origin, 1960; x units, 1 year; y, total
annual sales in thousands of dollars)

This equation has been calculated by the method of least squares for 1950 to 1960 data available from the company's records. The problem is to estimate (1) total sales for the year 1965, and (2) monthly sales for the same year.

In 1960 the trend value is $1,440,000 and the growth forces are producing an increase in sales of $72,000 per year. Thus, we shall extrapolate by substituting $x = 5$ into the equation and say that, based on the long-term growth forces alone, 1965 sales are expected to be $y' = 1,440 + 72(5) = 1,800$ or $1,800,000.

If the sales of the store were uninfluenced by seasonal fluctuations, we could estimate monthly sales in precisely the same way. Modifying the trend equation as we did on page 328, namely, by changing the x units to 1 month, y to average monthly sales, and the origin to January 1960, we obtain

$$y' = 117.25 + 0.50x$$

(origin, January 1960; x units, 1 month;
y, average monthly sales in thousands of dollars)

Substituting $x = 60, 61, 62, \ldots$, and 71 into this last equation and solving for y', we estimate the trend values for January 1965, February 1965, ..., and December 1965 as 147.25, 147.75, 148.25, 148.75, 149.25, 149.75, 150.25, 150.75, 151.25, 151.75, 152.25, and 152.75.

Since store sales are strongly affected by seasonal factors, it would hardly seem reasonable to predict sales of $147,250 for January 1965 or sales of $152,750 for December 1965. Indeed, a seasonal index calculated from the same data by the ratio-to-moving-average method shows that typical January sales are only 80 per cent of those of the average month, while typical December sales are 141 per cent of those of the average month. Multiplying the January trend figure by 0.80 we arrive at predicted sales of $117,800 for January 1965, and multiplying the December trend figure by 1.41 we arrive at predicted sales of $215,378 for December 1965. Calculating by this method a prediction for each month of 1965, we arrive at the sales figures shown in the following table:

Month	Trend Value	Seasonal Index	Predicted Monthly Sales for 1965
January	147.25	0.80	$117,800
February	147.75	0.75	$110,812
March	148.25	0.95	$140,838
April	148.75	0.98	$145,775
May	149.25	1.07	$159,698
June	149.75	0.96	$143,760
July	150.25	0.82	$123,205
August	150.75	0.89	$134,168
September	151.25	1.04	$157,300
October	151.75	1.23	$186,652
November	152.25	1.10	$167,475
December	152.75	1.41	$215,378

Here the trend values are the ones calculated above, the seasonal index was obtained from the company's records, and the predicted sales figures are the products of the monthly trend values and the corresponding values of the seasonal index. Note that what we are doing here is precisely *the opposite of deseasonalizing*. We introduce, rather than remove, seasonal patterns into our predictions by multiplying, rather than dividing, by the values of the seasonal index (written as proportions).

So far our predictions account for trend and seasonal patterns; we have not yet considered the effects of cyclical and irregular influences. The latter, we have suggested, are essentially unpredictable: freight lost in transit for 5 weeks, a fire in a competing store, the untimely death of an executive, etc., are things for which it is difficult to account. While the effects of such events may more or less average out in the long run, they may also substantially affect sales in particular months and cause even the best forecasts to go astray.

The problem of allowing in one's predictions for cyclical variations is a very difficult one and we shall not go into it in this book in any detail. Let us merely point out that in this area a great deal of help is available to everyone from both private and public sources. In addition to masses of other information furnished by the federal government, the Bureau of the Census publishes a monthly report, "Business Cycle Developments," which draws heavily on work done over many years by the (privately supported) National Bureau of Economic Research. The wealth of economic data contained in the report is in the form of *economic indicators*, that is, series of data intended to point the direction of general business activity.

EXERCISES

1. The following data show the monthly stocks of turkeys in cold storage (in millions of pounds) for the years 1957–1962:

	Jan	*Feb*	*Mar*	*Apr*	*May*	*Jun*	*Jul*	*Aug*	*Sep*	*Oct*	*Nov*	*Dec*
1957	170	150	137	109	98	92	90	102	149	241	220	177
1958	179	154	131	105	84	80	79	104	161	255	208	162
1959	160	141	112	87	68	65	67	87	134	220	183	149
1960	142	124	105	87	74	66	71	113	186	282	210	161
1961	169	152	126	108	94	106	128	189	270	382	318	263
1962	251	219	191	156	132	121	123	160	233	340	265	203

Compute a seasonal index for these data by the ratio-to-moving-average method, using the median to average the percentages of moving average obtained for the individual months.

2. Use the seasonal index obtained in Exercise 1 to deseasonalize the 1957 through 1962 stocks of turkeys as shown in the data directly above. Also plot the deseasonalized data together with the original data on one chart.

3. The following is a trend equation fit by the method of least squares to the figures on the cold-storage stocks of turkeys in Exercise 1: $y' = 181.48 + 1.04x$ *(origin, January 1962; x units, 1 month; y, average monthly stocks in millions of pounds)*. Use this equation and the

seasonal index computed in Exercise 1 to forecast the monthly stocks of turkeys in 1965.

4. The following data show the monthly production of slippers for housewear (in thousands of pairs) for the years 1957–1962:

	Jan	Feb	Mar	Apr	May	Jun	Jul	Aug	Sep	Oct	Nov	Dec
1957	2,986	4,563	5,304	5,361	5,782	5,598	5,649	8,044	7,772	8,657	7,426	3,759
1958	3,261	3,721	4,845	4,915	5,917	6,345	5,899	7,404	8,334	8,591	7,194	4,146
1959	3,426	4,911	5,489	6,455	6,132	6,453	6,546	8,154	9,208	9,142	7,913	4,872
1960	4,328	4,805	5,896	5,485	5,756	6,239	5,179	8,406	7,734	8,510	8,301	3,949
1961	3,115	3,328	4,915	4,795	5,490	6,235	4,682	8,483	8,526	9,568	9,206	5,136
1962	4,930	4,943	5,811	5,161	6,615	6,511	5,550	8,585	7,829	8,702	7,375	3,906

Compute a seasonal index for these data, using the modified mean (see page 336) to average the percentages of moving average obtained for the different months.

5. Use the seasonal index obtained in Exercise 4 to deseasonalize the 1962 production of slippers as shown in that exercise.

6. Often deseasonalized monthly data are multiplied by 12 and then referred to as *annual rates*. The use of seasonally adjusted annual rates is particularly helpful in facilitating the analysis of month-to-month changes in series of data which are best understood on an annual basis. Thus, we often see reported such statements as, "Americans had more income in June on an annual rate basis than in any other month in history." Based on the seasonally adjusted figure for March 1962 obtained in the preceding exercise, at what annual rate was the 1962 slipper production then running?

7. The trend of slipper production in the United States may be described by the following equation: $y' = 74{,}026 + 424x$ (*origin, 1959–1960; x units, 6 months; y, total annual production in thousands of pairs*). Use this equation (suitably modified) and the seasonal index computed in Exercise 4 to forecast the monthly production of slippers in 1966.

8. The following data show the monthly values of new public highway construction (in millions of dollars) put in place during the years 1957 through 1962:

	Jan	Feb	Mar	Apr	May	Jun	Jul	Aug	Sep	Oct	Nov	Dec
1957	247	206	224	329	434	513	491	544	584	589	403	328
1958	261	238	247	349	459	549	586	626	643	636	507	399
1959	296	269	316	422	511	631	659	643	655	591	467	410
1960	221	237	251	342	493	552	601	645	644	558	450	470
1961	291	267	271	338	435	574	562	651	685	651	603	490
1962	332	241	279	339	509	618	643	700	708	800	589	496

(a) Compute a seasonal index by the ratio-to-moving-average method, using the median to average the percentages of moving average obtained for the individual months.

(b) Plot the original data together with the values of the centered 12-month moving average on one diagram.

(c) Use the seasonal index obtained in part (a) to deseasonalize the 1962 data.

(d) Use the results of part (c) to determine the annual rate of new public highway construction for the last three months of 1962 (see Exercise 6).

(e) An equation measuring the trend in the value of public highway construction put in place is $y' = 6{,}140 + 196x$ (*origin, 1962; x units, 1 year; y, total annual construction in millions of dollars*). Use this equation (suitably modified) and the seasonal index computed in part (a) to forecast the monthly values of construction put in place for the year 1965.

9. A large furniture manufacturer estimates total 1965 sales to be $44,400,000. If the company's seasonal index for furniture sales is 78, 75, 100, 126, 138, 121, 101, 104, 99, 103, 80, and 75 for the twelve months of the year, draw up a tentative 1965 sales budget for the manufacturer, assuming that there is no trend.

10. Suppose that the furniture manufacturer referred to in Exercise 9 determines the trend in furniture sales by means of the equation $y' = 30{,}000{,}000 + 2{,}880{,}000x$ (*origin, 1960; x units, 1 year; y, total annual sales in dollars*).

(a) Use this equation, suitably modified, to calculate the trend values for monthly sales for each month of 1965.

(b) Use the trend values obtained in part (a) and the seasonal index given in Exercise 9 to forecast the company's monthly sales in 1965.

11. In a study of its sales a motor company obtained the following least squares trend equation: $y' = 2{,}800 + 200x$ (*origin, 1955; x units, 1 year; y, total number of units sold annually*). The company has physical facilities to produce only 6,000 units a year, and it believes that it is reasonable to assume that, at least for the next decade, the trend will continue as before.

(a) What is the average annual increase in the number of units sold?

(b) By what year will the company's expected sales have equalled its present physical capacity?

(c) How much in excess of the company's present capacity is the estimated sales figure for 1975?

12. A company selling swimming-pool supplies had sales of $20,000 and $24,000 in March and April of 1963. The company's seasonal index for these two months stands at 105 and 140. The president of the company expressed dissatisfaction with the April sales, but the sales manager said that he was quite pleased with the $4,000 increase. What argument should the president of the company use to reply to the sales manager? The sales manager also predicts on the basis of these two months' sales that the total 1963 sales will be $264,000, while the president of the company predicts that total sales will be $217,000 (rounded to the nearest $1,000). Criticize the sales manager's estimate and explain how the president may have arrived at his figure.

A Word of Caution

Among the topics discussed in this chapter there are many that lend themselves to abuses and misinterpretations. As we have already pointed out, one of the most serious mistakes in problems of correlation is to interpret a strong correlation, a high degree of association, as a cause-effect relationship. A classical example, which is often used to illustrate this fallacy, is the one in which a relationship is established between babies and storks. A strong positive correlation was obtained for the number of storks seen nesting in English villages and the number of children born in these same communities. The explanation, of course, is very simple: in large villages there are lots of houses, lots of chimneys for storks to nest in, lots of storks, and lots of babies; in small villages there are but few houses, few chimneys for storks to nest in, few storks, and few babies.

So far as forecasting is concerned, it must be remembered that any projection of past experience to the uncertain future is speculative and hazardous. Nevertheless, it must go on if business and government are to operate intelligently and successfully, and improved techniques of gathering, analyzing, and interpreting data are constantly being developed. Moreover, no one is irrevocably committed to a forecast, to survive or perish with it once it has been made. In the illustration of the preceding section, for example, adjustments may have to be made to take account of the impact of improved area transportation facilities, the opening of a new competing store, an increase in the sales tax, and other factors which may be unforeseeable at the time a forecast is made.

Forecasts are tentative things—special kinds of hypotheses, so to speak —which can always be modified or revised in response to changing conditions. When in the light of new information forecasts are revised, all who are concerned must take whatever steps are necessary to translate revised production, sales, or other goals into action. Intelligent forecasting and planning demand one's continual attention to changing conditions.

Generally speaking, it seems clear that realistic forecasts, which contribute greatly both to individual success and to the stability of the economy, are the results of applying sound business experience and judgment to relevant and timely statistical analyses.

Technical Note 11 (Limits of Prediction)

In order to judge the "goodness" of a prediction based on a least squares regression equation, we must, as always, have some estimate of *chance variation*. To this end, we assume that the y we obtain for any given value of x is a value of a random variable (a random sample of size 1) from a population which can be closely approximated by a normal curve. Furthermore, we assume that the standard deviation of this population is σ regardless of x. In fact, this σ is the required measure of chance variation and we estimate it by means of the quantity

$$s_e = \sqrt{\frac{\Sigma\,(y - y')^2}{n - 2}}$$

called the *standard error of estimate.* As is explained in the text on page 305, $\Sigma\,(y - y')^2$, the sum of the squared deviations represented by the solid line segments of Figure 10.4 is that portion of the total variation of the y's which can be attributed to chance. The divisor $n - 2$ is the *number of degrees of freedom* associated with this estimate of chance variation; it is $n - 2$ rather than the $n - 1$ we have used until now when estimating a variance, because the *two* constants a and b (instead of the one constant $\bar{y}$) had to be calculated first on the basis of the original data.

The quantity $\Sigma\,(y - y')^2$ is sometimes obtained by actually substituting the various values of y and y' (see page 314); in practice, it is simpler to calculate it by means of the short-cut formula

$$\Sigma\,(y - y')^2 = \Sigma\,y^2 - a \cdot \Sigma\,y - b \cdot \Sigma\,xy$$

so that the formula for the standard error of estimate becomes

$$s_e = \sqrt{\frac{\Sigma\,y^2 - a \cdot \Sigma\,y - b \cdot \Sigma\,xy}{n - 2}} \qquad \bigstar$$

Substituting $n = 10$, $a = 24.43$, $b = 10.53$, $\Sigma\ y = 2{,}140$, $\Sigma\ xy = 42{,}480$, and $\Sigma\ y^2 = 501{,}600$ (which are given on pages 306, 307, and 315), we find that for our example concerning the quality and the processing time of the given parts

$$s_e = \sqrt{\frac{501{,}600 - 24.43(2{,}140) - 10.53(42{,}480)}{10 - 2}}$$

$$= 15.8$$

Let us now demonstrate how this estimate of chance variation is used to evaluate the "goodness" of a prediction based on a least squares equation. If we are given a set of paired data for which we determine the equation of the least squares line, and if we use this equation to calculate the predicted value y_0' for a given value x_0 of x, we can assert with a probability of 0.95 that the value we will actually obtain will lie between $y_0' - A$ and $y_0' + A$, called the *limits of prediction*, where

$$A = t_{.025} \cdot s_e \sqrt{\frac{n + 1}{n} + \frac{(x_0 - \bar{x})^2}{\Sigma\ x^2 - n \cdot \bar{x}^2}}$$

and $t_{.025}$ is obtained from Table II with $n - 2$ degrees of freedom. Here x_0 is the value for which we want to make the prediction, y_0' is the value we obtain by substituting x_0 into the equation of the least squares line, while n, $\bar{x}$, and $\Sigma\ x^2$ pertain to the data for which the line was originally obtained. (If we want to change the probability from 0.95 to 0.98 or 0.99, we have only to replace $t_{.025}$ with $t_{.01}$ or $t_{.005}$ in the formula for A.)

Returning now to our numerical example, let us apply this theory to predict the quality of a part processed for $x_0 = 20$ minutes. Substituting this value into $y' = 24.43 + 10.53x$, we have already found on page 307 that the predicted quality rating is $y_0' = 235$. If we now substitute $s_e = 15.8$, $n = 10$, $\bar{x} = 180/10 = 18$, $\Sigma\ x^2 = 3{,}616$ (see page 306), and $t_{.025}$ (for 8 degrees of freedom) $= 2.306$ into the expression for A, we obtain

$$A = 2.306(15.8) \sqrt{\frac{11}{10} + \frac{(20 - 18)^2}{3{,}616 - 10(18)^2}} = 38$$

and the limits of prediction are $235 - 38 = 197$ and $235 + 38 = 273$. In other words, we can assert with a probability of 0.95 that the quality rating of a part processed for 20 minutes will be contained in the interval from 197 to 273.

This may seem like a fairly wide interval, and in practice it may or may not be adequate for predictive purposes. One reason for the width of the interval is that it is based on only 10 points, the processing times and quality ratings of the 10 parts. Another reason for the width of the interval is that s_e is 15.8, indicating considerable variation in quality even among parts processed for the same length of time. So long as the process used to manufacture the parts is not changed, there is nothing that can be done to get appreciably narrower limits of prediction.

Technical Note 12 (Runs Above and Below the Median)

There are several tests that can be used to determine whether an apparent trend in a series of data is significant or whether it can be attributed to chance. The one we shall discuss in this note is based on the idea that if there is an *upward trend* most of the small values come first and the large values come later, while if there is a *downward trend* most of the large values come first and the small values come later. To make the distinction between large values and small values precise, we divide the data into values falling *above the median* (represented by the letter a) and values falling *below the median* (represented by the letter b). We then base our decision on the resulting sequences of a's and b's; specifically, we base it on the *total number of runs* of a's or b's, where a run is defined as a sequence of identical letters (or other kinds of symbols) which is followed and preceded by different letters or no letters at all.

To illustrate this procedure, let us consider the data in the table on page 351 which represent the number of ordinary life insurance policies purchased in the United States in the years 1940 through 1961. The median of this set of figures is $\dfrac{5,756 + 5,776}{2} = 5,766$ and we have indicated for each year whether the corresponding figure is above or below the median. (If one of the figures had actually equalled the median it would have been omitted.)

Inspecting the table, we find that there is first a run of six b's, then a run of two a's, then a run of five b's, and finally a run of nine a's. The fact that there are so very few runs with most of the b's coming first is a clear indication that there is a trend, but to put the decision on a rigorous basis, we use the following criterion which actually tests the

Year	Number of Policies (000 omitted)	
1940	3,855	b
1941	4,163	b
1942	3,344	b
1943	3,718	b
1944	4,131	b
1945	4,343	b
1946	5,896	a
1947	5,776	a
1948	5,286	b
1949	4,996	b
1950	5,279	b
1951	5,521	b
1952	5,756	b
1953	6,465	a
1954	6,450	a
1955	7,572	a
1956	8,493	a
1957	8,783	a
1958	8,307	a
1959	8,683	a
1960	8,734	a
1961	8,702	a

null hypothesis that the arrangement of the a's and b's is random against the alternative that there is a trend (or some other systematic pattern):

the null hypothesis is rejected at a level of significance of 0.05 if u, the total number of runs above or below the median, is less than or equal to $u_{.05}$, where $u_{.05}$ is to be obtained from Table VII on page 445.

In our example we had $u = 4$ and the number of a's = the number of b's = 11. Since the corresponding value of $u_{.05}$ is 7 according to the table on page 445, we find that there is a *significant trend*. Had we wanted to use a level of significance of 0.01 in this example, we would have found from Table VII that $u_{.01} = 6$, so that the trend is significant also at this level. (Whether a non-random arrangement is indicative of a trend or, perhaps, a business cycle, will have to be judged by inspecting the data.)

ELEVEN
SHORT-CUT STATISTICS AND NONPARAMETRIC METHODS

Short-cut Statistics

None of the methods of this book requires calculations which are so complicated or involved that they cannot be handled with a desk calculator or even by hand. Hence, it would seem that there is no real need for short-cut techniques or other kinds of simplifications. In general this is true, but there are situations where it is important to get on-the-spot estimates of, say, the average quality of parts turned out by a machine, the variation in the thickness of plate glass, or the correlation between the input and the output of a certain process. We may thus want to use estimates which can be obtained with a minimum of arithmetic, even though there may be a corresponding loss of *efficiency*, that is, even though we may be exposing ourselves to greater chance fluctuations.

Under the heading of "short-cut statistics" we might thus estimate the mean of a population with a *sample median*, which usually requires less work than the sample mean, or we might use the *mid-range*, the average of the largest and smallest values in a sample, the *mid-quartile*

$\dfrac{Q_1 + Q_3}{2}$, where Q_1 and Q_3 are as defined on page 41, or some other formula based on the *fractiles* of a distribution.

The most popular short-cut statistic for estimating the standard deviation of a population is the *sample range*. To obtain such an estimate for a sample from a population whose shape is roughly that of a normal curve, we divide the sample range (the largest value minus the smallest) by an appropriate constant which depends on the size of the sample and which is usually denoted d_2 in industrial applications. This method is used mainly when n is very small, in which case the values of d_2 can be obtained from the following table:

n	2	3	4	5	6	7	8	9	10	11	12
d_2	1.13	1.69	2.06	2.33	2.53	2.70	2.85	2.97	3.08	3.18	3.26

To illustrate this technique, suppose that the following are the times (in minutes) that nine secretaries took to perform a certain task:

28.9   23.5   40.7   33.8   36.5   31.2   29.2   41.2   39.4

The median of this sample is 33.8 and the range is $41.2 - 23.5 = 17.7$. Since $d_2 = 2.97$ for $n = 9$, we estimate the true mean and standard deviation of the time it takes a secretary to perform the given task as 33.8 minutes and $17.7/2.97 = 6.0$ minutes, respectively. (It will be left to the reader in Exercise 7 on page 356 to compare these values with the corresponding mean and standard deviation of the sample.)

There are numerous other short-cut techniques for estimating standard deviations. When dealing with a fairly large set of data we might calculate the mean of the largest 5 per cent of the data, the mean of the smallest 5 per cent, and then make use of the fact that the difference between these two means estimates, roughly, four times the standard deviation. Also, if a distribution follows closely the pattern of a normal curve, we can make use of the fact that approximately 68 per cent of the data fall within one standard deviation on either side of the mean, and estimate σ by means of the quantity $\frac{1}{2}(P_{84} - P_{16})$ or by means of the difference $P_{84} - P_{50}$. These P's are the corresponding percentiles as defined on page 42, and by using the special *probability graph paper* of Technical Note 8 on page 217, they can even be read directly off the plot of a cumulative distribution.

When dealing with large sets of paired data, the calculation of a correlation coefficient can be quite involved. To simplify matters, we sometimes base r on the *ranks* of the observations instead of their actual numerical values. We first rank the x's among themselves, giving Rank 1 to the largest value, Rank 2 to the second largest, and so on; then we similarly rank the y's among themselves and calculate the *coefficient of rank correlation* by means of the formula

$$r' = 1 - \frac{6(\Sigma\, d^2)}{n(n^2 - 1)} \qquad \bigstar$$

Here n is the number of pairs of observations and the d's represent the differences between the ranks of the corresponding x's and y's. In case there are ties, we assign to each of the tied values the mean of the ranks which they jointly occupy. Thus, if the third and fourth largest values are identical we assign each a rank of $\dfrac{3 + 4}{2} = 3.5$, and if the fifth, sixth, and seventh highest values are identical we assign each a rank of $\dfrac{5 + 6 + 7}{3} = 6$.

To illustrate this technique, let us refer again to the example which dealt with the processing times and the quality ratings of certain parts. Performing the necessary operations, we obtain

x	y	Rank of x	Rank of y	d	d^2
15	180	7	7	0	0
12	140	8.5	9	−0.5	0.25
20	230	4	5	−1	1
17	190	6	6	0	0
12	160	8.5	8	0.5	0.25
25	300	2	2	0	0
22	270	3	3	0	0
9	110	10	10	0	0
18	240	5	4	1	1
30	320	1	1	0	0
					2.50

Substituting $n = 10$ and $\Sigma\, d^2 = 2.5$ into the formula for r', we get

$$r' = 1 - \frac{6(2.5)}{10(100 - 1)} = 0.985$$

and this is very close to 0.978, the value which we obtained for r on page 315. Note that we would have obtained the identical result for r' if we had applied the formula on page 315 directly to the ranks of the x's and the y's. That is, r' gives the exact correlation coefficient for the ranks.

If we use the ranks of the x's and the y's instead of their actual values, we are, of course, disregarding some information, but r' is usually very close to r. It is of interest to note that if we calculate r' instead of r, we can test the null hypothesis that there is no relationship between the two variables without having to make any assumptions about the nature of the populations from which the data are obtained. We reject this null hypothesis at a level of significance of 0.05 if r' exceeds $1.96/\sqrt{n - 1}$ or if it is less than $-1.96/\sqrt{n - 1}$. For our example, this critical value equals

$$\frac{1.96}{\sqrt{n - 1}} = \frac{1.96}{\sqrt{10 - 1}} = 0.65$$

and since this figure is exceeded by the value obtained for r', we can say that there is a *significant correlation*.

EXERCISES

1. Estimate the mean of the 40 job times on page 222 by using the median, and estimate the standard deviation by taking one-fourth of the difference between the mean of the highest 5 per cent of the data and the mean of the lowest 5 per cent of the data. Compare these values with those of $\bar{x}$ and s given on page 222.

2. Estimate the mean of the 100 downtimes on page 14 by using the mid-quartile (Q_1 and Q_3 are given on page 41), and estimate the standard deviation by taking one-fourth of the difference between the mean of the highest 5 per cent and the mean of the lowest 5 per cent of the data.

3. Estimate the standard deviation of the downtime distribution on page 15 by taking half the difference between the percentiles P_{84} and P_{16}. Repeat this process of estimation by reading the necessary percentiles off the graph obtained in Exercise 21 on page 210.

4. Estimate the standard deviation of whichever data you grouped among those of the exercises on pages 19 through 21 by taking half the difference between the percentiles P_{84} and P_{16}. Repeat this process of estimation by reading the necessary percentiles off the graph obtained in Exercise 22 on page 210.

5. Use the sample range and an appropriate value of the divisor d_2 to approximate the standard deviation of the donations made to the United Fund on page 52. Compare this value with the sample standard deviation obtained on that same page.

6. Eight cans of cleansing powder are randomly selected from a large production lot and their net weights determined with the following results: 13.9, 14.1, 14.2, 13.9, 14.0, 14.1, 14.0, and 13.9 ounces. Use the sample range and an appropriate value of d_2 to estimate the standard deviation of the population from which this sample was obtained.

7. Compute the mean and the standard deviation of the data on page 353 (pertaining to the time nine secretaries took to perform a certain task) and compare with the short-cut estimates obtained on that page.

8. A random sample of 6 daily scrap records (where scrap is expressed as a percentage of material requisitioned) shows 3.4, 4.0, 3.8, 6.0, 5.4, and 4.4 per cent scrap. Use the sample range and an appropriate value of d_2 to estimate the standard deviation and compare with the value of s obtained for these data in Exercise 18 on page 230.

9. Calculate r' for the relative humidity and moisture content readings of Exercise 1 on page 308 and test for significance with $\alpha = 0.05$. Also compare with the value of r obtained in Exercise 1 on page 318.

10. Calculate r' for the area burned and variable operating expenditure data of Exercise 3 on page 309 and test for significance with $\alpha = 0.01$. Also compare with the value of r obtained in Exercise 3 on page 318.

11. Calculate r' for the nicotine and tar content data of Exercise 5 on page 310 and test for significance with $\alpha = 0.05$.

12. The following data were collected in a study to measure the effects of various factors on the efficiency of an extraction operation. The variable x is the extraction time (in minutes) and the variable y is the extraction efficiency (in per cent):

Extraction Time, x	Extraction Efficiency, y
14	50
32	48
40	78
52	70
58	84
34	60
48	84
58	70
44	62
26	50
18	44
46	76
20	52
30	64
58	80
44	70
26	58
40	56
52	80
38	70

Calculate r' and test for significance at $\alpha = 0.05$.

13. As part of its product development work, a large company asks two judges (taste testers) to rank (in order of preference) samples of blueberry muffins made from 10 different trial mixes. The results they obtained are as follows:

Mix	Taste Tester 1	Taste Tester 2
A	1	2
B	2	4
C	3	5
D	4	1
E	5	7
F	6	3
G	7	6
H	8	9
I	9	10
J	10	8

Calculate r' as a measure of the *consistency* of the two judges and test for significance at $\alpha = 0.05$.

14. In a study devoted to the problem of salesmen turnover, an investigator takes a random sample of 11 large companies and ranks them according to hiring cost and separation rate (with the 1's assigned to the companies with the highest hiring cost and with the highest separation rate). Using the data which follow, is there evidence at the 0.01 level of significance that companies having the highest hiring cost have the lowest separation rate?

Company	Hiring Cost	Separation Rate
A	1	10
B	2	11
C	3	9
D	4	7
E	5	8
F	6	6
G	7	4
H	8	5
I	9	1
J	10	3
K	11	2

15. Taking into account a number of factors considered relevant (grades, intelligence, personality, interest, aspiration, and so on), a random sample of 10 members of the 1948 graduating class of a large collegiate graduate school of business is ranked by a faculty committee on their probable success (highest estimated success being ranked 1). In 1962 the men are ranked by another faculty committee on the actual degree of success attained, and the results are as shown in the following table:

	Estimated Success	Actual Success
Mr. A	1	5
Mr. B	2	4
Mr. C	3	1
Mr. D	4	7
Mr. E	5	10
Mr. F	6	2
Mr. G	7	9
Mr. H	8	3
Mr. I	9	8
Mr. J	10	6

Is there any evidence (at the 0.05 level of significance) of faculty ability to predict business success under the limited conditions of the study?

Nonparametric Tests

Most of the tests discussed in Chapter 9 required assumptions about the population (or populations) from which the samples were obtained; essentially, these tests concerned the *parameters* of populations, their means, their standard deviations, and so forth. Since there are many situations in which (among other things) the assumption that the population has roughly the shape of a normal curve cannot be met, statisticians have developed alternate techniques which have become known as *nonparametric* or *distribution-free* tests. Strictly speaking, these terms were not intended to be synonymous; the first was meant to apply to tests in which we make no hypothesis about specific values of parameters, and the second was meant to apply to tests in which we, furthermore, make no assumptions about the nature, shape, or form of the populations. Nowadays, it has become the custom to refer to either kind of test simply as *nonparametric*.

Several nonparametric tests have become quite popular since they also fall under the heading of "quick and easy" or "short-cut" tests. Not only are most of these tests simpler so far as arithmetical details are concerned, but they are often easier to explain and easier to understand than the standard techniques which they replace. Although the subject of nonparametric testing has become quite extensive in recent years, we shall limit our discussion to a few examples. Actually, we have already met two nonparametric tests: first there was the significance test for a trend in Technical Note 12 (the one based on runs above and below the median), and then there was the significance test for r' discussed in the preceding section. In addition to these, we shall now discuss a test which is called the *sign test*, and some tests based on *rank sums*.

The Sign Test

As we pointed out in Chapter 9, the small-sample test for the difference between two means cannot be used unless the populations from which the samples are obtained can be approximated closely by normal curves and unless these populations have equal standard deviations. If either of these assumptions cannot be met, we can employ a nonparametric test, called the *sign test*, which is based on the *signs* of the observed differences (whether they are positive or negative) instead of their actual magnitudes. The sign test also provides a convenient alternative to the method discussed in Exercise 19 on page 272, namely, to the case where the two samples are *not independent.*

To illustrate the sign test (as it is used in a problem where the two samples are *not independent*), let us consider the following data on the weights (in pounds) of 20 persons before and after they have tried out a new reducing diet:

	Weight Before	*Weight After*	*Sign of Change*
Mr. A	192	183	−
Mr. B	153	151	−
Mr. C	175	173	−
Mr. D	214	209	−
Mr. E	239	228	−
Mr. F	149	150	+
Mr. G	178	173	−
Mr. H	163	159	−
Mr. I	210	207	−
Mr. J	158	156	−
Mr. K	134	131	−
Mr. L	189	186	−
Mr. M	203	200	−
Mr. N	245	247	+
Mr. O	177	174	−
Mr. P	256	248	−
Mr. Q	227	222	−
Mr. R	189	189	
Mr. S	176	179	+
Mr. T	196	193	−

The right-hand column of this table shows whether there was an increase in weight, a decrease in .weight, or no change. Counting the signs, we find that there are 16 minus signs, 3 plus signs, and one case (the 18th) where there was no change at all.

Ignoring those cases where there is no change, the null hypothesis that the reducing diet is *not effective* is equivalent to the null hypothesis that we are as likely to get a minus sign as we are to get a plus. Hence, we test the null hypothesis that the probability of getting a minus sign is $p = 0.50$ against the one-sided alternative $p > 0.50$. (We use this one-sided alternative because $p > 0.50$ means that there is a better than fifty-fifty chance for losing weight; if p were less than 0.50, the diet would be a weight-gaining rather than a reducing diet.) We can now use

he method on page 274; we have "16 successes in 19 trials," and pro-
:eeding as on page 275 we find that for $n = 19$ and $p = 0.50$ the mean
ιnd the standard deviation of the binomial distribution are

$$\mu = 19(0.50) = 9.5$$

ιnd
$$\sigma = \sqrt{19(0.50)(0.50)} = 2.18$$

Basing the test on the normal curve approximation to the binomial dis-
.ribution, we get

$$z = \frac{16 - 9.5}{2.18} = 2.98$$

ιnd since this exceeds the critical value of 1.64 (for a one-sided test with a
evel of significance of 0.05), we reject the null hypothesis and accept the
ιlternative that the reducing diet is effective. (When n is very small, it
may be preferable to base this test on a table of binomial probabilities
·ather than the normal curve approximation; had we done so in this
ιxample, we would have found that the probability of getting 16 or more
successes in 19 trials with $p = 0.50$ is 0.0021, and the conclusions would
ηave been the same.)

This example illustrates one of the many uses of the sign test; several
ιther applications are given in the exercises on page 366. Note that
ιecause of its extreme simplicity the sign test is sometimes used as a
short-cut, even though standard techniques are applicable.

Tests Based on Rank Sums

We have already seen in several cases how short-cuts can be attained
ιy replacing measurements or observations by their ranks within
samples and how we can subsequently perform nonparametric signifi-
:ance tests, which do not require the usual restrictive assumptions. In
this section we shall discuss another technique based on ranks, which
can be used to decide whether two samples come from populations with
equal or unequal means, and which can also be used to decide whether
two samples come from populations with equal or unequal variances
(when there is no difference between the population means). The test
we are referring to is the U-test, also called the *Mann-Whitney test*,
named after the two statisticians who first suggested its use.

To illustrate how the U-test is used to test whether there is a difference between two population means, suppose we want to compare the annual incomes of salesmen of chemicals and salesmen of home appliances, and that random samples produced the following results (in dollars):

Salesmen of Chemicals

7,600	10,400	12,500	7,300	8,700
6,900	9,700	14,900	7,800	

Salesmen of Home Appliances

8,800	9,200	10,100	8,300	9,900	8,500
11,100	7,100	9,000	9,400	9,100	

The means of these two samples are $9,533 and $9,136, and the problem is to decide whether the difference between the two is significant. The standard way of handling this kind of problem is the t-test described in Technical Note 10 on page 292, but it can be seen from the data that it may well be unreasonable to assume that the two samples come from populations with equal standard deviations; the second sample seems to display considerably less variation than the first.

To perform the U-test, we first rank the data *jointly* (as if they were one sample) in an increasing (or decreasing) order of magnitude. Using the letters c and h, respectively, to indicate for each figure whether it comes from the sample of salesmen of chemicals or from the sample of salesmen of home appliances, we get

6,900	7,100	7,300	7,600	7,800	8,300	8,500	8,700	8,800
c	h	c	c	c	h	h	c	h
9,000	9,100	9,200	9,400	9,700	9,900	10,100	10,400	11,100
h	h	h	h	c	h	h	c	h
12,500	14,900
c	c

Assigning the data *in this order* the ranks 1, 2, 3, ..., and 20, we find that the values of the first sample occupy ranks 1, 3, 4, 5, 8, 14, 17, 19, 20, while those of the second sample occupy ranks 2, 6, 7, 9, 10, 11, 12, 13, 15, 16, and 18. (There are no *ties* in rank in this example, but if there are ties we treat them as on page 354; that is, we assign to each of the tied observations the mean of the ranks which they jointly occupy.)

The null hypothesis we shall want to test is that both samples come from the same population, and it stands to reason that in that case the means of the ranks assigned to the values of the two samples should be more or less the same. The alternative hypothesis is that the populations have unequal means, and if this difference is pronounced, most of the smaller ranks will go to the values of one sample while most of the higher ranks will go to those of the other sample.

Using *rank sums* (rather than average ranks), we shall base the test of this null hypothesis on the statistic

$$U = n_1 n_2 + \frac{n_1(n_1 + 1)}{2} - R_1 \qquad \star$$

where n_1 and n_2 are the sizes of the two samples and R_1 is the sum of the ranks assigned to the values of the first sample. (In practice, we find whichever rank sum is most easily obtained, as it is immaterial which sample is referred to as the "first.") In our example we have $n_1 = 9$, $n_2 = 11$, $R_1 = 1 + 3 + 4 + 5 + 8 + 14 + 17 + 19 + 20 = 91$, and hence

$$U = 9 \cdot 11 + \frac{9 \cdot 10}{2} - 91 = 53$$

Under the null hypothesis that the $n_1 + n_2$ observations come from one population (or equal populations), it can be shown that the sampling distribution of U has the mean

$$\mu_U = \frac{n_1 n_2}{2} \qquad \star$$

and the standard deviation

$$\sigma_U = \sqrt{\frac{n_1 n_2(n_1 + n_2 + 1)}{12}} \qquad \star$$

Furthermore, if n_1 and n_2 are both greater than 8 (some statisticians prefer that they be both greater than 10), the sampling distribution of U can be approximated closely with a normal curve. Hence, we can reject the null hypothesis at a level of significance of 0.05 if

$$z = \frac{U - \mu_U}{\sigma_U} \qquad \star$$

exceeds 1.96 or is less than -1.96. As was pointed out above, rejection of the null hypothesis will be taken as an indication that the two populations have unequal means. Incidentally, if either n_1 or n_2 is so small that the normal curve approximation cannot be used, the test can be based on special tables referred to in the Bibliography at the end of this book.

Returning now to our numerical example where $n_1 = 9$ and $n_2 = 11$, we find that

$$\mu_U = \frac{9 \cdot 11}{2} = 49.5$$

$$\sigma_U = \sqrt{\frac{9 \cdot 11 \cdot 21}{12}} = 13.16$$

and hence that

$$z = \frac{53 - 49.5}{13.16} = 0.27$$

Since this value falls between -1.96 and 1.96, we cannot reject the null hypothesis that the samples came from identical populations. Using this nonparametric test we were thus unable to obtain a significant difference in the annual incomes of the two kinds of salesmen.

The U-test has the important advantage that it requires fewer assumptions than the corresponding "standard" tests. In fact, the only assumption needed is that the populations from which we are sampling are continuous, and in actual practice even the violation of this assumption is usually not very serious. Another advantage of the U-test is that it is very easy to perform; like the sign test, it is thus often used for reasons of simplicity even though "standard methods" could be employed.

An interesting feature of the U-test is that, with a slight modification it can also be used to test the null hypothesis that the two samples come from the same population, or identical populations, against the alternative that the two populations have *unequal dispersions*, namely, that they differ in variability or spread. As before, the values of the two samples are arranged jointly in an increasing (or decreasing) order of magnitude, but now they are *ranked from both ends toward the middle*. We assign Rank 1 to the smallest value, Ranks 2 and 3 to the largest and second largest, Ranks 4 and 5 to the second and third smallest, Ranks 6 and 7 to the third and fourth largest, and so on. Subsequently, the calculation of U and the performance of the test are the same as before. The only difference is that with this kind of ranking a *small rank sum* tends to indicate that the population from which the sample was obtained has a *greater variation* than the other; its values occupy the more extreme positions. Returning to our example, we find that with the new kind of ranking the values of the first sample have ranks 1, 5, 8, 9, 16, 14, 7, 3, and 2. This yields $R_1 = 65$, $U = 79$, and

$$z = \frac{79 - 49.5}{13.16} = 2.24$$

since σ_U and μ_U have the same values as before. Since the value we have obtained for z exceeds 1.96, the null hypothesis must be rejected, and we conclude that there is a difference in variability between the two populations. In other words, there is a significant difference in the variability of the annual incomes of the two kinds of salesmen. (Since U is greater than expected, R_1 is smaller than expected, and this means that the first sample exhibits a greater variability than the second; this agrees with the observation made on page 362.)

EXERCISES

1. The following data represent the expenditures on research and development (in cents per common share) in 1952 and in 1962 for a random sample of 15 large manufacturing companies:

	1952	*1962*
Company A	12	14
Company B	8	9
Company C	14	17
Company D	9	8
Company E	17	20
Company F	20	22
Company G	7	11
Company H	11	11
Company I	12	15
Company J	11	13
Company K	8	10
Company L	5	10
Company M	13	17
Company N	22	27
Company O	17	16

Use the sign test and a level of significance of 0.05 to check whether there is actually an increase in research and development expenditures between the two time periods in the population of companies from which the sample was obtained.

2. In its quality control section, a large food manufacturer tests the consistency of a salad dressing by dropping a plummet from a standard height into 12 jars of the dressing randomly selected from a large production lot, and measuring the distance the plummet penetrates (which is proportional to the consistency of the mix). These jars are set aside for 10 days and then tested again for consistency. If the following are the penetration distances (in inches) on the two tests, is there any evidence of a change in consistency (as reflected by a change in the distance)?

	First Test	Second Test
Jar 1	3.4	3.5
Jar 2	3.2	3.1
Jar 3	3.7	3.5
Jar 4	3.1	3.2
Jar 5	3.5	3.5
Jar 6	3.9	3.7
Jar 7	3.4	3.2
Jar 8	3.4	3.5
Jar 9	3.6	3.3
Jar 10	3.5	3.3
Jar 11	3.8	3.9
Jar 12	3.2	3.1

3. On the first trial of a practice period 15 experienced code clerks scored 70, 74, 80, 84, 79, 82, 85, 82, 81, 86, 75, 80, 81, 79, and 83 points on a newly constructed digit symbol learning test, and on the tenth trial they scored 76, 79, 90, 92, 79, 88, 90, 90, 87, 82, 80, 88, 89, 84, and 88 points, respectively. Test at the 0.05 level whether the apparent gain in score is significant.

4. The sign test can also be used to test the hypothesis that the mean of a symmetrical population equals some constant μ_0 against a suitable one-sided or two-sided alternative. We simply use a *plus sign* to represent each sample value exceeding μ_0, a *minus sign* to represent each sample value less than μ_0, and we then test the hypothesis $p = 1/2$ on the basis of the number of plus signs (or minus signs) obtained in n trials. (If a value actually equals μ_0 it is discarded.) Use this method to test on the basis of the following sample data (in days) whether the average number of days wholesalers of drugs and drug sundries require to convert receivables into cash is $\mu_0 = 31$ days: 38, 40, 28, 30, 32, 33, 40, 28, 43, 50, 28, 33, 30, 51, 37, 50, 30, 35, 28, 26.

5. In addition to its use in credit analysis, the ratio analysis of working capital is important in determining how efficiently working capital is

being used. One important measure is the ratio of inventory to net working capital since it shows the extent to which owners have invested in the least liquid of all working-capital components. The following figures show the inventory-to-net-working-capital ratios (times 100) for the same 20 wholesalers referred to in Exercise 4 in a survey conducted in 1958: 77.4, 79.5, 70.4, 73.2, 68.9, 80.1, 74.4, 82.4, 81.0, 78.5, 79.0, 75.0, 82.3, 81.2, 75.4, 77.8, 79.3, 80.2, 75.0, and 75.7. Use this information to test at the 0.05 level whether the corresponding mean for all wholesalers of drugs and drug sundries is $\mu_0 = 79.3$.

6. Referring to Exercise 5, suppose that in a survey conducted in 1963 the corresponding ratios (times 100) for the 20 wholesalers (listed in the same order) were: 76.3, 82.5, 75.9, 75.6, 73.0, 79.2, 77.2, 82.4, 80.3, 81.2, 82.1, 74.9, 80.8, 82.4, 80.5, 75.0, 78.5, 80.0, 80.8, and 81.3. Use the sign test and a level of significance of 0.05 to check whether there has been a change from 1958 to 1963 in the mean ratio of inventory to net working capital in the population of wholesalers from which the samples were obtained.

7. In attempting to control various costs, a large company wants to compare the use of a certain complex, expensive carbon interleafed form used in the production departments of two separate plants. The completed form output of the two departments is virtually the same, and the company thinks that the number of forms requisitioned should also be about the same. In the absence of past detailed stock records, the company takes a 20-week period and finds that Department Q requisitioned, respectively, 4, 8, 8, 12, 6, 14, 15, 5, 7, 7, 13, 5, 9, 8, 10, 6, 10, 12, 9, and 6 boxes, while Department R requisitioned, respectively, 8, 3, 10, 5, 3, 7, 5, 6, 11, 7, 2, 4, 4, 6, 11, 4, 4, 4, 6, and 7 boxes of forms. Treating these data as constituting random samples of size 20 each, test at the 0.01 level of significance whether it is reasonable to treat the average weekly numbers of boxes of forms required by the two departments as being the same. (Note that when there are ties in rank, each of the tied observations is assigned the mean of the ranks which they jointly occupy.)

8. Before placing a large order for road flares to be carried by all company cars, a major fleet operator life-tests flares of Brand G and Brand H. The following data show the burning times (in minutes) of random samples of 12 flares of each kind:

Brand G: 18 20 14 16 15 15 19 21 20 22 18 20
Brand H: 15 14 23   9 12 14 14 13 11 16 14 14

Use the U-test and a level of significance of 0.01 to check whether it is reasonable to maintain that there is no difference in the true average burning times of the two kinds of flares.

9. It is desired to compare the strength of yarn made by two manufacturers on the basis of the following sample data representing the tensile strengths of ten strands (in pounds) of each kind of yarn:

$$\begin{array}{ll} \textit{Sample from} & 141.2,\ 138.2,\ 142.6,\ 139.2,\ 140.8,\ 138.8, \\ \textit{First Manufacturer:} & 140.0,\ 140.4,\ 140.0,\ 141.0 \end{array}$$

$$\begin{array}{ll} \textit{Sample from} & 141.8,\ 143.0,\ 139.6,\ 136.0,\ 138.0,1\ 44.0, \\ \textit{Second Manufacturer:} & 148.2,\ 137.6,\ 142.0,\ 138.4 \end{array}$$

Use the U-test and a level of significance of 0.05 to test the null hypothesis that the two samples come from identical populations against the alternative that the two populations have unequal means.

10. Referring to Exercise 9, use a level of significance of 0.05 to test the hypothesis that the two samples come from identical populations against the alternative that the two populations have unequal dispersions.

11. The following are the Rockwell hardness numbers obtained for 15 aluminum die castings randomly selected from Lot A, and for 12 castings randomly selected from Lot B:

Lot A: 56, 97, 89, 73, 59, 76, 87, 56, 74, 70, 81, 67, 75, 53, 71
Lot B: 75, 81, 67, 70, 71, 86, 55, 75, 94, 88, 52, 65

(a) Use a level of significance of 0.05 to test the null hypothesis that the samples came from identical populations against the alternative that the two populations have unequal means.

(b) Use a level of significance of 0.05 to test the null hypothesis that the samples came from identical populations against the alternative that the two populations have unequal dispersions.

A Word of Caution

As we have suggested earlier, methods which require no (or virtually no) assumptions concerning the form of population distributions are usually *less efficient* than the corresponding standard methods. To illustrate this, we have only to refer to the calculations of Chapter 7 where we showed that, by using Chebyshev's Theorem, we can say that there is a probability of "at least" 0.75 that the mean of a random sample of size 64 drawn from *some* (infinite) population with $\sigma = 20$ is not "off" by more than 5. However, given that the sample came from a population having the shape of a normal distribution with $\sigma = 20$, we can make the same statement with a probability of 0.95. To put it another way, assertions made with equal confidence require larger sample sizes if they are made without knowledge of the form of the underlying distribution than if they are made with such knowledge. It is generally true that *the more one is willing to assume, the more one can infer from a sample;* on the other hand, it is also true that *the more one assumes, the more one restricts the applicability of the method.*

TWELVE
PLANNING
BUSINESS
RESEARCH

Sources of Business Data

Regardless of whether we merely describe things numerically or whether we generalize beyond our data, locating, assembling, or collecting data can raise many problems. This is a serious matter because access to a good supply of high-quality data is fundamental to all of statistics. Data required to solve practical everyday business problems can come from many sources, sometimes classified broadly as *internal* and *external*. Internal data are generated from the activities within a firm; they may be taken from a firm's order book, or inventory, payroll, personnel, or accounting records; they may be collected in experiments and tests of product quality characteristics, or they may be gathered by agents, by telephone, or with questionnaires from customers as well as suppliers. External data are obtained from sources outside the firm; they may come from records of state, local, and national governments and their agencies and regulatory bodies, from trade associations, private institutions, other firms, and so on. Some problems require the combination of internal and external data, say, when a company compares its own operating performance with that of its competitors or the industry as a whole.

External data are sometimes classified as *primary*, meaning that the organization gathering the data also publishes or releases them, or as *secondary*, meaning that the data are published by an organization other than the one by which they were gathered. There are many important and highly respected sources of primary as well as secondary data. Among the nongovernmental sources we find private statistical services, trade associations, trade publications, university research bureaus, commercial and financial periodicals, and specialized reporting agencies. From these sources come data on employment, farm prices and marketings, construction contracts, store sales, bank debits, and the like, often broken down on a regional, county, or city basis. In addition, there are reports on prices, production, sales, employment, etc., in different industries, and all this information is supplied to fill the needs of individuals and groups for reliable statistics.

By far the biggest collector and publisher of business data, and generally the most important single source of external data, is the federal government. Within the great mass of statistical material flowing from the government it is possible to find information relating to virtually every aspect of the life of the nation. For instance, the Department of Commerce publishes each year the *Statistical Abstract of the United States*, an immense storehouse of data referring to many things and gathered from many sources. Through the Bureau of the Census, the Commerce Department periodically takes and publishes the results of censuses of population, manufactures, distribution, housing, and agriculture, and also publishes monthly trade reports giving data on inventories, sales, and so on, in various wholesale and retail lines of business for the entire country and for selected cities. The Office of International Trade, the Office of Industry and Trade, and the Bureau of Foreign and Domestic Commerce, all of the Commerce Department, collect and publish data on the trade of the United States and other countries. Through the Office of Business Economics, the Department issues one of the most important of all statistical publications, the monthly *Survey of Current Business* (which is supplemented by weekly data on some of the major series of data). The regular monthly issues contain indicators of general business conditions and series relating to wholesale and retail commodity prices and trade, construction activity, population and employment, payrolls, wages and hours, finance, foreign trade, transportation, and so on.

Without much doubt, this publication constitutes one of the most valuable collections of current business data.

Other important statistics are collected and published by the Department of Labor, whose Bureau of Labor Statistics issues the *Monthly Labor Review*, the primary source for the indexes of consumer prices and wholesale prices, and data on construction contracts and costs, employment, payrolls, wages and hours, and work stoppages. In addition to the publications of various other Departments, agencies, and commissions of the government, the Board of Governors of the Federal Reserve System publish monthly the *Federal Reserve Bulletin*, the *Federal Reserve Chart Book on Financial and Business Statistics*, and various other periodic releases. Besides containing a wealth of financial information, the monthly *Bulletin* is the primary source of the Index of Industrial Production.

Most of the data collected by the government are needed by the government itself in discharging its many reponsibilities; data relative to some phenomena are not needed specifically by the government, but are collected and published in response to the needs of such large groups of individuals as to justify their collection at public expense.

EXERCISES

1. Determine whether the *Survey of Current Business* is a primary or secondary source for the following data: exports of locomotives, registrations of new passenger cars, yields on common stocks, estimates of personal savings, industrial production, construction contracts awarded, retail prices of commodities, and sales of electronic digital computers.

2. Answer each of the following questions with respect to appropriate government publications:

   (a) Figures showing factory sales of motor vehicles are often thought to be identical with production. What is the official interpretation of these figures?

   (b) What types of vehicles are included in the designation "passenger cars"?

   (c) Discuss the comparability of the data shown in the passenger car sales series from 1929 to the present.

   (d) For purposes of reporting these figures, how are foreign car sales determined?

3. Referring to an appropriate government publication, determine the primary source of data on the labor force, employment, and unemployment. In the civilian labor force, is an unpaid family worker considered to be employed or not?

4. Referring to an appropriate government publication, determine the primary source of data on employment in nonagricultural establishments. What are the major industry divisions for which the total employment is regularly reported, and in what two forms are these data given?

5. As of the most recent date or period for which you can locate data, determine (a) how much currency was in circulation in the United States, (b) what was the total reported net profit after taxes of all manufacturing industries, and (c) what was the total number of publicly financed buildings authorized to be constructed by all permit-issuing places in the United States.

6. What was the total book value (unadjusted) of the inventories of nondurable goods industries in May 1956? Of this amount, how much represented goods in process, finished goods, and purchased materials?

Sampling

It is important to recognize that much of the published information available from government and private sources (indeed, much of the world's knowledge) is actually based on samples. Even in simple problems involving relatively small numbers of items or individuals, it is rarely feasible, practical, or economical to collect and analyze all relevant observations or measurements. As we have suggested earlier, there are usually time, cost, or other limitations which force one to take samples and generalize from them to the whole populations from which they came. Although the word "sample" is used somewhat loosely in everyday language, let us observe again that in statistics it has a very special meaning: it is interpreted more strictly to refer to data that can reasonably serve to make generalizations, or inferences, about the population from which they came.

In all studies based on samples, great care must be exercised to ensure that the samples will lend themselves to valid generalizations, and every precaution must be taken to avoid *biases* of some sort or another. This includes the unfortunate tendency of samples not to be representative of populations they are supposed to represent and thus to lead away from, rather than toward, the truth.

In most of the work we have done until now we have assumed that we were dealing with random samples. In everyday language "randomness" means a certain haphazardness or lack of bias, which is supposed to assure that no single item or groups of items belonging to a population are preferred, avoided, or distorted during the process of sampling. In this sense, randomness really refers to the methods we use in sampling, particularly, to the things we must avoid so that we can rightfully say that we have a random sample. This agrees with the rigorous definitions we gave for random sampling (from finite and infinite populations) in Chapter 7, where we suggested the use of gambling devices or, better, tables of random numbers. Correspondingly, such samples are referred to as *probability samples*.

In contrast to probability samples, we shall refer to samples as *judgment samples* if, in addition to (or instead of) chance, personal judgment plays a significant role in their selection. There are many situations where, for practical reasons, investigators use judgment samples to gain needed information. One important use of such sampling is in testing markets for new products. Because of the tremendous cost of market testing on a national scale, many products are first tested in one or a few cities. Such test cities are usually not selected at random; instead they are carefully chosen because in someone's considered judgment they are "typical" or "average" American cities. Subsequently, when generalizations are made to national markets, samples of public reaction to advertising, packaging, etc., constitute judgment samples.

Regardless of how the conclusions or actions based on judgment samples ultimately turn out, judgment samples have the undesirable feature that standard statistical theory cannot be applied to evaluate the accuracy and reliability of estimates or to calculate the probabilities of making various kinds of erroneous decisions. Whenever elements of judgment enter in the selection of a sample, the evaluation of the "goodness" of estimates or decisions based on the sample is again largely a matter of personal judgment.

Sample Designs

The subject of sample designs includes a great deal of material, to which we can present here at best an introduction. By a *sample design* we mean a definite plan, completely determined before any data are collected, for obtaining a sample from a given population. Thus, a plan to take a simple random sample of size 10 from among the 245 members of a trade association by using a table of random numbers in a prescribed way constitutes a sample design. Generally speaking, there are always many ways in which a sample can be taken from a given population; some of these are quite simple, while others are relatively involved. Sometimes two or more procedures are combined in sampling different parts of the same population. In what follows, we shall briefly discuss some of the most important kinds of sample designs; detailed treatments of this subject are referred to in the Bibliography at the end of this book.

Systematic sampling. There are many situations where the most practical way of sampling is to select, say, every 10th voucher in a file, every 20th name on a list, every 50th piece coming off an assembly line, and so forth. Sampling of this sort is referred to as *systematic sampling*, and an element of randomness is usually introduced into this kind of sample by using random numbers or some gambling device to pick the unit with which to start. Although a systematic sample may not be a random sample in accordance with our definitions, it is often reasonable to treat systematic samples as if they were random samples. Whether or not this is justified depends entirely on the structure (order) of the list, or arrangement, from which the sample is obtained. In many instances, systematic sampling actually provides an improvement over simple random sampling inasmuch as the sample is "spread more evenly" over the entire population.

— The real danger in systematic sampling lies in the possible presence of *hidden periodicities*. For instance, if we inspect every 40th piece made by a particular machine, our results would be quite biased if, because of a regularly recurring failure, it so happened that every 20th piece had blemishes. Also, a systematic sample might yield biased results if we interviewed the residents of every 10th house along a certain route and it so happened that every 10th house selected was a corner house on a double lot.

Stratified sampling. As we have seen in Chapters 7, 8, and 9, the "goodness" of a generalization or the "closeness" of an estimate depends entirely on the standard error of the statistic being used, which in turn depends on both the size of the sample and the variability of the population. Thus, one way of increasing the precision of a generalization is to increase the size of the sample, and if the cost of sampling is largely overhead and the items to be sampled are readily at hand, it may be about as easy to take a sample of size 200 as it is to take a sample of size 50. On the other hand, if the cost of sampling is more or less proportional to the size of the sample (as, for example, in destructive testing where the cost of sampling is largely the cost of the items tested), we have to look for other ways of increasing the precision, or reliability, of our sampling technique. One relatively simple scheme for reducing the size of the standard error of a statistic is *stratification*, that is, dividing the population into a number of nonoverlapping subpopulations, or strata, and then sampling separately from the different strata. If the items selected from each of the strata constitute a simple random sample, the entire procedure (first stratification and then simple random sampling) is called *stratified (simple) random sampling*. Although the concept of this kind of sampling is simple, a number of substantial problems immediately arise: How many strata should be formed? What should be the sample size for the different strata? How are the samples within the strata to be selected? Stratification does not guarantee good results, but if properly executed, stratified sampling generally leads to a higher degree of precision or reliability.

To illustrate the general idea behind stratified sampling, let us consider the following oversimplified, though concrete, example. Suppose we want to estimate the mean weight of 4 persons on the basis of a sample of size 2; the weights of the 4 persons are, respectively, 110, 130, 180, and 200 pounds, so that μ, the mean weight we are trying to estimate, is equal to 155 pounds. If we take an ordinary random sample of size 2 from this population and weigh two of these persons, it can easily be seen that $\bar{x}$ can vary from 120 to 190. In fact, the 6 possible samples of size 2 that can be taken from this population have means of 120, 145, 155, 155, 165, and 190, so that $\sigma_{\bar{x}} = 21.0$ (see Exercise 2 on page 379).

Now suppose that we make use of the fact that among the four persons there are 2 men and 2 women and that we *stratify* our sample by randomly selecting one of the 2 women and one of the 2 men. Assuming that the two smaller weights are those of the two women, we now find that $\bar{x}$ varies on the much smaller interval from 145 to 165. In fact, the means of the four possible samples are now 145, 155, 155, and 165, so that $\sigma_{\bar{x}} = 7.1$ (see Exercise 3 on page 379). *This illustrates how, by stratifying the sample, we were able to reduce $\sigma_{\bar{x}}$ from 21.0 to 7.1.*

Essentially, the goal of stratification is to form strata in such a way that there is some relationship between being in a particular stratum and the answer sought in the statistical study, and that within the separate strata there is as much homogeneity (uniformity) as possible. Note that in our example there was such a connection between sex and weight and that there was much less variability in weight within the two groups than there was within the entire population. A more detailed and more theoretical treatment of some of the problems of stratified sampling is taken up in Technical Note 13 on page 393.

In the above example, we stratified the sample only with respect to one characteristic. A further refinement consists of stratifying with respect to *several* characteristics, say, with respect to income, nationality background, age, and geographical location, in a survey designed to determine public opinion concerning a certain political issue. We would thus allocate part of the sample to persons with low incomes, who belong to nationality group A, are in the 20–30 year age bracket, and live in the Southeast; another portion to persons with high incomes, who belong to nationality group B, are in the over-65 years age bracket, and live in New England; and so forth. This process is called *cross-stratification* and it is quite widely used, particularly in public opinion polls and market surveys.

Quota sampling. In many applications of stratified sampling the selection of individuals within the various strata has traditionally been nonrandom. Instead, interviewers have been given quotas to be filled from the various strata, without too many restrictions as to how they are to be filled. For instance, in determining attitude toward increased foreign aid expenditures, an interviewer working a certain area for an opinion research organization might be told to interview 5 retail merchants of German origin who own homes, 10 wage-earners of Anglo-Saxon origin who live in rented apartments, 2 retired persons who live in trailers, etc., with the actual selection of the individuals being left to the interviewer's discretion. This is a convenient, relatively inexpensive, and often necessary procedure, but as it is usually executed, the resulting quota samples are not probability samples. Interviewers naturally tend to select individuals who are most readily available—persons who work in the same building, shop in the same store, or perhaps reside in the same general area. Quota samples are thus essentially judgment samples, and although it may be possible to guess at sampling errors by using experience or corollary information, quota samples generally do not lend themselves to any sort of formal statistical evaluation.

Cluster sampling. To illustrate another important kind of sampling, suppose that a large foundation wants to study the changing patterns of family expenditures in the Los Angeles area. In attempting to complete schedules for a sample of 2,000 families, the foundation runs into a number of difficulties; simple random sampling is practically impossible since suitable lists are not available and the cost of contacting families scattered over a wide area (sometimes with 2 or 3 call backs for the not-at-homes) can be very high. One way in which a sample can be taken in this example is to divide the total area of interest into a number of smaller, nonoverlapping areas, say, city blocks. A number of these blocks can then be chosen with the use of random numbers and all (or samples of) the families residing in these blocks are included in the sample. This kind of sampling is referred to as *cluster sampling;* that is, the total population is divided into a number of relatively small subdivisions, which are themselves *clusters* of still smaller units, and then some of these subdivisions, or clusters, are randomly selected for inclusion in the over-all sample. If the clusters are geographic subdivisions, as in our example, this kind of sampling is also called *area sampling.*

To give two further illustrations of cluster sampling, suppose that the management of a large chain-store organization wants to interview a sample of its employees to determine their attitude toward a proposed pension plan. If random methods were used to select, say, 5 stores from the list and if all employees of these stores were interviewed, the resulting sample would be a cluster sample. Also, if the Dean of Students of a university wanted to know how fraternity men at the school feel about a certain new regulation, he would obtain a cluster sample if he interviewed the members of several randomly selected fraternities.

Although estimates based on cluster samples are generally not as reliable as estimates based on simple random samples of the same size (see Exercise 4 on page 379), they are usually more reliable *per unit cost.* Referring again to the survey of family expenditures in the Los Angeles area, it is easy to see that it may well be possible to obtain a cluster sample several times the size of a simple random sample at the same expense. (It is much cheaper to visit and interview families living close together in clusters than families selected at random over a wide area.)

In practice, several of the methods we have discussed may well be used in the same survey. For instance, if government statisticians wanted to study the attitude of American farmers toward marketing cooperatives, they might first stratify the country by states or some other geographic subdivision. To obtain a sample from each stratum they might then use cluster sampling, subdividing each stratum into a number of smaller geographic subdivisions, and finally they might use simple random sampling or systematic sampling within each cluster.

EXERCISES

1. The following scores were made by 12 job applicants on a screening test administered by a large chemical manufacturer:

   52 90 61 76 55 67 27 68 38 43 20 51

   (a) List the three possible systematic samples of size 4 that can be taken from this list by starting with one of the first three scores and then taking each third score on the list.
   (b) Calculate the means of the three samples obtained in part (a) and, assuming that the starting point was randomly selected from among the first three scores, show that the mean of this sampling distribution of $\bar{x}$ equals the population mean μ, namely, the mean of all 12 scores.

2. Verify for the 6 sample means on page 376 (which are assigned equal probabilities of $1/6$) that $\sigma_{\bar{x}} = 21.0$.

3. Verify for the 4 sample means on page 376 (which are assigned equal probabilities of $1/4$) that $\sigma_{\bar{x}} = 7.1$.

4. To generalize the example given in the text, suppose that in a group of 6 persons there are 3 women whose weights are 110 lb, 120 lb, and 130 lb, and 3 men whose weights are 180 lb, 190 lb, and 200 lb.

   (a) List all possible random samples of size 2 from this population, calculate the means of these samples, and show that $\sigma_{\bar{x}} = 22.7$.
   (b) List all possible stratified random samples of size 2 obtained by selecting one man and one woman, calculate the means of these samples, and show that $\sigma_{\bar{x}} = 5.8$.
   (c) Suppose that the 6 persons are divided into clusters according to sex, each cluster is assigned a probability of $1/2$, and a random sample of size 2 is taken from the chosen cluster. List all possible samples, calculate their means, and show that $\sigma_{\bar{x}} = 35.2$.
   (d) Compare and discuss the results obtained for $\sigma_{\bar{x}}$ in parts (a), (b), and (c).

5. On the basis of annual volume of work, 60 sawmills in the Pacific Northwest are classified into 30 that are small, 20 that are medium, and 10 that are large.

(a) In how many ways can we choose a stratified 10 per cent sample of the 60 sawmills if one third of the sample is allocated to each of the three strata?

(b) In how many ways can we choose a stratified 10 per cent sample of the 60 sawmills if the portion of the sample allocated to each stratum is proportional to the size of the stratum?

(The exercises which follow are based on the material in Technical Note 13 on page 393.)

6. In a large factory with a number of similar machines, records are kept of the number of minutes required by an operator to get the machine restarted following machine failures of various kinds. Suppose that 1,400 records are on file, with 700 classed as "ordinary" stoppages, 400 as "moderate" stoppages, and 300 as "severe" stoppages. In order to estimate the mean restart time for the whole population, a 1 per cent stratified random sample (with proportional allocation) is taken from the file with the following results (times are in minutes):

> *Ordinary Stoppages:* 5, 2, 5, 7, 2, 4, and 3
> *Moderate Stoppages:* 8, 11, 9, and 8
> *Severe Stoppages:* 14, 18, and 16

(a) Use the weighted-mean formula given in Technical Note 13 on page 393 to estimate the mean restart time for the whole population.

(b) Verify that the identical result is obtained when the sample means are weighted with their respective sample sizes (rather than the sizes of the respective strata).

(c) Verify the fact that the estimates obtained in parts (a) and (b) are identical with the simple arithmetic mean of the 14 observations. (That is, verify that in a problem like this, proportional allocation is self-weighting.)

7. A population is divided into two strata so that $N_1 = 20,000$, $N_2 = 60,000$, $\sigma_1 = 30$, and $\sigma_2 = 40$. How should a sample of size 100 be allocated to the strata if we use (a) proportional allocation, and (b) optimum allocation?

8. A population is divided into four strata so that $N_1 = 6,000$, $N_2 = 2,000$, $N_3 = 3,000$, $N_4 = 1,000$, $\sigma_1 = 2$, $\sigma_2 = 4$, $\sigma_3 = 6$, and $\sigma_4 = 12$. How should a sample of size 600 be allocated to the four strata if we use (a) proportional allocation, and (b) optimum allocation?

Design of Experiments

Even those who have never been actively engaged in research should be able to visualize the problems involved in planning an experiment so that it can actually serve the purpose for which it is designed. It happens all too often that an experiment purported to test one thing tests another or that an experiment that is improperly designed cannot serve any useful purpose at all. Suppose, for instance, that we want to compare the cleansing action of two detergents and that 10 swatches of white cloth soiled with India ink and oil are washed in an agitator-type machine, 5 with a cup of each kind of detergent. Whiteness readings are made by the same machine and the results obtained are as follows:

Detergent Q: 80 74 78 83 75
Detergent R: 68 70 64 56 72

Using this information, we want to test at the 0.01 level of significance whether the difference between 78 and 66 (the two sample means) is significant. Proceeding as in Technical Note 10 on page 292, we formulate the hypothesis $\mu_1 = \mu_2$ and the alternative hypothesis $\mu_1 \neq \mu_2$, where μ_1 and μ_2 are the "true" average whiteness readings for the two populations. Calculating t according to the formula on page 294, we obtain $t = 3.67$, and since this exceeds $t_{.005} = 3.355$ for 8 degrees of freedom, we reject the null hypothesis. In other words, we conclude that there is a real difference in the actual average whiteness of the two populations.

Interpreting this result, we might arrive at the perfectly natural conclusion that Detergent Q is superior in cleansing action to Detergent R. However, a moment's reflection will make us realize that we may not really have a basis for such a conclusion. For all we know, the water temperature may have been different when testing the two detergents, one detergent could have been used in soft water and the other in hard water, the washing times might have differed substantially, and even the machine used to determine the whiteness readings might have gone out of adjustment after the readings were taken for the first detergent. Thus, what may have seemed an obvious conclusion at first, turns out to be highly questionable. It is entirely possible, of course, that the difference between the two means is due to quality differences in the two detergents, but we have just listed several other factors which could be held responsible. In fact, we could go on indefinitely listing possible causes, any of which—either singly or in combination with others— might be held accountable for the results. The significance test which we have performed convinces us that the difference is too large to be attributed to chance, but it does not tell us *why* this difference has occurred.

Questions of this sort are treated in a branch of statistics called the *design and analysis of experiments*. If we want to be able to show that one factor (among many possible ones) can definitely be considered as the *cause* of an observed phenomenon which has been shown to be significant, we must make sure somehow that none of the other factors could possibly be held responsible. In other words, if we hope to show that one particular factor caused certain results, we must make sure that other relevant factors are *controlled* in such a way that they could not reasonably be held accountable. One way of handling this kind of problem is to perform a rigorously controlled experiment in which all variables except the one with which we are concerned are held fixed. In our example, we might thus use the same washing machine (carefully inspected after each use), the same washing time, water of exactly the same temperature and hardness, and we might inspect all of the testing equipment after each use. Under these rigid conditions we know that a significant difference between the (whiteness) means is not due to differences in washing machines, washing times, water temperature or hardness, or the testing equipment. On the positive side, we know that one detergent performs better than the other *if it is used in this narrowly restricted way*. This does not tell us whether the same difference would exist if the tests were performed in a different kind of washer, if the washing time were longer or shorter, if the water had a different temperature or hardness, and so on. Generally speaking, this kind of controlled experiment really does not tell us very much about the phenomenon we want to investigate; after all, we cannot advertise a detergent as being better only if it is used under such highly restrictive conditions.

Another way of handling this kind of problem is to *design* the experiment in such a way that we can not only compare the merits of the two detergents under more general conditions but can also test whether other important variables might affect their performance. To illustrate how this might be done, suppose we decide that we want to investigate the effects of four factors on the cleanliness of cottons washed in an agitator-type machine: the detergent used, the washing time, the water temperature, and the water hardness. (Such other factors as water level are assumed to be rigorously controlled in the experiment.) Letting Q and R stand for a cup of the respective detergent, S and L for washing times of 10 minutes and 20 minutes, W and H for warm and hot water, and E and F for soft and hard water, there are altogether $2 \cdot 2 \cdot 2 \cdot 2 = 16$ ways in which these four factors can be combined. Using identical samples of

cloth and testing equipment that is rigorously checked, we might conduct
the following series of test washings in which each of the 16 possible
combinations is included once:

Test Washing	Detergent	Time	Temperature	Hardness
1	R	L	W	E
2	R	L	H	F
3	Q	L	W	E
4	R	S	W	F
5	Q	S	H	F
6	Q	S	W	E
7	R	S	W	E
8	Q	L	H	F
9	R	S	H	F
10	Q	S	H	E
11	Q	L	W	F
12	Q	S	W	F
13	R	L	H	E
14	R	S	H	E
15	Q	L	H	E
16	R	L	W	F

This means that the first test washing is performed with detergent R, a
washing time of 20 minutes, and warm soft water; the second test washing is performed with detergent R, a washing time of 20 minutes, and
hot hard water; and so on. A scheme like the above is said to be *completely
balanced* since each detergent is used once with each possible combination
of washing time, temperature, and hardness.

The seeming lack of order in the arrangement of the 16 tests is by no
means accidental. When we first wrote down the possible combinations,
we filled the "Detergent" column by writing eight Q's followed by
eight R's; then we filled the next column by alternately writing down
four L's and four S's, the "Temperature" column by alternately writing
down two W's and two H's, and the last column by alternating E's and
F's. If we actually performed the tests in this order, we would run the
first 8 tests with Detergent Q, the other 8 with Detergent R, and extrane-
ous factors might conceivably upset the results. For instance, there
might be a progressive deterioration in machine efficiency which could
not be detected by inspection. Similarly, we might get in trouble if we
deliberately conducted the first 8 test washings using the shorter washing
time, or the hot water, or the soft water. We protect ourselves against
biases which might inadvertently invalidate the results by *randomizing*

the order of the tests; after writing down the 16 possible combinations of the four factors, we selected the order shown in the above table with the use of random numbers.

Another important consideration in the design of an experiment is that of *replication* or *repetition*. Any time we want to decide whether an observed difference between sample means is significant or whether a sample mean differs significantly from some assumed value, we must have some idea, some estimate, of chance fluctuations. In experiments of the sort we have just described this kind of variation is called the *experimental error*, and it is usually estimated by repeating all (or part) of the entire experiment a number of times. In our example, we might conduct the 16 test washings in the given order, then rerandomize the order and conduct 16 more tests. The 32 tests thus made, including 2 each of the 16 possible combinations, would yield an estimate of the experimental error, and they would permit a rather detailed analysis of the effects of the four variables on the whiteness of cottons washed with the given kind of equipment.

The purpose of this example has been to introduce some of the basic ideas of experimental design. Generally speaking, the analysis of an experiment depends partly on the design itself, and partly on assumptions concerning the populations from which the data are obtained. Specification of these assumptions (for example, that the populations from which the data are obtained have normal distributions) thus constitutes another important aspect of the proper use of statistics in experimentation. The analysis of a four-factor experiment like the one described above is fairly complicated, but we shall illustrate the general procedure, called the *analysis of variance*, in the next section with reference to a simpler kind of problem.

One-way Analysis of Variance

To illustrate what is called a *"one-way" analysis of variance* (where we consider only one variable of classification), suppose that we want to compare the effectiveness of three methods of teaching the programming of a certain kind of electronic computer. Method A is straight teaching machine instruction, Method B involves personal instruction with considerable personal attention and some direct experience working with the machine, while Method C is the same as Method B except that the students have no opportunity to see or work with the computer itself. In each case the instruction time is equivalent to 35 classroom hours.

Now suppose that random samples of size 4 are taken from large groups of students taught by the three methods and that these students obtain the following scores on an appropriate achievement test:

	Method A	Method B	Method C
	62	77	72
	58	79	69
	68	73	70
	64	83	65
Means:	63	78	69

Looking at this table as three random samples from three different populations, we want to know whether the differences among the three means can be attributed to chance.

Designating the "true" average scores for students taught with the three methods μ_1, μ_2, and μ_3, we shall want to test the null hypothesis

$$Hypothesis: \quad \mu_1 = \mu_2 = \mu_3$$

against the alternative that μ_1, μ_2, and μ_3 are *not all equal*. Intuitively speaking, small differences among the $\bar{x}$'s may, as always, be attributed to chance, so that if the $\bar{x}$'s are very nearly the same size, this would support the null hypothesis that $\mu_1 = \mu_2 = \mu_3$. On the other hand, if the differences among the $\bar{x}$'s are large, too large to be reasonably attributed to chance, this would support the alternative hypothesis that the μ's are not all equal. Hence, we need a precise measure of the size of the discrepancies among the $\bar{x}$'s and, correspondingly, a well-defined criterion to test the null hypothesis with the use of this measure.

An obvious measure of the discrepancies among the $\bar{x}$'s is their variance, and if we calculate it according to the formula on page 52, we obtain

$$s_{\bar{x}}^2 = \frac{(63 - 70)^2 + (78 - 70)^2 + (69 - 70)^2}{3 - 1} = 57$$

Note that we used the subscript $\bar{x}$ to indicate that this quantity measures the variability of the $\bar{x}$'s. As we shall see later, this quantity plays an important role in our ultimate decision to accept or reject the null hypothesis concerning the means of the three populations.

Let us now make an assumption which is critical to the method of analysis we shall employ: *it will be assumed that the populations from* *which the samples were obtained can be closely approximated by normal curves having the same variance σ^2.* This means that we shall assume that if we tested many students taught by each of the three methods, the distributions of the respective test scores would follow the over-all pattern of normal distributions having the same variance σ^2.

Combining the assumption of the preceding paragraph with the assumption that the null hypothesis is true, we can now look upon the three samples as samples from one and the same population. Making use of the fact that $\sigma_{\bar{x}}^2 = \dfrac{\sigma^2}{n}$ according to Theorem R on page 191, we can look upon $s_{\bar{x}}^2$ as an estimate of $\sigma_{\bar{x}}^2$ and hence $n \cdot s_{\bar{x}}^2$ as an estimate of σ^2. Returning to our numerical example, we can thus use $4 \cdot 57 = 228$ as an estimate of the population variance σ^2.

If σ^2 were known, we could compare $n \cdot s_{\bar{x}}^2$ with σ^2 and reject the null hypothesis if $n \cdot s_{\bar{x}}^2$ were much larger than σ^2. However, in our example (as in most practical problems) σ^2 is unknown and we have no choice but to estimate it on the basis of the given data. Having assumed that the samples all come from populations with the same variance σ^2, we could use each of the sample variances (namely, s_1^2, s_2^2, and s_3^2) as an estimate of σ^2 and, hence, we could also use their average. Referring again to our numerical example, we shall thus estimate σ^2 by means of the quantity

$$
\begin{aligned}
\frac{s_1^2 + s_2^2 + s_3^2}{3} = \frac{1}{3} &\left[\frac{(62-63)^2 + (58-63)^2 + (68-63)^2 + (64-63)^2}{3} \right. \\
&+ \frac{(77-78)^2 + (79-78)^2 + (73-78)^2 + (83-78)^2}{3} \\
&\left. + \frac{(72-69)^2 + (69-69)^2 + (70-69)^2 + (65-69)^2}{3} \right] \\
&= 14.4
\end{aligned}
$$

We now have *two* estimates of σ^2, the first being $n \cdot s_{\bar{x}}^2 = 228$ and the second being the mean of the sample variances, namely,

$$
\frac{s_1^2 + s_2^2 + s_3^2}{3} = 14.4
$$

Comparing these two estimates, we can now assert that if the first (which is based on the variation *among* the means of the samples) is much larger

han the second (which is based on the variation *within* the samples), it
s reasonable to reject the null hypothesis.

Before we introduce the criterion which defines exactly what we mean
ıere by "much larger," let us first consider the rationale of the argument.
₋et us begin by asking the following question: *What is it that accounts
ʿor the differences among the scores of individuals taught by the same method?*
⸵or instance, how can we explain the 10-point difference between the
ⱶcores of the third and fourth individuals taught by Method B? In reply
₋o this question, we might suggest that the two individuals may have
liffered in intelligence, experience, interests, motivation, education, read-
ng comprehension, and so on. It is hard to say how many items we might
ɔut on this list, but there is one thing that is definitely *not* on the list,
ıamely, differences in teaching method. Combining all factors other
han the one pertaining to teaching method under the general heading of
ʿchance," our second estimate of σ^2, the one which equalled 14.4 in our
⸵xample, is an estimate of chance variation.

Let us now ask another question: *What is it that accounts for the differ-
ʾnces between the scores of individuals taught by different methods?* For
nstance, how can we explain the difference of 21 points in the scores
ɔf the second individuals listed under Methods A and B? If the null
ıypothesis is true, this difference is also due entirely to the factors which
ᵥe combined above under the heading of chance; if the null hypothesis is
alse, however, we must add to this list the additional factor which
ⱶccounts for differences in teaching method. Under the null hypothesis,
ɔur first estimate of σ^2, the one which equalled 228 in our example, is also
ⱶn estimate of chance variation. If the null hypothesis is false, it is an
ʾstimate of chance variation *plus* whatever variation there may exist
ⱶmong the population means.

To put the comparison of the two estimates of σ^2 on a precise basis, let
ⱶs now introduce the statistic

$$F = \frac{\text{Estimate of } \sigma^2 \text{ based on the variability among the } \bar{x}\text{'s}}{\text{Estimate of } \sigma^2 \text{ based on the variability within samples}} \qquad \bigstar$$

ⱥppropriately called a *variance ratio*. If the various assumptions made
ʾarlier (that the null hypothesis is true and that the samples come from
ıormal populations with equal variances) are true, the theoretical
ⱶampling distribution of this statistic is the so-called *F* distribution, an
ʾxample of which is shown in Figure 12.1. Since the null hypothesis

must be rejected when F is *large* (when the variability of the $\bar{x}$'s is too great to be reasonably attributed to chance), we shall be interested in values of $F_{.05}$ and $F_{.01}$, namely, in values which are such that the area under the F distribution to their right is, respectively, 0.05 and 0.01 (see Figure 12.1). These quantities, which depend on two parameters called the number of *degrees of freedom for the numerator of F* and the number of *degrees of freedom for the denominator of F*, are given in Tables IV(a) and IV(b). Comparing the means of k samples of size n, the number of degrees of freedom for the numerator of F is $k - 1$, while the number of degrees of freedom for the denominator of F is $k(n - 1)$.

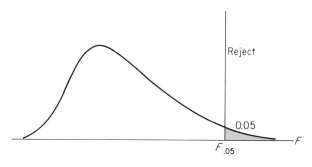

FIGURE 12.1

(So far as the formula for the degrees of freedom in the numerator is concerned, note that the numerator is essentially the variance of k means and that we thus have $k - 1$ degrees of freedom; so far as the formula for the degrees of freedom in the denominator is concerned, note that the denominator is the mean of k sample variances with each having $n - 1$ degrees of freedom.)

Returning now to our numerical example, we find that for $3 - 1 = 2$ and $3(4 - 1) = 9$ degrees of freedom $F_{.05}$ equals 4.26. Since

$$F = \frac{228}{14.4} = 15.8$$

in our example (which exceeds the critical value of 4.26), we find that the null hypothesis must be rejected. *We conclude that the three teaching methods are not equally effective.* Had we wanted to use a level of significance of 0.01 in this example, we would have found that for 2 and 9 degrees of freedom $F_{.01} = 8.02$, so that the null hypothesis could also have been rejected.

In the above example, the numerator of F was n times the variance of the sample means and the denominator was the mean of the variances of the individual samples. In actual practice, the calculations of the numerator and denominator of F may be simplified by using the short-cut formulas given in Exercise 6 on page 391.

The method we have described in this section is called the *analysis of variance*. To explain the meaning of this term, the reader will be asked in Exercise 5 below to show that the *total* variability of the data (in our example that of all 12 of the scores) may be analyzed, that is, expressed as the sum of two components, which are essentially the quantities appearing in the numerator and the denominator of F. The analysis of variance provides an extremely powerful tool for the analysis of experimental data, inasmuch as it enables us to analyze the total variability of a set of data into components which can be attributed to different "sources" or "causes" of variation.

EXERCISES

1. To test the effectiveness of four different preventive measures against the corrosion of cables, random samples of 5 pieces of cable are tested for each of the four preventive measures, and the extent of corrosion is measured by the depth of the maximum pits. The following are the results with the depth of maximum pits being given in thousandths of an inch:

Measure A	Measure B	Measure C	Measure D
62	38	62	58
42	44	57	70
48	58	68	62
56	58	60	60
62	52	58	65

Calculate F and (assuming that the necessary assumptions can be met) test at a level of significance of 0.05 whether the observed differences among the means obtained for the four preventive measures can be attributed to chance.

2. Four packages of frozen raspberries (supposedly of the same grade) are submitted by each of three packers to a large institutional buyer. The buyer grades the fruit (on a scale with 100 for perfection) with the following results:

A	B	C
94	72	80
89	68	79
92	76	85
85	64	88

Calculate F and (assuming that the necessary assumptions can be met) test at a level of significance of 0.05 whether the observed differences among the means obtained for the raspberries submitted by the three packers can be attributed to chance.

3. In order to compare the action of three different types of inorganic phosphorescent pigment coatings of airplane instrument dials, 5 dials each are coated with the three types. The dials are then excited by an ultraviolet light, and the following are the number of minutes each glowed after the exciting light source was turned off:

Type A	Type B	Type C
45	50	61
47	58	65
42	47	55
42	53	60
49	52	54

Calculate F and (assuming that the necessary assumptions can be met) test at a level of significance of 0.01 whether the observed difference between the sample means can be attributed to chance.

4. On page 63 we referred to an experiment in which a research organization compares three kinds of paint, taking five cans of each kind and measuring the number of square feet covered by each gallon can. Use the method of this section and a level of significance of 0.05 to test whether the differences among the sample means is significant.

5. The analysis-of-variance technique owes its name to the fact that in it a measure of the total variability of the data is broken down into components which can be attributed to different sources (or causes) of variation. Measuring the *total variability* of the data by means of the quantity $SST = \Sigma \Sigma (x_{ij} - \bar{x})^2$, where x_{ij} is the ith observation of the jth sample and $\bar{x}$ is the over-all mean of all the data, we can write

$$SST = SSB + SSE$$

Here $SSB = n \cdot \Sigma (\bar{x}_j - \bar{x})^2$, where $\bar{x}_j$ is the mean of the jth sample, is a measure of the variability among the sample means, and $SSE = \Sigma \Sigma (x_{ij} - \bar{x}_j)^2$ is a measure of the variability within the samples; namely, it is a measure of chance variation. Verify the identity $SST =$

$SSB + SSE$ for the example in the text, for which the data are given on page 385. (To explain the symbolism used in this exercise, let us point out that SST stands for "total sum of squares," SSB stands for "between samples sum of squares," while SSE stands for "error sum of squares." Also, the symbol $\Sigma\,\Sigma$ indicates that the summation extends over all values of i and j.)

6. The calculation of F can be simplified by writing the formula on page 387 as

$$F = \frac{k(n-1)SSB}{(k-1)SSE} \qquad \bigstar$$

with SSB and SSE as defined in Exercise 5 and calculated by means of the short-cut formulas

$$SSB = \frac{1}{n}\,\Sigma\,T_j^2 - \frac{1}{k\cdot n}\,T^2 \qquad \bigstar$$

where T_j is the total of the observations in the jth sample and T is the total of *all* the observations, and

$$SSE = \Sigma\,\Sigma\,x_{ij}^2 - \frac{1}{n}\,\Sigma\,T_j^2 \qquad \bigstar$$

Thus, to calculate F we have only to find $T_1, T_2, \ldots,$ and T_k, the totals for the individual samples, the grand-total T (the sum of all the observations), and $\Sigma\,\Sigma\,x_{ij}^2$, the sum of the squares of the individual observations. Use this method to recalculate F for the data of Exercise 1.

7. Use the method of Exercise 6 to recalculate F for Exercise 4.

8. When faced with tight acreage restrictions under the federal farm planning program, crop producers have often sought to increase outputs by dosing land with fertilizer, putting the seeds (or plants) closer together in rows, and narrowing the width between the rows themselves. The following data show the yields of soybeans (in bushels per acre) planted 2 inches apart on essentially similar plots with the rows 20, 24, 28, and 32 inches apart:

	Width Between Rows		
20″	24″	28″	32″
20.6	22.3	22.7	20.8
22.5	20.8	20.5	18.0
22.3	20.0	19.1	17.4
22.1	21.3	20.5	18.2

Calculate F by the method of Exercise 6 and (assuming that the necessary assumptions can be met) test at a level of significance of 0.05 whether the observed differences between the means obtained for the four distances between rows can be attributed to chance.

A Word of Caution

In view of the fantastic amount of "statistical" information that is disseminated to the public for one reason or another, we cannot overemphasize the point that such information must always be treated with extreme caution. To avoid serious mistakes in the use of published data, it is essential to check the precise definition of all terms (say, "employment," "sales," "shipments"), and this usually requires *looking behind* the words themselves. A careful search is often necessary to discover not only what the data are supposed to represent, but also what units are being used, how these units are defined, and whether the definitions are consistent throughout so that comparisons can be made. The availability of just such information as this is one of the most valuable features of data published by the federal government. For all series published by the government, it is possible to find somewhere a complete description of what data (rigorously defined) are contained, how, when, and where they were gathered, how they were processed, and so on. Unfortunately, such information is often unavailable for data supplied by other sources, in which case it is always advisable to proceed with care.

Another area in which one must proceed cautiously is the area of public opinion sampling. There are in the United States a number of highly reputable polls—the Gallup Poll, the Roper Poll, and the California Poll, for example—based on carefully designed and executed statistical surveys. The past few years, however, have seen a phenomenal growth of polls of all sorts, and there are now literally hundreds of polls whose existence is hard to justify. In countless radio station and newspaper polls people are invited to phone or write in and register votes for their favorite presidential candidate, and interviewers stationed at busy downtown locations ask people for their preferences. In "popcorn" polls, theater-goers "vote" for their choice by buying popcorn in bags displaying their candidate's picture; in "ice cream" polls, a purchase of chocolate ice cream in a supermarket is recorded as a vote for Candidate A while a purchase of vanilla ice cream is recorded as a vote for Candidate B. Actually, this might all come under the heading of good fun, if it were not for the tremendous and growing influence of public opinion sampling on politics.

Technical Note 13 (Stratified Sampling)

The two main problems in stratified sampling are (1) the choice of strata which show promise of making the sampling design effective, and (2) the allocation of the sample among the individual strata. The first of these two problems was already touched upon on page 377, where we pointed out that the strata should be (insofar as this is possible) *internally homogeneous*. In public opinion sampling we might thus stratify by income, as it has been shown that persons within different income groups tend to favor certain political parties. Similarly, we stratified by sex in determining weights, and we might stratify by educational experience in a study of the speed of promotions of executives.

To treat the second kind of problem, let us introduce the following notation: suppose we are sampling from a finite population of size N and that this population is subdivided into k strata whose respective sizes are N_1, N_2, $\ldots$, and N_k. Suppose, furthermore, that the mean of the whole population is μ and that the means of the individual strata are μ_1, μ_2, $\ldots$, and μ_k. If we now take a sample of size n_1 from the first stratum, a sample of size n_2 from the second stratum, $\ldots$, and a sample of size n_k from the kth stratum, and the means of these k samples are, respectively, $\bar{x}_1$, $\bar{x}_2$, $\ldots$, and $\bar{x}_k$, we can estimate the mean of the whole population with the formula

$$\frac{N_1\bar{x}_1 + N_2\bar{x}_2 + \ldots + N_k\bar{x}_k}{N} \qquad \bigstar$$

This is a *weighted mean* of the individual $\bar{x}$'s, with the weights equal to the sizes of the respective strata.

Since we shall want this estimate to be as reliable as possible, namely, make its standard error as small as possible, we shall have to be careful in choosing the sample sizes n_1, n_2, $\ldots$, and n_k. One way of handling this problem is to make the sample sizes proportional to the sizes of the corresponding strata. In *proportional allocation*, as this kind of allocation is called, we thus make

$$\frac{n_1}{N_1} = \frac{n_2}{N_2} = \ldots = \frac{n_k}{N_k} \qquad \bigstar$$

or we make these ratios as nearly equal as possible. For instance, if a random sample of size 30 is to be taken from a population of size 1,000 and the population is divided into strata whose respective sizes are 300, 600, and 100, we would take a sample of size 9 from the first stratum, a sample of size 18 from the second stratum, and a sample of size 3 from the third stratum. Note also that if a sample is allocated proportionally to the various strata, the mean of the whole population is estimated directly by the ordinary mean of all the data (see Exercise 6 on page 380).

In proportional allocation we account for the relative importance of each stratum in the whole population, but we do not account for the fact that there may be a *difference in variability* among the strata. For instance, there may be a greater variability among the weights of men than among the weights of women, and it would thus seem logical to devote a greater portion of the sample to men than to women, even though the two strata may have the same size. Considerations of this kind lead us to what is called *optimum allocation*, where we minimize the standard error of our estimates by taking into account the sizes as well as the standard deviations of the individual strata. If the standard deviations of the strata are $\sigma_1, \sigma_2, \ldots,$ and σ_k, this kind of allocation requires that we make

$$\frac{n_1}{N_1\sigma_1} = \frac{n_2}{N_2\sigma_2} = \cdots = \frac{n_k}{N_k\sigma_k} \qquad \bigstar$$

or we make these ratios as nearly equal as possible. In this fashion, the larger and the more variable strata will contribute relatively more items to the over-all sample. Referring again to the numerical example of the preceding paragraph, suppose that the standard deviations of the three strata are $\sigma_1 = 40$, $\sigma_2 = 20$, and $\sigma_3 = 60$. It can easily be verified that, using optimum allocation, the sample sizes for the three strata are now 12, 12, and 6. Note that the sample size allocated to the third stratum has *doubled* by virtue of the fact that it has the highest standard deviation.

One difficulty in using optimum allocation is that we must know the standard deviations of the different strata; another difficulty arises if we want to estimate several quantities on the basis of one and the same survey and the σ's differ, depending on the quantity with which we are concerned. In a situation like this it is usually best to use proportional allocation. Indeed, the gain in reliability due to optimum allocation is often not large enough to offset the obvious practical advantages of (self-weighting) proportional allocation.

THIRTEEN
INTRODUCTION
TO OPERATIONS
RESEARCH

Operations Research

In the past few years, the scale of business activity has expanded tremendously, its pace has quickened, corporations have grown in size, in variety of product, in extent of the market, and operations have been decentralized on a large scale. There is now less time between the occurrence of an event and the time when something must be done about it, and management on all levels requires "high quality" information as early as possible. However, even with good information and planning, the control of operations is becoming increasingly difficult; in short, there is emerging from an already complex business world an even more complex one in which few companies will be able to survive for long without both sound planning and enough flexibility to change plans rapidly in response to changing conditions.

Over the years, a great deal of research has been conducted on various aspects of business and industry. Besides practical investigations of problems concerning profitability (manufacturing processes, costs and productivity, product design and development, consumer and market characteristics, and so on), much research has been conducted in the field of administration itself. Despite all this work, however, it has been recognized in the last few decades that none of this research has contributed much to what is management's primary responsibility: the process of making and executing the "right" decisions necessary to attain enterprise goals. The recognition of this fact accounts partly for present efforts in attempting to strengthen the decision-making process by integrating the scientific study of operations, by pulling together various specialized techniques (for example, motion and time study, production planning and quality control) and other powerful analytical methods borrowed from the physical and social sciences.

This sort of omnibus effort is what we have called *operations research*, namely, the application of modern scientific techniques to problems involving the operations of a "system" looked upon as a whole. This new type of research—characterized by its concern with operating problems outside the usual fields of science, a broadened view of organizations as entities, and often the team approach to solving problems—is deliberately practical (unlike most "pure" research) and it is aimed specifically at providing a quantitative basis for decision making.

On page 7 we listed a number of important techniques which nowadays are classified under the general heading of "operations research." To some of these we have already been introduced in our discussion of "rational" decision making in the face of uncertainty, statistical sampling, and the Theory of Games. In this short chapter, we shall continue our introduction to elementary methods of operations research by discussing briefly the following four topics: linear programming, inventory, waiting lines, and Monte Carlo methods.

Linear Programming

Largely under the influence of military needs, much work has recently been done on the general problem of allocating limited resources so as best to meet desired objectives. Characteristically, the primary objective in such problems is to plan (or program) activities so that, for example, a required amount of work can be done most efficiently with a given labor force and given facilities. The programming methods we shall discuss apply to situations that can be described by *linear models*, that is, they apply to problems that can be stated using linear expressions, linear equations, and linear inequalities. In general, we are interested in maximizing a linear expression of the form

$$a_1x_1 + a_2x_2 + \ldots + a_kx_k$$

where the x's are unknowns while the a's are known, and where the x's are, furthermore, subject to restrictions expressed by means of linear equations or linear inequalities. This explains why we refer to these methods as *linear programming*.

The use of linear models in the study of economics goes back at least to the work of Francois Quesnay who, in 1758, published his *Tableau Economique*. In 1889, Leon Walras showed for the first time in his general equilibrium theory that (under perfect competition) full employment of resources was possible in a society where each individual sought to maximize the return from his own resources. Both in this and in Cassel's later formulation of the Walrasian system, it is assumed that production functions (which specify what combinations of amounts and kinds of inputs and outputs are possible) are linear and homogeneous, namely, they are linear expressions of the form indicated above. In 1928, the economist Wassily Leontief suggested describing an economy expanding at a constant rate in terms of a linear model. In further studies, he applied general equilibrium theory to certain problems of interindustry economics, providing a new technique called 'input-output analysis" to solve the systems of linear equations in terms of which the problems were formulated. This success in applying general equilibrium theory to the analysis of an economic reality greatly stimulated interest among economists in linear economic models.

A large class of linear programming problems consists of so-called "mixing" problems, which require that given resources be combined or "mixed" so as to produce specified outputs most efficiently. For many years such problems were analyzed by conventional marginal analysis, a technique of early nineteenth century origin. However, for various reasons this technique is not well suited to actual problems arising in today's complex technological environment, and a wide variety of mixing problems are much better solved by the powerful new analytical methods referred to generally as "linear programming."

To illustrate, let us consider a problem in the operations of a company making two models, Standard and Deluxe, of a large commercial-sized coffeemaker. The profits yielded by the two models are, respectively, $10 and $30, and the company can sell as many units as it can produce. Components of these coffeemakers are processed by two different machines, I and II, with the following table showing the number of hours required on each machine to process a unit of each of the two models:

| | Processing Time (hours) | |
	Machine I	Machine II
Standard model	1	1
Deluxe model	2	5

In other words, to process one Standard model requires 1 hour on Machine I and 1 hour on Machine II; to process one Deluxe model requires 2 hours on Machine I and 5 hours on Machine II. Now suppose that during the scheduling period there are 20 hours available on Machine I, 35 hours on Machine II, and we are asked to determine how many units to schedule of each model so as to maximize the company's profit.

In order to translate this problem into the language of mathematics, let us designate the number of units of Standard and Deluxe models produced by x and y. (When there are more than two unknowns it is preferable to write them as x_1, x_2, x_3, . . . , but for two-variable problems the reader is probably more familiar with the x and y notation.) Since x and y must both be positive integers or zero, the first two restrictions we impose on these variables are

$$x \geq 0 \quad \text{and} \quad y \geq 0$$

Also, referring to the above table, we find that $x + 2y$ hours of Machine I time (of which 20 hours are available) are required to process x Standard models and y Deluxe models. Hence, we have a third restriction of the form

$$x + 2y \leq 20$$

Since, similarly, $x + 5y$ hours of Machine II time (of which 35 hours are available) are required to process x Standard models and y Deluxe models, we finally have the restriction

$$x + 5y \leq 35$$

The inequality signs in these last two restrictions indicate that 20 and 35 hours are the *upper limits* on machine-time availability. This means that it would be all right to use less, but not more, than these given amounts of time.

So far there are various values of x and y which will satisfy the four requirements, and our problem is reduced to finding the ones which will maximize the company's profit. Since the company's profit for x Standard models and y Deluxe models is given by the linear expression

$$10x + 30y$$

we will have to find that pair of values of x and y which maximizes $10x + 30y$ subject to the restrictions imposed by the four inequalities.

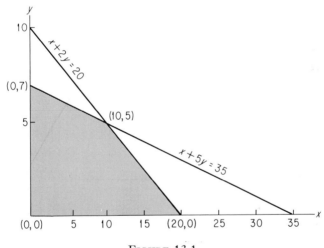

FIGURE 13.1

Let us begin by indicating geometrically the region into which the point (x, y), corresponding to a solution of the problem, must fall. The first two inequalities state that x and y cannot be negative, or in other words that a solution (x, y) must lie *on or above* the x-axis and *on or to the right of* the y-axis. Since $x + 2y \leq 20$ implies that (x, y) must lie *on or to the left of* the line whose equation is given by $x + 2y = 20$, and since $x + 5y \leq 35$ implies that (x, y) must lie *on or to the left of* the line whose equation is given by $x + 5y = 35$, we find that the region of permissible, or possible, solutions is given by the shaded region of Figure 13.1. *Thus, any point (x, y) lying in or on the edge of the shaded region of Figure 13.1 corresponds to values of x and y which satisfy the requirements of the problem.*

As can be seen from this diagram, there are many pairs of integers x and y which yield a point (x, y) inside the shaded region: there are $x = 0$ and $y = 0$, $x = 1$ and $y = 1$, $x = 2$ and $y = 3$, $x = 5$ and $y = 1$, and many more. Fortunately, there is no need to consider them all, as there exists the following theorem:

THEOREM T. *If there is a unique pair of values of x and y which maximizes (or minimizes) a linear expression of the form ax + by, then (x, y) must be a vertex (corner) of the polygon of permissible solutions; if there is more than one solution, at least two will have to correspond to vertices of this polygon.*

(This theorem extends immediately to the case where there are more than two unknowns.)

As a result of Theorem T, we have only to check the vertices of the shaded region of Figure 13.1. Three of these are easily found to be $(0, 0)$ $(0, 7)$, and $(20, 0)$, while the fourth, $(10, 5)$, is obtained by simultaneously solving the two linear equations $x + 2y = 20$ and $x + 5y = 35$. Substituting into $10x + 30y$ which gives the company's profit, we obtain the results shown in the following table:

Vertex	10x + 30y	Profit
(0, 0)	$10 \cdot 0 + 30 \cdot 0$	$ 0
(0, 7)	$10 \cdot 0 + 30 \cdot 7$	$210
(20, 0)	$10 \cdot 20 + 30 \cdot 0$	$200
(10, 5)	$10 \cdot 10 + 30 \cdot 5$	$250

Inspection of this table shows that $x = 10$ and $y = 5$ is the *optimum* (and also the unique) solution; that is, the company will realize a maximum profit of $250 by manufacturing 10 Standard models and 5 Deluxe models. (We were fortunate that the solution was in integers, since with this geometrical method we would otherwise have had to investigate points in the vicinity of the one yielding the "solution"; of course, it is not a requirement of all linear programming problems that the solution must be in terms of integers.)

Another important class of linear programming problems arises in situations where resources must be allocated to meet given demands—for instance, if goods from several sources must be delivered to a number of destinations at a minimum cost. To illustrate such *transportation* problems, suppose that a company operates three retail outlets, S_1, S_2, and S_3, in three different locations in the San Francisco Bay Region, supplying these stores from two different warehouses, W_1 and W_2. Suppose, furthermore, that the company has exactly 20 television sets in warehouse stock, 8 in W_1 and 12 in W_2, and that it must deliver 10 sets to store S_1, 4 sets to store S_2, and 6 sets to store S_3. It wants to *minimize* the cost of this operation, given that the cost of moving a set from W_1 to S_1, S_2, and S_3 is, respectively, \$12, \$15, and \$9, while the cost of moving a set from W_2 to S_1, S_2, and S_3 is, respectively, \$8, \$16, and \$11.

Letting x be the number of sets shipped from W_1 to S_1 and y the number of sets shipped from W_1 to S_2, it can easily be seen by constructing a 2-by-3 table that the number of sets shipped from W_1 to S_3 is $8 - x - y$, the number of sets shipped from W_2 to S_1 is $10 - x$, the number shipped from W_2 to S_2 is $4 - y$, and the number shipped from W_2 to S_3 is $x + y - 2$. Hence, the cost of this operation is

$$12x + 15y + 9(8 - x - y) + 8(10 - x) + 16(4 - y) + 11(x + y - 2)$$
$$= 6x + y + 194$$

and the quantity we want to minimize is $6x + y + 194$, or simply $6x + y$ since there is nothing we can do about the \$194. Since no shipment can be negative, the requirements we must impose on a solution are

$$x \geq 0, \qquad y \geq 0, \qquad y \leq 4$$
$$x + y \leq 8, \qquad x + y \geq 2$$

with the third, fourth, and fifth, particularly, arising from the fact that the number of sets shipped, respectively, from W_2 to S_2, from W_1 to S_3 and from W_2 to S_3 cannot be negative. Leaving it to the reader to work out the details in Exercise 1 on page 402, it can be shown that subject to the above restrictions the transportation cost is *minimum* for $x = 0$ and $y = 2$, where it equals \$196.

Both of the examples of this section could be solved by means of simple two-dimensional geometric figures. When we move to large and realistically complex problems, however, geometrical solutions become impossible and algebraic methods are required. Among these, the *Simplex Method*, devised by G. B. Dantzig in 1947, has found almost universal acceptance. This method is a highly efficient trial-and-error process which begins by finding a feasible solution and determining whether it maximizes (or minimizes) the linear expression with which we are concerned. If not, which is usually the case, the Simplex Method indicates the proper direction to take in searching for a maximizing (or minimizing) solution, and if such a solution exists, it will eventually be reached by this method.

Although there is no apparent connection between linear programming and the material discussed earlier in this book, it is a curious fact that the solution of a zero-sum two-person game (see Chapter 6) is actually equivalent to the solution of a linear program. As the reader will recall, each player in such a game tries to minimize his losses (or expected losses), and expressing these losses linearly in terms of the probabilities with which he selects the various strategies, he arrives at a linear program. We shall not go into this in any detail, but let us point out that games which are more complicated than the ones treated in Chapter 6 are practically always solved by means of the Simplex Method after they have been reformulated as linear programs. With this method we obtain optimum strategies for both players and also the value of the game.

EXERCISES

1. Referring to the example on page 401, draw the polygon of permissible solutions, find its five vertices, and show that $6x + y + 194$ (the transportation cost) has a minimum of $196.

2. A company makes two novelty cloth toys which must be cut and finished. To make one dozen of Toy A requires 60 minutes in each of the two departments, while 75 and 48 minutes, respectively, are required in the two departments to complete one dozen of Toy B. In the schedule period there are 50 hours available for cutting and 40 hours for finishing. The company will not put in production less than 10 dozen of either toy, and the profit is $8.00 and $11.00 per dozen on Toy A and Toy B.

   (a) If the company schedules to produce x dozen of Toy A and y dozen of Toy B, what linear expression should they try to maximize?

   (b) Show that the vertices of the polygon of permissible solutions are the points $(10, 10)$, $(10, 32)$, $(32, 10)$, and $(22\frac{6}{27}, 22\frac{6}{27})$.

   (c) Calculate the company's profit for each vertex and decide how they should schedule production to maximize their profit.

3. A manufacturer of a line of patent medicines is preparing a production run on Medicines A and B. There are sufficient ingredients on hand to make 20,000 bottles of A and 40,000 bottles of B, but there are only

45,000 bottles into which either of the medicines can be put. Furthermore, it takes 3 hours to prepare enough material to fill 1,000 bottles of Medicine A, it takes 1 hour to prepare enough material to fill 1,000 bottles of Medicine B, and there are 66 hours available for this operation. The profit is 8 cents per bottle for A and 7 cents per bottle for B.

(a) If the manufacturer plans to prepare x thousand bottles of Medicine A and y thousand bottles of Medicine B, what linear expression should he try to maximize in order to maximize his profit?

(b) Show that the vertices of the polygon of permissible solutions are the points $(0, 0)$, $(20, 0)$, $(0, 40)$, $(5, 40)$, $(10.5, 34.5)$. and $(20, 6)$.

(c) How should the manufacturer schedule production in order to maximize his profit?

4. A small manufacturer produces two items, Q and R, for which the demand exceeds his capacity. The production cost of Item Q is $6.00 per unit and the production cost of Item R is $3.00 per unit. The shipping costs are 20 cents per unit on Item Q and 30 cents per unit on Item R, and the items sell for $7.00 and $4.00, respectively. If because of a strict agreement covering the use of borrowed funds the manufacturer is forced to operate under a budget which allows a maximum production cost of $2,400 and a maximum shipping cost of $120, how many units of Q and R should be produced so as to maximize the excess of sales revenue over production and shipping costs?

5. In a critical review of its service work, a large company must analyze the activity in field parts inventories contained in 40 separate reports, of which 24 are in form R_1 and 16 are in form R_2. Three analysts, A_1, A_2, and A_3, are assigned 10, 19, and 11 reports, respectively, and it is known that they take 20, 24, and 32 minutes to analyze an R_1 report and 16, 18, and 35 minutes to analyze an R_2 report. The company wishes to assign the two kinds of reports to the analysts in such a way that the total time required to complete the 40 reports is minimized. How should they distribute the R_1 and R_2 reports among the three analysts, and what is the miminum required time?

Inventory Problems

For many years, businessmen have been as much concerned with problems of managing inventory as with any other problem of running a business. Inventory is listed in the balance sheet as a current asset and it is thus considered a part of working capital (the excess of current assets over current liabilities). Certainly, the 90-odd billion dollars of raw materials, work in progress, and finished-goods inventories held nowadays by American manufacturers, wholesalers, and retailers represents wealth of a sort. However, inventories are not an end in themselves; they are intended to be sold, not held, (hopefully) at a profit large enough to encourage enterprisers to continue to operate. On the other hand, inventories are often business "assets" in name only, being a severe drain on financial resources and one of the main causes of business failures.

Until recently, researchers have provided little help in solving inventory problems; about all any enterpriser could do was follow some vague, intuitive course leading (again, hopefully) to an inventory of such size that inventory costs were not "unreasonably high" and "not too many" sales were lost because of stockouts. In the last few years, however, the inventory problem has been studied extensively, and many recent developments such as centralized vendor control with decentralized procurement, blanket orders, direct releases, and cubic air space storage at point of use (rather than central storage) have greatly increased the efficiency of total materials management.

Beyond these developments, various quantitative techniques have helped greatly to improve materials handling ability. Restrictions imposed on early mathematical inventory models (which were largely concerned with cost minimization and ignored demand) have been relaxed to some extent, and more generally useful models have been derived. The statistical analysis of daily field sales reports, transmitted to a central computer over a teletype network, has enabled large manufacturers to reduce field, raw materials, and total inventories and to increase operating efficiency by relating manufacturing operations more closely to consumer demand. Aside from its direct contribution to individual companies, improved inventory control has had a stabilizing effect on the total economy; the increasing use of the new quantitative methods has been a major factor in preventing large inventory buildups, thus lessening the risk of an "inventory depression."

Model building techniques have nowadays advanced to the point where fairly sophisticated models of many practical inventory systems can be devised, leading to answers to the important questions of how much and when to order. The one we shall consider first is a simple *deterministic* item inventory model in which, say, over a period of one year a known number of units are to be supplied to "customers" at a constant rate, the time required to replenish stock (the "lead time") is negligible, and no shortage in the item will ever be allowed. After an amount is ordered and received, the stock is permitted to decline to zero, at which point another order (for items immediately available) is placed. During the year, this process is repeated a number of times—items are ordered, received, used up, ordered, received, used up, and so on, as illustrated in Figure 13.2. We referred to this model as *deterministic* since there are no random elements, that is, nothing is left to chance. The only question there is in this model is *how much to order each time;* when to order does not present a problem in this kind of situation.

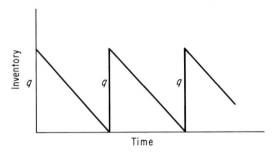

FIGURE 13.2

In order to derive a formula for the total variable cost C of maintaining inventory on the item for a year (or some other period), let us introduce the following notation: R is the total demand for the year (or other period), K is the order cost (the cost of placing each order regardless of size), I is the inventory carrying cost (the cost of carrying one unit in inventory for the given period of time), and q is the fixed quantity ordered at any one time.* Since the total demand for the year is R units and each order is of size q, the number of orders that will have to be placed is R/q, and the corresponding cost is $K(R/q)$. Furthermore, the average inventory size is $q/2$, as can be seen from Figure 13.2, so that the total inventory carrying cost for the year is $I(q/2)$ and the total variable cost of maintaining inventory on the item for a year is

$$C = \frac{1}{2} Iq + \frac{KR}{q} \qquad \bigstar$$

---

* In connection with I and K, we are concerned only with costs which may change with modifications in inventory policy. The principal costs which may enter into the carrying cost I are interest, insurance, taxes, depreciation, obsolescence, and storage costs; the order cost K is the sum of the various relevant costs of ordering materials or processing an order—forms, envelopes, stamps, personnel, and so on.

Having derived this formula expressing the total variable cost of maintaining inventory for a year (or some other period) in terms of I, K, R, and q, we can now ask for the value of q which will minimize this cost. Using elementary calculus we thus find that C is a minimum when

$$q = \sqrt{\frac{2RK}{I}} \qquad \bigstar$$

and substituting this expression for q into the formula for C, we also obtain the result that the minimum cost itself is

$$C = \sqrt{2RKI} \qquad \bigstar$$

To illustrate the use of these formulas, suppose that a large manufacturer annually requires 1,000 replacement parts for a certain type of machine. The fixed cost of placing an order is \$10, and the inventory carrying cost is \$0.50 per part per year. On the basis of this information we want to find the optimum size for each order and the minimum cost of inventorying the part for a year. Substituting $R = 1,000$, $K = 10$, and $I = 0.50$ into the formula for q, we obtain

$$q = \sqrt{\frac{2(1,000)(10)}{0.50}} = \sqrt{40,000} = 200 \text{ parts}$$

Substituting these same constants into the final formula for C, we obtain

$$C = \sqrt{2(1,000)(10)(0.50)} = \sqrt{10,000} = \$100$$

Hence, the parts should be ordered in lots of 200 and the total inventory cost for the part is \$100 annually, of which \$50 results from placing 5 orders and the other \$50 results from carrying an average inventory of 100 parts.

A serious shortcoming of the deterministic inventory model which we have discussed is that in practice the demand for an item as well as the speed with which an order can be filled depend (at least to some extent) on chance. We may thus have to work with figures pertaining to *average* demand, the *average* time it takes to get an order filled, or related probability distributions. To give an example where there is a *random demand* although the lead time, the time required to fill an order, is fixed, suppose a street vendor of corsages picks up his evening's supply from a wholesale florist who closes at 6 P.M.; consequently, the vendor cannot increase his supply during the sales period no matter how good early sales might be. The flowers are perishable and the vendor has no storage facilities, so that unsold items are a complete loss. The cost to the vendor is \$1.00 per corsage and the selling price is \$4.00.

If the daily demand were known, there would be no problem; the vendor would maximize his profits by stocking the exact quantity for which there will be a demand. However, in actual practice the demand is usually not known, and we shall assume that (on the basis of past experience) it is reasonable to use the following *demand distribution:*

Demand (Number of Corsages)	Probability
0	0.05
1	0.15
2	0.30
3	0.25
4	0.15
5	0.05
6 or more	0.05

Since we shall also need the probabilities that the demand will be for "1 or more corsages," "2 or more corsages," . . . , let us cumulate the above probabilities and exhibit the results in the following table:

Demand (Number of Corsages)	Probability
1 or more	0.95
2 or more	0.80
3 or more	0.50
4 or more	0.25
5 or more	0.10
6 or more	0.05

Using all this information, let us now determine how many corsages the vendor should stock each day so as to maximize his *expected profit,* a concept which we introduced first on page 156.

For no units stocked, the profit is obviously \$0, whatever the demand. For 1 unit stocked, the demand for "at least 1" or "1 or more" has a probability of 0.95, so that the expected profit is

$$4(0.95) - 1 = \$2.80$$

For 2 units stocked, the demand for exactly 1 corsage has a probability of 0.15, the demand for "2 or more" has a probability of 0.80, so that the expected profit is

$$4(0.15) + 8(0.80) - 2 = \$5.00$$

For 3 units stocked, the demand for exactly 1 corsage has a probability of 0.15, the demand for exactly 2 corsages has a probability of 0.30, the demand for "at least 3" or "3 or more" corsages has a probability of 0.50, so that the expected profit is

$$4(0.15) + 8(0.30) + 12(0.50) - 3 = \$6.00$$

Continuing in this fashion (see also Exercise 4 on page 409), we obtain the remaining values shown in the following table:

Number of Units Stocked	Expected Profit
0	$0
1	$2.80
2	$5.00
3	$6.00
4	$6.00
5	$5.40
6	$4.60

We did not go any further with these calculations, since the expected profit will continue to decrease. (Anyhow, we could not have gone further without knowing the probabilities that there will be a demand for exactly 6 corsages, exactly 7 corsages, and so on.)

Inspecting the above table, we find that the vendor can maximize his expected profit by stocking 3 or 4 corsages each day. Since he will turn fewer customers away if he stocks 4 rather than 3 and since unsatisfied demand may ultimately depress his market, it will be best if the vendor stocks 4 corsages each day.

The purpose of this simple example has been to show how chance elements can be handled in an inventory-type problem. If the lead time, the time it takes to fill an order or get a replacement, is also subject to chance variations, the problem becomes quite a bit more complicated; we shall not go into it at this time.

EXERCISES

1. Suppose that in the example given on page 406 the order cost is $10 for orders placed with a single vendor, but it is $14 if the parts are ordered from a multiple vendor. What is the optimum order quantity and the minimum total annual inventory cost on the item if orders are placed with a multiple vendor?

2. A company estimates that it will require 750 insulators of a certain type in a given period. The cost of carrying one unit in inventory for the period is 40 cents. The company buys the insulators from a wholesaler in the same town, sending its own truck to pick up the orders at a fixed cost of $6.00 per trip. Treating this cost as the order cost, what is the optimum number of insulators to buy at a time? How many times should lots of this size be bought during the period? What is the minimum cost of maintaining inventory on the item for the period? Of this total cost, how much is the carrying cost and how much is the order cost?

3. For the example given on page 406, $R = 1,000$, $K = 10$, and $I = 0.50$. Letting $q = 100, 120, 140, 160, 180, 200, 220, 240, 260, 280$, and 300, respectively, calculate the values of $\frac{1}{2}Iq$ $(= q/4)$ and plot them on a piece of ordinary graph paper with q measured along the horizontal scale. Calculate also the values of KR/q $(= 10,000/q)$ for the same values of q and plot them on the same diagram. Graphically adding the values obtained for $\frac{1}{2}Iq$ and KR/q for the various values of q, plot the corresponding total inventory costs and connect them with a smooth curve. Examination of this curve shows the relative insensitivity of this model. Within a range of ± 25 per cent of the optimum quantity the curve is relatively flat; thus, the order quantity could be adjusted to a quantity discount lot, or to the nearest standard or package lot (dozen, gross, etc.) without too much penalty in cost.

4. Referring to the example on page 408, show that the expected profit of the vendor is $6.00, $5.40, and $4.60 when he stocks 4, 5, and 6 units, respectively.

5. A vendor can buy an item for 70 cents and sell it for $1.50. The probabilities that 0, 1, 2, 3, 4, or "5 or more" items will be demanded are, respectively, 0.05, 0.15, 0.30, 0.25, 0.15, and 0.10. Show that the expected daily profits resulting from stocking 0, 1, 2, 3, 4, and 5 items are, respectively, $0, $0.725, $1.225, $1.275, $0.95, and $0.40. How many items should the vendor stock?

6. Suppose that as many as 2 "boosters" (with a lifetime of only 1 day) may have to be introduced into a certain chemical process each day. All unused boosters must be physically destroyed each day at a cost of $1.00 (for labor, transportation, etc.). It is estimated that the loss

resulting from not having a booster available when it is needed (and having to get one in a real hurry) is $5.00. The probabilities for a demand for 0, 1, or 2 boosters are, respectively, 0.50, 0.40, and 0.10. Find the stock level which will minimize the expected daily disposal and shortage cost. (*Hint:* If they stock 1 booster, the probability that it will have to be disposed of at a cost of $1.00 is 0.50, the probability that they will be 1 booster short and incur a cost of $5.00 is 0.10, and the expected cost is $1.00(0.50) + $5.00(0.10) = $1.00.)

7. Repeat Exercise 6 with the modification that the loss resulting from not having a booster available when needed is $10.00.

8. Referring to Exercise 6, show that it would be preferable not to stock any of the boosters if and only if the loss resulting from not having a booster available when needed is less than $1.00.

Waiting Lines

When a customer arrives at a cafeteria for service, he often finds the server busy with an earlier arrival and so he must wait; while he is waiting, others may arrive and a fairly long waiting line, or queue, can develop. Such waiting lines are not restricted to persons waiting for service at a food counter, a market checkout stand, an airline ticket office, a bank window, and so on, but they arise quite generally. Ships and trucks waiting to be unloaded at receiving docks, aircraft to be landed at airports, court cases to be heard, relief applications to be processed, machines to be repaired, to mention but a few, are all examples of waiting lines. If both the arrival times of "customers" and the service times at the "counter" were completely regular (say, a customer every 5 minutes and a service completed in exactly 4 minutes), proper scheduling could prevent waiting lines altogether. If, however, there is some chance element in arrival times, service times, or both (say, *on the average* a customer every 5 minutes and a service completed *on the average* in 4 minutes), waiting lines will sooner or later appear.

In all situations where units arrive at some facility which serves and eventually releases them, there are three basic elements in terms of which the servicing system can be described: (1) the *distribution of arrivals* (the input process), (2) the *service mechanism* including the distribution of service times, and (3) the *queue discipline*. Schematically, the over-all system may be pictured as in Figure 13.3.

Generally speaking, arrival times are irregular and more or less widely scattered over any fixed interval of time, and the way in which a queue forms may be described in either one of two ways. First, we may give an *arrival distribution* which specifies the probability that x customers will arrive during a given period of time. Among the various theoretical distributions which might describe such a process, the *Poisson distribution* (see Exercise 12 on page 141) is by far the most widely used; roughly speaking, it corresponds to the assumption that an arrival during one *small* interval of time is as likely as an arrival during any other *small* interval

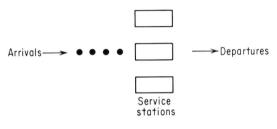

Arrivals⟶ ● ● ● ● ⟶Departures

Service
stations

FIGURE 13.3

of equal length, and the assumption that successive arrivals are independent. Using a formula similar to that of Exercise 12 on page 141, we have

$$f(x) = \frac{(\lambda t)^x \cdot e^{-\lambda t}}{x!}$$

for the probability that there will be x "Poisson arrivals" during a time interval of length t. Here λ *(lambda)* is the arrival rate, namely, the average number of arrivals per unit time, and e is the constant $2.71828\ldots$, which the reader may have met in the study of logarithms. Thus, if there are on the average 4 arrivals per hour and $t = 1$ hour, the probabilities for 0, 1, 2, 3, 4, 5, ... arrivals are, respectively, 0.02, 0.07, 0.15, 0.20, 0.20, 0.16, ... Probabilities like these are best obtained from special tables of Poisson probabilities; of course, they can be calculated directly with the use of the above formula, with $e^{-\lambda t}$ (in this case $e^{-4} = 0.018$) obtained from Table IX at the end of this book.

Instead of describing the way in which a queue forms by means of a probability distribution for the number of arrivals over a fixed period of time, an alternative (and often preferable) way is to give a distribution for the times (or delays) between arrivals for service. When dealing with "Poisson arrivals," we can obtain such a distribution, called an *inter-*

arrival distribution, by means of the following argument: to find the
probability that the time between two successive arrivals lies between
two arbitrary numbers, say, a and b, we have only to multiply the probability of 0 arrivals up to time a by the probability of at least 1 arrival
between a and b. Using the above formula for the Poisson distribution,
we find that the probability of 0 arrivals up to time a is $e^{-\lambda a}$, and that the
probability of at least 1 arrival on the interval from a to b (1 *minus* the
probability of 0 arrivals) is $1 - e^{-\lambda(b-a)}$. Multiplying these two probabilities we get

$$e^{-\lambda a}[1 - e^{-\lambda(b-a)}] = e^{-\lambda a} - e^{-\lambda b} \qquad \bigstar$$

for the probability that the time between two successive arrivals assumes
a value between a and b. We refer to such probabilities as *exponential*

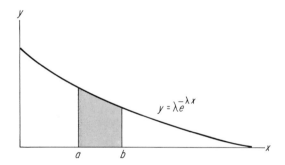

FIGURE 13.4. An exponential distribution.

probabilities, and to the corresponding interarrival distribution as an
exponential distribution. The graph of such an exponential distribution
is shown in Figure 13.4, where the probability of obtaining a value between
a and b is, as always, given by the area under the curve between a and b.
Referring again to the example where there were on the average 4 arrivals
per hour, we find, for instance, that the probability for a delay of less
than 6 minutes ($\frac{1}{10}$ of an hour) between successive arrivals is

$$e^{-0} - e^{-4(0.10)} = 1 - 0.67 = 0.33$$

after substituting $a = 0$ and $b = 0.10$. Similarly, substituting $a = 0.10$
and $b = 0.20$, we find that the probability for a delay between 6 and
12 minutes between successive arrivals is

$$e^{-4(0.10)} - e^{-4(0.20)} = 0.67 - 0.45 = 0.22$$

(The necessary values of e^{-x} were obtained from Table IX at the end of the book.)

So far as the service mechanism is concerned, there are essentially two problems: the first concerns the number of service lines that are available (the number of attendants, servers, unloading docks, bank windows, etc.) and the other concerns the length of time the service requires. Even though the service is nominally the same in a given problem, the actual times required to perform the service are usually not constant. Partly as a matter of mathematical convenience and partly because of its suitability to describe practical service-time situations, the exponential distribution we have just introduced is very often used also as the *service-time distribution*. The parameter μ is now used instead of λ, and it represents the average number of complete services that can be performed per unit time. In what follows, we shall restrict ourselves to situations where there is only one service line and the service distribution is exponential.

The way in which units in the queue are served when servicing facilities become available is called the "queue discipline." In many instances, service is on a "first come, first served" basis (as when airplanes are "stacked up" over an airfield in a holding pattern waiting to land), sometimes it is on a random basis (as when broken parts are tossed into a bin as they arrive and the next part repaired is selected more or less by chance), or on a "last come, first served" basis (as in bankruptcy proceedings of various sorts). Often, as in the case of messages waiting to be transmitted by telegraph, or work done by a computer, priorities are assigned to customers and some juggling takes place in the line as new arrivals appear. The exact type of discipline prescribed to govern a queue in a given situation is a matter of policy, and it is often chosen so as to meet certain goals.

Once the arrival distribution, the number of service lines, the service-time distribution, and the queue discipline have been specified, various probabilities and various averages can be calculated. In what follows, we shall consider a problem arising in a tool-repair center, where one attendant handles the service needs of a large number of machinists. It will be assumed that the arrivals have a Poisson distribution, the service-time distribution is exponential, queue discipline is "first come, first served," and all customers, from wherever they come, must form a single line for service. In the formulas which follow, λ will be the arrival rate (the average number of arrivals per unit time), μ will be the service rate (the average number of services per unit time), and their ratio

$h = \lambda/\mu$ (called the *utilization factor*) is the proportion of the time the service facilities are in use *or* the probability that a new arrival will have to wait. This assumes that $h < 1$, since otherwise the queue will grow indefinitely long. Using these assumptions, it can be shown that

$$\text{Average number of customers in the system at a given time} = \frac{h}{1 - h}$$

$$\text{Average time a customer spends in the system} = \frac{1}{\mu - \lambda}$$

$$\text{Average length of the waiting line} = \frac{h^2}{1 - h}$$

★

$$\text{Average time a customer must wait for service} = \frac{h}{\mu - \lambda}$$

Assuming that the arrival rate of machinists at the tool repair center is $\lambda = 2$ per hour and that the service rate is $\mu = 3$ per hour, we find that the facilities are in use $h = 2/3$ of the time, the average number of machinists waiting for service or being serviced at any given time is $\frac{h}{1 - h} = \frac{2/3}{1 - 2/3} = 2$, the average time a machinist spends waiting and being served is $\frac{1}{\mu - \lambda} = \frac{1}{3 - 2} = 1$ hour, the average number of men waiting is $\frac{h^2}{1 - h} = \frac{4/9}{1 - 2/3} = 4/3$, and the average time spent waiting for service is $\frac{h}{\mu - \lambda} = \frac{2/3}{3 - 2} = 2/3$ hours.

If we assume, furthermore, that the hourly wage paid the attendant is $1.50 and that the hourly cost of a machinist away from his work is $4.00, we find that the average cost of operating the system for an 8-hour day is

$$16 \cdot 1 \cdot 4 + 8 \cdot 1\tfrac{1}{2} = \$76$$

Here 16, the average number of arrivals per day, is multiplied by 1, the average time a machinist spends in the system, and then by 4, the hourly cost of a machinist away from his work; to this we added $8 \cdot 1\tfrac{1}{2}$, namely, the amount paid to the attendant.

Calculations like these are important because they enable us to decide, for example, whether it might be wise to replace the attendant with one whose hourly rate is \$3.50, but who can service on the average $\mu = 4$ customers per hour (see Exercise 4 below). Using a somewhat more complicated theory, we might also consider the possibility of hiring *two or more* attendants at \$1.50 an hour, with each being able to handle on the average 3 customers per hour. It is interesting to note that for two such attendants the cost of operating the system for an 8-hour day is reduced from \$76 to \$48; this is accounted for by the fact that with one attendant a machinist spends on the average 2/3 hours waiting and only 1/3 hours being served (see Exercise 2 below).

EXERCISES

1. Suppose that at a small stores supply room of a large company, service is provided by a single attendant on a "first come, first served" basis. Arrivals on the day shift have the Poisson distribution with a mean delay between arrivals of 8 minutes (and hence a mean arrival rate of 1/8 per minute). If service times have an exponential distribution with a mean service time of 5 minutes (and hence a mean service rate of 1/5 per minute), find

   (a) the average number of customers in the system (either in wait or in service) at a given time.

   (b) the average time a customer spends in the system.

   (c) the average length of the waiting line.

   (d) the average time a customer must wait for service.

2. The difference between the average time a customer spends in a service system and the average time a customer must wait for service is the average service time itself. Verify symbolically that, in fact,

$$\frac{1}{\mu - \lambda} - \frac{h}{\mu - \lambda} = \frac{1}{\mu}$$

3. The difference between the average number of customers in the system at a given time and the average length of the waiting line is the fraction of the time the service facility is in use. Verify this symbolically by showing that

$$\frac{h}{1 - h} - \frac{h^2}{1 - h} = h$$

4. In the example on page 414 we found that the average daily cost of operating the system described there was \$76. Determine whether or not it would be more economical to replace the attendant with another

man who can complete a service on the average in 15 minutes and whose hourly rate is $3.50.

5. For an 8-hour day, the mean arrival rate at a service facility is 4 per hour and the mean service rate is 5 per hour. The customers are machines and the cost of being in the service system and not in production is $10 per hour. If it is possible to increase the mean service rate to 6 per hour by making certain changes in personnel and equipment costing $15 a day, would this change be worthwhile?

6. Under the assumptions of the example on page 414, it can be shown that the probability that exactly n units are in the system at a given time is given by

$$P_n = (1 - h)h^n$$

for $n = 0, 1, 2, \ldots$. With reference to the example on page 414, find

(a) the probability that no machinists are in the system at a given time.

(b) the probability that exactly one machinist is in the system at a given time.

(c) the probability that exactly two machinists are in the system at a given time.

(d) the probability that three or more machinists are in the system at a given time.

7. Referring to Exercise 1, calculate the respective probabilities that at any given time 0, 1, 2, 3, 4, 5, 6, or 7 customers are in the system described in that exercise. Use these figures to calculate the approximate mean of this probability distribution and compare the result with that obtained in part (a) of Exercise 1. (Use formula of Exercise 6.)

Monte Carlo Methods

In Chapter 7, particularly in Technical Note 6, we indicated how tables of random digits (or other gambling devices) can be used to simulate sampling experiments. In recent years, similar techniques have been applied to a great variety of problems in the physical, social, and biological sciences under the general heading of *Monte Carlo methods.* They have been applied to the solution of problems leading to mathematical equations which actually cannot be solved by direct means, to the solution of problems whose solution would otherwise be too costly or require too much time, and to the solution of problems where experimental conditions simply cannot be reproduced. (Among the latter we find, for example, studies of the spread of cholera epidemics which, of course, cannot be experimentally induced.) Very often, the use of Monte Carlo methods eliminates the cost of building and operating expensive physical equipment; it is thus used in the study of collisions of photons with electrons, the scattering of neutrons, and other complicated phenomena.

A classical application of Monte Carlo methods to a problem of pure mathematics is the determination of π, the ratio of the circumference to the diameter of a circle, by probabilistic means. Early in the eighteenth century, the French naturalist George de Buffon proved that if a very fine needle of length L is thrown at random on a board ruled with equidistant parallel lines, the probability that the needle will intersect one of the lines is $2L/\pi a$, where a is the distance between the lines. The remarkable thing about this result is that it involves the constant $\pi = 3.1415926\ldots$, which in elementary geometry is approximated by the circumferences of regular polygons inscribed in a circle of radius $1/2$. Buffon's result implies that if such a needle is actually tossed a great many times, the proportion of the time it crosses one of the lines provides an estimate of $2L/\pi a$ and hence an estimate of π since L and a are known. Early experiments of this kind conducted in the middle of the nineteenth century yielded estimates of 3.1519 based on 5,000 trials and 3.155 based on 3,204 trials. Much more extensive experiments have been performed since, among them an exhibit at the 1939–40 New York World's Fair. (An alternate way of estimating π with a Monte Carlo method is given in Exercise 1 on page 424.)

Simulation by means of statistical sampling, that is, Monte Carlo techniques, has found wide applications in business research. Such methods are used to solve inventory problems, questions arising in connection with waiting lines, advertising, competition, the allocation of resources, scheduling of operations, and situations involving over-all planning and organization. To conclude our brief introduction to Operations Research, we shall illustrate the use of Monte Carlo techniques with a simple waiting-line problem arising in a company's planning of a production operation. The company wants to determine whether a certain automatic wash table, designed to perform a final wash of a product at the *constant* rate of one per minute, is adequate. Arrivals at the wash table are characterized by a Poisson distribution with a mean arrival rate of one every two minutes; that is, the arrival distribution is a Poisson distribution with $\lambda = 1/2$. There is a single service line, service is on a "first come, first served" basis, and the service time is *exactly* one minute.

The only aspect of this problem which has to be simulated Monte Carlo fashion is the arrival of the product at the wash table, and we shall do this by determining the times between successive arrivals with the use of a table of random digits. The method we shall use here is somewhat different from the one discussed on page 214, since the *exponential* interarrival distribution (see page 412), like the normal curve, is a continuous distribution. First we construct the cumulative interarrival distribution by calculating the probability that the time between arrivals will be less than t for various values of t. Substituting $a = 0$ and $b = t$ into the formula on page 412, we find that the probability for a delay between arrivals less than t is

$$e^{-\lambda \cdot 0} - e^{-\lambda t} = 1 - e^{-\lambda t}$$

and for our particular example this equals

$$1 - e^{-(1/2)t}$$

Substituting $t = 0, 1, 2, 3, \ldots$, and 10 into this last expression and using Table IX, we obtain the values shown in the following table·

Time Between Arrivals, t	Probability That Time Between Arrivals Is Less Than t
0	0.000
1	0.393
2	0.632
3	0.777
4	0.865
5	0.918
6	0.950
7	0.970
8	0.982
9	0.989
10	0.993

We did not go beyond $t = 10$ in this table, since the probability of getting an interarrival time greater than 10 minutes is, for all practical purposes, negligible.

Now we plot this cumulative probability distribution as we have done in Figure 13.5, and we are ready to sample interarrival times with the use of random numbers. To this end we draw two-digit random numbers, treating them as probabilities by placing a decimal point to the left of the first digit. Then we mark these probabilities on the vertical scale of

Figure 13.5 and read off the times between arrivals by first going *hori-*
zontally to the curve we fitted to the cumulative interarrival distribution
and then *down vertically* to the "time between arrivals" scale. Thus, if
we draw the random number 82, we mark 0.82 on the vertical scale and
obtain a time between arrivals of 3.50 minutes as indicated in Figure 13.5.

In the table on pages 420–423, it is assumed that we start out with an
arrival at time 0.00. The first column contains two-digit random numbers obtained from a table of random digits, the second column contains
the corresponding times between arrivals obtained with the use of Figure
13.5 as has just been indicated, and the figures in the remaining columns

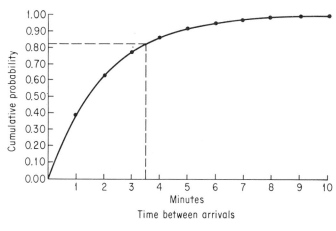

FIGURE 13.5

are self-explanatory. Thus, the item with which we begin our simulated
experiment is serviced from time 0.00 to time 1.00 and it did not have to
wait; the second item arrives at time 0.75, it is serviced from time 1.00
to 2.00, and it had to wait 0.25 minutes from the time of its arrival until
it began to get serviced. Note that time is measured in minutes in
this table, beginning with the arrival of the first item, and that it is given
to two decimals.

Not counting the first item which (by assumption) was served right
away, we find that the average time spent waiting in the queue was
$\frac{51.70}{100} = 0.517$ minutes, and this provides us with valuable information
about the performance of the wash table, about the congestion of arrivals,
and so on. We cannot check this value against the theory of the preceding

Random Number	Time Between Arrivals	Time of Arrival	Serviced from	until	Waiting Time in Queue
29	0.75	0.00	0.00	1.00	0.00
45	1.25	0.75	1.00	2.00	0.25
80	3.25	2.00	2.00	3.00	0.00
19	0.50	5.25	5.25	6.25	0.00
13	0.35	5.75	6.25	7.25	0.50
67	2.25	6.10	7.25	8.25	1.15
37	0.95	8.35	8.35	9.35	0.00
57	1.75	9.30	9.35	10.35	0.05
08	0.20	11.05	11.05	12.05	0.00
36	0.90	11.25	12.05	13.05	0.80
13	0.35	12.15	13.05	14.05	0.90
01	0.05	12.50	14.05	15.05	1.55
45	1.25	12.55	15.05	16.05	2.50
12	0.30	13.80	16.05	17.05	2.25
70	2.45	14.10	17.05	18.05	2.95
98	8.00	16.55	18.05	19.05	1.50
12	0.30	24.55	24.55	25.55	0.00
11	0.25	24.85	25.55	26.55	0.70
82	3.50	25.10	26.55	27.55	1.45
55	1.65	28.60	28.60	29.60	0.00
76	2.85	30.25	30.25	31.25	0.00
29	0.75	33.10	33.10	34.10	0.00
91	4.75	33.85	34.10	35.10	0.25
41	1.12	38.60	38.60	39.60	0.00
51	1.50	39.72	39.72	40.72	0.00
26	0.67	41.22	41.22	42.22	0.00
		41.89	42.22	43.22	0.33

Random Number	Time Between Arrivals	Time of Arrival	Serviced from	until	Waiting Time in Queue
73	2.65				
87	4.00	44.54	44.54	45.54	0.00
11	0.25	48.54	48.54	49.54	0.00
25	0.65	48.79	49.54	50.54	0.75
29	0.75	49.44	50.54	51.54	1.10
28	0.70	50.19	51.54	52.54	1.35
19	0.50	50.89	52.54	53.54	1.65
57	1.75	51.39	53.54	54.54	2.15
25	0.65	53.14	54.54	55.54	1.40
01	0.05	53.79	55.54	56.54	1.75
46	1.30	53.84	56.54	57.54	2.70
37	0.95	55.14	57.54	58.54	2.40
34	0.87	56.09	58.54	59.54	2.45
89	4.62	56.96	59.54	60.54	2.58
82	3.50	61.58	61.58	62.58	0.00
86	3.90	65.08	65.08	66.08	0.00
60	1.87	68.98	68.98	69.98	0.00
72	2.62	70.85	70.85	71.85	0.00
00	0.00	73.47	73.47	74.47	0.00
66	2.20	73.47	74.47	75.47	1.00
15	0.37	75.67	75.67	76.67	0.00
71	2.50	76.04	76.67	77.67	0.63
34	0.87	78.54	78.54	79.54	0.00
66	2.20	79.41	79.54	80.54	0.13
37	0.95	81.61	81.61	82.61	0.00
33	0.85	82.56	82.61	83.61	0.05
		83.41	83.61	84.61	0.20

Random Number	Time Between Arrivals	Time of Arrival	Serviced from	until	Waiting Time in Queue
22	0.58	83.99	84.61	85.61	0.62
95	6.00	89.99	89.99	90.99	0.00
08	0.20	90.19	90.99	91.99	0.80
56	1.70	91.89	91.99	92.99	0.10
49	1.40	93.29	93.29	94.29	0.00
95	6.00	99.29	99.29	0.29*	0.00
43	1.15	0.44	0.44	1.44	0.00
81	3.30	3.74	3.74	4.74	0.00
18	0.45	4.19	4.74	5.74	0.55
78	3.10	7.29	7.29	8.29	0.00
81	3.30	10.59	10.59	11.59	0.00
46	1.30	11.89	11.89	12.89	0.00
54	1.60	13.49	13.49	14.49	0.00
16	0.38	13.87	14.49	15.49	0.62
49	1.40	15.27	15.49	16.49	0.22
29	0.75	16.02	16.49	17.49	0.47
12	0.30	16.32	17.49	18.49	1.17
01	0.05	16.37	18.49	19.49	2.12
78	3.10	19.47	19.49	20.49	0.02
94	5.70	25.17	25.17	26.17	0.00
25	0.65	25.82	26.17	27.17	0.35
88	4.20	30.02	30.02	31.02	0.00
33	0.85	30.87	31.02	32.02	0.15
09	0.22	31.09	32.02	33.02	0.93
29	0.75	31.84	33.02	34.02	1.18

* To simplify the notation, we return to 0.00 after time 100.00.

Random Number	Time Between Arrivals	Time of Arrival	Serviced from	Serviced until	Waiting Time in Queue
62	1.95				
		33.79	34.02	35.02	0.23
74	2.70				
		36.49	36.49	37.49	0.00
69	2.40				
		38.89	38.89	39.89	0.00
79	3.15				
		42.04	42.04	43.04	0.00
69	2.40				
		44.44	44.44	45.44	0.00
08	0.20				
		44.64	45.44	46.44	0.80
88	4.15				
		48.79	48.79	49.79	0.00
12	0.30				
		49.09	49.79	50.79	0.70
75	2.75				
		51.84	51.84	52.84	0.00
69	2.40				
		54.24	54.24	55.24	0.00
36	0.90				
		55.14	55.24	56.24	0.10
52	1.55				
		56.69	56.69	57.69	0.00
25	0.65				
		57.34	57.69	58.69	0.35
61	1.90				
		59.24	59.24	60.24	0.00
94	5.70				
		64.94	64.94	65.94	0.00
58	1.80				
		66.74	66.74	67.74	0.00
54	1.60				
		68.34	68.34	69.34	0.00
29	0.75				
		69.09	69.34	70.34	0.25
28	0.70				
		69.79	70.34	71.34	0.55
75	2.75				
		72.54	72.54	73.54	0.00
86	3.95				
		74.49	76.49	77.49	0.00
98	8.00				
		84.49	84.49	85.49	0.00
90	4.70				
		89.19	89.19	90.19	0.00

section, since the service time was fixed and not exponentially distributed. However, appropriate theory shows that the *exact* value for the average waiting time in the queue is 0.50, and this shows that the approximation is very good even though the number of "trials" was fairly small. As in other sampling experiments, the precision of Monte Carlo results will, of course, increase with the number of trials.

So far we have used the sampling experiment only to estimate the average time spent waiting in the queue, but we might observe that there is additional information available on other aspects of the service system. Some of these are discussed in Exercises 2 and 3 below, and we might merely mention that the maximum time spent waiting was just under 3 minutes, the maximum time spent in the system was just under 4 minutes, and about 48 per cent of the "customers" did not have to wait for service.

EXERCISES

1. The following is an interesting and simple Monte Carlo technique for estimating π: with reference to Figure 13.6, suppose that we randomly

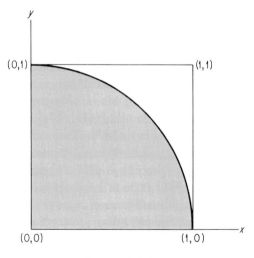

FIGURE 13.6

select points inside the indicated unit square and that we note in each case whether or not the point falls inside the circle whose center is at the origin and whose radius is 1. The probability that such a point will fall inside the circle is the ratio of the area of the sector (quarter) of the circle to the area of the square, namely, $\pi/4$ divided by 1, or simply $\pi/4$. Thus, the proportion of points falling inside the circle provides an estimate of $\pi/4$ and hence four times this proportion is an estimate of π. The points are selected as follows: we take four consecutive random digits, say, 8016, and we look upon these digits as representing the point (0.80, 0.16), namely, the point whose x-coordinate is 0.80 and whose y-coordinate is 0.16. To check whether the point falls in or on the circle we have only to see whether $x^2 + y^2 \leqslant 1$; for the point (0.80, 0.16) we get $0.80^2 + 0.16^2 = 0.6656$, and it follows that the point lies in the circle. Similarly, the four random digits 8174 are interpreted as the point (0.81, 0.74) which lies outside the circle, since $0.81^2 + 0.74^2 = 1.2037$. Use this method to estimate π on the basis of 100 points selected in this fashion.

2. Considering the first 20 minutes of the Monte Carlo experiment of this section, it can be verified that there were no "customers" in the system for a total of 4.00 minutes, there was exactly one "customer" in the system for a total of 7.50 minutes, there were exactly two for a total of 4.30 minutes, three for a total of 2.50 minutes, and four for a total of 1.70 minutes. Use these figures to estimate the average number of "customers" in the system at any given time.

3. Using the figures of Exercise 2, show that for the given period the average length of the waiting line was 0.72 customers.

4. Suppose that we have an inventory item which costs $2 and sells for $4. Unsold items have no value and are destroyed at 0 cost at the end of the day. The probabilities that 0, 1, 2, 3, 4, 5, or 6 or more items will be demanded on any one day are 0.05, 0.15, 0.30, 0.25, 0.15, 0.05, and 0.05, respectively.

   (a) Devise a Monte Carlo sampling scheme for simulating the daily demand for this item in a 200-day period. (*Hint:* Proceed as we did in Technical Note 6 on page 214.)

   (b) Conduct the sampling experiment and construct a frequency table showing the number of days on which the demand was for 0, 1, 2, ..., 6 or more items.

   (c) Referring to the sampling experiment of part (b) determine the respective profits over the 200-day period if the number of items stocked each day was 0, 1, 2, 3, 4, 5, or 6. Judging by this experiment, which stock level seems to maximize the expected profit?

5. As a prestige item, a pastry shop has decided to produce for general sale a very elegant kind of cake formerly available only by special order. The plan is to put the cake on sale each Saturday morning and

destroy all unsold cakes after closing since they will not hold over the weekend. Due to the availability of ingredients, the number of cakes they can bake varies somewhat, and the probabilities that they will have 2, 3, 4, 5, or 6 cakes available on any given Saturday are 0.05, 0.30, 0.40, 0.15, and 0.10, respectively. Analysis of past orders leads the shop to believe that the weekly demand for the cakes can be approximated by a Poisson distribution with a mean of 4, so that the probabilities of a demand for 0, 1, 2, ..., or 9 cakes are, respectively, 0.02, 0.07, 0.15, 0.20, 0.20, 0.16, 0.10, 0.06, 0.03, and 0.01.

(a) Use the method described in Technical Note 6 on page 214 to simulate the production and sales of the cakes on 200 Saturdays.

(b) If it costs 50 cents to produce one of these cakes, it sells for $1.75, and there is a 10-cent loss in good will for each customer turned away after the cakes are all sold, use the results of part (a) to estimate the pastry shop's average weekly profit on this item.

6. Suppose that in the quality control example of Exercise 11 on page 270 it is decided to use the medians of random samples of size 5 instead of their means.

(a) Use Table I to draw a graph of the cumulative normal distribution having $\mu = 1.50$ and $\sigma = 0.02$ (similar to that of Figure 13.5).

(b) Use the graph obtained in part (a) and the method discussed on page 418 to simulate taking 100 random samples of size 5 from the given normal population.

(c) Calculate the medians of the 100 samples obtained in part (b) and group them into a suitable frequency table. Then calculate the percentiles $P_{2.5}$ and $P_{97.5}$ (see page 42), which will serve as approximate 0.95 *control limits*. Using these limits, would the process be judged out of control if the median of a random sample of size 5 equalled 1.78?

A Word of Caution

The importance of creative management in the effective utilization of operations research cannot be overemphasized. Aside from such problems as organizing for operations research, managers must ask the right questions and suggest the proper criteria for evaluating results. Excessive concern with operating efficiency and the failure to think broadly and to plan wisely can be extremely damaging. Operating efficiency is always important, but unless it follows sound planning it is essentially useless: nothing can be gained by producing most efficiently the wrong product for the wrong market.

The goal of operations research is not to make decisions itself, but it is definitely intended to serve as an aid in decision making. Indeed, unless an operations research study influences a decision, brings about some change, or leads to action of some sort, it is not fulfilling its primary function. In this sense, it is the function of operations research to tell an executive some of the consequences of a change in advertising or discount policy, or of building a new plant in a new area, but *not* what he must necessarily do about these matters.

BIBLIOGRAPHY

A. Statistics for the Layman

Bross, I. D. J., *Design for Decision.* New York: Macmillan, 1953.

Franzblau, A. N., *A Primer of Statistics for Non-Statisticians.* New York: Harcourt, Brace, 1958.

Huff, D., *How to Lie with Statistics.* New York: W. W. Norton, 1954.

Huff, D., and Geis, I., *How to Take a Chance.* New York: W. W. Norton, 1959.

Levinson, H. C., *Chance, Luck, and Statistics.* New York: Dover Publications, Inc., 1963.

Moroney, M. J., *Facts from Figures.* London: Pelican Books, 1951.

Reichmann, W. J., *Use and Abuse of Statistics.* London: Methuen Ltd., 1961.

Slonim, M. J., *Sampling in a Nutshell.* New York: Simon and Schuster, 1960.

Tippett, L. H. C., *Statistics.* Fair Lawn, N.J.: Oxford University Press, 1943.

Wallis, W. A., and Roberts, H. V., *The Nature of Statistics*. New York: Collier Books, 1962.

Weaver, W., *Lady Luck—The Theory of Probability*. New York: Anchor Books, 1963.

Williams, J. D., *The Compleat Strategyst*. New York: McGraw-Hill, 1954.

B. Some General Texts on Business Statistics

Bryant, E. C., *Statistical Analysis*. New York: McGraw-Hill, 1960.

Croxton, F. E., and Cowden, D. J., *Practical Business Statistics*, 3rd ed. Englewood Cliffs, N.J.: Prentice-Hall, Inc., 1960.

Ekeblad, F. A., *The Statistical Method in Business*. New York: John Wiley, 1962.

Freund, J. E., and Williams, F. J., *Modern Business Statistics*. Englewood Cliffs, N.J.: Prentice-Hall, Inc., 1958.

Hirsch, W. Z., *Introduction to Modern Statistics*. New York: Macmillan, 1957.

Kurnow, E., Glasser, G. J., and Ottman, F. R., *Statistics for Business Decisions*. Homewood, Ill.: R. D. Irwin, Inc., 1959.

Merrett, A. J., and Bannock, G., *Business Economics and Statistics*. Englewood Cliffs, N.J.: Prentice-Hall, Inc., 1962.

Mills, F. C., *Statistical Methods*, 3rd ed. New York: Holt, Rinehart and Winston, 1955.

Neiswanger, W. A., *Elementary Statistical Methods*, rev. ed. New York: Macmillan, 1956.

Neter, J., and Wasserman, W., *Fundamental Statistics for Business and Economics*, 2nd ed. Boston: Allyn and Bacon, Inc., 1961.

Richmond, S. B., *Principles of Statistical Analysis*. New York: Ronald Press, 1957.

Schlaifer, R., *Introduction to Statistics for Business Decisions*. New York: McGraw-Hill, 1961.

Sprowls, R. C., *Elementary Statistics for Students of Social Science and Business*. New York: McGraw-Hill, 1955.

Stockton, J. R., *Business Statistics*. Cincinnati: South-Western Publishing Co., 1958.

Spurr, W. A., Kellogg, L. S., and Smith, J. H., *Business and Economic Statistics*, 2nd ed. Homewood, Ill.: R. D. Irwin, Inc., 1961.

Tuttle, A. M., *Elementary Business and Economic Statistics*. New York: McGraw-Hill, 1957.

C. Some Books on the Theory of Probability and Statistics

(*Most of these books require considerably more mathematical preparation than this text.*)

Alexander, H. W., *Elements of Mathematical Statistics*. New York: John Wiley, 1961.

Brunk, H. D., *An Introduction to Mathematical Statistics*. Boston: Ginn and Co., 1960.

Cramer, H., *The Elements of Probability Theory and Some of Its Applications*. New York: John Wiley, 1955.

Freund, J. E., *Mathematical Statistics*. Englewood Cliffs, N.J.: Prentice-Hall, Inc., 1962.

Goldberg, S., *Probability—An Introduction*. Englewood Cliffs, N.J.: Prentice-Hall, Inc., 1960.

Hoel, P. G., *Introduction to Mathematical Statistics*, 3rd ed. New York: John Wiley, 1962.

Keeping, E. S., *Introduction to Statistical Inference*. Princeton, N.J.: D. Van Nostrand Co., 1962.

Lindgren, B. W., and McElrath, G. W., *Introduction to Probability and Statistics*. New York: Macmillan, 1959.

Munroe, M. E., *Theory of Probability*. New York: McGraw-Hill, 1951.

Mood, A. M. and Graybill, F. A., *Introduction to the Theory of Statistics*, 2nd ed. New York: McGraw-Hill, 1963.

Mosteller, F., Rourke, R. E. K., and Thomas, G. B., *Probability with Statistical Applications*. Reading, Mass.: Addison-Wesley, 1961.

Wilks, S. S., *Elementary Statistical Analysis*. Princeton, N.J.: Princeton University Press, 1949.

D. Some Books Dealing with Special Problems of Statistics and Special Applications

Brown, R. G., *Statistical Forecasting for Inventory Control*. New York: McGraw-Hill, 1959.

Cowden, D. J., *Statistical Methods in Quality Control*. Englewood Cliffs, N.J.: Prentice-Hall, Inc., 1957.

Cox, D. R., *Planning of Experiments*. New York: John Wiley, 1958.

Cochran, W. G., *Sampling Techniques*. New York: John Wiley, 1953.

Davis, H. T., *The Analysis of Economic Time Series*. Bloomington, Indiana: Principia Press, 1941.

Deming, W. E., *Some Theory of Sampling*. New York: John Wiley, 1950.

Ferber, R., *Statistical Techniques in Market Research*. New York: McGraw-Hill, 1949.

Finney, D. J., *Experimental Design and its Statistical Basis*. Chicago: University of Chicago Press, 1955.

Hansen, M. H., Hurwitz, W. N., and Madow, W. G., *Sample Survey Methods and Theory*, vol. 1. New York: John Wiley, 1953.

Modley, R., and Lowenstein, D., *Pictographs and Graphs*. New York: Harper & Row, 1952.

Mudgett, B. D., *Index Numbers*. New York: John Wiley, 1951.

Myers, J. H., *Statistical Presentation*. Littlefield, Adams and Co., 1956.

Quenouille, M. H., *Rapid Statistical Calculations*. New York: Hafner Publishing Co., 1959.

Schmid, C. F., *Handbook of Graphical Presentation*. New York: Ronald Press, 1954.

Siegel, S., *Nonparametric Statistics*. New York: McGraw-Hill, 1956.

Snyder, R. M., *Measuring Business Changes*. New York: John Wiley, 1955.

E. Some Books on Operations Research

Bennion, E. G., *Elementary Mathematics of Linear Programming and Game Theory*. East Lansing, Mich.: Michigan State University, 1960.

Buchan, J. F., and Koenigsberg, E., *Scientific Inventory Management*. Englewood Cliffs, N.J.: Prentice-Hall, Inc., 1962.

Charnes, A., and Cooper, W. W., *Management Models and Industrial Applications of Linear Programming*, vols. I and II. New York: John Wiley, 1961.

Churchman, C. W., Ackoff, R. L., and Arnoff, E. L., *Introduction to Operations Research*. New York: John Wiley, 1957.

Dorfman, R., Samuelson, P. A., and Solow, R. M., *Linear Programming and Economic Analysis*. New York: McGraw-Hill, 1958.

Dresher, M., *Games of Strategy: Theory and Applications.* Englewood Cliffs, N.J.: Prentice-Hall, Inc., 1961.

Garvin, W. W., *Introduction to Linear Programming.* New York: McGraw-Hill, 1960.

Guetzkow, H., ed., *Simulation in Social Science: Readings.* Englewood Cliffs, N.J.: Prentice-Hall, Inc., 1962.

Hadley, G., and Whitin, T. M., *Analysis of Inventory Systems.* Englewood Cliffs, N.J.: Prentice-Hall, Inc., 1963.

Luce, R. D., and Raiffa, H., *Games and Decisions.* New York: John Wiley, 1958.

McCloskey, J. F., and Trefethen, F. N., *Operations Research for Management.* Baltimore: Johns Hopkins Press, 1954.

McCloskey, J. F., and Coppinger, J. M., *Operations Reesarch for Management,* vol. II. Baltimore: Johns Hopkins Press, 1956.

McKinsey, J. C. C., *Introduction to the Theory of Games.* New York: McGraw-Hill, 1952.

Miller, D. W., and Starr, M. K., *Executive Decisions and Operations Research.* Englewood Cliffs, N.J.: Prentice-Hall, Inc., 1960.

Sasieni, M., Yaspan, A., and Friedman, L., *Operations Research—Methods and Problems.* New York: John Wiley, 1959.

Starr, M. K., and Miller, D. W., *Inventory Control: Theory and Practice.* Englewood Cliffs, N.J.: Prentice-Hall, Inc., 1962.

Vajda, S., *The Theory of Games and Linear Programming.* London: Methuen Ltd., 1956.

Whitin, T. N., *The Theory of Inventory Management.* Princeton: Princeton University Press, 1953.

F. Some Statistical Tables

Fisher, R. A., and Yates, F., *Statistical Tables.* New York: Hafner Publishing Co., 1949.

Kendall, M. G., and Smith, B. B., *Tables of Random Numbers, Tracts for Computers No. XXIV.* Cambridge: Cambridge University Press, 1939.

National Bureau of Standards, *Tables of the Binomial Distribution.* Washington, D.C.: U.S. Government Printing Office, 1950.

Owen, D. B., *Handbook of Statistical Tables.* Reading, Mass.: Addison-Wesley, 1962.

Pearson, E. S., and Hartley, H. O., *Biometrika Tables for Statisticians*. Cambridge: Cambridge University Press, 1954.

RAND Corporation, *A Million Random Digits with 100,000 Normal Deviates*. Glencoe, Ill.: Free Press, 1955.

Romig, H. G., *50–100 Binomial Tables*. New York: John Wiley, 1953.

Table of 105,000 Random Decimal Digits. Interstate Commerce Commission, Bureau of Transport Economics and Statistics, Washington, D.C., 1949.

G. Some Sources of Statistical Data

(*The following books list such various sources of statistical data as periodicals, yearbooks and annuals, books and pamphlets, directories, and special reports.*)

Coman, E. T., Jr., *Sources of Business Information*. Englewood Cliffs, N.J.: Prentice-Hall, Inc., 1949.

Hauser, P. M., and Leonard, W. R., *Government Statistics for Business Use*, 2nd ed. New York: John Wiley, 1956.

Wasserman, P., *Information for Administrators*. Ithaca, N.Y.: Cornell University Press, 1956.

Wasserman, P., *et. al.*, eds., *Statistical Sources*. Detroit: Gale Research Company, 1962.

(*The following are some annual publications devoted largely to presenting statistical data of various sorts.*)

Agricultural Statistics. United States Department of Agriculture.

Commodity Yearbook. New York: Commodity Research Bureau, Inc.

Consumer Markets. Evanston, Ill.: Standard Rate and Data Service, Inc.

Demographic Yearbook. Statistical Office of the United Nations.

Industrial Marketing (Annual Market Data and Directory Number). Chicago: Advertising Publications, Inc.

Statistical Abstract of the United States. United States Bureau of the Census.

Statistical Yearbook. Statistical Office of the United Nations.

Survey of Buying Power. New York: Sales Management.

The Economic Almanac. New York: National Industrial Conference Board.

The Market Guide. New York: Editor and Publishing Co., Inc.

The World Almanac. New York: New York World-Telegram and The Sun.

STATISTICAL TABLES

Table I   NORMAL CURVE AREAS

z	.00	.01	.02	.03	.04	.05	.06	.07	.08	.09
0.0	.0000	.0040	.0080	.0120	.0160	.0199	.0239	.0279	.0319	.0359
0.1	.0398	.0438	.0478	.0517	.0557	.0596	.0636	.0675	.0714	.0753
0.2	.0793	.0832	.0871	.0910	.0948	.0987	.1026	.1064	.1103	.1141
0.3	.1179	.1217	.1255	.1293	.1331	.1368	.1406	.1443	.1480	.1517
0.4	.1554	.1591	.1628	.1664	.1700	.1736	.1772	.1808	.1844	.1879
0.5	.1915	.1950	.1985	.2019	.2054	.2088	.2123	.2157	.2190	.2224
0.6	.2257	.2291	.2324	.2357	.2389	.2422	.2454	.2486	.2517	.2549
0.7	.2580	.2611	.2642	.2673	.2704	.2734	.2764	.2794	.2823	.2852
0.8	.2881	.2910	.2939	.2967	.2995	.3023	.3051	.3078	.3106	.3133
0.9	.3159	.3186	.3212	.3238	.3264	.3289	.3315	.3340	.3365	.3389
1.0	.3413	.3438	.3461	.3485	.3508	.3531	.3554	.3577	.3599	.3621
1.1	.3643	.3665	.3686	.3708	.3729	.3749	.3770	.3790	.3810	.3830
1.2	.3849	.3869	.3888	.3907	.3925	.3944	.3962	.3980	.3997	.4015
1.3	.4032	.4049	.4066	.4082	.4099	.4115	.4131	.4147	.4162	.4177
1.4	.4192	.4207	.4222	.4236	.4251	.4265	.4279	.4292	.4306	.4319
1.5	.4332	.4345	.4357	.4370	.4382	.4394	.4406	.4418	.4429	.4441
1.6	.4452	.4463	.4474	.4484	.4495	.4505	.4515	.4525	.4535	.4545
1.7	.4554	.4564	.4573	.4582	.4591	.4599	.4608	.4616	.4625	.4633
1.8	.4641	.4649	.4656	.4664	.4671	.4678	.4686	.4693	.4699	.4706
1.9	.4713	.4719	.4726	.4732	.4738	.4744	.4750	.4756	.4761	.4767
2.0	.4772	.4778	.4783	.4788	.4793	.4798	.4803	.4808	.4812	.4817
2.1	.4821	.4826	.4830	.4834	.4838	.4842	.4846	.4850	.4854	.4857
2.2	.4861	.4864	.4868	.4871	.4875	.4878	.4881	.4884	.4887	.4890
2.3	.4893	.4896	.4898	.4901	.4904	.4906	.4909	.4911	.4913	.4916
2.4	.4918	.4920	.4922	.4925	.4927	.4929	.4931	.4932	.4934	.4936
2.5	.4938	.4940	.4941	.4943	.4945	.4946	.4948	.4949	.4951	.4952
2.6	.4953	.4955	.4956	.4957	.4959	.4960	.4961	.4962	.4963	.4964
2.7	.4965	.4966	.4967.	.4968	.4969	.4970	.4971	.4972	.4973	.4974
2.8	.4974	.4975	.4976	.4977	.4977	.4978	.4979	.4979	.4980	.4981
2.9	.4981	.4982	.4982	.4983	.4984	.4984	.4985	.4985	.4986	.4986
3.0	.4987	.4987	.4987	.4988	.4988	.4989	.4989	.4989	.4990	.4990

Table II   VALUES OF t^*

d.f.	$t_{.100}$	$t_{.050}$	$t_{.025}$	$t_{.010}$	$t_{.005}$	d.f.
1	3.078	6.314	12.706	31.821	63.657	1
2	1.886	2.920	4.303	6.965	9.925	2
3	1.638	2.353	3.182	4.541	5.841	3
4	1.533	2.132	2.776	3.747	4.604	4
5	1.476	2.015	2.571	3.365	4.032	5
6	1.440	1.943	2.447	3.143	3.707	6
7	1.415	1.895	2.365	2.998	3.499	7
8	1.397	1.860	2.306	2.896	3.355	8
9	1.383	1.833	2.262	2.821	3.250	9
10	1.372	1.812	2.228	2.764	3.169	10
11	1.363	1.796	2.201	2.718	3.106	11
12	1.356	1.782	2.179	2.681	3.055	12
13	1.350	1.771	2.160	2.650	3.012	13
14	1.345	1.761	2.145	2.624	2.977	14
15	1.341	1.753	2.131	2.602	2.947	15
16	1.337	1.746	2.120	2.583	2.921	16
17	1.333	1.740	2.110	2.567	2.898	17
18	1.330	1.734	2.101	2.552	2.878	18
19	1.328	1.729	2.093	2.539	2.861	19
20	1.325	1.725	2.086	2.528	2.845	20
21	1.323	1.721	2.080	2.518	2.831	21
22	1.321	1.717	2.074	2.508	2.819	22
23	1.319	1.714	2.069	2.500	2.807	23
24	1.318	1.711	2.064	2.492	2.797	24
25	1.316	1.708	2.060	2.485	2.787	25
26	1.315	1.706	2.056	2.479	2.779	26
27	1.314	1.703	2.052	2.473	2.771	27
28	1.313	1.701	2.048	2.467	2.763	28
29	1.311	1.699	2.045	2.462	2.756	29
inf.	1.282	1.645	1.960	2.326	2.576	inf.

* This table is abridged from Table IV of R. A. Fisher, *Statistical Methods for Research Workers*, published by Oliver and Boyd, Ltd., Edinburgh, by permission of the author and publishers.

Table III VALUES OF χ^2*

$d.f.$	$\chi^2_{.05}$	$\chi^2_{.025}$	$\chi^2_{.01}$	$\chi^2_{.005}$	$d.f.$
1	3.841	5.024	6.635	7.879	1
2	5.991	7.378	9.210	10.597	2
3	7.815	9.348	11.345	12.838	3
4	9.488	11.143	13.277	14.860	4
5	11.070	12.832	15.086	16.750	5
6	12.592	14.449	16.812	18.548	6
7	14.067	16.013	18.475	20.278	7
8	15.507	17.535	20.090	21.955	8
9	16.919	19.023	21.666	23.589	9
10	18.307	20.483	23.209	25.188	10
11	19.675	21.920	24.725	26.757	11
12	21.026	23.337	26.217	28.300	12
13	22.362	24.736	27.688	29.819	13
14	23.685	26.119	29.141	31.319	14
15	24.996	27.488	30.578	32.801	15
16	26.296	28.845	32.000	34.267	16
17	27.587	30.191	33.409	35.718	17
18	28.869	31.526	34.805	37.156	18
19	30.144	32.852	36.191	38.582	19
20	31.410	34.170	37.566	39.997	20
21	32.671	35.479	38.932	41.401	21
22	33.924	36.781	40.289	42.796	22
23	35.172	38.076	41.638	44.181	23
24	36.415	39.364	42.980	45.558	24
25	37.652	40.646	44.314	46.928	25
26	38.885	41.923	45.642	48.290	26
27	40.113	43.194	46.963	49.645	27
28	41.337	44.461	48.278	50.993	28
29	42.557	45.722	49.588	52.336	29
30	43.773	46.979	50.892	53.672	30

* This table is abridged from Table III of R. A. Fisher, *Statistical Methods for Research Workers*, published by Oliver and Boyd, Ltd., Edinburgh, by permission of the author and publishers.

Table IV(a) VALUES OF $F_{.05}$*

Degrees of freedom for numerator

	1	2	3	4	5	6	7	8	9	10	12	15	20	24	30	40	60	120	∞
1	161	200	216	225	230	234	237	239	241	242	244	246	248	249	250	251	252	253	254
2	18.5	19.0	19.2	19.2	19.3	19.3	19.4	19.4	19.4	19.4	19.4	19.4	19.4	19.5	19.5	19.5	19.5	19.5	19.5
3	10.1	9.55	9.28	9.12	9.01	8.94	8.89	8.85	8.81	8.79	8.74	8.70	8.66	8.64	8.62	8.59	8.57	8.55	8.53
4	7.71	6.94	6.59	6.39	6.26	6.16	6.09	6.04	6.00	5.96	5.91	5.86	5.80	5.77	5.75	5.72	5.69	5.66	5.63
5	6.61	5.79	5.41	5.19	5.05	4.95	4.88	4.82	4.77	4.74	4.68	4.62	4.56	4.53	4.50	4.46	4.43	4.40	4.37
6	5.99	5.14	4.76	4.53	4.39	4.28	4.21	4.15	4.10	4.06	4.00	3.94	3.87	3.84	3.81	3.77	3.74	3.70	3.67
7	5.59	4.74	4.35	4.12	3.97	3.87	3.79	3.73	3.68	3.64	3.57	3.51	3.44	3.41	3.38	3.34	3.30	3.27	3.23
8	5.32	4.46	4.07	3.84	3.69	3.58	3.50	3.44	3.39	3.35	3.28	3.22	3.15	3.12	3.08	3.04	3.01	2.97	2.93
9	5.12	4.26	3.86	3.63	3.48	3.37	3.29	3.23	3.18	3.14	3.07	3.01	2.94	2.90	2.86	2.83	2.79	2.75	2.71
10	4.96	4.10	3.71	3.48	3.33	3.22	3.14	3.07	3.02	2.98	2.91	2.85	2.77	2.74	2.70	2.66	2.62	2.58	2.54
11	4.84	3.98	3.59	3.36	3.20	3.09	3.01	2.95	2.90	2.85	2.79	2.72	2.65	2.61	2.57	2.53	2.49	2.45	2.40
12	4.75	3.89	3.49	3.26	3.11	3.00	2.91	2.85	2.80	2.75	2.69	2.62	2.54	2.51	2.47	2.43	2.38	2.34	2.30
13	4.67	3.81	3.41	3.18	3.03	2.92	2.83	2.77	2.71	2.67	2.60	2.53	2.46	2.42	2.38	2.34	2.30	2.25	2.21
14	4.60	3.74	3.34	3.11	2.96	2.85	2.76	2.70	2.65	2.60	2.53	2.46	2.39	2.35	2.31	2.27	2.22	2.18	2.13
15	4.54	3.68	3.29	3.06	2.90	2.79	2.71	2.64	2.59	2.54	2.48	2.40	2.33	2.29	2.25	2.20	2.16	2.11	2.07
16	4.49	3.63	3.24	3.01	2.85	2.74	2.66	2.59	2.54	2.49	2.42	2.35	2.28	2.24	2.19	2.15	2.11	2.06	2.01
17	4.45	3.59	3.20	2.96	2.81	2.70	2.61	2.55	2.49	2.45	2.38	2.31	2.23	2.19	2.15	2.10	2.06	2.01	1.96
18	4.41	3.55	3.16	2.93	2.77	2.66	2.58	2.51	2.46	2.41	2.34	2.27	2.19	2.15	2.11	2.06	2.02	1.97	1.92
19	4.38	3.52	3.13	2.90	2.74	2.63	2.54	2.48	2.42	2.38	2.31	2.23	2.16	2.11	2.07	2.03	1.98	1.93	1.88
20	4.35	3.49	3.10	2.87	2.71	2.60	2.51	2.45	2.39	2.35	2.28	2.20	2.12	2.08	2.04	1.99	1.95	1.90	1.84
21	4.32	3.47	3.07	2.84	2.68	2.57	2.49	2.42	2.37	2.32	2.25	2.18	2.10	2.05	2.01	1.96	1.92	1.87	1.81
22	4.30	3.44	3.05	2.82	2.66	2.55	2.46	2.40	2.34	2.30	2.23	2.15	2.07	2.03	1.98	1.94	1.89	1.84	1.78
23	4.28	3.42	3.03	2.80	2.64	2.53	2.44	2.37	2.32	2.27	2.20	2.13	2.05	2.01	1.96	1.91	1.86	1.81	1.76
24	4.26	3.40	3.01	2.78	2.62	2.51	2.42	2.36	2.30	2.25	2.18	2.11	2.03	1.98	1.94	1.89	1.84	1.79	1.73
25	4.24	3.39	2.99	2.76	2.60	2.49	2.40	2.34	2.28	2.24	2.16	2.09	2.01	1.96	1.92	1.87	1.82	1.77	1.71
30	4.17	3.32	2.92	2.69	2.53	2.42	2.33	2.27	2.21	2.16	2.09	2.01	1.93	1.89	1.84	1.79	1.74	1.68	1.62
40	4.08	3.23	2.84	2.61	2.45	2.34	2.25	2.18	2.12	2.08	2.00	1.92	1.84	1.79	1.74	1.69	1.64	1.58	1.51
60	4.00	3.15	2.76	2.53	2.37	2.25	2.17	2.10	2.04	1.99	1.92	1.84	1.75	1.70	1.65	1.59	1.53	1.47	1.39
120	3.92	3.07	2.68	2.45	2.29	2.18	2.09	2.02	1.96	1.91	1.83	1.75	1.66	1.61	1.55	1.50	1.43	1.35	1.25
∞	3.84	3.00	2.60	2.37	2.21	2.10	2.01	1.94	1.88	1.83	1.75	1.67	1.57	1.52	1.46	1.39	1.32	1.22	1.00

Degrees of freedom for denominator

* This table is reproduced from M. Merrington and C. M. Thompson, "Tables of percentage points of the inverted beta (F) distribution," *Biometrika*, vol. 33 (1943), by permission of the *Biometrika* trustees.

Table IV(b) VALUES OF $F_{.01}$*

Degrees of freedom for denominator (rows) × Degrees of freedom for numerator (columns)

den \ num	1	2	3	4	5	6	7	8	9	10	12	15	20	24	30	40	60	120	∞
1	4,052	5,000	5,403	5,625	5,764	5,859	5,928	5,982	6,023	6,056	6,106	6,157	6,209	6,235	6,261	6,287	6,313	6,339	6,366
2	98.5	99.0	99.2	99.2	99.3	99.3	99.4	99.4	99.4	99.4	99.4	99.4	99.4	99.5	99.5	99.5	99.5	99.5	99.5
3	34.1	30.8	29.5	28.7	28.2	27.9	27.7	27.5	27.3	27.2	27.1	26.9	26.7	26.6	26.5	26.4	26.3	26.2	26.1
4	21.2	18.0	16.7	16.0	15.5	15.2	15.0	14.8	14.7	14.5	14.4	14.2	14.0	13.9	13.8	13.7	13.7	13.6	13.5
5	16.3	13.3	12.1	11.4	11.0	10.7	10.5	10.3	10.2	10.1	9.89	9.72	9.55	9.47	9.38	9.29	9.20	9.11	9.02
6	13.7	10.9	9.78	9.15	8.75	8.47	8.26	8.10	7.98	7.87	7.72	7.56	7.40	7.31	7.23	7.14	7.06	6.97	6.88
7	12.2	9.55	8.45	7.85	7.46	7.19	6.99	6.84	6.72	6.62	6.47	6.31	6.16	6.07	5.99	5.91	5.82	5.74	5.65
8	11.3	8.65	7.59	7.01	6.63	6.37	6.18	6.03	5.91	5.81	5.67	5.52	5.36	5.28	5.20	5.12	5.03	4.95	4.86
9	10.6	8.02	6.99	6.42	6.06	5.80	5.61	5.47	5.35	5.26	5.11	4.96	4.81	4.73	4.65	4.57	4.48	4.40	4.31
10	10.0	7.56	6.55	5.99	5.64	5.39	5.20	5.06	4.94	4.85	4.71	4.56	4.41	4.33	4.25	4.17	4.08	4.00	3.91
11	9.65	7.21	6.22	5.67	5.32	5.07	4.89	4.74	4.63	4.54	4.40	4.25	4.10	4.02	3.94	3.86	3.78	3.69	3.60
12	9.33	6.93	5.95	5.41	5.06	4.82	4.64	4.50	4.39	4.30	4.16	4.01	3.86	3.78	3.70	3.62	3.54	3.45	3.36
13	9.07	6.70	5.74	5.21	4.86	4.62	4.44	4.30	4.19	4.10	3.96	3.82	3.66	3.59	3.51	3.43	3.34	3.25	3.17
14	8.86	6.51	5.56	5.04	4.70	4.46	4.28	4.14	4.03	3.94	3.80	3.66	3.51	3.43	3.35	3.27	3.18	3.09	3.00
15	8.68	6.36	5.42	4.89	4.56	4.32	4.14	4.00	3.89	3.80	3.67	3.52	3.37	3.29	3.21	3.13	3.05	2.96	2.87
16	8.53	6.23	5.29	4.77	4.44	4.20	4.03	3.89	3.78	3.69	3.55	3.41	3.26	3.18	3.10	3.02	2.93	2.84	2.75
17	8.40	6.11	5.19	4.67	4.34	4.10	3.93	3.79	3.68	3.59	3.46	3.31	3.16	3.08	3.00	2.92	2.83	2.75	2.65
18	8.29	6.01	5.09	4.58	4.25	4.01	3.84	3.71	3.60	3.51	3.37	3.23	3.08	3.00	2.92	2.84	2.75	2.66	2.57
19	8.19	5.93	5.01	4.50	4.17	3.94	3.77	3.63	3.52	3.43	3.30	3.15	3.00	2.92	2.84	2.76	2.67	2.58	2.49
20	8.10	5.85	4.94	4.43	4.10	3.87	3.70	3.56	3.46	3.37	3.23	3.09	2.94	2.86	2.78	2.69	2.61	2.52	2.42
21	8.02	5.78	4.87	4.37	4.04	3.81	3.64	3.51	3.40	3.31	3.17	3.03	2.88	2.80	2.72	2.64	2.55	2.46	2.36
22	7.95	5.72	4.82	4.31	3.99	3.76	3.59	3.45	3.35	3.26	3.12	2.98	2.83	2.75	2.67	2.58	2.50	2.40	2.31
23	7.88	5.66	4.76	4.26	3.94	3.71	3.54	3.41	3.30	3.21	3.07	2.93	2.78	2.70	2.62	2.54	2.45	2.35	2.26
24	7.82	5.61	4.72	4.22	3.90	3.67	3.50	3.36	3.26	3.17	3.03	2.89	2.74	2.66	2.58	2.49	2.40	2.31	2.21
25	7.77	5.57	4.68	4.18	3.86	3.63	3.46	3.32	3.22	3.13	2.99	2.85	2.70	2.62	2.53	2.45	2.36	2.27	2.17
30	7.56	5.39	4.51	4.02	3.70	3.47	3.30	3.17	3.07	2.98	2.84	2.70	2.55	2.47	2.39	2.30	2.21	2.11	2.01
40	7.31	5.18	4.31	3.83	3.51	3.29	3.12	2.99	2.89	2.80	2.66	2.52	2.37	2.29	2.20	2.11	2.02	1.92	1.80
60	7.08	4.98	4.13	3.65	3.34	3.12	2.95	2.82	2.72	2.63	2.50	2.35	2.20	2.12	2.03	1.94	1.84	1.73	1.60
120	6.85	4.79	3.95	3.48	3.17	2.96	2.79	2.66	2.56	2.47	2.34	2.19	2.03	1.95	1.86	1.76	1.66	1.53	1.38
∞	6.63	4.61	3.78	3.32	3.02	2.80	2.64	2.51	2.41	2.32	2.18	2.04	1.88	1.79	1.70	1.59	1.47	1.32	1.00

* This table is reproduced from M. Merrington and C. M. Thompson, "Tables of percentage points of the inverted beta (F) distribution," *Biometrika*, vol. 33 (1943), by permission of the *Biometrika* trustees.

Table V(a)   0.95 CONFIDENCE INTERVALS FOR PROPORTIONS*

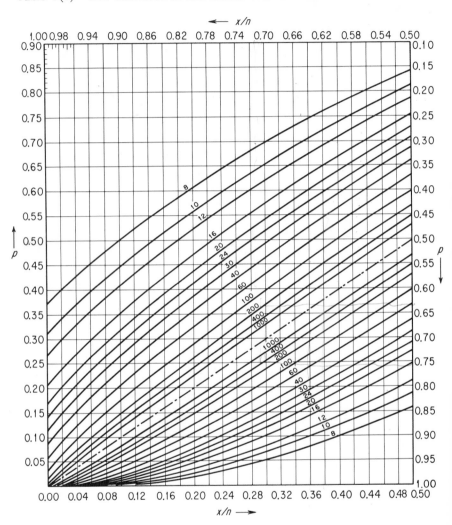

Table V(b) 0.99 CONFIDENCE INTERVALS FOR PROPORTIONS*

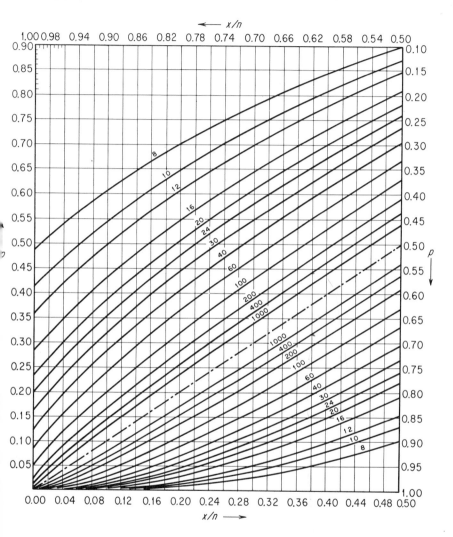

Table VI CRITICAL VALUES OF r^*

n	$r_{.025}$	$r_{.010}$	$r_{.005}$	n	$r_{.025}$	$r_{.010}$	$r_{.005}$
3	0.997			18	0.468	0.543	0.590
4	0.950	0.990	0.999	19	0.456	0.529	0.575
5	0.878	0.934	0.959	20	0.444	0.516	0.561
6	0.811	0.882	0.917	21	0.433	0.503	0.549
7	0.754	0.833	0.875	22	0.423	0.492	0.537
8	0.707	0.789	0.834	27	0.381	0.445	0.487
9	0.666	0.750	0.798	32	0.349	0.409	0.449
10	0.632	0.715	0.765	37	0.325	0.381	0.418
11	0.602	0.685	0.735	42	0.304	0.358	0.393
12	0.576	0.658	0.708	47	0.288	0.338	0.372
13	0.553	0.634	0.684	52	0.273	0.322	0.354
14	0.532	0.612	0.661	62	0.250	0.295	0.325
15	0.514	0.592	0.641	72	0.232	0.274	0.302
16	0.497	0.574	0.623	82	0.217	0.256	0.283
17	0.482	0.558	0.606	92	0.205	0.242	0.267

* This table is abridged from Table VI of R. A. Fisher and F. Yates, *Statistical Tables for Biological, Agricultural, and Medical Research*, published by Oliver and Boyd, Ltd., Edinburgh, by permission of the author and publishers.

Table VII   CRITICAL VALUES OF u (RUNS)*

Number of a's = Number of b's	$u_{.05}$	$u_{.01}$
5	3	2
6	3	2
7	4	3
8	5	4
9	6	4
10	6	5
11	7	6
12	8	6
13	9	7
14	10	8
15	11	9
16	11	10
17	12	10
18	13	11
19	14	12
20	15	13
25	19	17
30	24	21
35	28	25
40	33	30
45	37	34
50	42	38
60	51	47
80	70	65
100	88	84

* This table is based on F. S. Swed and C. Eisenhart, "Tables for testing randomness of grouping in a sequence of alternatives," *Annals of Mathematical Statistics*, vol. 14, p. 66.

Table VIII · RANDOM NUMBERS*

6063	2353	8531	8892	4109	5782	2283	1385	0699	5927
6305	1326	4551	2815	8937	2908	0698	5509	4303	9911
0143	0187	8127	2026	8313	8341	2479	4722	6602	2236
1031	0754	7989	4948	1804	3025	0997	9562	3674	7876
2022	3227	2147	5613	2857	8859	4941	7274	9412	0620
9149	0806	9751	8870	9677	9676	1854	8094	7658	7012
5863	0513	1402	3866	8696	9142	6063	2252	7818	2477
8724	0806	9644	8284	7010	0868	9076	4915	5751	9214
6783	4207	2958	5295	3175	3396	8117	5918	1037	4319
0862	1620	4690	0036	9654	4078	1918	8721	8454	7671
9394	2466	6427	5395	9393	0520	7074	0634	5578	4023
3220	3058	7787	7706	4094	5603	3303	8300	6185	8705
1491	3503	0584	7221	6176	0116	0309	1975	0910	3535
4368	5705	8579	5790	7244	6547	8495	7973	1805	7251
2325	4026	2919	8327	0267	2616	6572	8620	8245	6257
0591	1775	5134	8709	7373	3332	0507	5525	7640	2840
3471	1461	1149	6798	6070	9930	1862	3672	6718	3849
2600	9885	6219	3668	1005	5418	5832	0416	4220	4692
9572	7874	6034	4514	2628	1693	0628	2200	9006	3795
0822	2790	9386	5783	2689	2565	1565	0349	3410	5216
4329	3028	2549	2529	9434	3083	6800	8569	9290	8298
9289	5212	2355	9367	1297	1638	9282	3720	7178	2695
3932	9960	3399	1700	8253	1375	4594	6024	1223	5383
2282	0648	7561	7528	5870	7907	0713	8608	9682	8576
9933	3416	5957	2574	5553	5534	4707	3206	0963	2459
9015	6416	6603	2967	7591	5013	2878	8424	5452	4659
1539	0719	2637	9969	8450	4489	3528	3364	1459	9708
6849	5595	7969	2582	5627	1920	9772	8560	0892	6500
2523	7769	3536	9611	1079	1694	1254	4195	5799	5928
0701	7355	0587	8878	3446	1137	7690	0647	1407	6362
2163	8543	4594	6022	0496	8648	2999	1262	6702	0811
0327	5727	1070	5996	8660	9024	2135	9799	8414	9136
2169	3160	8707	6361	6339	4054	3251	7397	3480	5805
8393	8147	5360	4150	2990	3380	1789	7436	4781	0337
9726	9151	2064	0609	5878	9095	9737	2897	6510	8891
0515	2296	2636	9756	5313	7754	0916	6066	3905	1298
0649	8398	5614	0140	3155	2211	4988	3674	7663	0620
0026	9426	8005	8579	5774	7962	5092	5856	1626	0980
3422	0092	1626	1298	2475	1997	9796	7076	1541	1731
8191	1983	9164	1885	5468	8216	4327	8109	5880	9804
7408	0486	7654	4829	2711	6592	4785	5901	7147	9314
8261	9440	8118	6338	8157	9052	9093	8449	4066	4894
9274	8838	8342	3114	0455	6212	8862	6701	0099	0501
2699	0383	1400	3484	1492	4683	5369	3851	5870	0903
8740	0349	3502	3971	9960	6325	6727	4715	2945	9938
0247	2372	0424	0578	0036	1619	4479	7108	8520	1487
5136	9444	8343	1152	3615	1420	8923	7307	3978	5724
4844	8931	0964	2878	8212	9328	2656	1965	4805	0634
0205	8457	4333	2555	5353	9201	1606	2715	4014	1877
2517	5061	7642	3891	7713	7066	5435	1200	7455	5562

* From Donald B. Owen, *Handbook of Statistical Tables.* Reading, Mass.: Addison-Wesley, 1962

Table VIII   RANDOM NUMBERS *(Continued)*

2271	2572	8665	3272	9033	8256	2822	3646	7599	0270
3025	0788	5311	7792	1837	4739	4552	3234	5572	9885
3382	6151	1011	3778	9951	7709	8060	2258	8536	2290
7870	5799	6032	9043	4526	8100	1957	9539	5370	0046
1697	0002	2340	6959	1915	1626	1297	1533	6572	3835
3395	3381	1862	3250	8614	5683	6757	5628	2551	6971
6081	6526	3028	2338	5702	8819	3679	4829	9909	4712
3470	9879	2935	1141	6398	6387	5634	9589	3212	7963
0432	8641	5020	6612	1038	1547	0948	4278	0020	6509
4995	5596	8286	8377	8567	8237	3520	8244	5694	3326
8246	6718	3851	5870	1216	2107	1387	1621	5509	5772
7825	8727	2849	3501	3551	1001	0123	7873	5926	6078
6258	2450	2962	1183	3666	4156	4454	8239	4551	2920
3235	5783	2701	2378	7460	3398	1223	4688	3674	7872
2525	9008	5997	0885	1053	2340	7066	5328	6412	5054
5852	9739	1457	8999	2789	9068	9829	1336	3148	7875
0440	3769	7864	4029	4494	9829	1339	4910	1303	9161
0820	4641	2375	2542	4093	5364	1145	2848	2792	0431
7114	2842	8554	6881	6377	9427	8216	1193	8042	8449
6558	9301	9096	0577	8520	5923	4717	0188	8545	8745
0345	9937	5569	0279	8951	6183	7787	7808	5149	2185
7430	2074	9427	8422	4082	5629	2971	9456	0649	7981
8030	7345	3389	4739	5911	1022	9189	2565	1982	8577
6272	6718	3849	4715	3156	2823	4174	8733	5600	7702
4894	9847	5611	4763	8755	3388	5114	3274	6681	3657
2676	5984	6806	2692	4012	0934	2436	0869	9557	2490
9305	2074	9378	7670	8284	7431	7361	2912	2251	7395
5138	2461	7213	1905	7775	9881	8782	6272	0632	4418
2452	4200	8674	9202	0812	3986	1143	7343	2264	9072
8882	3033	8746	7390	8609	1144	2531	6944	8869	1570
1087	9336	8020	9166	4472	8293	2904	7949	3165	7400
5666	2841	8134	9588	2915	4116	2802	6917	3993	8764
9790	2228	9702	1690	7170	7511	1937	0723	4505	7155
3250	8860	3294	2684	6572	3415	5750	8726	2647	6596
5450	3922	0950	0890	6434	2306	2781	1066	3681	2404
5765	0765	7311	5270	5910	7009	0240	7435	4568	6484
8408	1939	0599	5347	2160	7376	4696	6969	0787	3838
8460	7658	6906	9177	1492	4680	3719	3456	8681	6736
4198	7244	3849	4819	1008	6781	3388	5253	7041	6712
9872	4441	6712	9614	2736	5533	9062	2534	0855	7946
6485	0487	0004	5563	1481	1546	8245	6116	6920	0990
2064	0512	9509	0341	8131	7778	8609	9417	1216	4189
9927	8987	5321	3125	9992	9449	5951	5872	2057	5731
4918	9690	6121	8770	6053	6931	7252	5409	1869	4229
8099	5821	3899	2685	6781	3178	0096	2986	8878	8991
1901	4974	1262	6810	4673	8772	6616	2632	7891	9970
8273	6675	4925	3924	2274	3860	1662	7480	8674	4503
2878	8213	3170	5126	0434	9481	7029	8688	4027	3340
6088	1182	3242	0835	1765	8819	3462	9820	5759	4189
5773	6600	5306	0354	8295	0148	6608	9064	3421	8570

* From Donald B. Owen, *Handbook of Statistical Tables.* Reading, Mass.: Addison-Wesley, 1962.

Table VIII RANDOM NUMBERS (*Continued*)

5500	2276	6307	2346	1285	7000	5306	0414	3383	2137
3251	8902	8843	2112	8567	8131	8116	5270	5994	7445
4675	1435	2192	0874	2897	0262	5092	5541	4014	2086
3543	6130	4247	4859	2660	7852	9096	0578	0097	4746
3521	8772	6612	0721	3899	2999	1263	7017	8057	4983
5573	9396	3464	1702	9204	3389	5678	2589	0288	4633
7478	7569	7551	3380	2152	5411	2647	7242	2800	6183
3339	2854	9691	9562	3252	9848	6030	8472	2266	1270
5505	8474	3167	8552	5409	1556	4247	4652	2953	5394
6381	2086	5457	7703	2758	2963	8167	6712	9820	5654
6975	5239	0762	5846	2431	0543	4956	8787	9651	2605
7185	4019	7332	2820	4853	8636	9505	6575	0365	6648
4510	1658	5615	2194	1901	4975	1895	4383	0415	3771
7752	0105	4769	2994	7445	0781	4960	4253	9451	6518
4834	4043	6591	3646	8918	4603	1970	9145	7615	3905
8866	6036	9755	4508	9061	2080	3406	9856	1298	6281
6622	4612	2030	7299	8414	8822	5176	9443	6054	6462
9094	8973	3335	2183	5192	1630	0959	8143	9182	8012
5618	6445	2983	0375	2540	2735	4901	5515	4787	7058
2705	2693	1944	8074	2015	3261	5529	7193	5401	9531
1797	4334	3293	2632	3770	1675	9363	7795	3331	8995
9448	5174	5869	0448	8613	4400	6938	5161	8691	2838
3461	1304	9682	8577	4449	1896	8328	1698	7138	1141
7092	5007	5596	8522	2580	4495	4728	8948	4434	2438
5533	4294	0939	4050	1225	6414	5895	0148	7053	5935
7852	8988	5951	4919	7404	2426	4450	2358	3082	4561
8313	8456	9892	0981	6736	8021	6226	5573	1664	9489
1158	2241	9861	7588	2669	5480	9160	4267	1690	7278
9338	7226	0025	8844	8181	5565	2418	9394	0837	3106
7711	1336	3251	8902	8425	5766	3262	5848	3545	7073
2656	1863	3884	6516	6922	1808	1896	8853	0964	3089
7980	9370	2850	3818	7281	8352	9637	0618	2430	6525
1409	7865	5908	4296	1888	2792	4014	1667	1295	0814
7657	6630	5000	1493	5459	5869	0315	8134	9587	2184
2863	5450	1329	8787	8795	4604	2615	0075	1433	7707
3988	2042	2906	8995	0818	9288	1650	0803	8319	2533
4551	2815	8941	4893	8612	4844	0042	3890	7069	8512
5772	4732	2829	3931	9540	6256	5420	2179	9448	5489
9150	1435	3817	8975	4276	9569	0175	6663	0045	5549
5764	7914	8280	1337	3779	8197	9105	5985	1054	2866
5895	0044	5021	3846	7599	0398	5212	9509	0134	4656
6857	1174	8085	6503	5355	3027	1708	3626	7059	0167
2538	2669	3746	3270	1214	9983	8434	1344	1160	3292
9983	1387	1410	8891	2523	8705	9190	2986	7654	5142
5061	9529	2922	2199	8310	6954	8090	5371	0672	6281
9999	4226	2815	8817	5606	5190	0495	7867	9968	5951
9078	5936	2393	7875	6871	3163	9203	2863	5693	9973
4823	2291	8925	6306	1717	0320	2549	3107	5488	0303
1232	1384	5698	9313	3501	3238	7227	0220	6118	7655
7694	6484	0279	8528	7214	1750	0577	8418	0698	5403

* From Donald B. Owen, *Handbook of Statistical Tables*. Reading, Mass.: Addison-Wesley, 1962.

Table VIII RANDOM NUMBERS (*Continued*)

0366	6390	2107	3875	4488	2911	1727	8108	3484	6370
3686	8812	8754	2758	3079	2994	3642	1580	1475	0366
4195	4602	1481	7324	8570	6913	6228	1934	6165	0554
8180	5460	0134	4469	8619	7723	8084	3293	1895	4886
1498	7883	5280	0692	7202	1273	3334	1554	3303	8569
9428	8633	9606	7679	4182	4035	6849	5593	6712	9822
9630	5879	9342	9618	8513	4399	9734	7744	4600	0224
1086	8918	7713	5909	2620	6612	0616	1298	2476	2386
2478	3551	1247	8004	0301	6672	6176	0682	2493	6381
2808	1133	5853	8737	9804	2404	7400	5904	8803	0377
8934	2047	4963	4531	6391	9064	3526	2482	9328	5556
1156	1191	1182	3032	8640	4681	3932	6975	4926	4870
5677	7494	0987	8870	4837	5267	4119	4163	1953	3553
3719	3586	5775	7309	5111	0919	7721	7032	1164	2105
6556	8472	1848	1056	3670	7509	0854	7210	9336	8127
1246	3476	4027	3654	2444	9040	5331	2363	4738	9822
6591	3387	4109	7956	5837	6914	6435	2624	8610	4005
8197	9026	4868	6372	2695	7143	2783	1925	3383	9060
5035	4569	7158	8531	8891	0975	6329	1329	8746	0989
1563	9650	2139	7696	7511	1725	7292	0664	8440	8593
6034	4512	1505	3857	0290	3270	8389	9612	1892	8707
2435	0238	6478	5727	0862	1621	5228	5038	2000	0433
9418	4486	5992	7172	8353	6516	6605	6387	8126	1603
3116	1295	0563	6475	4382	9902	6621	9209	8060	1787
5426	5517	5603	3722	4965	5892	8135	5214	9877	6429
2494	6696	5881	1198	2055	4624	4592	4788	7477	7149
1362	2650	8867	6503	5250	7622	5989	5909	2623	7875
5622	8415	9553	7882	1402	4723	7101	1917	8305	0440
6687	5386	9837	9111	8123	3859	1134	6321	4756	1325
0045	5546	2340	7068	6692	3802	8740	0563	8253	1589
3441	4562	1126	6427	7674	6564	1996	9167	4995	6200
9354	3914	6037	7309	5111	3080	3616	2152	2426	4450
8655	6422	1264	7859	3622	8979	7253	4257	5523	4808
0143	0292	0220	2205	4773	4964	5055	5460	0240	7505
5860	4714	6437	3670	5881	1131	7609	9690	3736	7266
8400	6939	5684	7116	3472	4006	1069	5272	5209	8271
3262	4214	5901	1064	7064	4286	1038	1178	3658	4628
2220	1426	2920	8956	8142	4642	3008	9816	5548	7753
9734	7954	9700	1489	3213	8400	7043	7552	4019	9938
3178	1061	8942	8397	4898	3793	6603	2864	6014	5225
4189	6015	5328	8242	0427	1270	1992	4789	8075	7632
4774	5282	1202	5496	8949	8940	9032	6872	3581	6631
9541	6606	6881	4916	5257	3207	9530	4546	9880	0479
4560	8877	8779	1690	6959	1916	2049	7214	0761	5111
2719	2098	7631	2574	5660	8600	2922	1570	6442	8082
7081	8366	4236	6582	9193	4328	8842	1588	1391	7714
2300	5410	2186	6846	4440	6180	6021	5258	3080	3723
4090	3091	2193	1295	0563	6579	6249	9151	1959	8949
2656	1861	2833	0067	2726	3697	5862	6058	8434	1240
9465	8924	6068	1461	0656	2718	1468	5401	9638	0931

* From Donald B. Owen, *Handbook of Statistical Tables*. Reading, Mass.: Addison-Wesley, 1962.

Table IX VALUES OF e^{-x}

x	e^{-x}	x	e^{-x}	x	e^{-x}	x	e^{-x}
0.0	1.000	2.5	0.082	5.0	0.0067	7.5	0.00055
0.1	0.905	2.6	0.074	5.1	0.0061	7.6	0.00050
0.2	0.819	2.7	0.067	5.2	0.0055	7.7	0.00045
0.3	0.741	2.8	0.061	5.3	0.0050	7.8	0.00041
0.4	0.670	2.9	0.055	5.4	0.0045	7.9	0.00037
0.5	0.607	3.0	0.050	5.5	0.0041	8.0	0.00034
0.6	0.549	3.1	0.045	5.6	0.0037	8.1	0.00030
0.7	0.497	3.2	0.041	5.7	0.0033	8.2	0.00028
0.8	0.449	3.3	0.037	5.8	0.0030	8.3	0.00025
0.9	0.407	3.4	0.033	5.9	0.0027	8.4	0.00023
1.0	0.368	3.5	0.030	6.0	0.0025	8.5	0.00020
1.1	0.333	3.6	0.027	6.1	0.0022	8.6	0.00018
1.2	0.301	3.7	0.025	6.2	0.0020	8.7	0.00017
1.3	0.273	3.8	0.022	6.3	0.0018	8.8	0.00015
1.4	0.247	3.9	0.020	6.4	0.0017	8.9	0.00014
1.5	0.223	4.0	0.018	6.5	0.0015	9.0	0.00012
1.6	0.202	4.1	0.017	6.6	0.0014	9.1	0.00011
1.7	0.183	4.2	0.015	6.7	0.0012	9.2	0.00010
1.8	0.165	4.3	0.014	6.8	0.0011	9.3	0.00009
1.9	0.150	4.4	0.012	6.9	0.0010	9.4	0.00008
2.0	0.135	4.5	0.011	7.0	0.0009	9.5	0.00008
2.1	0.122	4.6	0.010	7.1	0.0008	9.6	0.00007
2.2	0.111	4.7	0.009	7.2	0.0007	9.7	0.00006
2.3	0.100	4.8	0.008	7.3	0.0007	9.8	0.00006
2.4	0.091	4.9	0.007	7.4	0.0006	9.9	0.00005

$$n^2 = 2 \quad \text{of} \quad \sqrt{2} \quad \sqrt{\sqrt{2}} = \wedge$$

Table X SQUARES AND SQUARE ROOTS

n	n^2	$\sqrt{n}$	$\sqrt{10n}$	n	n^2	$\sqrt{n}$	$\sqrt{10n}$
1.00	1.0000	1.000000	3.162278	1.50	2.2500	1.224745	3.872983
1.01	1.0201	1.004988	3.178050	1.51	2.2801	1.228821	3.885872
1.02	1.0404	1.009950	3.193744	1.52	2.3104	1.232883	3.898718
1.03	1.0609	1.014889	3.209361	1.53	2.3409	1.236932	3.911521
1.04	1.0816	1.019804	3.224903	1.54	2.3716	1.240967	3.924283
1.05	1.1025	1.024695	3.240370	1.55	2.4025	1.244990	3.937004
1.06	1.1236	1.029563	3.255764	1.56	2.4336	1.249000	3.949684
1.07	1.1449	1.034408	3.271085	1.57	2.4649	1.252996	3.962323
1.08	1.1664	1.039230	3.286335	1.58	2.4964	1.256981	3.974921
1.09	1.1881	1.044031	3.301515	1.59	2.5281	1.260952	3.987480
1.10	1.2100	1.048809	3.316625	1.60	2.5600	1.264911	4.000000
1.11	1.2321	1.053565	3.331666	1.61	2.5921	1.268858	4.012481
1.12	1.2544	1.058301	3.346640	1.62	2.6244	1.272792	4.024922
1.13	1.2769	1.063015	3.361547	1.63	2.6569	1.276715	4.037326
1.14	1.2996	1.067708	3.376389	1.64	2.6896	1.280625	4.049691
1.15	1.3225	1.072381	3.391165	1.65	2.7225	1.284523	4.062019
1.16	1.3456	1.077033	3.405877	1.66	2.7556	1.288410	4.074310
1.17	1.3689	1.081665	3.420526	1.67	2.7889	1.292285	4.086563
1.18	1.3924	1.086278	3.435113	1.68	2.8224	1.296148	4.098780
1.19	1.4161	1.090871	3.449638	1.69	2.8561	1.300000	4.110961
1.20	1.4400	1.095445	3.464102	1.70	2.8900	1.303840	4.123106
1.21	1.4641	1.100000	3.478505	1.71	2.9241	1.307670	4.135215
1.22	1.4884	1.104536	3.492850	1.72	2.9584	1.311488	4.147288
1.23	1.5129	1.109054	3.507136	1.73	2.9929	1.315295	4.159327
1.24	1.5376	1.113553	3.521363	1.74	3.0276	1.319091	4.171331
1.25	1.5625	1.118034	3.535534	1.75	3.0625	1.322876	4.183300
1.26	1.5876	1.122497	3.549648	1.76	3.0976	1.326650	4.195235
1.27	1.6129	1.126943	3.563706	1.77	3.1329	1.330413	4.207137
1.28	1.6384	1.131371	3.577709	1.78	3.1684	1.334166	4.219005
1.29	1.6641	1.135782	3.591657	1.79	3.2041	1.337909	4.230839
1.30	1.6900	1.140175	3.605551	1.80	3.2400	1.341641	4.242641
1.31	1.7161	1.144552	3.619392	1.81	3.2761	1.345362	4.254409
1.32	1.7424	1.148913	3.633180	1.82	3.3124	1.349074	4.266146
1.33	1.7689	1.153256	3.646917	1.83	3.3489	1.352775	4.277850
1.34	1.7956	1.157584	3.660601	1.84	3.3856	1.356466	4.289522
1.35	1.8225	1.161895	3.674235	1.85	3.4225	1.360147	4.301163
1.36	1.8496	1.166190	3.687818	1.86	3.4596	1.363818	4.312772
1.37	1.8769	1.170470	3.701351	1.87	3.4969	1.367479	4.324350
1.38	1.9044	1.174734	3.714835	1.88	3.5344	1.371131	4.335897
1.39	1.9321	1.178983	3.728270	1.89	3.5721	1.374773	4.347413
1.40	1.9600	1.183216	3.741657	1.90	3.6100	1.378405	4.358899
1.41	1.9881	1.187434	3.754997	1.91	3.6481	1.382027	4.370355
1.42	2.0164	1.191638	3.768289	1.92	3.6864	1.385641	4.381780
1.43	2.0449	1.195826	3.781534	1.93	3.7249	1.389244	4.393177
1.44	2.0736	1.200000	3.794733	1.94	3.7636	1.392839	4.404543
1.45	2.1025	1.204159	3.807887	1.95	3.8025	1.396424	4.415880
1.46	2.1316	1.208305	3.820995	1.96	3.8416	1.400000	4.427189
1.47	2.1609	1.212436	3.834058	1.97	3.8809	1.403567	4.438468
1.48	2.1904	1.216553	3.847077	1.98	3.9204	1.407125	4.449719
1.49	2.2201	1.220656	3.860052	1.99	3.9601	1.410674	4.460942

Table X SQUARES AND SQUARE ROOTS (*Continued*)

n	n^2	$\sqrt{n}$	$\sqrt{10n}$	n	n^2	$\sqrt{n}$	$\sqrt{10n}$
2.00	4.0000	1.414214	4.472136	2.50	6.2500	1.581139	5.000000
2.01	4.0401	1.417745	4.483302	2.51	6.3001	1.584298	5.009990
2.02	4.0804	1.421267	4.494441	2.52	6.3504	1.587451	5.019960
2.03	4.1209	1.424781	4.505552	2.53	6.4009	1.590597	5.029911
2.04	4.1616	1.428286	4.516636	2.54	6.4516	1.593738	5.039841
2.05	4.2025	1.431782	4.527693	2.55	6.5025	1.596872	5.049752
2.06	4.2436	1.435270	4.538722	2.56	6.5536	1.600000	5.059644
2.07	4.2849	1.438749	4.549725	2.57	6.6049	1.603122	5.069517
2.08	4.3264	1.442221	4.560702	2.58	6.6564	1.606238	5.079370
2.09	4.3681	1.445683	4.571652	2.59	6.7081	1.609348	5.089204
2.10	4.4100	1.449138	4.582576	2.60	6.7600	1.612452	5.099020
2.11	4.4521	1.452584	4.593474	2.61	6.8121	1.615549	5.108816
2.12	4.4944	1.456022	4.604346	2.62	6.8644	1.618641	5.118594
2.13	4.5369	1.459452	4.615192	2.63	6.9169	1.621727	5.128353
2.14	4.5796	1.462874	4.626013	2.64	6.9696	1.624808	5.138093
2.15	4.6225	1.466288	4.636809	2.65	7.0225	1.627882	5.147815
2.16	4.6656	1.469694	4.647580	2.66	7.0756	1.630951	5.157519
2.17	4.7089	1.473092	4.658326	2.67	7.1289	1.634013	5.167204
2.18	4.7524	1.476482	4.669047	2.68	7.1824	1.637071	5.176872
2.19	4.7961	1.479865	4.679744	2.69	7.2361	1.640122	5.186521
2.20	4.8400	1.483240	4.690416	2.70	7.2900	1.643168	5.196152
2.21	4.8841	1.486607	4.701064	2.71	7.3441	1.646208	5.205766
2.22	4.9284	1.489966	4.711688	2.72	7.3984	1.649242	5.215362
2.23	4.9729	1.493318	4.722288	2.73	7.4529	1.652271	5.224940
2.24	5.0176	1.496663	4.732864	2.74	7.5076	1.655295	5.234501
2.25	5.0625	1.500000	4.743416	2.75	7.5625	1.658312	5.244044
2.26	5.1076	1.503330	4.753946	2.76	7.6176	1.661325	5.253570
2.27	5.1529	1.506652	4.764452	2.77	7.6729	1.664332	5.263079
2.28	5.1984	1.509967	4.774935	2.78	7.7284	1.667333	5.272571
2.29	5.2441	1.513275	4.785394	2.79	7.7841	1.670329	5.282045
2.30	5.2900	1.516575	4.795832	2.80	7.8400	1.673320	5.291503
2.31	5.3361	1.519868	4.806246	2.81	7.8961	1.676305	5.300943
2.32	5.3824	1.523155	4.816638	2.82	7.9524	1.679286	5.310367
2.33	5.4289	1.526434	4.827007	2.83	8.0089	1.682260	5.319774
2.34	5.4756	1.529706	4.837355	2.84	8.0656	1.685230	5.329165
2.35	5.5225	1.532971	4.847680	2.85	8.1225	1.688194	5.338539
2.36	5.5696	1.536229	4.857983	2.86	8.1796	1.691153	5.347897
2.37	5.6169	1.539480	4.868265	2.87	8.2369	1.694107	5.357238
2.38	5.6644	1.542725	4.878524	2.88	8.2944	1.697056	5.366563
2.39	5.7121	1.545962	4.888763	2.89	8.3521	1.700000	5.375872
2.40	5.7600	1.549193	4.898979	2.90	8.4100	1.702939	5.385165
2.41	5.8081	1.552417	4.909175	2.91	8.4681	1.705872	5.394442
2.42	5.8564	1.555635	4.919350	2.92	8.5264	1.708801	5.403702
2.43	5.9049	1.558846	4.929503	2.93	8.5849	1.711724	5.412947
2.44	5.9536	1.562050	4.939636	2.94	8.6436	1.714643	5.422177
2.45	6.0025	1.565248	4.949747	2.95	8.7025	1.717556	5.431390
2.46	6.0516	1.568439	4.959839	2.96	8.7616	1.720465	5.440588
2.47	6.1009	1.571623	4.969909	2.97	8.8209	1.723369	5.449771
2.48	6.1504	1.574802	4.979960	2.98	8.8804	1.726268	5.458938
2.49	6.2001	1.577973	4.989990	2.99	8.9401	1.729162	5.468089

Table X SQUARES AND SQUARE ROOTS (*Continued*)

n	n^2	$\sqrt{n}$	$\sqrt{10n}$	n	n^2	$\sqrt{n}$	$\sqrt{10n}$
3.00	9.0000	1.732051	5.477226	3.50	12.2500	1.870829	5.916080
3.01	9.0601	1.734935	5.486347	3.51	12.3201	1.873499	5.924525
3.02	9.1204	1.737815	5.495453	3.52	12.3904	1.876166	5.932959
3.03	9.1809	1.740690	5.504544	3.53	12.4609	1.878829	5.941380
3.04	9.2416	1.743560	5.513620	3.54	12.5316	1.881489	5.949790
3.05	9.3025	1.746425	5.522681	3.55	12.6025	1.884144	5.958188
3.06	9.3636	1.749286	5.531727	3.56	12.6736	1.886796	5.966574
3.07	9.4249	1.752142	5.540758	3.57	12.7449	1.889444	5.974948
3.08	9.4864	1.754993	5.549775	3.58	12.8164	1.892089	5.983310
3.09	9.5481	1.757840	5.558777	3.59	12.8881	1.894730	5.991661
3.10	9.6100	1.760682	5.567764	3.60	12.9600	1.897367	6.000000
3.11	9.6721	1.763519	5.576737	3.61	13.0321	1.900000	6.008328
3.12	9.7344	1.766352	5.585696	3.62	13.1044	1.902630	6.016644
3.13	9.7969	1.769181	5.594640	3.63	13.1769	1.905256	6.024948
3.14	9.8596	1.772005	5.603570	3.64	13.2496	1.907878	6.033241
3.15	9.9225	1.774824	5.612486	3.65	13.3225	1.910497	6.041523
3.16	9.9856	1.777639	5.621388	3.66	13.3956	1.913113	6.049793
3.17	10.0489	1.780449	5.630275	3.67	13.4689	1.915724	6.058052
3.18	10.1124	1.783255	5.639149	3.68	13.5424	1.918333	6.066300
3.19	10.1761	1.786057	5.648008	3.69	13.6161	1.920937	6.074537
3.20	10.2400	1.788854	5.656854	3.70	13.6900	1.923538	6.082763
3.21	10.3041	1.791647	5.665686	3.71	13.7641	1.926136	6.090977
3.22	10.3684	1.794436	5.674504	3.72	13.8384	1.928730	6.099180
3.23	10.4329	1.797220	5.683309	3.73	13.9129	1.931321	6.107373
3.24	10.4976	1.800000	5.692100	3.74	13.9876	1.933908	6.115554
3.25	10.5625	1.802776	5.700877	3.75	14.0625	1.936492	6.123724
3.26	10.6276	1.805547	5.709641	3.76	14.1376	1.939072	6.131884
3.27	10.6929	1.808314	5.718391	3.77	14.2129	1.941649	6.140033
3.28	10.7584	1.811077	5.727128	3.78	14.2884	1.944222	6.148170
3.29	10.8241	1.813836	5.735852	3.79	14.3641	1.946792	6.156298
3.30	10.8900	1.816590	5.744563	3.80	14.4400	1.949359	6.164414
3.31	10.9561	1.819341	5.753260	3.81	14.5161	1.951922	6.172520
3.32	11.0224	1.822087	5.761944	3.82	14.5924	1.954483	6.180615
3.33	11.0889	1.824829	5.770615	3.83	14.6689	1.957039	6.188699
3.34	11.1556	1.827567	5.779273	3.84	14.7456	1.959592	6.196773
3.35	11.2225	1.830301	5.787918	3.85	14.8225	1.962142	6.204837
3.36	11.2896	1.833030	5.796551	3.86	14.8996	1.964688	6.212890
3.37	11.3569	1.835756	5.805170	3.87	14.9769	1.967232	6.220932
3.38	11.4244	1.838478	5.813777	3.88	15.0544	1.969772	6.228965
3.39	11.4921	1.841195	5.822371	3.89	15.1321	1.972308	6.236986
3.40	11.5600	1.843909	5.830952	3.90	15.2100	1.974842	6.244998
3.41	11.6281	1.846619	5.839521	3.91	15.2881	1.977372	6.252999
3.42	11.6964	1.849324	5.848077	3.92	15.3664	1.979899	6.260990
3.43	11.7649	1.852026	5.856620	3.93	15.4449	1.982423	6.268971
3.44	11.8336	1.854724	5.865151	3.94	15.5236	1.984943	6.276942
3.45	11.9025	1.857418	5.873670	3.95	15.6025	1.987461	6.284903
3.46	11.9716	1.860108	5.882176	3.96	15.6816	1.989975	6.292853
3.47	12.0409	1.862794	5.890671	3.97	15.7609	1.992486	6.300794
3.48	12.1104	1.865476	5.899152	3.98	15.8404	1.994994	6.308724
3.49	12.1801	1.868154	5.907622	3.99	15.9201	1.997498	6.316645

Table X SQUARES AND SQUARE ROOTS (*Continued*)

n	n^2	$\sqrt{n}$	$\sqrt{10n}$	n	n^2	$\sqrt{n}$	$\sqrt{10n}$
4.00	16.0000	2.000000	6.324555	4.50	20.2500	2.121320	6.708204
4.01	16.0801	2.002498	6.332456	4.51	20.3401	2.123676	6.715653
4.02	16.1604	2.004994	6.340347	4.52	20.4304	2.126029	6.723095
4.03	16.2409	2.007486	6.348228	4.53	20.5209	2.128380	6.730527
4.04	16.3216	2.009975	6.356099	4.54	20.6116	2.130728	6.737952
4.05	16.4025	2.012461	6.363961	4.55	20.7025	2.133073	6.745369
4.06	16.4836	2.014944	6.371813	4.56	20.7936	2.135416	6.752777
4.07	16.5649	2.017424	6.379655	4.57	20.8849	2.137756	6.760178
4.08	16.6464	2.019901	6.387488	4.58	20.9764	2.140093	6.767570
4.09	16.7281	2.022375	6.395311	4.59	21.0681	2.142429	6.774954
4.10	16.8100	2.024846	6.403124	4.60	21.1600	2.144761	6.782330
4.11	16.8921	20.27313	6.410928	4.61	21.2521	2.147091	6.789698
4.12	16.9744	2.029778	6.418723	4.62	21.3444	2.149419	6.797058
4.13	17.0569	2.032240	6.426508	4.63	21.4369	2.151743	6.804410
4.14	17.1396	2.034699	6.434283	4.64	21.5296	2.154066	6.811755
4.15	17.2225	2.037155	6.442049	4.65	21.6225	2.156386	6.819091
4.16	17.3056	2.039608	6.449806	4.66	21.7156	2.158703	6.826419
4.17	17.3889	2.042058	6.457554	4.67	21.8089	2.161018	6.833740
4.18	17.4724	2.044505	6.465292	4.68	21.9024	2.163331	6.841053
4.19	17.5561	2.046949	6.473021	4.69	21.9961	2.165641	6.848357
4.20	17.6400	2.049390	6.480741	4.70	22.0900	2.167948	6.855655
4.21	17.7241	2.051828	6.488451	4.71	22.1841	2.170253	6.862944
4.22	17.8084	2.054264	6.496153	4.72	22.2784	2.172556	6.870226
4.23	17.8929	2.056696	6.503845	4.73	22.3729	2.174856	6.877500
4.24	17.9776	2.059126	6.511528	4.74	22.4676	2.177154	6.884766
4.25	18.0625	2.061553	6.519202	4.75	22.5625	2.179449	6.892024
4.26	18.1476	2.063977	6.526868	4.76	22.6576	2.181742	6.899275
4.27	18.2329	2.066398	6.534524	4.77	22.7529	2.184033	6.906519
4.28	18.3184	2.068816	6.542171	4.78	22.8484	2.186321	6.913754
4.29	18.4041	2.071232	6.549809	4.79	22.9441	2.188607	6.920983
4.30	18.4900	2.073644	6.557439	4.80	23.0400	2.190890	6.928203
4.31	18.5761	2.076054	6.565059	4.81	23.1361	2.193171	6.935416
4.32	18.6624	2.078461	6.572671	4.82	23.2324	2.195450	6.942622
4.33	18.7489	2.080865	6.580274	4.83	23.3289	2.197726	6.949820
4.34	18.8356	2.083267	6.587868	4.84	23.4256	2.200000	6.957011
4.35	18.9225	2.085665	6.595453	4.85	23.5225	2.202272	6.964194
4.36	19.0096	2.088061	6.603030	4.86	23.6196	2.204541	6.971370
4.37	19.0969	2.090454	6.610598	4.87	23.7169	2.206808	6.978539
4.38	19.1844	2.092845	6.618157	4.88	23.8144	2.209072	6.985700
4.39	19.2721	2.095233	6.625708	4.89	23.9121	2.211334	6.992853
4.40	19.3600	2.097618	6.633250	4.90	24.0100	2.213594	7.000000
4.41	19.4481	2.100000	6.640783	4.91	24.1081	2.215852	7.007139
4.42	19.5364	2.102380	6.648308	4.92	24.2064	2.218107	7.014271
4.43	19.6249	2.104757	6.655825	4.93	24.3049	2.220360	7.021396
4.44	19.7136	2.107131	6.663332	4.94	24.4036	2.222611	7.028513
4.45	19.8025	2.109502	6.670832	4.95	24.5025	2.224860	7.035624
4.46	19.8916	2.111871	6.678323	4.96	24.6016	2.227106	7.042727
4.47	19.9809	2.114237	6.685806	4.97	24.7009	2.229350	7.049823
4.48	20.0704	2.116601	6.693280	4.98	24.8004	2.231591	7.056912
4.49	20.1601	2.118962	6.700746	4.99	24.9001	2.233831	7.063993

Table X SQUARES AND SQUARE ROOTS (*Continued*)

n	n^2	$\sqrt{n}$	$\sqrt{10n}$	n	n^2	$\sqrt{n}$	$\sqrt{10n}$
5.00	25.0000	2.236068	7.071068	5.50	30.2500	2.345208	7.416198
5.01	25.1001	2.238303	7.078135	5.51	30.3601	2.347339	7.422937
5.02	25.2004	2.240536	7.085196	5.52	30.4704	2.349468	7.429670
5.03	25.3009	2.242766	7.092249	5.53	30.5809	2.351595	7.436397
5.04	25.4016	2.244994	7.099296	5.54	30.6916	2.353720	7.443118
5.05	25.5025	2.247221	7.106335	5.55	30.8025	2.355844	7.449832
5 06	25.6036	2.249444	7.113368	5.56	30.9136	2.357965	7.456541
5.07	25.7049	2.251666	7.120393	5.57	31.0249	2.360085	7.463243
5.08	25.8064	2.253886	7.127412	5.58	31.1364	2.362202	7.469940
5.09	25.9081	2.256103	7.134424	5.59	31.2481	2.364318	7.476630
5.10	26.0100	2.258318	7.141428	5.60	31.3600	2.366432	7.483315
5.11	26.1121	2.260531	7.148426	5.61	31.4721	2.368544	7.489993
5.12	26.2144	2.262742	7.155418	5.62	31.5844	2.370654	7.496666
5.13	26.3169	2.264950	7.162402	5.63	31.6969	2.372762	7.503333
5.14	26.4196	2.267157	7.169379	5.64	31.8096	2.374868	7.509993
5.15	26.5225	2.269361	7.176350	5.65	31.9225	2.376973	7.516648
5.16	26.6256	2.271563	7.183314	5.66	32.0356	2.379075	7.523297
5.17	26.7289	2.273763	7.190271	5.67	32.1489	2.381176	7.529940
5.18	26.8324	2.275961	7.197222	5.68	32.2624	2.383275	7.536577
5.19	26.9361	2.278157	7.204165	5.69	32.3761	2.385372	7.543209
5.20	27.0400	2.280351	7.211103	5.70	32.4900	2.387467	7.549834
5.21	27.1441	2.282542	7.218033	5.71	32.6041	2.389561	7.556454
5.22	27.2484	2.284732	7.224957	5.72	32.7184	2.391652	7.563068
5.23	27.3529	2.286919	7.231874	5.73	32.8329	2.393742	7.569676
5.24	27.4576	2.289105	7.238784	5.74	32.9476	2.395830	7.576279
5.25	27.5625	2.291288	7.245688	5.75	33.0625	2.397916	7.582875
5.26	27.6676	2.293469	7.252586	5.76	33.1776	2.400000	7.589466
5.27	27.7729	2.295648	7.259477	5.77	33.2929	2.402082	7.596052
5.28	27.8784	2.297825	7.266361	5.78	33.4084	2.404163	7.602631
5.29	27.9841	2.300000	7.273239	5.79	33.5241	2.406242	7.609205
5.30	28.0900	2.302173	7.280110	5.80	33.6400	2.408319	7.615773
5.31	28.1961	2.304344	7.286975	5.81	33.7561	2.410394	7.622336
5.32	28.3024	2.306513	7.293833	5.82	33.8724	2.412468	7.628892
5.33	28.4089	2.308679	7.300685	5.83	33.9889	2.414539	7.635444
5.34	28.5156	2.310844	7.307530	5.84	34.1056	2.416609	7.641989
5.35	28.6225	2.313007	7.314369	5.85	34.2225	2.418677	7.648529
5.36	28.7296	2.315167	7.321202	5.86	34.3396	2.420744	7.655064
5.37	28.8369	2.317326	7.328028	5.87	34.4569	2.422808	7.661593
5.38	28.9444	2.319483	7.334848	5.88	34.5744	2.424871	7.668116
5.39	29.0521	2.321637	7.341662	5.89	34.6921	2.426932	7.674634
5.40	29.1600	2.323790	7.348469	5.90	34.8100	2.428992	7.681146
5.41	29.2681	2.325941	7.355270	5.91	34.9281	2.431049	7.687652
5.42	29.3764	2.328089	7.362065	5.92	35.0464	2.433105	7.694154
5.43	29.4849	2.330236	7.368853	5.93	35.1649	2.435159	7.700649
5.44	29.5936	2.332381	7.357636	5.94	35.2836	2.437212	7.707140
5.45	29.7025	2.334524	7.382412	5.95	35.4025	2.439262	7.713624
5.46	29.8116	2.336664	7.389181	5.96	35.5216	2.441311	7.720104
5.47	29.9209	2.338803	7.395945	5.97	35.6409	2.443358	7.726578
5.48	30.0304	2.340940	7.402702	5.98	35.7604	2.445404	7.733046
5.49	30.1401	2.343075	7.409453	5.99	35.8801	2.447448	7.739509

Table X SQUARES AND SQUARE ROOTS (*Continued*)

n	n^2	$\sqrt{n}$	$\sqrt{10n}$	n	n^2	$\sqrt{n}$	$\sqrt{10n}$
6.00	36.0000	2.449490	7.745967	6.50	42.2500	2.549510	8.062258
6.01	36.1201	2.451530	7.752419	6.51	42.3801	2.551470	8.068457
6.02	36.2404	2.453569	7.758866	6.52	42.5104	2.553429	8.074652
6.03	36.3609	2.455606	7.765307	6.53	42.6409	2.555386	8.080842
6.04	36.4816	2.457641	7.771744	6.54	42.7716	2.557342	8.087027
6.05	36.6025	2.459675	7.778175	6.55	42.9025	2.559297	8.093207
6.06	36.7236	2.461707	7.784600	6.56	43.0336	2.561250	8.099383
6.07	36.8449	2.463737	7.791020	6.57	43.1649	2.563201	8.105554
6.08	36.9664	2.465766	7.797435	6.58	43.2964	2.565151	8.111720
6.09	37.0881	2.467793	7.803845	6.59	43.4281	2.567100	8.117881
6.10	37.2100	2.469818	7.810250	6.60	43.5600	2.569047	8.124038
6.11	37.3321	2.471841	7.816649	6.61	43.6921	2.570992	8.130191
6.12	37.4544	2.473863	7.823043	6.62	43.8244	2.572936	8.136338
6.13	37.5769	2.475884	7.829432	6.63	43.9569	2.574879	8.142481
6.14	37.6996	2.477902	7.835815	6.64	44.0896	2.576820	8.148620
6.15	37.8225	2.479919	7.842194	6.65	44.2225	2.578759	8.154753
6.16	37.9456	2.481935	7.848567	6.66	44.3556	2.580698	8.160882
6.17	38.0689	2.483948	7.854935	6.67	44.4889	2.582634	8.167007
6.18	38.1924	2.485961	7.861298	6.68	44.6224	2.584570	8.173127
6.19	38.3161	2.487971	7.867655	6.69	44.7561	2.586503	8.179242
6.20	38.4400	2.489980	7.874008	6.70	44.8900	2.588436	8.185353
6.21	38.5641	2.491987	7.880355	6.71	45.0241	2.590367	8.191459
6.22	38.6884	2.493993	7.886698	6.72	45.1584	2.592296	8.197561
6.23	38.8129	2.495997	7.893035	6.73	45.2929	2.594224	8.203658
6.24	38.9376	2.497999	7.899367	6.74	45.4276	2.596151	8.209750
6.25	39.0625	2.500000	7.905694	6.75	45.5625	2.598076	8.215838
6.26	39.1876	2.501999	7.912016	6.76	45.6976	2.600000	8.221922
6.27	39.3129	2.503997	7.918333	6.77	45.8329	2.601922	8.228001
6.28	39.4384	2.505993	7.924645	6.78	45.9684	2.603843	8.234076
6.29	39.5641	2.507987	7.930952	6.79	46.1041	2.605763	8.240146
6.30	39.6900	2.509980	7.937254	6.80	46.2400	2.607681	8.246211
6.31	39.8161	2.511971	7.943551	6.81	46.3761	2.609598	8.242272
6.32	39.9424	2.513961	7.949843	6.82	46.5124	2.611513	8.258329
6.33	40.0689	2.515949	7.956130	6.83	46.6489	2.613427	8.264381
6.34	40.1956	2.517936	7.962412	6.84	46.7856	2.615339	8.270429
6.35	40.3225	2.519921	7.968689	6.85	46.9225	2.617250	8.276473
6.36	40.4496	2.521904	7.974961	6.86	47.0596	2 619160	8.282512
6.37	40.5769	2.523886	7.981228	6.87	47.1969	2.621068	8.288546
6.38	40.7044	2.525866	7.987490	6.88	47.3344	2.622975	8.294577
6.39	40.8321	2.527845	7.993748	6.89	47.4721	2.624881	8.300602
6.40	40.9600	2.529822	8.000000	6.90	47.6100	2.626785	8.306624
6.41	41.0881	2.531798	8.006248	6.91	47.7481	2.628688	8.312641
6.42	41.2164	2.533772	8.012490	6.92	47.8864	2.630589	8.318654
6.43	41.3449	2.535744	8.018728	6.93	48.0249	2.632489	8.324662
6.44	41.4736	2.537716	8.024961	6.94	48.1636	2.634388	8.330666
6.45	41.6025	2.539685	8.031189	6.95	48.3025	2.636285	8.336666
6.46	41.7316	2.541653	8.037413	6.96	48.4416	2.638181	8.342661
6.47	41.8609	2.543619	8.043631	6.97	48.5809	2.640076	8.348653
6.48	41.9904	2.545584	8.049845	6.98	48.7204	2.641969	8.354639
6.49	42.1201	2.547548	8.056054	6.99	48.8601	2.643861	8.360622

Table X   SQUARES AND SQUARE ROOTS (*Continued*)

n	n^2	$\sqrt{n}$	$\sqrt{10n}$	n	n^2	$\sqrt{n}$	$\sqrt{10n}$
7.00	49.0000	2.645751	8.366600	7.50	56.2500	2.738613	8.660254
7.01	49.1401	2.647640	8.372574	7.51	56.4001	2.740438	8.660026
7.02	49.2804	2.649528	8.378544	7.52	56.5504	2.742262	8.671793
7.03	49.4209	2.651415	8.384510	7.53	56.7009	2.744085	8.677557
7.04	49.5616	2.653300	8.390471	7.54	56.8516	2.745906	8.683317
7.05	49.7025	2.655184	8.396428	7.55	57.0025	2.747726	8.689074
7.06	49.8436	2.657066	8.402381	7.56	57.1536	2.749545	8.694826
7.07	49.9849	2.658947	8.408329	7.57	57.3049	2.751363	8.700575
7.08	50.1264	2.660827	8.414274	7.58	57.4564	2.753180	8.706320
7.09	50.2681	2.662705	8.420214	7.59	57.6081	2.754995	8.712061
7.10	50.4100	2.664583	8.426150	7.60	57.7600	2.756810	8.717798
7.11	50.5521	2.666458	8.432082	7.61	57.9121	2.758623	8.723531
7.12	50.6944	2.668333	8.438009	7.62	58.0644	2.760435	8.729261
7.13	50.8369	2.670206	8.443933	7.63	58.2169	2.762245	8.734987
7.14	50.9796	2.672078	8.449852	7.64	58.3696	2.764055	8.740709
7.15	51.1225	2.673948	8.455767	7.65	58.5225	2.765863	8.746428
7.16	51.2656	2.675818	8.461678	7.66	58.6756	2.767671	8.752143
7.17	51.4089	2.677686	8.467585	7.67	58.8289	2.769476	8.757854
7.18	51.5524	2.679552	8.473488	7.68	58.9824	2.771281	8.763561
7.19	51.6961	2.681418	8.479387	7.69	59.1361	2.773085	8.769265
7.20	51.8400	2.683282	8.485281	7.70	59.2900	2.774887	8.774964
7.21	51.9841	2.685144	8.491172	7.71	59.4441	2.776689	8.780661
7.22	52.1284	2.687006	8.497058	7.72	59.5984	2.778489	8.786353
7.23	52.2729	2.688866	8.502941	7.73	59.7529	2.780288	8.792042
7.24	52.4176	2.690725	8.508819	7.74	59.9076	2.782086	8.797727
7.25	52.5625	2.692582	8.514693	7.75	60.0625	2.783882	8.803408
7.26	52.7076	2.694439	8.520563	7.76	60.2176	2.785678	8.809086
7.27	52.8529	2.696294	8.526429	7.77	60.3729	2.787472	8.814760
7.28	52.9984	2.698148	8.532292	7.78	60.5284	2.789265	8.820431
7.29	53.1441	2.700000	8.538150	7.79	60.6841	2.791057	8.826098
7.30	53.2900	2.701851	8.544004	7.80	60.8400	2.792848	8.831761
7.31	53.4361	2.703701	8.549854	7.81	60.9961	2.794638	8.837420
7.32	53.5824	2.705550	8.555700	7.82	61.1524	2.796426	8.843076
7.33	53.7289	2.707397	8.561542	7.83	61.3089	2.798214	8.848729
7.34	53.8756	2.709243	8.567380	7.84	61.4656	2.800000	8.854377
7.35	54.0225	2.711088	8.573214	7.85	61.6225	2.801785	8.860023
7.36	54.1696	2.712932	8.579044	7.86	61.7796	2.803569	8.865664
7.37	54.3169	2.714774	8.584870	7.87	61.9369	2.805352	8.871302
7.38	54.4644	2.716616	8.590693	7.88	62.0944	2.807134	8.876936
7.39	54.6121	2.718455	8.596511	7.89	62.2521	2.808914	8.882567
7.40	54.7600	2.720294	8.602325	7.90	62.4100	2.810694	8.888194
7.41	54.9081	2.722132	8.608136	7.91	62.5681	2.812472	8.893818
7.42	55.0564	2.723968	8.613942	7.92	62.7264	2.814249	8.899438
7.43	55.2049	2.725803	8.619745	7.93	62.8849	2.816026	8.905055
7.44	55.3536	2.727636	8.625543	7.94	63.0436	2.817801	8.910668
7.45	55.5025	2.729469	8.631338	7.95	63.2025	2.819574	8.916277
7.46	55.6516	2.731300	8.637129	7.96	63.3616	2.821347	8.921883
7.47	55.8009	2.733130	8.642916	7.97	63.5209	2.823119	8.927486
7.48	55.9504	2.734959	8.648699	7.98	63.6804	2.824889	8.933085
7.49	56.1001	2.736786	8.654479	7.99	63.8401	2.826659	8.938680

Table X SQUARES AND SQUARE ROOTS (*Continued*)

n	n^2	$\sqrt{n}$	$\sqrt{10n}$	n	n^2	$\sqrt{n}$	$\sqrt{10n}$
8.00	64.0000	2.828427	8.944272	8.50	72.2500	2.915476	9.219544
8.01	64.1601	2.830194	8.949860	8.51	72.4201	2.917190	9.224966
8.02	64.3204	2.831960	8.955445	8.52	72.5904	2.918904	9.230385
8.03	64.4809	2.833725	8.961027	8.53	72.7609	2.920616	9.235800
8.04	64.6416	2.835489	8.966605	8.54	72.9316	2.922328	9.241212
8.05	64.8025	2.837252	8.972179	8.55	73.1025	2.924038	9.246621
8.06	64.9636	2.839014	8.977750	8.56	73.2736	2.925748	9.252027
8.07	65.1249	2.840775	8.983318	8.57	73.4449	2.927456	9.257429
8.08	65.2864	2.842534	8.988882	8.58	73.6164	2.929164	9.262829
8.09	65.4481	2.844293	8.994443	8.59	73.7881	2.930870	9.268225
8.10	65.6100	2.846050	9.000000	8.60	73.9600	2.932576	9.273618
8.11	65.7721	2.847806	9.005554	8.61	74.1321	2.934280	9.279009
8.12	65.9344	2.849561	9.011104	8.62	74.3044	2.935984	9.284396
8.13	66.0969	2.851315	9.016651	8.63	74.4769	2.937686	9.289779
8.14	66.2596	2.853069	9.022195	8.64	74.6496	2.939388	9.295160
8.15	66.4225	2.854820	9.027735	8.65	74.8225	2.941088	9.300538
8.16	66.5856	2.856571	9.033272	8.66	74.9956	2.942788	9.305912
8.17	66.7489	2.858321	9.038805	8.67	75.1689	2.944486	9.311283
8.18	66.9124	2.860070	9.044335	8.68	75.3424	2.946184	9.316652
8.19	67.0761	2.861818	9.049862	8.69	75.5161	2.947881	9.322017
8.20	67.2400	2.863564	9.055385	8.70	75.6900	2.949576	9.327379
8.21	67.4041	2.865310	9.060905	8.71	75.8641	2.951271	9.332738
8.22	67.5684	2.867054	9.066422	8.72	76.0384	2.952965	9.338094
8.23	67.7329	2.868798	9.071935	8.73	76.2129	2.954657	9.343447
8.24	67.8976	2.870540	9.077445	8.74	76.3876	2.956349	9.348797
8.25	68.0625	2.872281	9.082951	8.75	76.5625	2.958040	9.354143
8.26	68.2276	2.874022	9.088454	8.76	76.7376	2.959730	9.359487
8.27	68.3929	2.875761	9.093954	8.77	76.9129	2.961419	9.364828
8.28	68.5584	2.877499	9.099451	8.78	77.0884	2.963106	9.370165
8.29	68.7241	2.879236	9.104944	8.79	77.2641	2.964793	9.375500
8.30	68.8900	2.880972	9.110434	8.80	77.4400	2.966479	9.380832
8.31	69.0561	2.882707	9.115920	8.81	77.6161	2.968164	9.386160
8.32	69.2224	2.884441	9.121403	8.82	77.7924	2.969848	9.391486
8.33	69.3889	2.886174	9.126883	8.83	77.9689	2.971532	9.396808
8.34	69.5556	2.887906	9.132360	8.84	78.1456	2.973214	9.402127
8.35	69.7225	2.889637	9.137833	8.85	78.3225	2.974895	9.407444
8.36	69.8896	2.891366	9.143304	8.86	78.4996	2.976575	9.412757
8.37	7.00569	2.893095	9.148770	8.87	78.6769	2.978255	9.418068
8.38	70.2244	2.894823	9.154234	8.88	78.8544	2.979933	9.423375
8.39	70.3921	2.896550	9.159694	8.89	79.0321	2.981610	9.428680
8.40	70.5600	2.898275	9.165151	8.90	79.2100	2.983287	9.433981
8.41	70.7281	2.900000	9.170605	8.91	79.3881	2.984962	9.439280
8.42	70.8964	2.901724	9.176056	8.92	79.5664	2.986637	9.444575
8.43	71.0649	2.903446	9.181503	8.93	79.7449	2.988311	9.449868
8.44	71.2336	2.905168	9.186947	8.94	79.9236	2.989983	9.455157
8.45	71.4025	2.906888	9.192388	8.95	80.1025	2.991655	9.460444
8.46	71.5716	2.908608	9.197826	8.96	80.2816	2.993326	9.465728
8.47	71.7409	2.910326	9.203260	8.97	80.4609	2.994996	9.471008
8.48	71.9104	2.912044	9.208692	8.98	80.6404	2.996665	9.476286
8.49	72.0801	2.913760	9.214120	8.99	80.8201	2.998333	9.481561

Table X   SQUARES AND SQUARE ROOTS (*Continued*)

n	n^2	$\sqrt{n}$	$\sqrt{10n}$	n	n^2	$\sqrt{n}$	$\sqrt{10n}$
9.00	81.0000	3.000000	9.486833	9.50	90.2500	3.082207	9.746794
9.01	81.1801	3.001666	9.492102	9.51	90.4401	3.083829	9.751923
9.02	81.3604	3.003331	9.497368	9.52	90.6304	3.085450	9.757049
9.03	81.5409	3.004996	9.502631	9.53	90.8209	3.087070	9.762172
9.04	81.7216	3.006659	9.507891	9.54	91.0116	3.088689	9.767292
9.05	81.9025	3.008322	9.513149	9.55	91.2025	3.090307	9.772410
9.06	82.0836	3.009983	9.518403	9.56	91.3936	3.091925	9.777525
9.07	82.2649	3.011644	9.523655	9.57	91.5849	3.093542	9.782638
9.08	82.4464	3.013304	9.528903	9.58	91.7764	3.095158	9.787747
9.09	82.6281	3.014963	9.534149	9.59	91.9681	3.096773	9.792855
9.10	82.8100	3.016621	9.539392	9.60	92.1600	3.098387	9.797959
9.11	82.9921	3.018278	9.544632	9.61	92.3521	3.100000	9.803061
9.12	83.1744	3.019934	9.549869	9.62	92.5444	3.101612	9.808160
9.13	83.3569	3.021589	9.555103	9.63	92.7369	3.103224	9.813256
9.14	83.5396	3.023243	9.560335	9.64	92.9296	3.104835	9.818350
9.15	83.7225	3.024897	9.565563	9.65	93.1225	3.106445	9.823441
9.16	83.9056	3.026549	9.570789	9.66	93.3156	3.108054	9.828530
9.17	84.0889	3.028201	9.576012	9.67	93.5089	3.109662	9.833616
9.18	84.2724	3.029851	9.581232	9.68	93.7024	3.111270	9.838699
9.19	84.4561	3.031501	9.586449	9.69	93.8961	3.112876	9.843780
9.20	84.6400	3.033150	9.591663	9.70	94.0900	3.114482	9.848858
9.21	84.8241	3.034798	9.596874	9.71	94.2841	3.116087	9.853933
9.22	85.0084	3.036445	9.602083	9.72	94.4784	3.117691	9.859006
9.23	85.1929	3.038092	9.607289	9.73	94.6729	3.119295	9.864076
9.24	85.3776	3.039737	9.612492	9.74	94.8676	3.120897	9.869144
9.25	85.5625	3.041381	9.617692	9.75	95.0625	3.122499	9.874209
9.26	85.7476	3.043025	9.622889	9.76	95.2576	3.124100	9.879271
9.27	85.9329	3.044667	9.628084	9.77	95.4529	3.125700	9.884331
9.28	86.1184	3.046309	9.633276	9.78	95.6484	3.127299	9.889388
9.29	86.3041	3.047950	9.638465	9.79	95.8441	3.128898	9.894443
9.30	86.4900	3.049590	9.643651	9.80	96.0400	3.130495	9.899495
9.31	86.6761	3.051229	9.648834	9.81	96.2361	3.132092	9.904544
9.32	86.8624	3.052868	9.654015	9.82	96.4324	3.133688	9.909591
9.33	87.0489	3.054505	9.659193	9.83	96.6289	3.135283	9.914636
9.34	87.2356	3.056141	9.664368	9.84	96.8256	3.136877	9.919677
9.35	87.4225	3.057777	9.669540	9.85	97.0225	3.138471	9.924717
9.36	87.6096	3.059412	9.674709	9.86	97.2196	3.140064	9.929753
9.37	87.7969	3.061046	9.679876	9.87	97.4169	3.141656	9.934787
9.38	87.9844	3.062679	9.685040	9.88	97.6144	3.143247	9.939819
9.39	88.1721	3.064311	9.690201	9.89	97.8121	3.144837	9.944848
9.40	88.3600	3.065942	9.695360	9.90	98.0100	3.146427	9.949874
9.41	88.5481	3.067572	9.700515	9.91	98.2081	3.148015	9.954898
9.42	88.7364	3.069202	9.705668	9.92	98.4064	3.149603	9.959920
9.43	88.9249	3.070831	9.710819	9.93	98.6049	3.151190	9.964939
9.44	89.1136	3.072458	9.715966	9.94	98.8036	3.152777	9.969955
9.45	89.3025	3.074085	9.721111	9.95	99.0025	3.154362	9.974969
9.46	89.4916	3.075711	9.726253	9.96	99.2016	3.155947	9.979980
9.47	89.6809	3.077337	9.731393	9.97	99.4009	3.157531	9.984989
9.48	89.8704	3.078961	9.736529	9.98	99.6004	3.159114	9.989995
9.49	90.0601	3.080584	9.741663	9.99	99.8001	3.160696	9.994999

ANSWERS

TO ODD-NUMBERED
EXERCISES

Page 17

1. (a) 1,272; (b) no; (c) no; (d) 951; (e) no; (f) no.

3. 70.0–89.9, 90.0–109.9, 110.0–129.9, 130.0–149.9, 150.0–169.9.

5. Boundaries: 4.5, 9.5, 14.5, 19.5, 24.5, 29.5; Marks: 7, 12, 17, 22, 27; Interval: 5.

9. This firm offers the highest trade-in of $4,965.

11. 68 per cent.

15. The class frequencies are 12, 28, 19, 10, 7, 3, and 1.

Page 43

3. 14.0.

5. (a) mean, 7.74, median, 7.9, modes, 7.9 and 8.0; (b) mean, 30.77, median, 30.9; (c) mean, 1.0, median, 1.1, modes, 1.1 and 1.2.

7. mean, 115.2; median, 98; modes, 80, 98, and 100.

11. Using $-12°$ instead of $348°$, $-5°$ instead of $355°$, etc., the mean is $0°$.

13. \$70.04.   15. \$271.03.   17. 0.286.

21. Median, \$4,422.1; $Q_1 = \$2,449.4$; $Q_3 = \$6,843.4$.

23. (a) 49.0; (b) 48.9.   29. (a) 9; (b) 19.

31. (a) $x_1 + x_2 + x_3 + x_4 + x_5$; (b) $w_1^2 + w_2^2 + w_3^2 + w_4^2$;
    (c) $(x_2 + y_2) + (x_3 + y_3) + (x_4 + y_4)$; (d) $x_3^2 f_3 + x_4^2 f_4 + x_5^2 f_5 + x_6^2 f_6$

Page 57

1. 0.086.   3. 0.237.   5. 1.88.

7. 150.   9. 10.5.   13. (a) 75 per cent; (b) 88.8 per cent.

15. At most 4 per cent.

17. A is selling at 1.5 standard deviations above average while B is selling at
    3 standard deviations above average; leaving other considerations aside,
    it would be better to sell Stock B.

19. 0.61 per cent.

Page 62

3. 0.864.

Page 81

1. (a) 100.0, 96.0, 94.8, 94.2; (d) 93.1.

3. (a) 100.0, 97.6, 97.5, 97.1; (b) 99.5; (c) 89.8 and 81.8; (d) 90.4; (e) 104.5.

5. (a) 27.1, 152.8, 184.1, 65.7, 36.8, 100.0; (b) 107.2; (c) 85.7.

9. 73.3.

11. (a) 99.9 and 102.6; (b) 99.9 and 102.5; (c) 102.6; (d) 102.6; (e) 102.6;
    (f) 102.9.

Page 91

5. No.   7. 73.22, 73.25, 73.66, 74.01, 74.19, 74.48, 73.98.

11. 74.1, 77.8, 90.4, 94.8, 100.0, 111.1, 114.1, 120.0.

13. Simple aggregative index, geometric mean of price relatives, and Ideal
    Index; others do not.

Page 102

1. (b) 3 and 2.   5. 60.   7. (a) 6; (b) 36; (c) 30.
9. 720.   11. 6.   13. 792.
17. (a) 10; (b) 10; (c) 1.   19. (a) 12; (b) 20.

Page 112

5. TTT, TTH, THT, HTT, THH, HTH, HHT, HHH.
9. (a) (4, 1), (3, 2); (b) (1, 1), (2, 2), (3, 3); (c) (2, 1), (2, 2); (d) (2, 1); (e) (2, 1), (2, 2), (3, 1), (3, 2), (4, 1), (4, 2), (4, 3); (f) none; (g) (2, 1), (3, 1), (4, 1), (3, 2), (4, 2), (4, 3); (h) same as (g); K and L are not mutually exclusive, K and M are mutually exclusive, L and M are not mutually exclusive.
15. No.

Page 122

1. The sum of the first broker's probabilities is less than 1, those of the second broker are possible, the sum of the third broker's probabilities exceeds 1.
3. (a) 0.70; (b) 0.55; (c) 0.75; (d) 0; (e) 0.25.
5. (a) The firm does not offer for public sale an unregistered new stock.
   (b) The firm offers for public sale an unregistered new stock and the SEC issues a stop order.
   (c) The firm offers for public sale an unregistered new stock and the SEC does not issue a stop order.
   (d) The firm does not offer for public sale an unregistered new stock and the SEC does not issue a stop order.
7. (a) $\frac{4}{20}$; (b) $\frac{7}{10}$; (c) $\frac{5}{20}$; (d) $\frac{7}{10}$; (e) 0; (f) $\frac{8}{10}$; (g) 0; (h) $\frac{1}{5}$.
9. (a) $\frac{1}{26}$; (b) $\frac{3}{13}$; (c) $\frac{1}{13}$; (d) $\frac{4}{13}$.
11. (a) 0.47; (b) 0.60; (c) 0.95.

Page 133

1. $\frac{52}{67}$ and $\frac{15}{22}$.
3. (a) 0.25; (b) 0.10; (c) 0.55; (d) 0.45.
5. (a) 0; (b) $\frac{3}{5}$; (c) $\frac{2}{7}$; (d) $\frac{5}{16}$.
7. (a) $\frac{2}{3}$; (b) $\frac{17}{60}$; (c) $\frac{11}{15}$; (d) $\frac{13}{60}$; (e) $\frac{4}{15}$; (f) $\frac{13}{17}$; (g) $\frac{13}{40}$; (h) $\frac{1}{5}$; (i) $\frac{16}{43}$.
9. $\frac{7}{8}$.   11. $\frac{1}{2}$.   13. $\frac{3}{13}$.
15. $\frac{980}{1979}$.

Page 139

1. (a) 0.161; (b) 0.965; (c) 0.109; (d) 0.145.
3. 0.14.   5. 0.232.   7. 0.279.
9. 0.336 and 0.329.   11. 0.14.   13. 0.8955 and 0.1045.
15. 0.327, 0.475, and 0.198.

Page 152

1. $26,400.   3. (a) $\frac{1}{15}$, $\frac{7}{15}$, $\frac{7}{15}$; (b) $17.00; (c) $7.00.
5. $555.56.   7. (a) 0.58; (b) 4.95.
9. $7.00.   11. 1.40 and 0.61.
13. (a) 200 and 10; (b) 3 and 1.71; (c) 100 and 9.49.
15. The probability is less than $\frac{1}{9}$.
17. We can assert with a probability of at least $\frac{8}{9}$ that anywhere from 72 to 128 of the 1,000 cars stopped will have faulty brakes.

Page 159

1. (a) Continue drilling; (b) stop drilling; (c) randomize with $p = \frac{13}{19}$ to stop drilling; (d) continue drilling; (e) continue drilling.
3. (a) Lease the facilities; (b) continue to operate the resort; (c) lease the facilities; (d) he might be inclined to gamble on making $35,000 by continuing to operate.
5. Continue drilling.
7. (a) He should not market the lot.

Page 172

1. (a) Strategies II and 2, value is 5; (b) strategies II and 2, value is 3; (c) strategies I and 1, value is -2.
3. (a) Saddle point is the entry in the second row and third column, value is 2; (b) saddle points are the entries in the third row and first column, third row and fourth column, fourth row and first column, fourth row and fourth column, value is 3.
5. (a) 0, $\frac{13}{18}$, $\frac{5}{18}$; 0, $\frac{2}{3}$, $\frac{1}{3}$; value is $\frac{10}{3}$; (b) 0, $\frac{2}{9}$, $\frac{7}{9}$, 0; $\frac{4}{9}$, $\frac{5}{9}$; value is $\frac{17}{9}$.
9. Both should bring out a new computer.
11. (a) First player should use probabilities of $\frac{11}{16}$ and $\frac{5}{16}$, and second player should use probabilities of $\frac{11}{16}$ and $\frac{5}{16}$; (b) $\frac{23}{16}$.
13. Method 4.   15. $p = \frac{7}{10}$.

Page 183

1. (a) 15; (b) 45; (c) 1,225.
3. $a, b, c; a, b, d; a, b, e; a, c, d; a, c, e; a, d, e; b, c, d; b, c, e; b, d, e; c, d, e$; yes.

Page 192

3. The mean and the variance are 3.5 and $\frac{7}{12}$, respectively.
5. The mean is 9.5 and the standard deviation is 0.79.
7. (a) The frequencies are 11, 15, 7, 6, 0, 0, and 1; (b) mean is 9.13.
9. It is divided by 3.

Page 207

1. (a) 0.0294; (b) 0.9394; (c) 0.8051; (d) 0.1056; (e) 0.0734; (f) 0.0601; (g) 0.7620.
3. (a) 0.6826; (b) 0.9544; (c) 0.9974; (d) 0.9500; (e) 0.9802; (f) 0.9902.
5. 1244.   7. 9.2 per cent and 2.3 per cent.
9. Supplier B's springs are preferable.
13. (a) negligible; (b) 0.9452; (c) 0.1156; (d) 0.7793.
15. (a) 0.1934; (b) 0.1937.   17. 0.2327.   19. 0.0197.

Page 226

1. One can assert with a probability of 0.95 that the error will be less than 2.94 days.
3. (a) One can assert with a probability of 0.98 that the error is less than 0.0466 seconds; (b) 12.10–12.20.
5. 0.89.   7. $n = 49$.
9. It can be asserted with a probability of 0.95 that the error will be less than $5.38; without the finite population correction the figure is $6.20.
11. 95 per cent.   13. $21.10–$27.62.
15. 2959–3461.   17. 0.6488–0.6502.

Page 236

1. 0.693–0.747   3. 0.02–0.065.
5. (a) 0.73–0.87; (b) 0.727–0.873; (c) 18,980–22,620.

7. They can assert with a probability of 0.98 that the error of the estimate is less than 0.029.

9. 666.   11. (a) 601; (b) 505.

Page 241

1. 13.2–17.4 days.

Page 254

1. A Type I error is committed if it is claimed erroneously that the average price is not \$14,500; a Type II error is committed if it is claimed erroneously that the average price is \$14,500.

3. A Type I error will be committed if they assert that manual sorting is more efficient than automatic sorting when it is not; a Type II error will be committed if they assert that automatic sorting is more efficient than manual sorting when it is not.

7. (a) 0.0026; (b) 0.0228, 0.1587, 0.5000, 0.8413, 0.9772, 0.9772, 0.8413, 0.5000, 0.1587, 0.0228.

Page 260

1. (a) $\mu_2 > \mu_1$; (b) $\mu_1 > \mu_2$; (c) $\mu_1 \neq \mu_2$.

3. (a) $r > 0.04$; (b) $r < 0.04$.

Page 268

1. $z = -3.93$; reject hypothesis; that is, there is evidence that new pins have adversely affected his score.

3. $z = 1.43$; not significantly higher.

5. $z = -2.12$; yes.

7. (a) $\bar{x}$ less 14.31; (b) 0.464.

9. $z = -1.37$; difference is not significant.

11. Control limits are 1.473 and 1.527; process is out of control with samples 8, 9, 10, 11, and 14.

13. $t = -4.11$; they are not operating at the desired level.

15. $t = -2.09$; the mean is less than 3,000.

17. $t = -1.30$; difference is not significant.

19. $t = -3.15$; difference is significant.

Page 280

1. $z = -3.84$; the claim is exaggerated.
3. $z = 4.15$; the claim is too low.
5. $z = 1.73$; accept the claim.
7. $\chi^2 = 12.36$; reject the null hypothesis.
9. $\chi^2 = 0.79$; null hypothesis cannot be rejected.
11. $z = 4.43$; accept the claim.
13. Central line is 0.20; control limits are 0.08 and 0.32. The process is out of control at the time of the last sample.

Page 288

1. $\chi^2 = 24.29$; there is a relationship.
3. $\chi^2 = 6.03$; no significant relationship.
5. $\chi^2 = 4.2$; no reason to doubt that the die is balanced.
7. $\chi^2 = 0.29$; excellent fit.

Page 308

1. (b) $y' = -0.1689 + 0.2451x$; (c) 10.9.
3. (a) $y' = 0.5756 - 0.1571x$; (c) 0.26.
5. (a) $y' = 10.31 + 5.81x$; (c) 19.0.
7. $y' = -12.9596 + 0.0044x$.
9. 0.06–7.64.   11. 10.1–27.9.   13. 2.56–5.14.

Page 318

1. $r = 0.91$; significant.   3. $r = -0.92$; significant.
5. $r = 0.95$; significant.   7. $r = 0.96$; significant.
11. -0.40–1.20.

Page 331

1. (b) $y' = 5 - 0.69x$ (Origin, 1958–59; x units, 6 months; y, number of manufacturing companies); (c) The trend values are 8.45 and 1.55.
3. (b) $y' = 582.4 + 8.9x$ (Origin, 1957; x units, 1 year; y, annual production in millions of pairs); (c) The trend values are 537.9 and 626.9.

5. (a) $y' = 8.8 - 0.096x$ (Origin, 1956–57; x units, 6 months; y, annual shipments in billions of board feet); (b) $y' = 0.69 - 0.0013x$ (Origin, June 1954; x units, 1 month; y, average monthly shipments in billions of board feet).

7. (a) $y' = 699.9 + 16.4x$ (Origin, 1956–57; x units, 6 months; y, total annual cost of magazine advertising in millions of dollars). (b) $y' = 72.2 + 0.23x$ (Origin, January 1962; x units, 1 month; y, average monthly cost of magazine advertising in millions of dollars).

11. The values for 1932–1960 are: 52.8, 51.2, 56.0, 65.4, 70.6, 77.0, 83.8, 96.8, 111.0, 145.6, 183.8, 221.4, 245.6, 270.8, 277.8, 272.6, 282.8, 312.0, 337.2, 365.0, 391.0, 418.6, 430.8, 444.8, 451.0, 476.2, 483.6, 489.8, 503.8.

13. (a) The values for 1926–1961 are: 588033, 591910, 602083, 527771, 496432, 439963, 463096, 462410, 480011, 504821, 560345, 567334, 574726, 592344, 722455, 835332, 907935, 883077, 819408, 796265, 792231, 790948, 736514, 739390, 765549, 801875, 792763, 750909, 747709, 737619, 732772, 706828, 707348, 717375, 728160, 721127; (b) The values for 1928–1959 are: 543010, 526158, 520527, 489171, 478202, 478843, 503131, 508589, 536599, 558523, 620037, 688879, 731286, 758350, 796911, 826232, 844016, 826265, 783881, 771782, 775896, 776367, 770282, 758186, 757836, 770755, 755350, 732670, 730244, 723040, 722920, 718852.

15. No significant trend.   17. A significant trend.

Page 344

1. 119.1, 103.0, 86.8, 68.8, 56.0, 56.5, 56.4, 74.9, 117.1, 185.9, 153.7, 121.7.

3. 261, 227, 192, 153, 125, 127, 127, 169, 266, 424, 352, 280 millions of pounds.

5. 8328, 6992, 6765, 6144, 6905, 6415, 5974, 6524, 5816, 6035, 5686, and 5604 thousands of pairs.

7. 3905, 4667, 5676, 5555, 6341, 6725, 6160, 8734, 8941, 9588, 8631, and 4642.

9. 2,886,000; 2,775,000; 3,700,000; 4,662,000; 5,106,000; 4,477,000; 3,737,000; 3,848,000; 3,663,000; 3,811,000; 2,960,000; 2,775,000.

11. (a) 200; (b) 1971; (c) 800.

Page 355

1. median, 40.45; standard deviation, 8.59.

3. 16.4.   5. 3.95.

7. mean, 33.8; standard deviation, 6.1.

9. $r' = 0.88$; significant.   11. $r' = 0.39$; not significant.

13. $r' = 0.77$; significant.   15. $r' = 0.27$; no.

Page 365

1. $z = 2.67$; there is a significant increase.
3. $z = 3.21$; the gain is significant.
5. $z = -1.15$; cannot reject the hypothesis that the mean is 79.3.
7. $z = 2.86$; means are not the same.
9. $z = 0.15$; accept the null hypothesis.
11. (a) $z = 0.05$; accept the null hypothesis; (b) $z = -0.46$; no significant difference in dispersions.

Page 379

1. (a) 52, 76, 27, and 43; 90, 55, 68, and 20; 61, 67, 38, and 51.
5. (a) 3,719,250; (b) 7,714,000.
7. (a) 25 and 75; (b) 20 and 80.

Page 389

1. $F = 3.72$; significant.   3. $F = 15.8$; significant.
5. $SSB = 456$, $SSE = 130$, $SST = 586$.
7. $F = 0.41$; as before.

Page 402

3. (a) $80x + 70y$; (c) 10,500 bottles of A and 34,500 bottles of B.
5. The company should assign 10 R_1 reports to A_1, 3 R_1 and 16 R_2 reports to A_2, and 11 R_1 reports to A_3; total minimum time is 912 minutes.

Page 409

1. $q = 237$ and $C = \$118.32$.
5. 3 items.   7. Stock 2 boosters.

Page 415

1. (a) $\frac{5}{3}$; (b) $\frac{40}{3}$; (c) $\frac{25}{24}$; (d) $\frac{25}{3}$.
5. Yes; total cost would be reduced by $145.
7. 0.375, 0.234, 0.146, 0.092, 0.057, 0.036, 0.022, 0.014; mean is 1.44 (exact value of the mean is 1.67).

INDEX